The North Sea

A Highway of Economic and Cultural Exchange
Character – History

Editors:
Arne Bang-Andersen
Basil Greenhill
Egil Harald Grude

Norwegian University Press
Stavanger – Oslo – Bergen – Tromsø

Norwegian University Press (Universitetsforlaget AS), 0608 Oslo 6
Distributed world-wide excluding Scandinavia by
Oxford University Press, Walton Street, Oxford OX2 6DP

London   New York   Toronto
Delhi   Bombay   Calcutta   Madras   Karachi
Kuala Lumpur   Singapore   Hong Kong   Tokyo
Nairobi   Dar Es Salaam   Cape Town
Melbourne   Auckland

and associated companies in
Beirut   Berlin   Ibadan   Mexico City   Nicosia

© Universitetsforlaget AS 1985
ISBN 82-00-07267-3
Cover: Eirik Moe

Printed in Norway
by Industritrykk A/s

Contents

Character of the North Sea

EGIL BERGSAGER

Introduction

The North Sea as it is observed today is the result of a long geologic history. Up till very recently it was basically unknown. Based on the many wells which have been drilled in connection with exploration for hydrocarbons over the last twenty years, a fairly detailed picture has emerged. This shows a wide variation of environments, ranging from periods with dry and hot deserts to a cold and wet climate when thick ice covered the area. Volcanic activity has also occurred.

This chapter will discuss the geologic history with special emphasis on the Quaternary period since that had the major effect on the character of the North Sea as it is observed today. Recent sedimentation, bathymetry, current systems, tidal range and eustatic/isostatic movements will also be discussed.

The main conclusions are based on reports and material available in the Norwegian Petroleum Directorate. A number of external publications are also important. Many of the questions discussed are still debated and the present author's conclusions are not necessarily the same as those from authors of previous publications, even if their results have been used.

Publications and discussions of special value for this paper have been P. Ziegler regarding pre-Quaternary development, T. Løken and J. Mangerud regarding glaciation, H. Thomsen regarding post glacial age datings from the Jæren – Stavanger area and G. Maisey regarding pock marks. A special thanks to P. Blystad for his constructive remarks on the Quaternary development.

The most interesting aspect of the work with this chapter, however, has been the cooperation with archaeologists from countries around the North Sea. One could perhaps be tempted to say that it has been a fareway between two cultures – that of the oil industry and that of the historical academic sphere. Future joint ventures of this kind are to be recommended – to the benefit of both.

The paper does not intend to present basically new research results. It is intended to give a summary of the present knowledge of the evolution and processes of the North Sea. It is furthermore intended to be read also by non geologists. Some of the more basic geologic aspects, like the time scale presented in fig. 1, have therefore been included.

Tectonic Framework

In a platetectonic context, the Post Precambrian period can be subdivided into two major phases in the North Sea. The

PERIODE	MILL YEARS	
QUATERNARY		PLEISTOCENE
	1,7	PLIOCENE
	12	MIOCENE
	25	OLIGOCENE
TERTIARY	35	EOCENE
	53	PALEOCENE
		DANIAN
	70	MAASTRICHTIAN
CRETACEOUS		
	145	
JURASSIC	190	
TRIASSIC		
	225	
PERMIAN		ZECHSTEIN
		ROTLIEGENDES
	280	
CARBONFERIUS	345	
DEVONIAN	405	
SILURIAN		
	425	
ORDOVICIAN	500	
CAMBRIAN		
	570	
PRECAMBRIAN		
	4700	

Figure 1. Geologic time table.

first is Cambrian-Devonian and the second Carboniferous-Recent. During the first phase it formed a margin of an open sea between the Laurentian-Greenland and Fennoscandian Baltic shields, as shown in fig. 2. This phase culminated with the Caledonian orogeny, which had the main activity during late Silurian to Early Devonian.

The major fold belt was in the northern North Sea. Isotopic age determinations on metamorphic and intrusive rocks encountered in exploration wells show the link between the metamorphic Caledonides known in Norway and Scotland. Isotopic age determinations on similar rocks from wells in Denmark, Germany and Holland show that a branch of the fold belt

must have extended "southwards" through the North Sea.

Rocks of Caledonian age form the economic basement over major parts of the North Sea.

After the Caledonian orogeny, the North Sea has developed as an intracratonic sedimentary basin at the rim of the Fennoscandian shield. It was part of a larger basin, which extended from Poland through Germany, Denmark, Holland, England and through the North Sea to the Atlantic. During the mesozoic period the North Sea was exposed to a rift phase. The

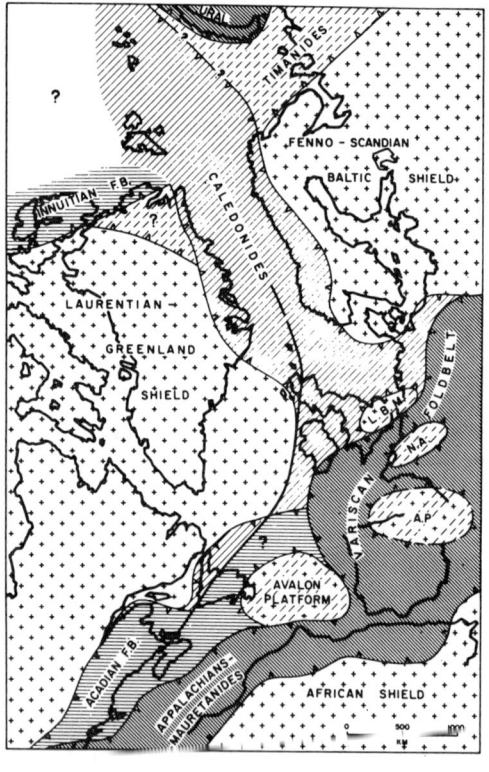

TIME OF CONSOLIDATION

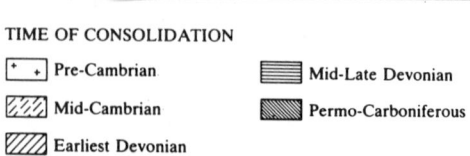

Figure 2. Spatial relationship of Palaeozoic orogenic belts in the Arctic-North Atlantic realm. (Ziegler 1982.)

a lively shipping traffic, it was also one of the richest sea basins in the world for production of seafood in abundant variety, and this bred a rase of tough and daring fishermen in the countries around the North Sea.

Quite lately a remarkable thing has happened. In addition to the amazing riches of seafood, the North Sea appeared to have other riches as well, enormous riches of gas and oil.

The exploitation of these riches below the bottom of a very windy and turbulent sea, belongs to one of the most exciting and remarkable chapters in the story of the North Sea, a story which has been recorded in this book by scholars and writers from the countries around the North Sea.

This survey was arranged by Stavanger Maritime Museum and National Maritime Museum, and was sponsored by British Council and International Commission of Maritime History.

The group has had two discussion meetings, from 18th to 22nd June 1978 at Utstein Monastery near Stavanger and from 7th to 11th October 1979 at Sandbjerg Castle, Denmark. The first meeting was attended by Dr. Christopher Grayson from the Secretariat General of the Council of Europe.

The cost of the publication of this book has been covered by Statoil, Stavanger, and we are very thankful for this contribution.

Arne Bang-Andersen
Director of Stavanger
Museum, ret.

Basil Greenhill
Director of National
Maritime Museum, ret.

Egil Harald Grude
Curator of Stavanger
Maritime Museum

Introduction

Nothing is so roomy as the Sea, nothing is so patient. On its broad back it carries, like a good-natured elephant, the small manikins who inhabit the Earth. In its vast and cold deep there is room enough for all the misery of the world. It is not true that the Sea is unfaithful – it has never promised anything. Its great heart beats steadily and without pretention – the last element of soundness in a sick world.

It was the great Norwegian writer, Alexander Kielland, who opened one of his books with these words. He belonged to a wealthy family in Stavanger which had gained prosperity from shipping and trade for generations.

The Sea was not far from their windows – the North Sea, which opened the gates to the great world, first of all to the countries around it's shores, but also to the vast Atlantic Ocean and the cold Arctic regions.

The North Sea also opened the gates to the Baltic, which in the days of the sailing ships was of great importance for the seafaring people around the North Sea.

This region was an essential source of supply of commodities which no maritime nation could be without, such as: timber for the ship's hulls, mast and yards, hemp for making sails and pitch and tar for making the hulls, rope and rigging, resistant against rot and decay.

For a very long time the North Sea has been a highway of trade and commerce. It has, however, also been the scene of material raids, invasions and more or less peaceful emigrations. In a certain period it seemed that the possibilities that a North Sea kingdom was within reach when the Danish King Canute in 1016 became king of England as well as Norway. But his plan of making the North Sea and Anglo-Norse lake in a kingdom stretching from Ireland to the Baltic failed, and has never again been revived.

The people around the North Sea have continued to be politically divided, but all the same united in a web of shipping and trade connections, which again opened the possibility of a lively cultural exchange and possibility for human contact and understanding.

This understanding was from time to time disturbed by warefare, which to a considerable extent was fought in violent sea battles where considerable bravery and old fashioned chivalry were demonstrated. These wars did not create long lasting hatred between the North Sea countries. They were soon forgotten and replaced with the traditional peaceful connections in shipping and trade.

When the days of sail came to an end and the North Sea was crossed by iron built steamships, with high and thin funnels, a new era started in the North Sea. It's turbulent waters had till then from hundreds of years been crossed by ships using the wind as motive power, from the long and slender clinker built ships with a single square sail to the solid and bulky windjammers with several masts and a complicated rig. However, the steam ship period lasted for only about a century and was followed by the era of motor driven ships, and there we still are to-day.

The North Sea was not only a highway of

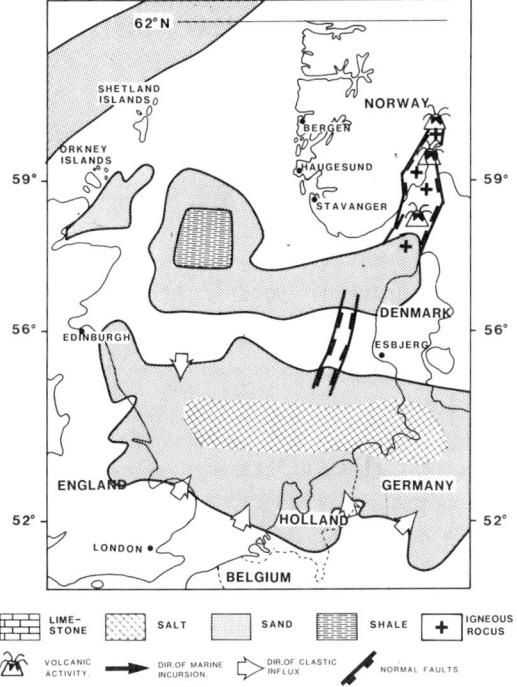

Figure 5. Lower Permian.

ging from conglomerate to silt and shale have been recognized. The sedimentary environment is less known than that in the south because of very scanty well control. The Rotliegendes deposits occur at great depths in the northern part. The basin extends from the Moray Firth to the Oslo Graben. The latter did probably start to open in Carboniferous time. Thin Rotliegendes silt and sandstone of a characteristic red colour, overlain by thick beds of lava, are exposed today in the Oslo area.

Rotliegendes thicknesses of more than 1000 m have been found in the central part of the southern basin. The northern basin is thinner, but thicknesses of more than 500 m have been encountered.

Zechstein

The climate continued to be warm and the 2 E-W running southern and northern basins are still existing, but the sediments are very different from those of Rotliegen-

Permian

Rotliegendes

The lower part of Permian is called Rotliegendes (fig. 1), but at the same time the term is often used to characterize the sediments from this period. It was a hot and dry period, and the sediments were of desert type with aeolian and sabkha sand deposits. The Permian basin of the southern North Sea was running in an E-W direction at the foothills of the Variscan highlands. Sandstone from Rotliegendes is a very important reservoir rock for most of the gas fields of the southern North Sea and Holland.

The northern North Sea was characterized by another sedimentary basin separated from that in the south by the Ringkøbing-Fyn and Mid North Sea highs. Rotliegendes red beds of a similar type to those observed in the southern basin have been found. Wide variations of grain sizes ran-

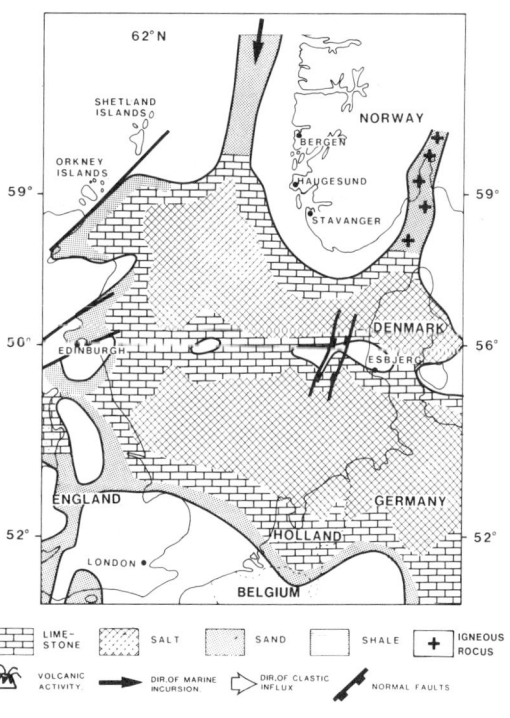

Figure 6. Upper Permian.

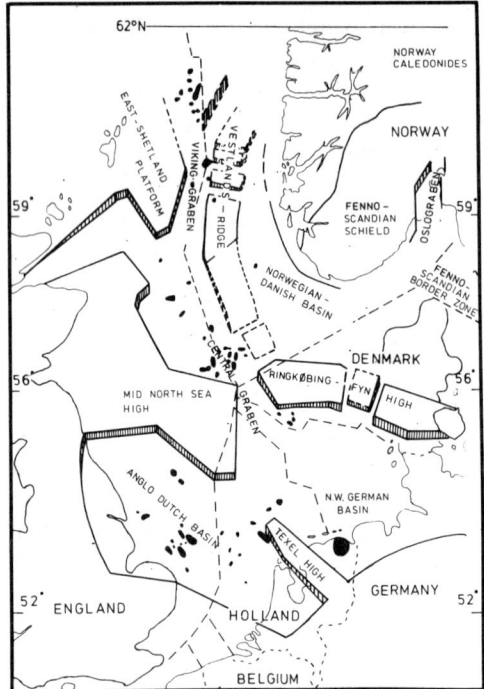

Figure 3. Major mesozoic structural elements of the North Sea.

major tectonic elements are shown in fig. 3. The rift phase never did develop into a drift (ocean floor spreading) phase like we have along the mid Atlantic ridge today. It culminated in lower Eocene with a period of major volcanic activity. This corresponds to the onset of ocean floor spreading in the North Atlantic.

It was at about this time the North Sea as we observe it today came into existence. During the Tertiary it developed as a quietly subsiding basin with the shape of a large symmetrical saucer. The final touch came with the glaciations during Quaternary time.

Sedimentary Environments

The sedimentary environment has varied through the geologic history. A summary of the lithostratigraphy as it has developed during the last 300 million years is shown in fig. 4.

The different periods are discussed below.

Carboniferous

Sediments from this period are known only from the southern and partly west central North Sea. Occasional marine transgressions from the Variscan ocean in the south occurred, but paralic conditions dominated. Those gave rise to thick upper Carboniferous coal-measures, which are the source rocks for the huge gas discoveries in the southern North Sea, as well as the onshore Groningen Field in Holland (see fig. 3).

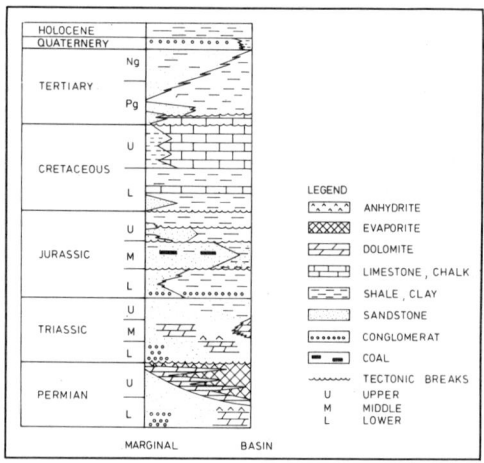

Figure 4. Composite lithostratigraphy for the northern North Sea.

11

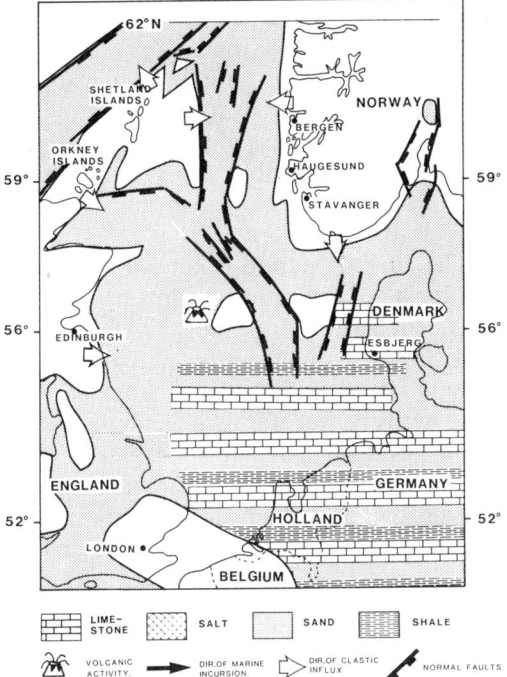

Figure 7. Triassic.

Triassic

Towards the end of Permian, the seaway to the "arctic" ocean was closed. It was possibly caused by doming related to rift movements in the Proto Atlantic. This led to an arid continental depositional regime. Continued subsidence of the basins coupled with extensive sediment transportation are the reasons for the thick sediments which are found today.

North of Ringkøbing-Fyn and Mid North Sea highs the entire Triassic sequence is characterized by red beds of typical continental character over most of the area. Drilling in the very northern part of the Norwegian shelf revealed marine sediments. This may be the southern part of an area where marine facies dominate. Continental red beds are also dominating in the southern North Sea, but transgressions from the Tethys in the south are the reasons for marine beds with limestones etc. As a result of this, the southern North Sea can be compared with the classical tripartite facies of Germany.

Triassic sediments reach thicknesses of 3000 m in the northern as well as in the southern basin.

Continental deposits are in most areas no prime target in hydrocarbon exploration. Triassic in the North Sea is no exception to this general rule. Some discoveries have been made, with gas fields in the southern North Sea as the most prominent. There are, however, indications that Triassic may become more important. This is particularly related to discoveries in the very northern part where marine deposits have been encountered.

Jurassic

In the lower part of the Jurassic there is a change from the Triassic red bed facies to more marine deltaic deposits. This is related to a regional tectonic pulse often referred to as "Early Kimmerian phase" The

des. A seaway extending to the oceans of the present arctic area was established and a marine transgression covering most of the North Sea took place. The sediments are characterized by thick salt deposits. Zechstein is also frequently used as a facies description of such deposits. Along the basin margins and on highs like Ringkøbing-Fyn and Mid North Sea highs, deep water carbonates have been recognized.

Due to late diapirism the real thicknesses of the Zechstein deposits are uncertain, but more than 1000 m have been encountered on several locations in the southern as well as in the northern basin. The carbonates are reservoir rocks for a few small discoveries. The importance of the Zechstein sediments in a hydrocarbon context is mainly related to two aspects:

- Salt diapirism is an important trapping mechanism of structures in younger beds.
- Salt act as cap rock for gas fields in the southern North Sea.

13

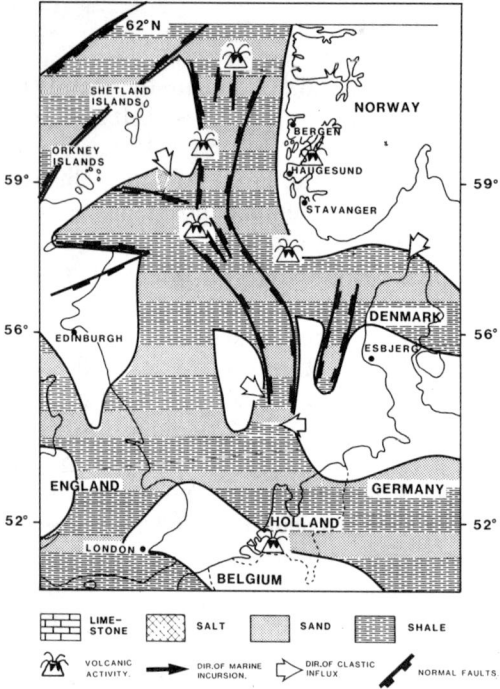

Figure 8. Jurassic.

In the northern North Sea there are good reasons to assume that Upper Jurassic Heather and Lower Jurassic Dunlin shales were also contributing substantially.

The total thickness of the Jurassic deposits varies considerably, but thicknesses of 1000-2000 m are reached in the northern as well as in southern part.

The Jurassic period is considered to be the most important in a hydrocarbon context. The large delta deposits in the northern North Sea include large oil fields like Brent, Beryll and Statfjord from middle and partly lower Jurassic, and the huge Troll gas field from upper Jurassic. The Norwegian Petroleum Directorate assumes furthermore that the majority of the undiscovered reserves on the Norwegian part of the North Sea are to be found in Jurrassic sandstones in the area between 60° and 62°N. That is probably the most prospective play in the North Sea at present.

Not only is the Jurassic important for its reservoirs. Organic rich shales from Jurassic is probably source rock for most of the hydrocarbons discovered in the Central and northern North Sea.

Cretaceous

Lower Cretaceous

The transgressive phase of the Jurassic continued into the Cretaceous. From that time the North Sea has remained open marine and gradually approached its geographic shape of today. The lowest part of Cretaceous coincides with a major rifting pulse, the late Kimmerian phase, which affected the whole North Sea area as well as the entire North Atlantic – Arctic rift system.

Sedimentologically there is a marked difference between the lower and upper Cretaceous. The lower part consists of clastic sediments over the whole of the North Sea. Shale is the most abundant. The water depths in the central North Sea were probably 1000–2000 m. Sand has

seaway towards the arctic oceans was re-opened and has stayed open ever since.

The sediments consist of huge clastic deposits being sourced from the fringing plateaus. More local limestones fringing the high areas have also been encountered.

The sandstone occurs mainly as thick deltas and nearshore deposits. The sources of the sand have changed through time. In lower Jurassic a N-S basin with sand coming in from different sides of the basin is proposed. Following an uplift to the south at the onset of middle Jurassic, large constructive deltas were building out northwards. In upper Jurassic the deltas are more wave dominated with the major sand source assumed to be the "Norwegian" mainland to the east. Local highs were also sources of sand deposits.

The main source rock for most of the hydrocarbon discovered in the North Sea is assumed to be Jurassic black shale with Kimmeridge shale from upper Jurassic as the most prominent in the southern part.

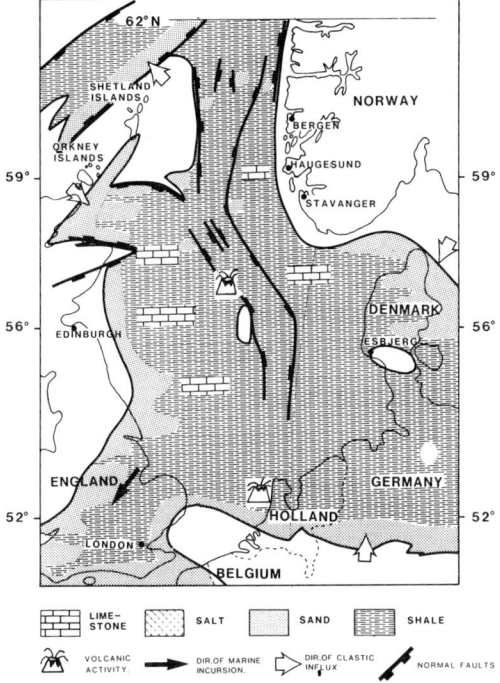

Figure 9. Lower Cretaceous.

a tectonically quiet period and the limestones and chalks covered the old highs.

The deposits are very pure over most of the area, except the very northern part, where it becomes more clastic.

Thicknesses of more than 1000 m have been encountered in the Central and Viking graben, while 2–300 m is the maximum over the highs. The hydrocarbon interest is, up till now, confined to the Ekofisk area in the SW part of the Norwegian shelf and the W part of the Danish shelf.

A combination of salt diapirs/tectonic movements causing extensive fracturation and redeposition, in combination with high pressure causing the preservation of abnormally high porosity, is assumed to be the main reasons for the favourable reservoir conditions. The right combination of such conditions has not been found in other parts of the widespread chalk deposits.

been encountered in limited areas. There may be a good chance of finding more sand. Such sand may be fringing the old late Kimmerian highs. Those are rotated fault blocks. Possible lower Cretaceous sand sourced by erosion of such highs will have a more synclinal position today, and few wells have been drilled in such positions.

Shale thicknesses of 1200 m have been encountered in the central part and 1000 m in the more marginal areas.

Only a few reservoirs have been discovered in lower Cretaceous.

Upper Cretaceous

The upper Cretaceous is characterized by thick limestone and chalk deposits over almost the entire North Sea. Such limestone and chalk deposits occur onshore Denmark, Germany, Belgium, Holland, Luxemburg, France and the eastern part of England. Magnificent exposures can be seen in the cliffs of Dover in England. It is

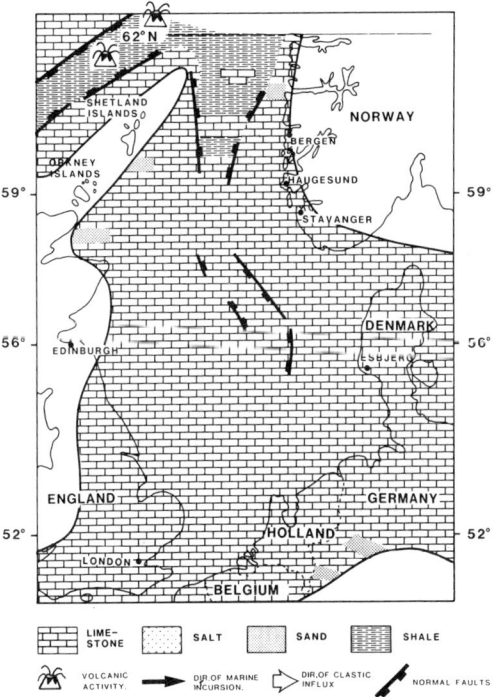

Figure 10. Upper Cretaceous – Danian.

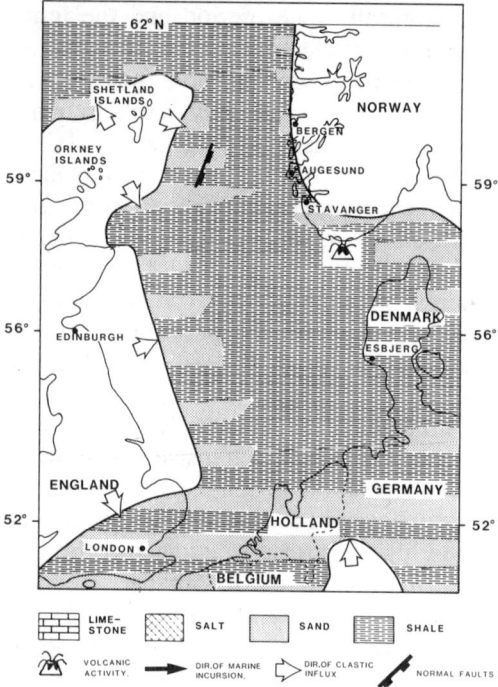

Figure 11. Tertiary (Palaeocene – Plio-cene).

Tertiary

The same sedimentary environment as that of upper Cretaceous prevailed into Danian, the lowest part of Tertiary. (See fig. 10.)

In the upper part of Paleocene it changed to more clastic facies. This change corresponds to the Laramide tectonic movements. A result of that was an uplift and eastward tilting of the West Shetland platform. This gave rise to substantial sediment transport towards the Viking and Central grabens. A variety of sedimentary deposits are found ranging from nearshore deltas and beaches to distant turbidites and shale deposited at water depths of several hundred metres.

The widespread volcanic activity in the lower part of Eocene marks the conclusion of the Laramide tectonism. It is recognized as thick lava benches in western Scotland, numerous ash beds in northern Denmark,

and a tuffaceous zone giving rise to characteristic markers on the Sonic and Gamma logs in the great majority of wells all over the North Sea. A volcano has been proposed in Skagerak, south of Kristiansand in Norway. Other volcanic sources related to magnetic anomalies along the Norwegian coast are also probable. The widespread tuffs and ash beds and the similarity in the observations indicate that the North Sea at that time must have been a quiet sea, which allowed the wind blown volcanic sediments to be settled like a carpet.

The sediments of the rest of the Tertiary period are clastics. They range from shale to coarse sandstones with the more fine-grained silt and shales as the dominant deposits. Such facies are to be expected in an intracratonic, quietly subsiding basin. Sedimentologically this has continued through the Quaternary period. The sedimentary basin is roughly symmetrical along a N-S axis along the central North Sea. It reaches thicknesses of more than 3000 m along the central part around the Ekofisk area.

There is considerable hydrocarbon interest in the Tertiary beds. This is mainly related to the sand deposits of the Paleocene and Eocene, where the Forties oil field in UK and the Frigg gas field straddling the UK-Norway borderline are the most prominent. Danian chalk in the Ekofisk area has proven highly prospective.

Quaternary

In the context of "North Sea as a cultural fareway" the Quaternary period is very important since that represents the most recent influence. The North Sea has gradually developed through millions of years, but the detailed distribution of land and sea-bottom topography as we observe it to-day is mainly caused by the more recent developments. Major influencing agents are the glaciations.

The average thickness of the Quaternary

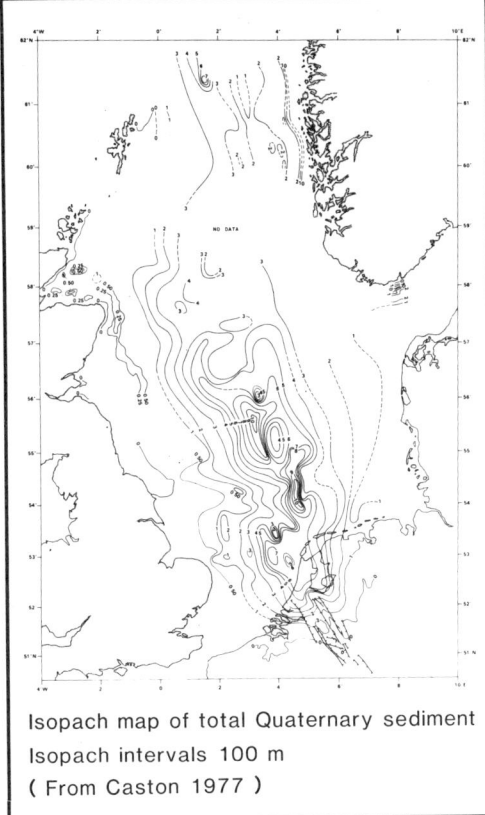

Isopach map of total Quaternary sediment
Isopach intervals 100 m
(From Caston 1977)

Figure 12.

There are, however, other sources of information such as:

Shallow wells drilled to 100–200 m below sea bottom and completely cored in connection with geotechnical analysis of the sea bottom below possible offshore production facilities.

– Bottom samples and shallow wells related to pipeline routes, geological and geochemical mapping.

– Extensive shallow seismic related to drilling and production activities.

In addition to the oil related sources there has been extensive bottom mapping by scientific institutions in the North Sea countries for years.

sediments are 5–700 m in the central North Sea, but more than 1000 m has been encountered in the southern part. (See fig. 12.)

All the wells in the North Sea penetrate the Quaternary, but the information is limited. The upper part is normally penetrated without any return of geologic samples since mud circulation is not established till after the first casing is set. That is normally at depths of 50–100 m below sea bottom. The lack of prospective interest for Quaternary allows minimum expenses for logs and additional geological samples, even after the mud return system is established. So, there are not too many samples from Quaternary.

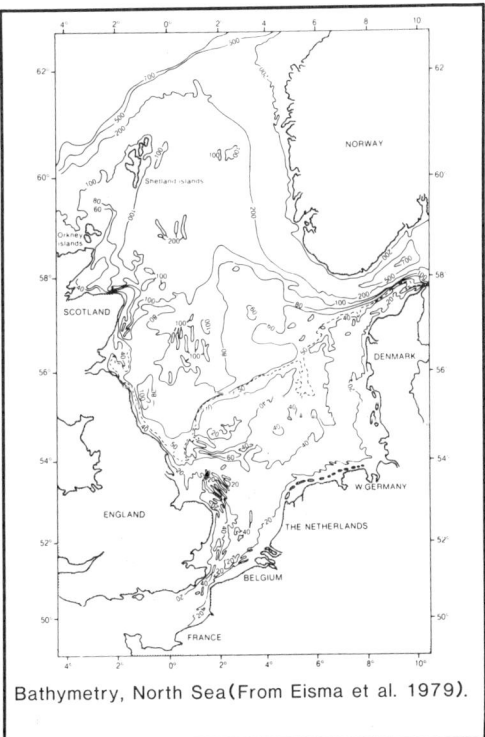

Bathymetry, North Sea (From Eisma et al. 1979).

Figure 13.

17

Physical conditions

Bathymetry

Fig. 13 shows the water depths as recognized today. The most prominent feature is the Norwegian channel with depths of more than 500 m. Seismic sections across the channel west of Norway indicate that it has a glacial origin. Whether this is the case east of southern Norway is not established. It follows the southern and western margin of the crystalline basement of Norway, and it is therefore reasonable to assume some relation to older features even if the ice were the most important agent.

Tidal range

The vertical tidal range is shown in fig. 14. It is more or less negligible along the Nor-

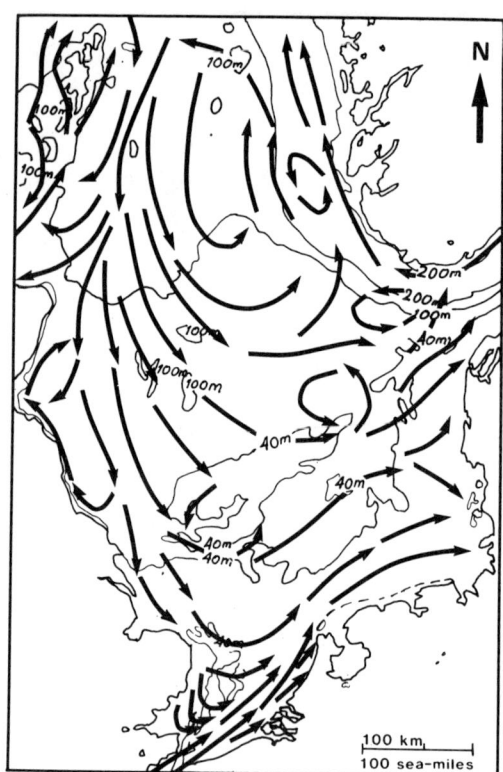

Figure 15. Average surface ocean currents.

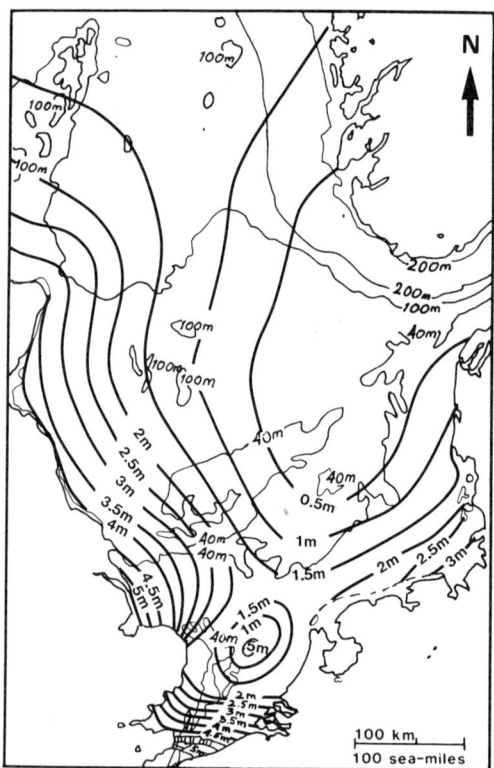

Figure 14. Vertical tidal range.

wegian coast, while very much affecting the eastern and southern coast of UK, the southern Dutch coast and the coast of Belgium.

Ocean currents

The current system is shown in fig. 15. The main influence is the Gulf stream. Two main branches of the stream enter the North Sea, one through the British channel and one from north around the Shetland islands. The main picture shows a circular movement with a southern direction east of UK, an eastern direction along Belgium, Holland, Germany and a northern direction along the west coast of Norway. A westward current between the Bergen area and the Shetland islands is not of interest in this context.

Sea bed sediments

Fig. 16 shows the sea bed sediments as they are exposed today. It will probably change as more information becomes available, but it gives a good indication of the main elements. Of special interest are the sediments on the banks. They are mainly sand and gravel and have been interpreted as outwash fans related to relicts of glacial moraines. The series of banks along the western margin of the Norwegian channel have been interpreted as terminal moraines deposited during a temporary stop and possible glacial advance during the deglaciation of the Weichselian Scandinavian ice sheet. Postglacial mud is found in depressions and covers a large part of the Norwegian Trench.

Pockmarks

A description of the bottom sediments is not complete without mentioning some peculiar observations called pockmarks. They are depressions, circular to oval, up to 300 m wide and 15 m deep. They are found in areas of soft silty clay. A number of theories have been proposed to explain them,

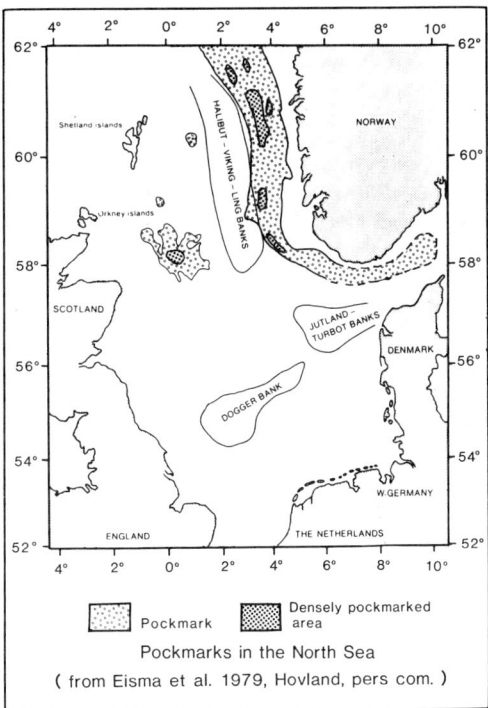

Figure 17.

and discussion is still continuing. The most probable process seems to be slow seepage from shallow gas "pockets". Over the years the gas bubbles erode the fine–grained bottom sediments and create the observed depressions. Fig. 17 shows the distribution of pockmarks in the North Sea today.

Eustatic and Isostatic Movements

The effect of glaciation on the surrounding sea and land areas is strong during glacial as well as inter-glacial times. Large ice sheets will lower the sea level of the world oceans. If the glacier of the Antarctic melted today, the world's sea level would rise more than 50 m. Estimations have been made that the lowering during the Quaternary glaciations were 80–150 m.

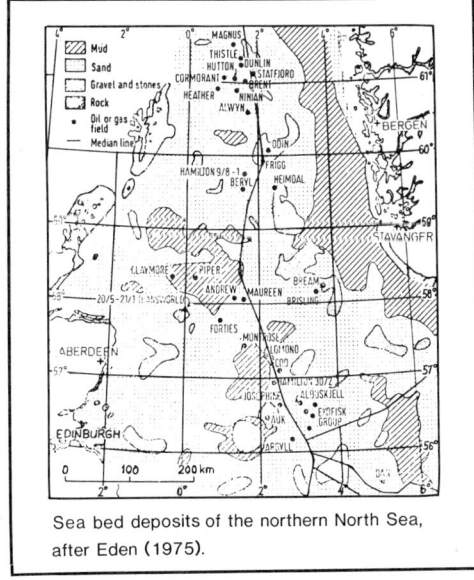

Sea bed deposits of the northern North Sea, after Eden (1975).

Figure 16.

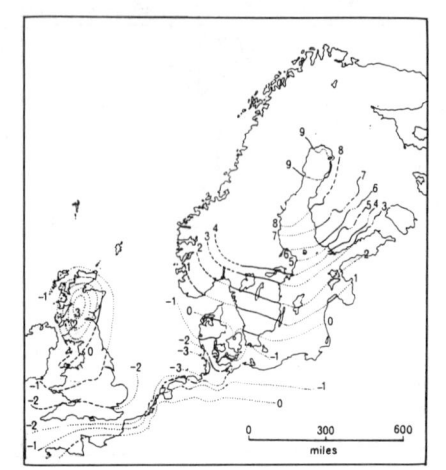

Contemporary uplift and downwarping in the North Sea area. The isobases represent rate of cange (+ or −) in mm/year, West (1968). (After From, 1953 and Valentin, 1954).

Figure 18.

The weight of the ice resulted in an isostatic downwarping. Ice thicknesses of more than 3000 m over the central part of the Scandinavian ice sheet during glacial maximum have been indicated. A small uplift of the surrounding marginal areas occurred due to isostatic effects.

During and after the deglaciation opposite movements to restore isostatic balance took place. An observed effect of that are post-glacial marine deposits at Skaadalen in Oslo which have been found 221 m above present sea level. Calculations indicate an uplift of 500 m in northern Sweden where the center of the last Weichselian glacial advance was. Isostatic balance has not been reached yet, and there are still small crustal movements in and around the North Sea. They are shown in fig. 18.

The Weichselian Glaciation

This is the latest glaciation. It succeeded the Saale which is assumed to represent the most extensive Quaternary glaciation. Saale occurred around 200 000 years ago, and the ice cap covered almost the whole part of the North Sea, Great Britain, Scandinavia, and the northern parts of Germany and Holland. One of the indications of such an extension is ice-transported volcanic rocks of characteristic Oslo graben type, which have been found as far away as Berlin and London.

The Weichselian glaciation was less extensive, but since it was the latest it is the most important with regard to the present character of the North Sea. Fig. 19 shows the climatic changes over the last 70 000 years. The last major features reflecting an active ice sheet are the moraine deposits called Ra along the Norwegian coast, Mid Swedish moraines in Sweden and Sal-

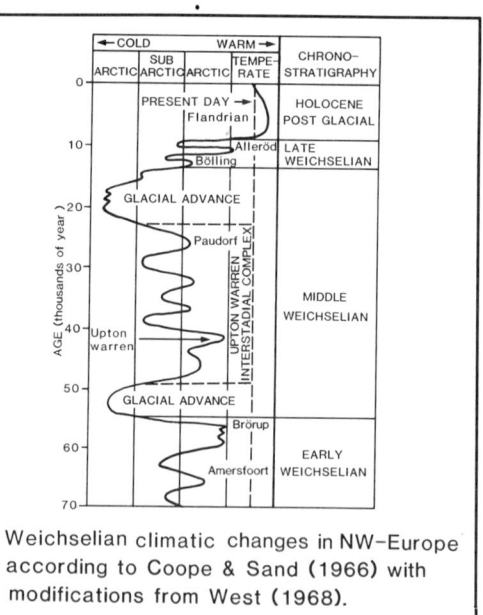

Weichselian climatic changes in NW-Europe according to Coope & Sand (1966) with modifications from West (1968).

Figure 19.

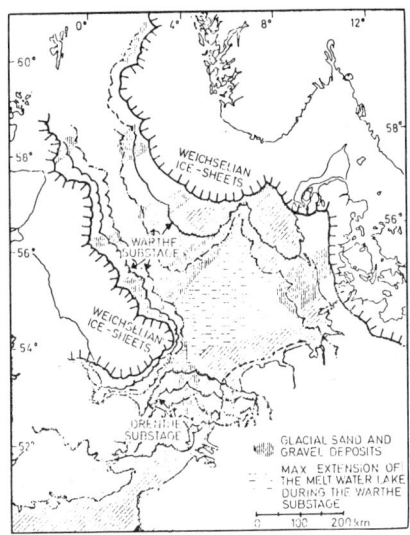

Figure 20. The maximum Weichselian glaciation in the North Sea (Reinhardt 1974). A minimum view.

pausselka in Finland. They were all formed during the period 11–10 000 years B. P. (Before Present). The glaciation ended about 10 000 years ago.

Two cold periods with glacial advances are recognized around 50 000 and 20 000 years B.P. with a warmer interstadial complex between them. Extensive deglaciation took place during this interstadial. During the warmest period (40–45 000 years B.P.) it was probably only the northernmost part of Scandinavia and the mountain ranges which were ice covered. The rest was probably ice free.

A number of observations, including C[14]-datings, along the west coast of Norway indicate that at least part of the area was ice free several times during the major part of the Weichselian glaciation. It is therefore reasonable to assume that the North Sea was ice free during the interstadial periods.

The last major glacial advance at around 20 000 years B.P. is considered to be the coldest, giving rise to the most extensive ice coverage. An important question, which still remains uncertain, is whether there was

complete ice coverage between Norway and UK over the northern North Sea during maximum Weichselian glaciation. Fig. 20 and fig. 21 illustrate two alternative interpretations of the North Sea 17–18 000 years B.P.

The interpretation of the southern North Sea is relatively clear. A substantial part was land area and a number of archeological registrations reveal clear indications of late Weichselian and Holocene settlements in areas which are now subsea. Rivers from the European mainland preceding present rivers like the Rhine and the Elbe, were the main sources of sediment transportation.

The interpretation of the northern part is more questionable. Important arguments and observations are:

– *Striations showing glacial movements toward west* have been observed on the east coast of Shetland.

This should indicate that the thick Scandinavian ice sheet forced the smaller ice over Shetland to move westwards.

Figure 21. The North Sea during Weichselian maximum (Valentin 1957). A maximum view.

21

It could, however, be a local phenomenon without the need of a large Scandinavian ice sheet as a "pusher".

– Overconsolidated sandy and silty clay
Several shallow wells drilled for geotechnical analyses, show overconsolidated sandy and silty clay under a thin (less than 10 m) sand bed. The water content of the clay is below the plastic limit. The wells are located on the Norwegian shelf around 60°N, close to the UK borderline. The most probable explanation seems to be that the observed phenomenon is caused by thick ice during the last advance of the Weichselian glaciation.

Conclusion
The question of whether the British and Scandinavian glaciers met across the north-

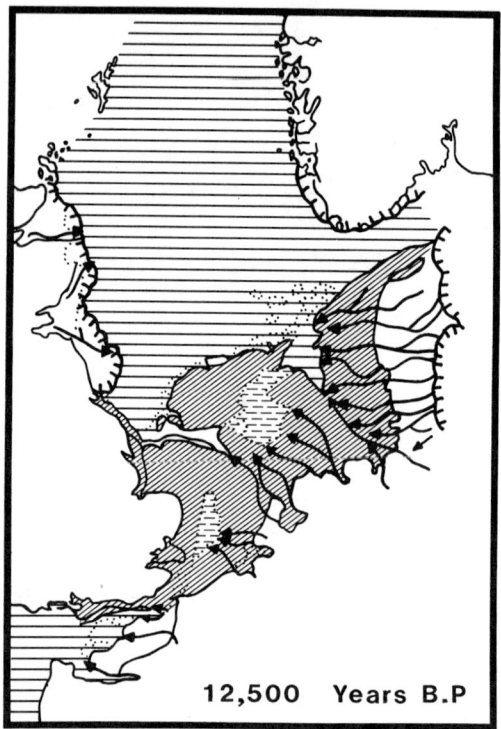

12,500 Years B.P

Figure 23.

ern North Sea during the last glacial advance is still uncertain, but the observations in the northern areas are easiest to explain if there was a complete ice coverage. The geotechnical observations are considered to be of particular importance in this context.

Deglaciation period

A number of questions related to the deglaciation are still debated, especially regarding periodic stops and small advances.

A main stop is known from Denmark dated to approximately 15 000 years B.P. A very possible interpretation would be to assume that the series of glacial relicts along the western margin of the Norwegian channel are from the same period. The picture could then be as shown in fig. 22.

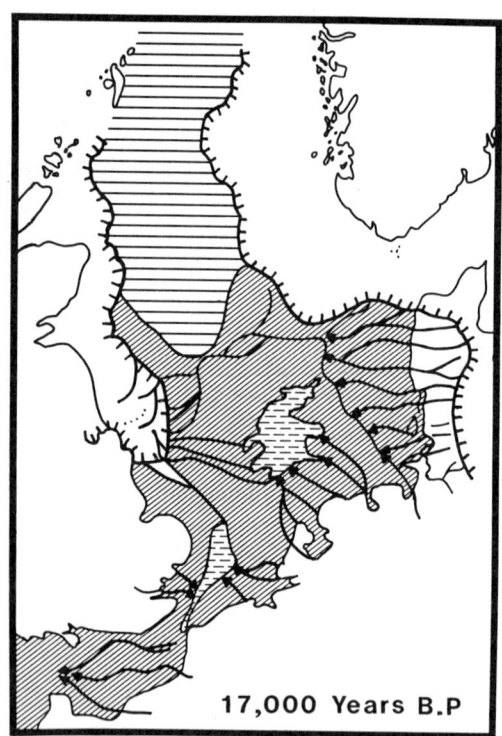

17,000 Years B.P

Figure 22.

C[14]-dating and pollen analyses from around the Stokka water in the Stavanger and the Kårstø areas, show that they must have been ice free earlier than 13 300 years B.P. This would imply that the ice must have withdrawn rather fast, faster than has been assumed by some authors, from the main stop at 15 000 years B.P.

When the deglaciation continued after the main stop, the ice would probably start to float over the deep Norwegian channel. Once this occurred the ice probably broke up and sailed away as large ice-bergs in a very short time, probably only a few years. It is therefore possible to explain a very rapid withdrawal of the ice. Widespread and prominent scouring in the bottom sediments have been recorded, particulary on the NW'ern part of the Norwegian Trench.

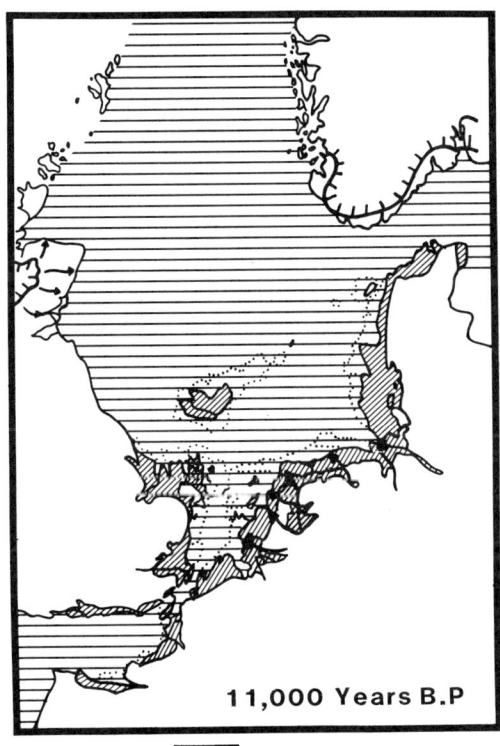

11,000 Years B.P

Figure 24.

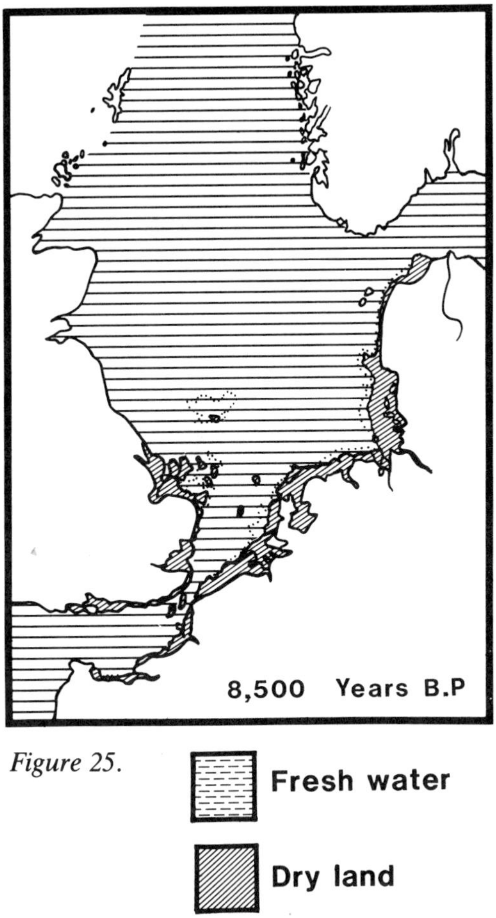

▤ **Seawater**

⌒ **Front of glacier**

8,500 Years B.P

Figure 25.

▦ **Fresh water**

▨ **Dry land**

It is reasonable to assume that the land–sea distribution widely referred to as 12 500 years B.P. in previous publications (fig. 23) would probably better be referred back to 13 500–14 000 years B.P.

The deglaciation as shown in figs. 22–25 is mainly based on geomorphological concepts. However, recent investigations in the northern North Sea, and the bordering countries, have shown that this is probably and oversimplification. The geotechnical observations discussed above can best be explained by ice coverage across the northern North Sea during Weichselian. Shore line deposits in the Statfjord area have been C[14]-dated to about 13 000–11 000 years B.P. These observations indicate that a major part of the North Sea was probably

23

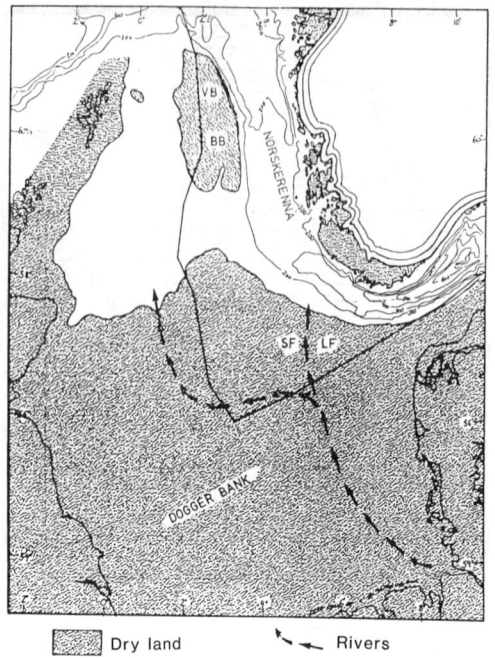

| ▨ Dry land | ↖↙ Rivers |

Figure 26. The North Sea area 13 – 11000 years B.P. (from Blystad 1984).

Syn & Post Glacial Habitation

A number of finds in the southern North Sea show that people were living there during the Weichselian glacial advance. Large parts of the southern North Sea were dry land during periods of several thousand years. The deltaic environment was probably an area with rich animal wild life and accordingly a good area for people basing their living on hunting.

Whether there were land areas in the northern North Sea where people could live is more doubtful. The most probable area in the Norwegian North Sea where such habitation could occur is the Ekofisk area.

The observations discussed above indicate that environments allowing human habitation could have occurred, but no finds indicating such habitation have been reported anywhere in the Norwegian North Sea – until now.

dry land during this period. A tentative interpretation is shown in fig. 26.

The whole of Denmark was probably ice-free before 12 000 years B.P. The southern part of the North Sea, including the Dogger-bank area, was dry land untill around 7 500 years B.P.

Based on the observations known today, I consider the deglasiation as shown in fig. 27-30 to be the most reasonable interpretation.

Four stages of deglaciation and transgression in the North Sea area. (Updated from Løken, T. 1983).

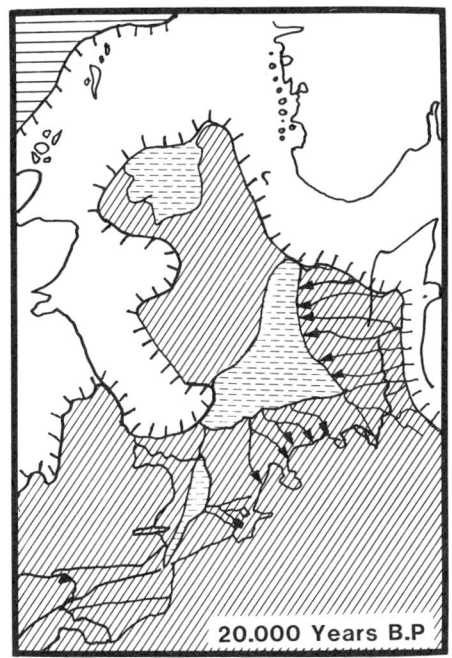

Figure 27.

Figure 28.

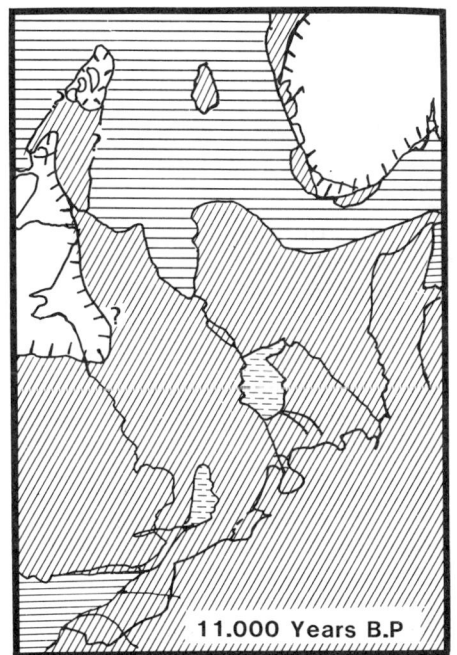

Figure 29.

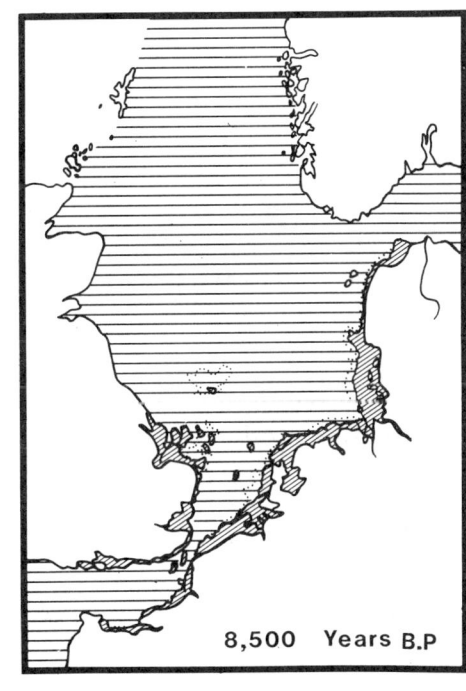

Figure 30.

 Front of glacier ▤ Seawater ▤ Fresh water ▨ Dry land

Bibliography

Anderson, B.G. 1979: The deglaciation of Norway 15.000 – 10.000 B.P. *Boreas, 8,* 79–87.

Andersen, B.G. 1981: Late Weichselian Ice Sheets in Eurasia and Greenland. *In:* Denton, G.H. & Hughes, T.J. (eds.). *The Last Great Ice Sheets.* pp. 1–65. John Wiley & Sons, N.Y.

Bergsager, E. 1983: Exploration results, Production and Development Plans on the Norwegian Continental Shelf. *NPD Contributions No 13.*

Blystad, P. 1981: *Nordsjøens seinkvartære historie, med særlig vekt på isutbredelse og havnivåendringer i den sentrale og nordlige del av Nordsjøen. En litteraturstudie.* Intern rapport. Arkeologisk Museum i Stavanger.

Blystad, P. 1984: *Forprosjekt Nordsjøen.* Intern rapport Arkeologisk Museum, Stavanger.

Boulton, G. 1979: A model of Weichselian glacier variation in the North Atlantic region. *Boreas 8,* 373–395.

Caston, V.N.D. 1979: The Quaternary Sediments of the North Sea. *In* Banner, F.T., Collins, M.B. & Massie, K.S. (eds.); *The North-West European Shelf Seas: the Sea Bed and the Sea in Motion. I Geology and Sedimentology,* 195–270. Elsevier Oceanography Series 24A. Elsevier Scientific Publishing Company, Amsterdam, Oxford, New York.

Eden, R.A., Holmes, R & Fannin, N.G.T. 1978; Quaternary deposits of the Central North Sea. 6. Depositional environment of offshore Quaternary deposits of the Continental Shelf around Scotland. *Rep. inst. Geol. Sci.,* No. 77/15. 18 pp.

Eisma, D., Jansen, J.H.F & van Weering, Tj. C.E. 1979: Sea-floor morphology and recent sediment movement in the North Sea. In: E. Oele, R.T.E. Schuttenhelm & A.J. Wiggers (eds.): The quaternary History of the North Sea, 217–231. *Acta Univ. Us. Symp. Univ. Ups. Annum Quingentesimum Celebrantis: 2, Uppsala.*

Faber, E., & Stahl, W. 1984: *Geochemical Surface Exploration for Hydrocarbons in North Sea.* AAPG. Bull. Vol. 68, No 3, pp 363–386.

Feyling-Hanssen, R.W. 1981: *Foraminifera indication of Eemian interglacial in the northern North Sea. Bull. geol. Soc. Denmark, 129;* 175–189.

Feyling-Hanssen, R.W. 1982: Foraminifera zonation of a boring in Quaternary deposits of the northern North Sea. *Bull. geol. Soc. Denmark 31,* 29–47.

Flinn, D., 1978: The erosional history of Shetland: a review. *Proc. Geol. Ass. 88,* 129–146.

Hoppe, G. 1974: The glacial history of the Shetland Isles. *Spec. publ. Ass. 88,* 129–146.

Jansen, J.H.F. & Hensey, A.M. 1981: Interglacial and Holocene sedimentation in the northern North Sea: an example of Eemian deposits in the Tartan Field. *In:* Nio S.D., Schuttenhelm R.T.E. & van Weering Tj.C.E. (eds.): *Holocene Marine Sedimentation in the North Sea Basin. Spec. Publs. int. Ass Sediment, 5,* 323–334.

Løken, T. 1976: Geology of superficial sediments in the northern North Sea. pp. 45–59. *In: Proceedings from the symposium BOSS' 76: Behavior of Off-shore structures.*

Løken, T. 1983: Kvartærgeologiske forhold på norsk kontinentalsokkel *In: Fundamentering av Offshore-konstruksjoner.* Norske Sivilingeniørers Forening.

Mangerud, J. & Berglund, B. 1978: The Subdivision of the Quaternary of Norden: a discussion. *Boreas, 7,* 179–181.

Rønnevik, H., Bergsager E.I., Moe, A., Øvrebø, O., Navrestad, T. and Stangenes, J. 1975. The Geology of the Norwegian Continental Shelf. *In:* Woodland, A.O. (ED.). *Petroleum and the Continental Shelf of North West Europe.*

Pratje, O. 1951: Die Deutung der Steingrunde in der Nordsee als Endmoranen. *Deutsche hydrographische Zeitschrift 4 (3),* 106–114.

Reinhard, H. 1974: Genese des Nordseeraumes im Quartar. *Fennia 129,* 96 pp.

Thomsen, M.E. & Eden, R.A. 1977: *Quaternary deposits in the North Sea, 3.* The Quaternary sequence in the west-central North Sea. *Rep. Inst. Geol. Sci.,* No. 77/12, 18 pp.

Valentin, H. 1957: Die Grenze der letzen Vereizung im Nordseeraum. *Abh. dl. Geogr. tg. Hamburg, 30,* 359–366.

Ziegler, P.A. & Louwerens, C.J. 1979: Tectonics of the North Sea. In E. Oele, R.T.E. Schuttenhelm & A.J. Wiggers (eds.): The Quaternary History of the North Sea, 7–22. *Acta Univ. Ups. Symp. Univ. Ups. Annum Quingentesium Celebrantis: 1,* Uppsala.

Ziegler, P.A. 1982: *Geological Atlas of Western and Central Europe.* Shell Internationale Petroleum Maatscharppij B.V.

Ziegler, W. 1975: Outline of the Geological History of the North Sea. *In.:* Woodland, A.O., *Petroleum and the Continental Shelf of the North West Europe. Vol. I.*

Climate and its Variability in the North Sea – Northeast Atlantic Region

HUBERT H. LAMB

This aspect concerns the mobile elements – atmosphere and ocean – in the environment in which human history unfolds itself in the region.

The mainstream of the circulation of the atmosphere is the great circumpolar current of principally upper westerly winds, in a somewhat meandering flow covering a broad zone and dominating a great depth (which includes some 70% of the mass) of the atmosphere. The continual succession of developing cyclones, the travelling "depressions" (low pressure systems), which bring the familiar alternations of passing rain or snow-belts followed by some hours or some days of clearing and fine weather, is produced and steered by the massive upper wind system. During the course of the regular seasonal round of the year, and during apparently irregular variations of both shorter and longer duration, the circumpolar vortex expands and contracts and at times becomes more or less distorted. These variations cause the storms to pass now further south, now further north, or to be steered along more unusual paths northward or southward, and occasionally to be halted for some time.

The tracks followed by the depression centres are somewhat affected by the geography of land and sea, tending for instance to avoid mountainous barriers and extensive cold land surfaces. The most frequent paths of the storm centres pass from west to east near the northern edge of our region, passing sometimes north of Iceland and far to the northeast towards the Barents Sea. But at other times, and more frequently in some periods of history than others, depressions pass right across the middle of our region or even to the south of it. The region owes its mild climate in comparison with the average for the same latitudes to the westerly winds from the Atlantic Ocean, which prevail on the southern side of the travelling depressions, and it is to the southern side of the centres that the belts of cloud and rain, and sometimes squally winds, accompanying the fronts between windstreams of unlike origin, are most commonly found. The surface winds are liable to be particularly strong close to the front and also where the front has become swept around the northern part of the centre of the depression (particularly where this happens close to mountainous coasts).

Historians have commonly tried to interpret past events, including for instance old sailing routes, in terms of the prevailing winds and storm tracks of the present day. That this is a dangerous proceeding, which may produce quite midleading conclusions, is easily seen from observation of the differences in the relative frequencies of passage of depression centres along different paths, and at different latitudes, from one year and one decade to another (even

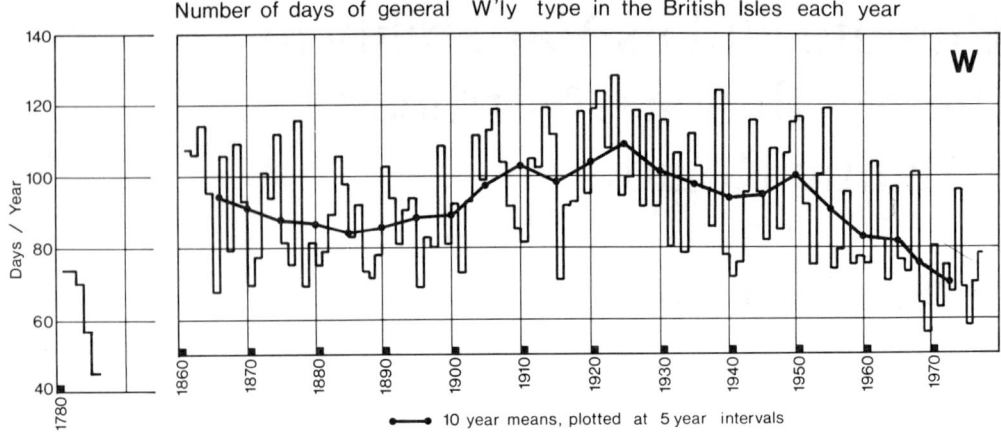

Figure 1. The number of days each year with general Westerly winds over the British Isles, 1781–85 and 1861 to 1978.
10-years averages are indicated by the bold line.

from one long spell of weather to another) at the present day.

Although the prevailing winds over the North Sea region have been generally Westerly probably at all times since the end of the last ice age, a history of the frequency of Westerly days over the British Isles, as in fig. 1, shows that the frequency varies greatly. The variations of the frequency of Northwesterlerly winds seen in fig. 2 (and similarly for some other wind directions) are more or less inverse to those of the more general Westerly winds. It is to be noticed that Northwesterly winds

tend to bring rougher seas and bigger swells (owing to the long fetch over open water) into the North Sea. In some cases of severe storms from NW or N the water level in the North Sea is raised sufficiently (up to three, or even four, metres in the narrower waters in the southern part) to produce disastrous sea floods over the low-lying coastlands.

Fig. 3 summarizes the recorded history of the incidence of sea flood disasters over many centuries past. Some of these floods rank among the greatest weather disasters ever reported anywhere in the world, with

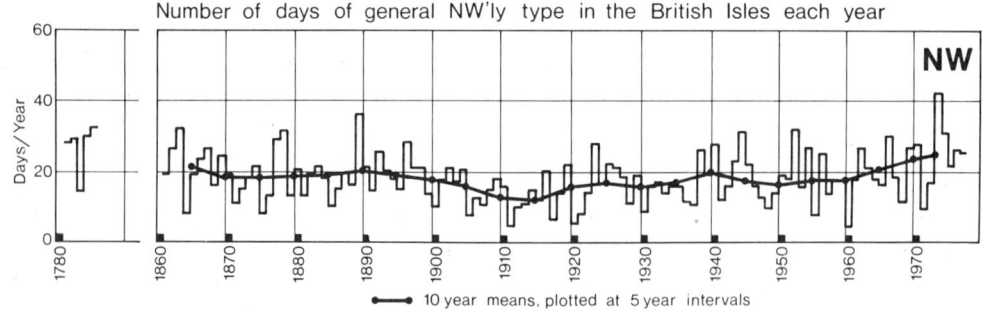

Figure 2. The number of days each year with general Northwesterly winds over the British Isles 1781–85 and 1861 to 1978.
10-year averages are indicated by the bold line.

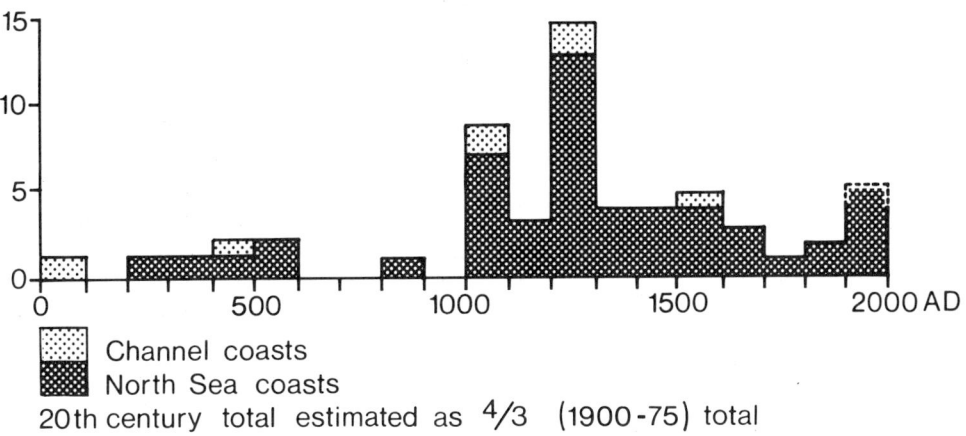

Number of reported SEVERE SEA FLOODS per century

Channel coasts
North Sea coasts
20th century total estimated as 4/3 (1900-75) total

Figure 3. The numbers of recorded severe sea-flooding disasters around the North Sea coasts and the Channel century by century.

death tolls in some cases estimated at 100,000 to 400,000 (Lamb, 1977). Despite inevitable incompleteness of the reports which have survived from the earlier centuries – a defect not likely, however, to affect the main incidents with great losses of life, to which the diagram relates, as much as the less important cases – it seems clear that the thirteenth century was particularly marked by North Sea flood disasters. In addition to the great storminess, which is clearly recorded, it seems likely that the situation was aggravated by a somewhat higher general sea level (perhaps by 50 cm to one meter) after several centuries of notably warm climate over much of the world. On the coasts around the southern North Sea in the Netherlands and England the sixteenth and seventeenth centuries also produced a notably high incidence of sea floods. Since the climate was then in a notably cold phase and glaciers were growing in most parts of the world, the general sea level is unlikely to have been high at that time, so that the frequent breaches of sea defences and flooding of the lowlands must be taken as a mark of the severity of the storms at that

epoch. The relative concentration of the events in those centuries in the southern North Sea is interesting and must be associated with particularly frequent Northerly and Northwesterly winds and/or some concentration of the cyclonic activity at a lower latitude than in most other centuries. That a "preferred" direction of the storm winds plays a part is apparent from the fact that in the twelfth, thirteenth and fourteenth centuries and the middle part of the fifteenth century, when there were also some severe sea floods, the worst incidents occurred further north, on the Danish and German coasts (Gottschalk, 1971, 1975, 1977; Lamb, 1981, 1982).

In fig. 4 we see estimates based on measurements from the isobars on daily weather maps of the frequencies of gale situations over the North Sea and the British Isles and Atlantic waters between latitudes 50 and 60°N as far as longitude 10°W, decade by decade from 1880 to 1977. There is little doubt that the decline of gale frequency in this region to a minimum period between about 1910 and the 1950s and its subsequent increase to about the level of 1880 must be associated with the

GALE INDEX SURVEY BASED ON
PRESSURE DISTRIBUTION

(a) Over the North Sea

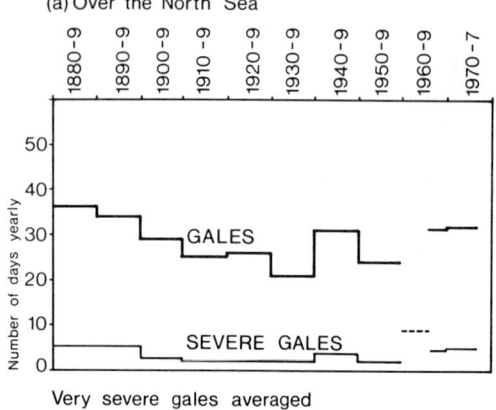

Very severe gales averaged
1 per year in the 1890s
1 in 2 years in the 1880s and 1970s
1 per decade between 1910 and 1939

(b) Over the British Isles / East Atlantic

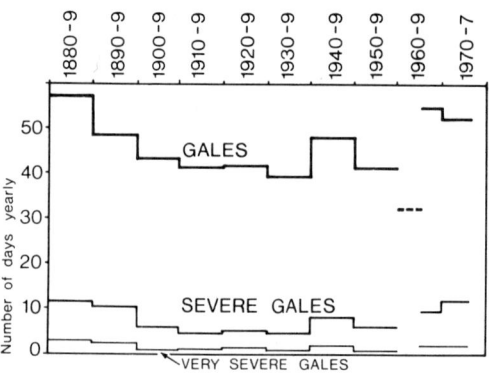

Figure 4. The frequencies of gale situations over the North Sea and over the British Isles and adjacent waters 50–60°N 0–10°W by decades from 1880 to 1977.

fact that the cyclonic activity had shifted to an average position further north in the decades when the gales in the latitude zone 50–60°N were less frequent. Subsequently low pressure centres in the fifties have become more frequent again.

These shifts of the depression tracks in quite recent decades (see, for example, Lamb 1982 figs. 19–22) indicate that there

is no warrant for assuming in historical research – for instance, in connection with the winds and weather experienced on the principal sailing routes in Viking times – that the average wind pattern was identical with recent years. One must have some better basis for reconstructing the wind patterns of the past. In fact, the succession of three or four warm decades in the Arctic after 1920, accompanied by a great recession of the Arctic sea ice, began to produce a situation which had some obvious analogy with the warmth of Viking times, when ice was very seldom mentioned on the sea routes between Norway, Iceland and southern Greenland. It seems reasonable therefore to regard the 1930s, when the main cyclonic activity was furthest north and often penetrated the Arctic as far as Spitsbergen – with a rise in the frequency of gales there which was the counterpart of their decline in latitudes south of Iceland – as the likeliest analogue we have for the situation around AD 1000–1200. Certainly there were some differences: for instance, the records of the English medieval vineyards (and others north of the present limit on the continent) suggest that there was significantly less trouble with late spring frosts in the high middle ages than in the 1930s (Lamb, 1977). But this only amounts to saying that the situation in the medieval warm period was somewhat more deviant from most later experience, although evidently in the same direction as developments in and around the 1930s were tending.

Climatic changes are brought about, however, not only by variations in the prevailing patterns of the wind circulation. They are also affected by corresponding changes in the ocean surface currents.

Much less is known about this than the variations of the winds. It is more difficult to reconstruct past variations in the ocean current pattern because data are scarce. Fortunately, the North Sea and adjacent waters have long been among the busiest shipping regions of the world and are

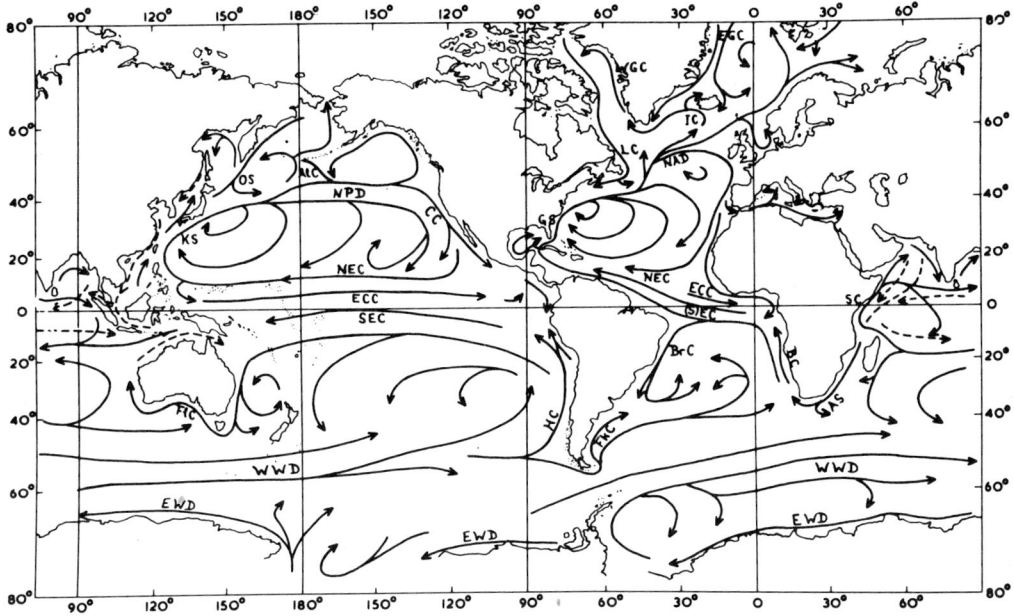

Figure 5. The prevailing surface currents in the world's oceans (twentieth century).

unique in the abundance of many different kinds of record.

A map of the apparent average pattern of the world's ocean surface currents is shown in fig. 5. There are two points in the Atlantic sector where we may suspect that quite small variations in the ocean currents could have important climatic effects. The Equatorial Current, which crosses the ocean from east to west, is forced to divide before the "nose" of Brazil into two branches, one going south parallel to the coast of South America and the other passing into the northern hemisphere where it enters the Caribbean and ultimately feeds the Gulf Stream. If the Equatorial Current system were to shift bodily a little to the north or a little to the south in response to a corresponding shift of the winds that drive it by their drag upon the sea surface, correspondingly more or less equatorial water could be expected to pass into the northern hemisphere to supply the Gulf Stream. Fig. 6 shows that the 40-year average positions of the main features of

the wind circulation over the Atlantic in both hemispheres have indeed undergone displacement north and south by more than one degree of latitude during the period, since the middle of the nineteenth century, for which adequate maps exist.

The other region which must engage our attention is much nearer northwest Europe. The channel between Scotland and Iceland is seen on fig. 5 as occupied by the main branch of the warm saline North Atlantic Drift water of Gulf Stream origin passing into the Norwegian Sea and on towards the Barents Sea and the Arctic Ocean, where it sinks beneath the ice-bearing surface layer of much fresher water. But it will be noticed that a very different current, consisting of polar water, a branch of the East Greenland ice-bearing current, comes very close to the region of the Scotland-Iceland channel at the east side of Iceland. Examination of the record of sea surface temperatures measured at the Faeroe Islands (61 to 62°N, in the middle of the channel referred to), which happily is one of the longest records of sea

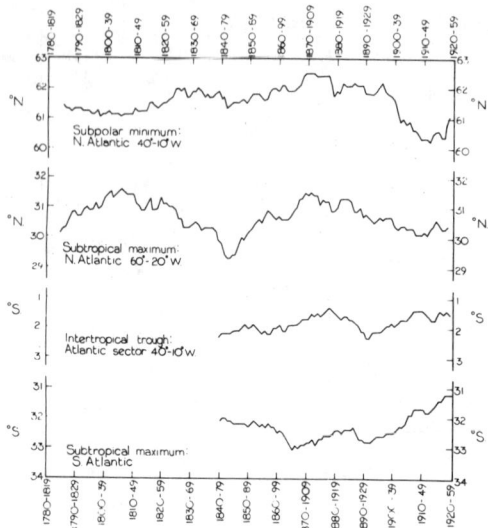

Figure 6. The varying latitude positions maintained by features of the global atmosphere pressure distribution and corresponding surface wind pattern over the Atlantic Ocean.

The graphs show 40-year average positions for (A) January, (B) July.

temperature measured at one place anywhere in the world, shows that the polar water occasionally penetrates the region, ousting the warm North Atlantic water for the time being and bringing a lowering of the sea surface temperature by up to 5°C. Such a visitation occurred for several weeks in April–May 1968 and again in 1969, and similar advances of the cold water occurred again in 1979. At such times a tongue of the polar ice is liable to advance along the east and southeast coast of Iceland or towards the Faeroe Islands, where the ice was last sighted in 1888.

The sea surface temperature measurements at the Faeroe Islands, beginning in 1967, show that the difference of ocean surface temperature between the warmest 5-year period and the coldest 5-year period there amounted to 1.0°C. This is a variation twice as great as that registered by the prevailing air temperatures inland in England

and in central Europe over the same period of time. Thus our concept of the ocean as a moderating influence on climate, almost as a "thermostat", needs some amendment. Where replacement of one ocean current by another is involved, the changes in the ocean may even be greater than on the surrounding lands.

Study of the geography of the changes of prevailing temperatures which have occurred during the present century shows that the general warming of climates in the first half of the century was much greater over the Norwegian and Barents Seas than over Europe or North America (Lamb, 1979). The warming increased towards the north, amounting to +2.5°C from the 1910–19 decade to the 1920s (and to +6.0°C for the winters) in an area near Spitsbergen, indicating clearly that an important part was played by an increase of warm Atlantic water entering the Arctic, driven by increased southwesterly winds. The subsequent cooling from the period 1945–54 to 1955–64 registered an almost identical pattern, the cooling amounting to –2.5°C (and –6.0°C for the winters) in the northern part of the Barents Sea. Icelandic oceanographic surveys since the 1940s have shown that the volume of cold water delivered southwards by the East Greenland Current in latitudes between 75 and 65°N can vary by a factor of 10, and at times of strong flow the polar water is liable to dominate the ocean surface near Iceland (Aagard, 1969; Malmberg et al., 1972; Sverdrup, 1945).

A map (fig. 7) of the deviation of ocean surface temperatures at the climax of the last ice age from modern values, derived in the United States CLIMAP research project of recent years from species analysis (McIntyre et al., 1976) of the microfauna and flora represented in the ocean bed deposits, shows that the greatest differences were broadly spread over the eastern North Atlantic, where the polar water evidently dominated the ocean to south of latitude 45°N, culminating with deviations of close to –12°C near the southern part of the Bay of

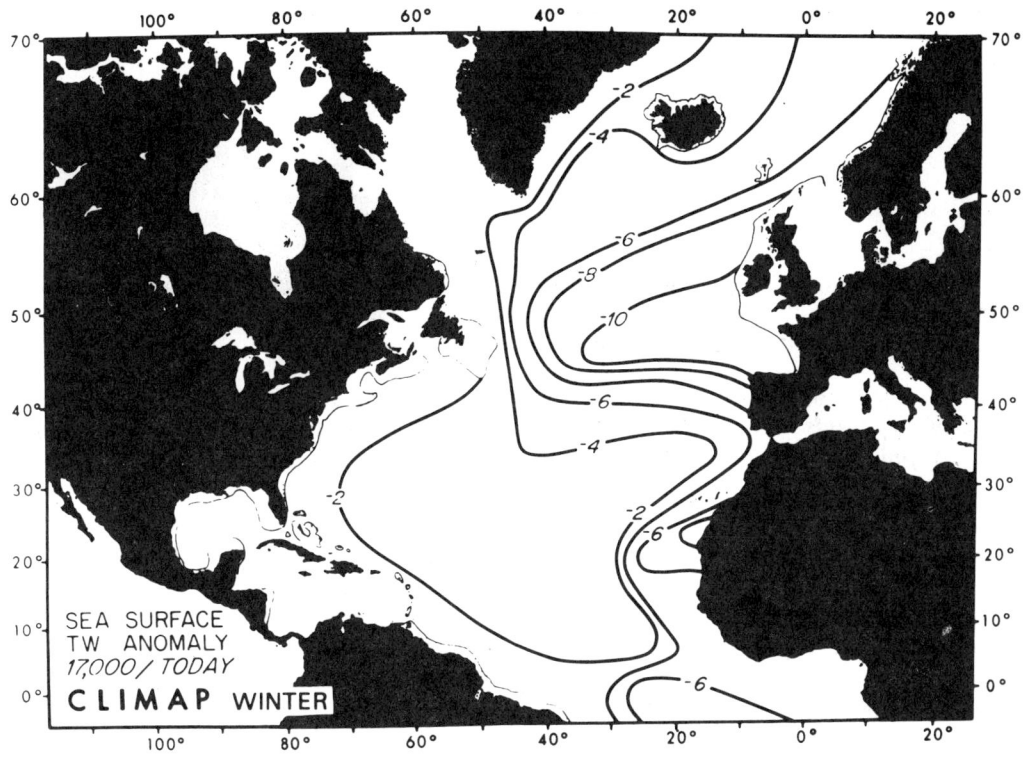

Figure 7. The prevailing depression of ocean surface temperatures (°C) in February below modern values at the climax of the last ice age about 20,000 years ago. (From McIntyre et al., 1976.)

Biscay. This is more than twice the deduced average deviation for the whole world and was probably only exceeded near where the great inland ice-sheets extended into middle latitudes over Europe and North America. The map reveals that the Gulf Stream water at that time spread more or less due east across the Atlantic towards the Strait of Gibraltar and was effectively ousted from the ocean surface everywhere north of 42°N. Related studies by A. McIntyre (1972) and W.F. Ruddiman (1975) in the CLIMAP project have indicated that a cold surface current proceeded south from Iceland and that over the past 225,000 years there have been as many as eight occasions when the polar water covered the ocean surface near longitude 20°W as far south as 42 to 46°N. Only twice – for about 10,000 years in the last

interglacial and over a period of similar length up to now in postglacial times – has the warm Atlantic water dominated the surface as far north as its present day limit (near 74 to 76°N at 20°W).

We can extend our survey of the recent history of this water current boundary in the northeast Atlantic by consideration of the records of the ice and the fisheries. Fig. 8 shows the variations of the Arctic ice at the coasts of Iceland by 20-year periods over the last 1,100 years as indicated by surviving Icelandic reports. It is certain that there were virtually no occurrences of the ice for a long period in the middle ages. Its subsequent increase is quite clearly reported in a number of surviving documents. The maximum towards which the reports build up after about 1600 is probably accurately por-

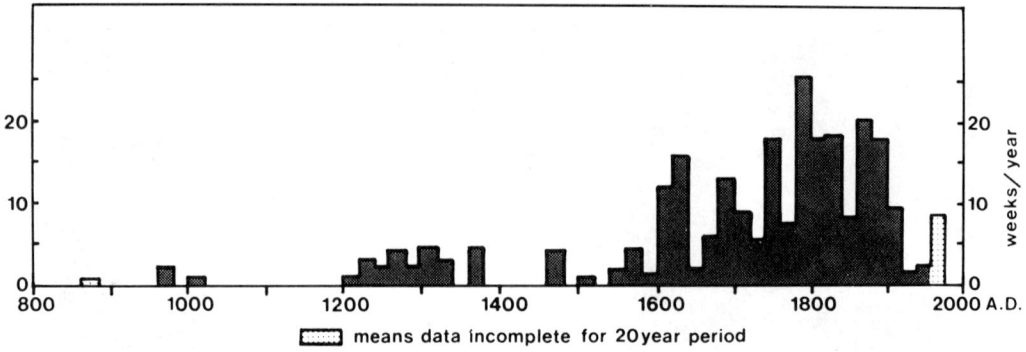

Figure 8. The average number of weeks each year with Arctic sea ice at the coasts of Iceland, by 20-years periods from AD 860 to 1960–75. (After Koch, 1945, updated with information kindly supplied by the Iceland Weather Bureau.)

trayed around 1780–1800 and after, as are the more recent variations. It is known, however, from other reports that there was more ice than the diagram indicates already by the late 1500s, and it seems certain that the greatest incidence (exceeding that of the 1780s) should appear in and around the 1690s.

Fig. 9 shows the geographical positions of the average ice limit at the end of the winter season at various periods around 1800 compared with the years of least ice in the present century. This may be compared with the earliest sample survey of sea surface temperatures (fig. 10), measured by a small expedition of biologists between May and October 1789, which sailed from Leith (Edinburgh) to the Faeroe Islands and (clockwise) around Iceland, and thence to near south Norway and Denmark before returning to Scotland. The summer of that year in Europe was somewhat warmer than the average of the cold climate period of that time, so the deviations of sea surface temperature seen are likely to be modest by comparison with the severer parts of the so-called Little Ice Age, which set in after about AD 1550. What we see is that the whole width of the Norwegian Sea seems to have been colder than the average for this century, the deviation reaching –1.5°C near the Faeroe Islands, but water up to 1.5°C

warmer than modern averages was just reaching southwest Iceland from the south.

The fisheries records enable us to extend our estimates back to the climax stages of the Little Ice Age in and about the seventeenth

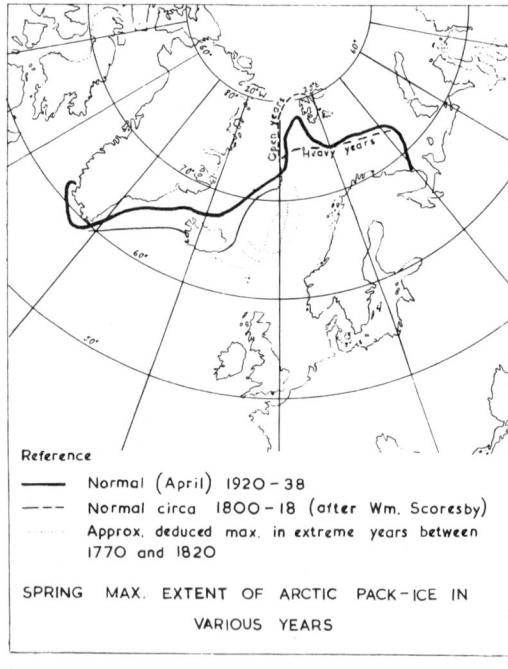

Figure 9. The limit of the Arctic sea ice at its late-winter seasonal maximum in various periods of years from the eighteenth to the twentieth century.

34

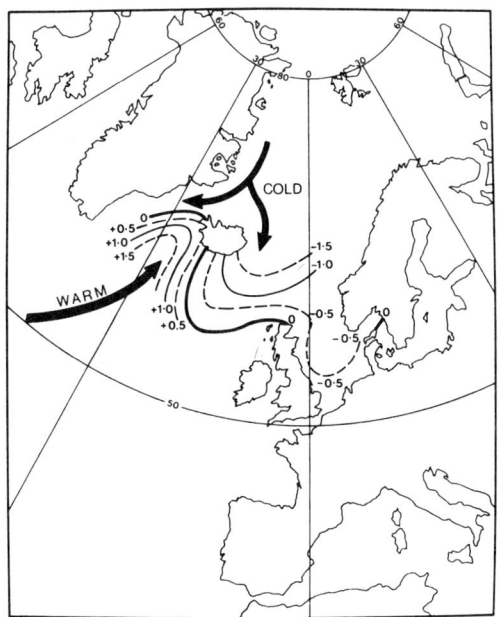

Figure 10. The sea surface temperatures observed in the summer of 1789 by the Stanley expedition around Iceland and in the North Sea, expressed as departures in °C from modern averages for the same months of the year. The arrows indicate apparent ocean surface current anomalies.

century. The cod provide a very useful indicator, because they are so finely tuned to the water temperatures (Beverton & Lee, 1965). Their optimum conditions are in waters between about 4 and 7°C, yet they effectively cannot exist in water colder than 2°C because their kidneys fail. A detailed report on the Faeroes fisheries by Svabo (1782) tells us that the cod fishery was never known to fail there before about 1615, when complaints began of there not being enough, with foreign fishing in the area. In 1625 and 1629, however, there were no cod at all, and such failures continued intermittently until for thirty years, from 1675 to 1704, there were never cod to be had. The improvement that followed was also a halting and intermittent affair, and it was not until after 1839 that there were regularly enough cod to provide a surplus for export. Rather as the pattern of

the 1789 map (fig. 10) would suggest, the cod fishery in southwest Iceland did not fail as soon or for as long as at the Faeroe Islands: from 1685 to 1704 the fishery failed there also, but foreign vessels fishing 20 km out from the coast of southwest Iceland did obtain cod. The most extreme year was clearly 1695 over the whole region. Iceland was entirely surrounded by the Arctic ice, apart from one locality on the west coast, for most of that year, and the ice extended out to sea further than the eye could see from the coastal mountains. In the same year the cod fishery failed along the whole coast of Norway, apart from one part of inner Trondheim fjord, presumably a "pocket" of Atlantic water and an isolated cod population cut off and surviving there from previous years. Cod also became scarce at the Shetland Islands (60°N). The most likely explanation seems to be that the polar water had spread over the entire surface of the Norwegian Sea and south almost to Shetland.

There seems to be verification of this analysis in the numerous reports of permanent snow on the tops of the Scottish mountains in the seventeenth century and much of the eighteenth century, as well as in the great glacier advances in Iceland and formation of small, new glaciers in southern Norway (Hardangervidda) at that time. There are also one or two reports of small lakes in the mountains in northern Scotland which bore permanent ice. This last report and the Scottish snow reports seem to require prevailing temperatures in northern Scotland about 2.5°C colder than modern averages. A lowering of rather more than 2°C is also indicated for southern Norway. These values are such as may be explained by a deviation of the ocean surface between Iceland and the Faeroe Islands amounting to −5°C during the 30-year period when the polar water was dominant there. For many decades before and after 1700 the ocean surface was probably 3 to 4°C colder than today over an area extending only somewhat less far out

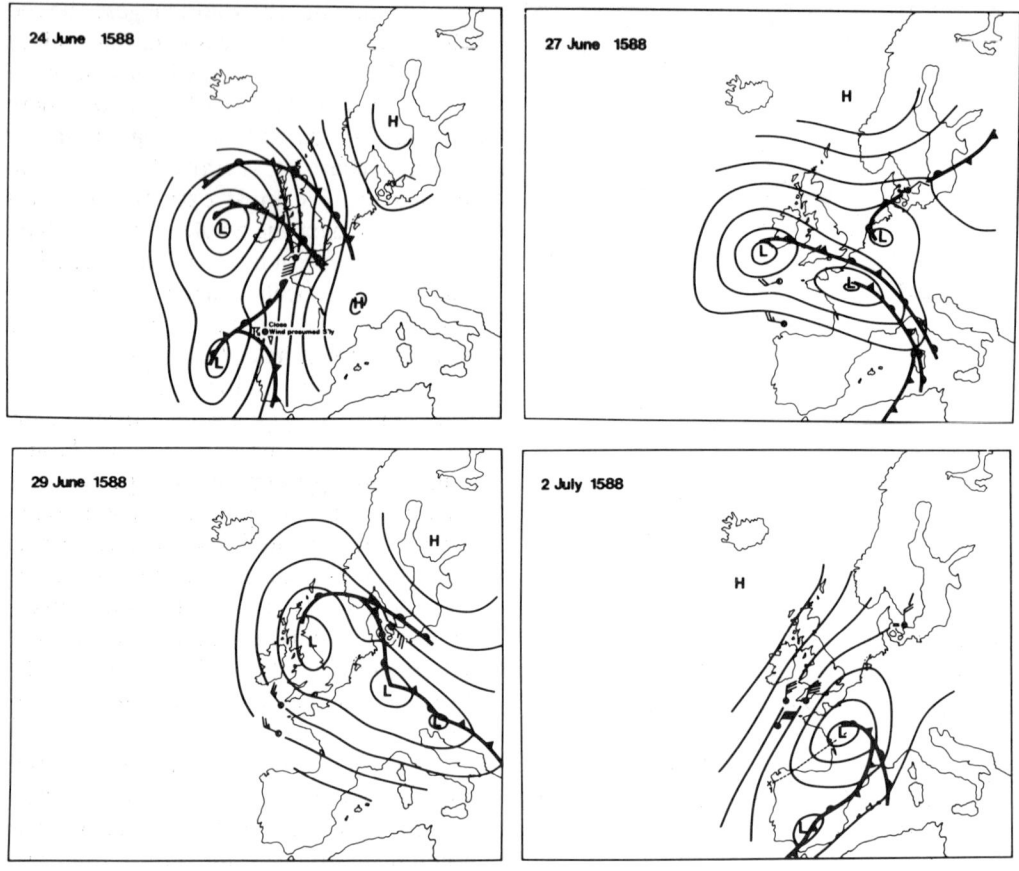

Figure 11. A sample sequence of daily weather maps from the summer of 1588 based on the weather reports from the ships of the Spanish Armada and other sources.

from the southeast and east coast of Iceland, while in 1695 the anomaly was more extensive and probably even somewhat more than –5°C.

An implication of importance to shipping on the northern seas is that there must have been on average a stronger gradient of temperature than nowadays between about latitude 50°N and 60–65°N, giving a potential energy source for stronger windstorms. An analysis by Douglas, Lamb & Loader (1978) of the Spanish Armada storms, using the abundant weather reports from the ships to produce daily weather maps for sixty days between May and October 1588, concluded that six times in August and September of that one year the

distances travelled by depression centres in twenty-four hours indicated jet streams at or slightly above the limit of probable occurrence for those months of the year based on twentieth century statistics. This tends to confirm that the whole wind system (at the surface and aloft) was repeatedly stronger than could be expected to develop in the environment familiar in the present century. It could, however, be explained by a summer situation with the main Arctic ice limit as far south as Iceland, where it is reported to have been in the years 1585–87 and probably still was in 1588, judging by the persistent wind patterns appearing on the daily weather map analysis.

Fig. 11 illustrates a sample daily weather map sequence from the analysis of 1588. That year is believed to have produced the wettest summer of record in the Swiss Alps and contributed to the rapid glacier advances then going on there. There are, however, records from many other years in the centuries of colder and rougher climate, particularly between 1550 and 1720 (but to some extent from about 1310 to the 1890s), of windstorms on the coasts of northwest Europe of a strength probably unmatched in the twentieth century. These storms left their mark not only in shipwrecks but in breached dykes and great sea floods over the low-lying coastlands and at other places alterations to the coasts (and in a few places inland) by huge drifts of blown sand which buried farmland and townships.

Present understanding of meteorology hardly permits scientific forecasting of climate, and very divergent opinions have been expressed in recent years depending in some cases upon entirely theoretical diagnoses of probable side-effects of human activities such as the adding of great quantities of carbon dioxide to the atmosphere. What is clear is that the North Sea and northeast Atlantic region is liable to bigger variations of its climate than have hitherto been appreciated. Moreover, these changes are contributed to by variations of the ocean currents which cause the boundary between water of Gulf Stream origin and the polar water, with its big temperature shift, to swing far to the north in times of warming and far to the south in times of cooling, these shifts, sustained over many years, being greater over the Norwegian Sea and neighbouring ocean areas than over Europe or North America.

Figure 12. Storm waves breaking over the small island of Heligoland on 10. October 1926. In AD 800 Heligoland is believed to have been 40 miles in diameter, today it measures 1 mile by 1/3 mile. Photo: Copyright Schensky. With acknowledgement H. Rohde of Hamburg.

Bibliography

Aagard, K., The wind-driven circulation of the Greenland and Norwegian Seas and its variability. *ICES Dublin 1969 Symposium on Physical Variability in the North Atlantic*. Copenhagen (International Council for the Exploration of the Sea) 1969

Bevertom, R.J.H. & Lee, A.J., "Hydrographic fluctuations in the North Atlantic Ocean and some biological consequences". In *The biological significance of climatic changes in Britain* (C.G. Johnson & L.P. Smith, Editors). London (Institute of Biology and Academic Press) 1965

Douglas, K.S.; Lamb, H.H. & Loader, C., A meteorological study of July to October 1588: the Spanish Armada storms. Norwich (University of East Anglia, Climatic Research Unit CRU RP 6 – see also supplement covering May to July 1588, CRU RP 6a) 1978

Gottschalk, M.K.E., *Stormvloeden en rivieroverstromingen in Nederland: Deel I, II, III.* Assen/Amsterdam (Van Gorkum) 1971, 1975 and 1977

Koch, L., "The East Greenland ice", *Meddelelser om Grønland, Bd. 130 Nr. 3.* Copenhagen 1945

Lamb, H.H., *Climate present, past and future – Vol. 2: Climatic History and the Future.* London (Methuen) and New York (Barnes & Noble). 835 pp. 1977

Lamb, H.H., "Climatic variation and changes in the wind and ocean circulation: the Little Ice Age in the northeast Atlantic". *Quaternary Research,* Vol. 11, pp 1–20. London and New York (Academic Press) 1979

Lamb, H.H., "Climatic fluctuations in historical times and their connexion with transgressions of the sea, storm-floods and other coastal changes". Pp 251–290 in *Transgressies en occupatiegeschiedenis in de kustgebieden van Nederland en Belgie: Interdisciplinair Colloquium* 5–7 September 1978. (Edited by A. Verhulst and M.K.E. Gottschalk) 1981

Lamb, H.H., *Climate, History and the Modern World.* London (Methuen) 1982

Malmberg, Sv.A.; Gade, H.G. & Sweers, H.E., "Current velocities and volume transports in the East Greenland Current off Cape Nordenskjöld in August – September 1965". In: *Sea-Ice Conference Proceedings,* Reykjavik, pp 130–9. 1972

McIntyre, A.; Kipp, N.G.; Be, A.W.H.; Crowley, T.; Kellogg, T.; Gardner, J.V.; Prell, W. & Ruddiman, W.F., "Glacial North Atlantic 18,000 years ago: a CLIMAP reconstruction". In: *Investigation of Late Quaternary Paleoceanography and Paleoclimatology* (R.M. Cline & J.D. Hays, Editors), pp 43–76. *Geological Society of America Memoir 145.* Boulder, Colorado. 1976

McIntyre, A.; Ruddiman, W.F. & Jantzen, R., "Southward penetrations of the North Atlantic polar front: faunal and floral evidence of large-scale surface watermass movements over the last 225,000 years", *Deep Sea Research, Vol. 5, pp 361–389.* London and New York (Academic Press)

Ruddiman, W.F. & Glover, L.K., "Subpolar North Atlantic circulation at 9,300 years B.P.: faunal evidence". *Quaternary Research,* Vol. 5, pp 361–389. London and New York (Academic Press) 1975

Svabo, J.C., *Indberetninger fra en Reise i Faerøe 1781 og 1782.* Copenhagen. (Republished 1959 by Selskabet til Udgivelse af Faerøiske Kildeskrifter og Studier) 1782

Sverdrup, H.V., *Oceanography for meteorologists.* London (Allen and Unwin) 1945

The North Sea: A Highway of Invasions, Immigration and Trade
Fifth to Ninth Centuries A.D.

HELEN CLARKE

In recent years archaeologists have been turning their attention increasingly towards the study of the so-called 'Dark Ages'. This period, from the collapse of the Roman Empire to the flowering of the high Middle Ages, earned its popular title because surviving written evidence for its history is slight and often difficult to understand. Archaeologists, however, concentrate not on the written record (although they need to be aware of it) but on the material remains of civilizations, now often hidden below the ground but still in many cases capable of investigation, excavation and interpretation. Their work has shown that it is possible to flesh out the documentary evidence and shed light on the 'Dark Ages' by studying the dwellings, graves and other physical remains of the people who lived during those years, now more often, but less evocatively, known as the 'Early Middle Ages'. In this chapter recent understanding of the contacts between the countries surrounding the North Sea from the fifth to ninth centuries will be surveyed and emphasis will be placed on the results of archaeological excavations, most of them carried out during the past twenty years.

The Anglo-Saxon Invasions: England and the Continent in the Fifth and Sixth Centuries

Early in the fifth century the Roman legions withdrew from Britain to concentrate on the defence of the continental Empire. This left England exposed to attacks from the Picts and Scots of Scotland and Ireland, and to invasion and settlement by Germanic peoples notably the Angles, Saxons and Jutes from across the North Sea. A south Gallic chronicle with its final entry in A.D. 452 is the only exactly contemporary account of this turbulent time (Miller 1978) but an historical outline can be compiled by combining its evidence with the writings of historians and chroniclers who lived three or more centuries later (Bede, Nennius and the compilers of the *Anglo-Saxon Chronicle*) and, most importantly, with the *Ruin of Britain (De Excidio Britanniae)* written by a British monk, Gildas, who lived only a generation or so after the fifth-century events which he described and whose writings probably formed the basis for much of the later histories.

The historians relate that the perilous state of the country after the departure of the Romans caused the native leaders of the Britons to send a petition, 'the groans of the Britons', to Aëtius, the mid-fifth century military commander of the western Roman Empire, asking for aid against threats from the barbarians of the north, that is, the Picts. Perhaps because no aid was forthcoming from the Romans, Vortigern, apparently the foremost leader of the Britons and described as 'proud tyrant' *(superbus tyrannus)* by Gildas, called for help from Germanic mercenaries who, under the leadership of Hengest and Horsa, came in three ships from their homeland in Saxony, eventually to settle in Thanet, east Kent. After defeating the Picts, the Germanic mercenaries (Saxons) summoned reinforcements from across the North Sea, rebelled against their British overlords, and set out to conquer and occupy most of southern and eastern England. Throughout the second half of the fifth century ever-increasing numbers of Germanic peoples came from the Continent, settling both in eastern and southern England and also penetrating far into the west, driving the native Britons before them.

Gildas relates that 'All the major towns were laid low by the repeated battering of enemy rams; laid low, too, were all the inhabitants – church leaders, priests and people alike, as the swords glinted all around and the flames crackled'. The Britons, however, rallied and won a great victory at *Mons Badonicus* at the end of the fifth century. The victory heralded a period of peace between Briton and Saxon which continued throughout the first half of the sixth century. During that time the Germanic immigrants consolidated their hold on the areas in which they had already settled and began to organise themselves into kingdoms.

Archaeological work has recently modified the historical picture in a number of ways and in particular by suggesting that some Germanic peoples must have arrived in Britain as early as the second half of the fourth century, almost a hundred years before Vortigern's legendary summons to Hengest and Horsa. These Germanic peoples formed part of the Roman military forces, known as *foederati*, who garrisoned the forts on the east and south coasts of England, which already needed to be defended in the fourth century against attacks by barbarians from the Continent (Johnston 1977). Some *foederati* were also stationed inland (Hawkes and Dunning 1961) and by the beginning of the fifth century there was an appreciable, if not very large, Germanic military presence in lowland England. It has recently been suggested that certain coastal or riverine settlements, such as Mucking, Essex (Jones 1968, 1974a, 1974b, 1978) or the settlement whose cemetery is known at Highdown in Sussex (Welch 1976), were founded in the early fifth century as look-out posts from which the *foederati* could see incoming sea-borne traffic from the Continent, and perhaps control the Germanic immigrants who, once the Romans had left, came in increasing numbers, finally forming the backbone of the Anglo-Saxon invasions of the later fifth century.

The fourth century Germanic population, introduced into Britain by the Romans, stayed behind and increased in numbers after the departure of the Roman legions in about A.D. 410. The native British rulers, who found themselves in charge of the country once the Roman army of occupation had gone, may have encouraged immigration from the Continent and deliberately settled the Germanic immigrants in areas such as East Anglia where they could act as defensive forces against the unfriendly Pictish and continental invaders who attacked England after the departure of the Romans. This may be the origin of the Anglo-Saxon historians' account of Vortigern, Hengest and Horsa. Certainly, the number of Germanic settlers in England increased rapidly during the second half of the fifth century, in what has been called the 'period of uncontrolled Anglo-Saxon settlement' (Myres 1969).

It is agreed by archaeologist and historian alike that the Germanic peoples came by ship from across the North Sea. Is it possible to discover precisely where the immigrants came from and how they travelled to England?

Bede, who wrote in the early eighth century, tells us at one point (I. 15) that the reinforcements to Hengest's forces were Saxons, Angles and Jutes.

From the Jutes are descended the people of Kent and the Isle of Wight, and those in the province of Wessex opposite the Isle of Wight who are called Jutes to this day. From the Saxons, that is the country now known as Old Saxony, came the East, South and West Saxons. And from the Angles – that is the country known as Angulus, which lies between the provinces of the Jutes and the Saxons, and remains unpopulated to this day – are descended the East and Middle Angles, the Mercians, all the Northumbrian peoples, that is those people living north of the river Humber, and other English peoples.

So Bede implies that the immigrants came from well-defined areas on the Continent (Jutland, Saxony and Angeln) and that they kept together in distinct groups after their arrival in England. Evidence from cemetery and settlement sites on the Continent, however, suggests that racial and tribal distinctions were already blurred by the beginning of the fifth century, before the main emigration westwards, and Bede's equation of people with areas is unlikely to be true. But there is archaeological evidence to support his general hypothesis about the areas from which the Germanic settlers came. It is probable that most set out from the Elbe-Weser region of Lower Saxony, north Germany, and the lands which flanked that district to north and south. Objects found in late fourth and fifth-century settlements and graves in that area of the Continent are very close in style and type to those discovered in only slightly later contexts in England.

For example, some pottery from the fifth-century Anglo-Saxon settlement site at Mucking in Essex, England, is almost identical to pottery used by the inhabitants of the settlement of Feddersen Wierde in Lower Saxony, Germany (Jones 1969) and some of the pottery from the Anglo-Saxon cremation cemeteries at Spong Hill, and Caistor-by-Norwich, Norfolk, is decorated with patterns very similar to those found on pottery from the Elbe-Weser region (Hills 1980). Jewellery and other objects buried with the dead in Anglo-Saxon cemeteries in England can also be very similar to those found in roughly contemporary graves in Germany, Holland and southern Denmark. Other objects discovered in England, however, imply that some of the immigrants came from elsewhere on the Continent; in particular, fifth-century weapons and belt buckles found in Kent suggest that their owners came originally from northern France (Evison 1965) and some brooches found in England seem to have been brought from as far away as southern Norway (Bøe 1931), perhaps by people who travelled the south Scandinavian sea route along the west coast of Jutland to the Dover straits, and then along the shortest open sea passage to England.

It is possible, therefore, for archaeologists to point to the original homelands of the Anglo-Saxons by comparing objects which have been found on either side of the North Sea. Small, portable objects such as pottery and jewellery may have been brought by the immigrants themselves, or may have been made in traditional continental styles soon after the Anglo-Saxons settled on English soil. Similarly, the buildings which the Anglo-Saxons erected on their arrival in England might be expected to have been constructed according to the traditional building methods current in the Germanic areas during the fourth and fifth centuries A.D. The so-called aisled long-house (a rectangular timber building, longitudinally divided into three by two rows of roof-supporting posts and housing cattle at one end and people at the other) was the classic type of building in the settlements of the Anglo-Saxons' continental homeland. They have been found on sites such as Ezinge in the Netherlands (van Giffen 1936) and Feddersen Wierde (Haarnagel 1979) and Flögeln (Zimmermann 1974) in Germany. A development away from the classic type has been discovered at Wijster in the Netherlands (van Es 1967). There, the roof-supporting posts lay closer to the walls, giving a larger unimpeded area within the buildings, but cattle and men were still housed under the same roof. These and many other similar settlements were occupied up to the fifth century A.D. and then deserted, perhaps because their inhabitants emigrated to England taking their traditional forms of pottery, jewellery and, presumably, building types with them. Excavations on Anglo-Saxon settlement sites in England, however, have shown that the most common dwellings used by the immigrants in the fifth to seventh centuries were not the long-houses of the Continent but rectangular, timber structures with the weight of their roofs carried by posts forming part of the walls, and without discernible divisions into animal and human quarters.

The difference between continental and English buildings of this period is very striking; the reasons for it are less obvious. The 'English' type of dwelling may have developed because new building materials in the form of sturdier timbers were available to the Anglo-Saxon immigrants once they arrived in England, because the English climate made it less necessary to house men and animals under the same roof, or because the modifications shown by the buildings at Wijster came to fruition in England. It is also possible that the immigrant Anglo-Saxons used native British labour to build their houses and that the buildings of early Anglo-Saxon England represent a fusion of continental Germanic and native British styles.

Another type of building which was common on both sides of the North Sea in the fifth to seventh centuries was the *Grubenhaus* or 'sunken hut'. This was a hut, normally no more than 6m long and 4.5m wide, whose floor was sunk up to 1m below the ground surface. In the Anglo-Saxons' continental homeland such huts were usually associated with large timber buildings of the classic aisled type and are thought to have been ancillary buildings, for example, workshops or slaves' sleeping quarters, rather than permanent dwellings.

Excavations in England, however, have shown that some Anglo-Saxon settlements contained great numbers of sunken huts and comparatively few larger timber buildings. Over two hundred *Grubenhäuser* were found in the Anglo-Saxon settlement at Mucking, for example, and about sixty at West Stow, Suffolk (West 1969) where they were associated with, but far outnumbered, post-built structures. At Bishopstone, Sussex, though, only three out of the twenty-two buildings which were excavated were sunken huts, the rest were the conventional type of Anglo-Saxon timber building (Bell 1977). Only few English settlements of the fifth to seventh centuries have so far been excavated so it is as yet impossible to draw any firm conclusions about the building types found on them, but the present evidence suggests that, contrary to continental practice, some of the *Grubenhäuser* on English sites served as dwellings. The differences between the Anglo-Saxon buildings in England and the dwellings of the Angles, Saxons and Jutes on the Continent suggest that the immigrants brought with them the traditional building practices of their homelands, but they modified them on arrival in England, perhaps for the reasons suggested above.

The ships which the immigrants may have used on their journeys across the North Sea will be dealt with elsewhere. They were probably of the open, clinker-built type propelled by oars and without sail (Ellmers 1978). A fourth-century example of this type of vessel has been dicovered at Nydam, Germany (Åkerlund 1963) and the Sutton Hoo ship displays similar characteristics. Unfortunately, we have as yet little knowledge of the size or carrying capacity of the ships in use precisely at the time of the main Anglo-Saxon immigration. Cemetery and settlement evidence can give us some idea of the density of Anglo-Saxon settlement in England in the fifth and sixth centuries, but we cannot even hazard a guess at the numbers of Anglo-Saxons who came across the North Sea, the numbers of ships needed to transport them, nor, precisely, the sea routes most favoured by the immigrants, although coastal routes with the shortest possible open-sea crossings are most likely.

Christianity, Invasions and Trade: England and the Continent in the Seventh to Ninth Centuries

With the arrival of St. Augustine in Thanet in 597 and the subsequent conversion of England to Christianity, we move on to the next phase of contacts across the North Sea. This was a time when England became as closely connected with the Christian countries of southern Europe as with the Germanic countries north of the Rhine. Masons came from Gaul, for example, to build early churches in Kent, and Gallic masons and glaziers were employed at Wearmouth and Jarrow in Northumbria when monasteries were built there in the late seventh century (Cramp 1969). Benedict Biscop, their founder, who travelled extensively on the Continent, was just one of the many Christian Englishmen who crossed the North Sea as missionaries to unconverted northern Europe or as pilgrims to the south. They often left England through the few newly-founded ports on the south and east coasts, such as Saxon Southampton which was mentioned as 'that mart called Hamwih' by St. Willibald in about 721 (Keen 1975), and entered the Continent through Quentovic in northern France or Domburg on the island of Walcheren at the mouth of the Rhine.

Settlements such as these grew up not only to serve as missionary ports but also to take advantage of trade between the British Isles, Scandinavia and continental Europe. Commercial activities at this time were stimulated by the stability of the Merovingian and later the Carolingian Empires on the Continent, and the eighth and ninth centuries saw the greatest resurgence of European trade since the fall of the Roman Empire. Much of this trade relied on water transport, and urban settlements began to grow up alongside rivers and close to, although often not precisely on, the coast. On the Continent, Dorestad (van Es 1969) on the Rhine was the most important trading centre until the middle of the ninth century when it was superseded by the Scandinavian ports of Hedeby, now in Germany, and Birka in Sweden. Dorestad's importance was based on transit traffic along the Rhine, and Frisian merchants voyaged from it in their cogs carrying goods to the British Isles, Scandinavia and the western seaboard of Europe. Archaeological evidence shows that the Frisian merchants travelled as far north as Birka and Hedeby, which were beginning to prosper as international market centres in the early ninth century, and as early as the eighth century documents record Frisian colonies in London and York. These, with Southampton and Ipswich, are the four ports which are known to have existed in England by the early eighth century. There is good reason to suppose that others such as Sandwich and Dover were beginning to grow at this time, but little more can be said on the basis of present evidence.

Eighth-century York and London (Museum of London 1980) are known mainly through their documentary records. Ipswich (Dunmore 1975, 1976) is not referred to in documents until the tenth century but pottery which has been found in archaeological excavations in the modern town shows that it was already a flourishing port in the eighth century, with trading connections across the North Sea to the Rhineland. Southampton, however, is the best known Anglo-Saxon port, because of the excavations which have taken place there since the end of the Second World War (Addyman & Hill 1968, 1969).

By the eighth century it was both the main exit port for missionaries travelling from southern England to the Continent, and a commercial centre involved in trade with northern France (perhaps through the port of Quentovic) and, to a much lesser extent, the Low Countries (Hodges 1977, 1978a, 1978b). Pottery made in workshops on the Continent has been found in excavations in Southampton; it was probably brought to England along with the wine which was one of the most important products imported into Anglo-Saxon England both from northern France and Rhineland (Holdsworth 1976, 1980).

The seventh and eighth centuries were mainly ones of peace which allowed commerce to flourish and prosper and ports to develop into undefended urban complexes. But there were dangers to both ports and shipping even at this time of relative peace and these took the form of piracy, which had been rife in the North Sea and English Channel since before the end of the Roman Empire. Many ports of this period were situated at some distance from the coast, on rivers, inlets or deltas (Clarke 1979), and their sites may have been chosen with an eye to possible threats from pirates. Their inland sites, however, may also reflect the volume and type of goods which were being traded. The cargoes which were carried then seem to have been of small volume but high value (such as the precious wine imported into Saxon Southampton), which could be accommodated in fairly small vessels of shallow draught able to negotiate the approaches to riverine ports. This essentially peaceful picture where pirates were the only danger was suddenly shattered in the ninth century by the eruption of the Scandinavian Vikings into western Europe. They themselves first appeared as pirates, looting undefended monasteries and towns in lightning attacks, and then retiring back to Scandinavia with their booty. Their activities effectively disrupted trade between the British Isles and Europe in the ninth century, and may have been instrumental in the desertion of a number of formerly important ports, suchs as Dorestad, sacked by the Vikings in 834.

The history of the Viking attacks in Western Europe is well known (Sawyer 1975, 1978; Smyth 1977) and need not be dealt with in detail here. In England the *Anglo-Saxon Chronicle* records the first arrival of a Viking raiding party in Dorset in *c*. 789, when three ships were greeted as merchantmen by Beaduheard, the reeve of the king of Wessex, who was promptly murdered for his pains. An attack on the monastery of Lindisfarne followed in 793 and from then onwards the number of attacks increased, mainly on coastal monastic sites. Such attacks continued sporadically until the middle of the ninth century when we have the first reference to Scandinavians overwintering, in Thanet in 850 and the Isle of Sheppey in 855. This was the beginning of the second phase of the Viking attacks on England, with the obvious intention of colonization. Such an intention was realized in 876, when part of Yorkshire was occupied by Scandinavians, and by 881, when the Danelaw was established.

The archaeological evidence for the Vikings in ninth-century England is regrettably slight (Wilson 1976), limited to a few scattered burials, some stone crosses carved in Scandinavian art styles, a few pieces of jewellery and one or two settlements. The most important of these is the town of York, which was captured by the Vikings in 867 and which subsequently became the capital of that area of England which was under Scandinavian rule. Recent excavations in Coppergate (Hall 1978) have shown York to have been a flourishing commercial centre with workshops devoted to leatherworking, woodworking, glassmaking and jewellery production, among other things. In addition, York seems to have been a centre of international trade, perhaps the west European equivalent of the Scandinavian ports of Hedeby and Birka. The town was accessible by water from the North Sea, and is characteristic of the period in its position as a port situated some distance from the coast. Lincoln has also recently been shown to have been of importance in Scandinavian England, with excavations at Flaxengate (Colyer & Jones 1979) revealing a series of timber buildings in which trades similar to those at York were practised. Lincoln, on the River Witham, was also a port with international connections and, although it never rivalled York in importance, it was obviously a centre of Scandinavian activity in the ninth and tenth centuries.

Further north in the British Isles the Scandinavians had colonized the northern isles, the Hebrides and parts of mainland Scotland by the early ninth century. The sea route followed by the Viking ships to these areas must have been that westwards from southwest Norway to Shetland, a route also followed when the Norwegian Vikings sailed to Iceland and Greenland. The contrast between these bold forays across the open seas and the routes pursued by the Anglo-Saxons in the fifth and sixth centuries is a vivid illustration of the improved ship-building technique practised by the Scandinavian Vikings (Binns 1980).

Modifications of the hull shape, and the addition of a sail meant that by the ninth century the Viking ship was capable of sailing long distances on the high seas, and methods of navigation seem to have kept pace with the development of the ships. As a result, the Vikings were much more mobile than their predecessors, and could therefore extend their contacts from America in the west to Byzantium in the east. A number of different types of ships were probably used by the Vikings in their North Sea voyages, although they all conformed to the same basic design of an open, clinker-built vessel which could be propelled both by oars and by sail. The discovery of five tenth-century Viking ships at Skuldelev, near Roskilde, Denmark (Olsen & Crumlin-Pedersen 1978) has shown something of the variety of ships known to the Vikings: merchantmen, warships, coasters, for example, and we should imagine similar types of vessels plying the North Sea in the ninth century, some carrying warriors for forays against the coasts of England and western Europe, some carrying passengers who were to colonize the lands around the North Sea, others coming peacefully, laden with goods for exchange in markets such as York and Lincoln.

The fifth to the ninth centuries saw immense changes in the lands around the North Sea, beginning with the great movements of Germanic peoples from the Continent to England, continuing with the adoption of Christianity by those same peoples, the formation of states under royal rule, and the resurgence of international trade. Finally, the Vikings erupted from Scandinavia, sailing the seas as pirates, colonizers and merchants. Throughout the period the North Sea served as a unifier, not a barrier. The peoples living around its coasts exploited the sea as a means of communication, and were linked closely together culturally, economically, and to some extent even politically.

Bibliography

Addyman P.V. and Hill D.H., "Saxon Southampton: a review of the evidence I", *Proc. Hants. Field Club and Archaeol. Soc.* 25, 1968, 61–93

Addyman P.V. and Hill D.H., "Saxon Southampton: a review of the evidence II", *Proc. Hants. Field Club and Archaeol. Soc.* 26, 1969, 61–96

Anglo-Saxon Chronicle see Garmonsway 1972

Bede see Sherley-Price 1955

Bell M., Excavations at Bishopstone, Sussex, *Sussex Archaeological Collections* 115, 1977

Binns A., *Viking Voyagers*, London 1980

Bøe J., «Jernalderens keramikk i Norge», *Bergen Museums Skrifter* 14, 1931

Clarke H., "The archaeology, history and architecture of the medieval ports of the east coast of England", in McGrail (ed.), 1979, 55–65

Colyer C. and Jones M.J., "Excavations at Lincoln. Second interim report: excavations in the lower town", *The Antiquaries Journal* 59, 1979, 50–91

Cramp R., "Excavations at the Saxon monastic sites of Wearmouth and Jarrow, Co. Durham: an interim report", *Medieval Archaeology* 13, 1969, 21–66

Dunmore S. *et al.*, "The origin and development of Ipswich: an interim report", *East Anglian Archaeology* 1, 1975, 57–67

Dunmore S. *et al.*, "Ipswich archaeological survey: the second interim report", *East Anglian Archaeology* 3, 1976, 135–40

Ellmers D., "Die Schiffe der Angelsachsen", *Sachsen und Angelsachsen, Veröffenlichungen des Helms-Museums 32*, 1978, 495–509

van Es W.A., "Wijster. A native village beyond the imperial frontier", *Palaeohistoria XI*, 1967

van Es W.A., "Excavations at Dorestad: a preliminary report: 1967–1968" *Berichten van de Rijksdienst voor het Oudheidkundig Bodemonderzoek* 19, 1969, 183–208

Evison V.I., *The Fifth-Century Invasions South of the Thames*, London 1965

Garmonsway G.N. (ed.), *The Anglo-Saxon Chronicle*, London 1972

van Giffen A.E., "Der Warf in Ezinge, Provinz Groningen, Holland, und seine westgermanischen Häuser", *Germania* 20, 1936, 40–7

Gildas see Winterbottom 1978

Green *et al.* (eds.) *Social Archaeology and Settlement*, British Archaeological Reports International Series 47, Oxford 1978

Haarnagel W., *Die Grabung Feddersen Wierde*, Neumünster 1979

Hall R.A., *Viking Age York and the North*, Council for British Archaeology Research Report 27, London 1978

Hawkes S.C. and Dunning G.C., "Soldiers and settlers in Britain, fourth to fifth century", *Medieval Archaeology 5*, 1961, 1–70

Hills C., "The Anglo-Saxon settlement of England", in Wilson (ed.) 1980, 81–94

Hodges R., "Trade and urban origins in dark age England: an archaeological critique of the evidence", *Berichten van de Rijksdienst voor het Oudheidkundig Bodemonderzoek* 27, 1977, 191–215

Hodges R., "Ports of trade in early medieval Europe", *Norwegian Archaeological Review* 11: 2, 1978a, 97–101

Hodges R., "State formation and the role of trade in middle Saxon England", in Green *el al.* (eds.) 1978b, 439–53

Holdsworth P., "Saxon Southampton: a new review", *Medieval Archaeology* 20, 1976, 26–61

Holdsworth P., *Excavations at Melbourne Street, Southampton, 1971–76*, Council for British Archaeology Research Report 33, London 1980

Johnston D.E. (ed.), *The Saxon Shore*, Council for British Archaeology Research Report 18, London 1977

Jones M.U., "Crop-mark sites at Mucking, Essex", *The Antiquaries Journal* 48, 1968, 210–30

Jones M.U., "Saxon pottery from a hut at Mucking, Essex", *Berichten van de Rijksdienst voor het Oudheidkundig Bodemonderzoek* 19, 1969, 145–56

Jones M.U., "Excavations at Mucking, Essex: a second interim report", *The Antiquaries Journal* 54, 1974a, 183–99

Jones M.U. and W.T., "The early Saxon landscape at Mucking, Essex", in Rowley (ed.) 1974b, 20–35

Jones M.U., "Die Siedlung Mucking in Essex", *Sachsen und Angelsachsen, Veröffenlichungen des Helms-Museums 32*, 1978, 413–22

Keen L., "Illa mercimonia qui dicitur Hamwih: a study in early medieval urban development", *Archaeologia Atlantica* 1, 1975, 165–90

McGrail S. (ed.), *Medieval Ships and Harbours in Northern Europe*, British Archaeological Reports International Series 66, Oxford 1979

Miller M., "The last British entry in the Gallic Chronicles", *Britannia* 9, 1978, 315–8

Museum of London, *Archaeology of the City of London*, London 1980

Myres J.N.L., *Anglo-Saxon Pottery and the Settlement of England*, Oxford 1969

Nennius see Stevenson 1838

Olsen O. and Crumlin-Pedersen O., *Five Viking Ships from Roskilde Fjord,* Roskilde 1978

Rowley R. T. (ed.), *Anglo-Saxon Settlement and Landscape, British Archaeological Reports 6,* Oxford 1974

Sawyer P.H., *The Age of the Vikings,* London 1975

Sawyer P.H., *From Roman Britain to Norman England,* London 1978

Smyth A.P., *Scandinavian Kings in the British Isles, 850–880,* Oxford 1977

Sherley-Price L., *Bede. A History of the English Church and People,* Harmondsworth 1955

Stevenson J., *Nennii Historia Brittonum,* English Historical Society, London 1838

Welch M., "Highdown and its Saxon cemetery". *Worthing Museum and Art Gallery Publications,* 1976

West S.E., "The Anglo-Saxon village of West Stow: an interim report of the excavations 1965–68", *Medieval Archaeology* 13, 1969, 1–20

Wilson D.M. (ed.), *The Archaeology of Anglo-Saxon England,* London 1976

Wilson D.M. (ed.), *The Northern World,* London 1980

Winterbottom M. (ed.), *Gildas, The Ruin of Britain and Other Works,* London and Chichester, 1978

Zimmermann W.H., "A Roman iron age and early migration settlement at Flögeln", Kr. Westermünde, Lower Saxony, in Rowley (ed.), 1974, 56–73

Towards a North Sea Kingdom? Viking Age Incursions and later Attempts to Establish Scandinavian Rule "West over the Sea"

ALAN BINNS

There can scarcely have been any other period until our own in which the North Sea was as important, and so much depended upon skill in crossing it, as in the period of just over two centuries covered in this chapter. It is common knowledge that the Viking settlements in Britain had a great influence upon our placenames, our legal system and our language (including all our plural pronouns, they, their and them). The influence is thoroughgoing enough to demonstrate the importance of the settlements, however much historians have argued (with not a little special pleading, on both sides) about the numbers involved. The theme of this volume requires consideration of two questions less often raised, and much less easily answered. How far did these two centuries of Anglo-Scandinavian interaction, often though not always hostile, in the end produce an understanding and some common interests which might have produced a North Sea kingdom instead of an Anglo-Norman Britain turned towards France? And what was the determining role in this interaction of the ships, seamen and techniques involved?

Discussion about feelings, motives and roles is speculative; the objective evidence of ship-finds or documented dates does not illuminate them, and one has to turn to language for evidence of two different kinds. Language is the medium through which contemporary observers communicate to us their prejudices and assumptions as well as statements of motive or feeling, and we have to make due allowance for the former if we are to use the latter without being misled by it. Language is also evidence itself, as when the O.E. distinction between *fierd* the English army and *here* the hostile (Viking) army is no longer observed in the O.E. Chronicle entry E 1048, where an English king, Edward, calling out the English levies is said to *bannan ut here*. Similarly, the joint Anglo-Danish force attacking the Normans in York after the Conquest is described as *lith*. This is very different from terms like *wælwulfas* (slaughter-wolves) used before the year 1000AD, though even in the mid-tenth century poem on the re-taking of the Five Boroughs in the Chronicle the language used about the Christian Danes of the Midlands presents them as allies of the West Saxons against irreconcilably pagan Norse. The advantage of using the language itself as evidence is that it does not require us to consider how far chroniclers such as Ælnoth or Æthelweard aimed to tell the truth or what they believed to be true. We should recall that the great historian Bede meant by the "vera lex historiae" the obligation to inspire readers!

Steblin-Kamenskii in *The Saga Mind* has suggested that sagas deal in what he calls "syncretic truth", an interesting concept about which many have reservations. We certainly cannot assume that even the King's sagas are reliable guides to motive and view of the leaders in this period. The words used however, by writers in all three languages, have their own history, and can reveal the changing views built into the language even when their users are lying. And of course some statements dismissed by former historians as untrue can from this point of view be no less interesting, and sometimes, if one correctly understands the implication of the words used, may even prove to be true, or at least plausible, after all.

I have given as Appendix IV a highly selective group of texts which I find offer this sort of evidence: there is no question of rehabilitating historical sources, only of offering a useful reading of them. I think in the end it must remain very doubtful how far there was ever a real desire or serious attempt to found a North Sea Kingdom in either Norway, Denmark or England.

It is impossible to disagree with Professor G.N. Garmonsway when he observed in his 1963 Coke lecture on Canute and his Empire: "In reading the various records which describe his reign and character one rarely receives the impression that Canute at any time during his career deliberately made up his mind to play the game of power politics in order to win for himself an extensive empire across the northern seas. As long as his brother Harald ruled in Denmark, it is unlikely that any such ambition influenced his mind or his policies, and his subsequent intervention in Norwegian affairs seems mostly prompted by the importunities of those Norwegians who had fled to his court from St. Olaf's tyranny . . . Had he wished it, the most obvious path to a greater domination would have been into the Baltic, in active rivalry with the Swedes, if necessary . . . Just as it is false, in M. Louis Halphen's opinion, to regard Charlemagne as a great politician who planned and perfected his grand designs before embarking on his

enterprises, so too it is probably wrong to suppose that Canute's actions were dictated by any consistent policy of aggrandisement: they were rather those of an opportunist, one not particularly gifted with acumen and political sense to be able to anticipate the turn of events but decisive in action in pursuit of his interests when opportunity arose and the situation demanded it.''

Subsequent studies of the marine aspects of the question since Professor Garmonsway's judicious summing up seem to me to support his views. The shipping routes for whose regular use we have real evidence at the beginning of the eleventh century would scarcely have permitted the consolidation of a North Sea empire, even if it had been desired. The distances and difficulties involved are of a different order from those of William the Conqueror's frequent cross-Channel journeys. The northern route ran from west Norway between Bergen and Stavanger to the Shetlands, and thence via the Western Isles and down the Irish Sea to the French Atlantic coast, or more rarely down the east coast of Britain to the Humber. The southern route ran from Denmark, through the Limfjord and down the coast via the Frisian islands and the Rhine delta to the Thames estuary. Communication with the heart of Scandinavian England round the rivers flowing into the Humber was by both these routes circuitous and vulnerable to outside interference. It is noticeable that the old-style earldoms in the isles along the northern route survived very well, past the end of this period, but they certainly did not welcome the extension of royal power from either Scotland or Scandinavia, and survived precisely because they were at too great a distance for any contemporary organised seaborne force to have much hope of subduing them or controlling them once subdued.

The apparently vastly wealthier and more powerful Viking kingdom of York (often joined with Dublin) declined immediately its route to the sea via the Humber was no longer securely Scandinavian after the English reconquest of the Scandinavian Five Boroughs in the Midlands. At the end of the period, after the Norman Conquest, the Humber significantly provided the battleground between Dane and Norman as it had done between Harald Hardrada's Norwegians and the Anglo-Saxons: it was the access to the intensely Scandinavian area of England which had to provide the foundation of the authority of any king with ambitions to rule on both sides of the North Sea. The rejection of Harald Hardrada by the Scandinavian population of this region as we see it in the saga accounts of the Stamford Bridge campaign at once explains his failure and suggests how far the English and Scandinavians of northern England had indeed as the Latin chronicler observes "run together into one nation" conscious of common interests which divided them from Scandinavia as well as from the purely English south of Britain. Those placenames with the element "Owst" are perhaps not merely an Old Norse form of "east" but reflect a usage among the Scandinavian speakers parallel to that in Iceland, where recently arrived and temporary residents from mainland Scandinavia were nicknamed "Austman".

When we turn from the question of feelings and community of interest in a possible North Sea Kingdom, to that of the ships and seamanship, we may find a reason why the numerous and rewarding contacts of the ninth and tenth centuries did not grow into a stable kingdom in the eleventh. I think it is possible to detect a strong suggestion of changing ship types in the sources, and such changes are not always improvements in every way: usually the improved performance in one direction has to be bought at the expense of worse performance in another judged (sometimes with disastrous results) to be less important. In my opinion the entries in the Old English chronicle and the references to longships in Ragnar's saga are consistent with a replacement of the earlier less specialised handier and smaller craft, after about 1000AD by larger, more powerful in battle, but less seaworthy and shorter-range craft. Tuxen's old idea that these craft had largely developed out of the experience of the Viking raids on England seems to me to deserve much more attention than it has received in our century.

The seaworthy and adaptable little ships of the early Viking voyages in the ninth century were by its end increasingly vulnerable to the much larger ships with twice as many rowers which King Alfred built against them, as the Old English Chronicle entry for 896 tells us. The captains of these dreadnoughts were often Frisian, but we do not know who supervised their building. Were the shipwrights also Frisians? Alfred describes the hull form as neither Frisian nor Danish and we should not exclude the possibility that Anglo-Saxon traditions of boatbuilding lent themselves, by heavier scantlings and more rigid hulls, to the production of larger warships than the Scandinavian techniques were well adapted to producing. I know of no archaeological evidence for this speculation (Graveney can scarcely be legitimately brought into the argument?) but it seems consistent with the language of the Chronicle.

Once capital ships of this type existed on the English side of the North Sea attacks intended to conquer the country and not simply gather booty from a rapid raid had to include at least some vessels capable of meeting them, for it seems that at any time after the 880's it was English doctrine to attack (preferably from seaward) Viking fleets in their chosen river mouth, perhaps to cut off the first wave onto the beach from any further support, perhaps as the surest way of bringing them to action once they were fully committed to an objective.

The capacity of such war vessels for long open sea crossings was suspect and the larger crews were much more difficult to supply, but these disadvantages were of no great moment either for coastal defence work in England or for campaigning in the Baltic or along the coast of Norway. To transfer them however from one of these fields to the other evidently was only possible by the circuitous coastal routes recorded in the Chronicle. It is not possible to go into greater detail here but the contrast with the earlier Viking period is dealt with in my *Viking Voyagers,* Heinemann, 1980.

The Old English Chronicle is in these two centuries contemporary, either an official source or a regional one taking a jaundiced view of authority, but not all important events were registered (e.g. Viking fleet C, taken from Æthelweard). The sagas are later, and cannot be taken automatically to represent a Scandinavian view taken by participants in the events. Often their view of events in England seems more likely to be derived from post-Conquest Anglo-Norman clerics, strongly prejudiced against the Anglo-Saxon royal house the Normans had replaced. *Knytlinga saga* for instance was probably composed in Iceland between 1241 and 1259 by Lawman Olafr Thortharson and largely based on his uncle's Heimskringla. Its superior account of Canute's campaigns, and its greater accuracy in rendering English names, are not evidence that it derives in any way from the memories of any of Canute's campaigners except for those embedded in skaldic verse. The improvements more probably came from some Latin chronicle of English events recently received in Iceland; probably it resembled closely Roger of Wendover's, as the version of events seems to be derived from his, and it is not the true version which we find in the O.E. Chronicle, but a legendary one which we can follow developing in the course of the eleventh and twelfth centuries, in the multitude of interdependent chroniclers.

Of these I have examined William of Malmesbury, Benedict of Peterborough, Florence of Worcester, Symeon of Durham, Henry of Huntingdon, Matthew Paris, John of Wallingford and Roger of Wendover. The general story is the same in all of them, as they built one upon another, though of course they chose to omit and include different things. I choose Roger of Wendover for purposes of comparison rather than Roger of Hoveden or John of Wallingford because his version of events is the closest to Knytlinga's and because I think there are other grounds for supposing that the Gesta Anglorum accessible to Snorri and used by him for events in England, was more like Roger of Wendover than any of the other 12th century chronicles. In App. I I have set out the main events in the order in which they occur in Wendover and Knytlinga, starting with Cnut's arrival in England (Knytlinga) or return to England (Wendover).

The most interesting features of agreement to me are those which are probably unhistorical and certainly first appear comparatively late in the development of the English historical tradition. There is no hint in the O.E. Chronicle of a confused flight by some of the English at the battle of Sherston because they thought Edmund was dead, though some knew he wasn't. I have not found the story before Henry of Huntingdon (ca. 1130). The same is true of the idea of a hand-to-hand combat between Edmund and Cnut, which indeed has been seen as a misunderstanding of the O.E. phrase *comon togædere* by a later writer. The attribution of Swein's death to St Edmund, and of Edmund Ironside's death to Eadric Streona first appears in the historical tradition in Henry of Huntingdon, but is found earlier (about 1100) in *De Miraculis Sancti Eadmundi* by Herman Archdeacon, a text which his distinguished *nafni* Herman Pálsson has shown was early absorbed into Icelandic historical tradition. Even if it is assumed that the saga version of events in England goes back to an earlier Old Norse stage before 1150AD in the writing of Ari Frodi, it would still be recognisably derived from Anglo-Norman writers evidently the last to propagate evidence in favour of the North Sea Kingdom alternative to their own state.

The Latin sources used in compiling my calendar show the international role of Latin at this period. Ethelweard translates about 975AD into his own almost impenetrable Latin (see App. 2) a version of the O.E. Chronicle better than any surviving one. Florence of Worcester, before 1118-AD does the same. Both have information about Viking matters surviving in no other text. The Encomium Emmæ has some splendid descriptions of Viking ships in orotund Latin which (like Æthelweard or Ælnoth on the ships) occasionally reminds one of Skaldic verses. I doubt if there is any connection, but find it reassuring that contemporaries of such different backgrounds share similar attitudes to similar vessels. Unfortunately the Encomium Emmæ also shows that a really prejudiced contemporary can be quite as misleading and unreliable as any later romancer.

Ordericus Vitalis, though a Norman cleric committed to William, is aware of his faults and failures and gives a detailed account of Saint Cnut's skilled campaigning around and across the Humber, which Knytlinga saga rather strangely ignores. To me this demonstrates conclusively that it has no sort of connection with the memories of any participants in that campaign, who would scarcely have ignored completely their own triumphs over the most famous and succesful general of their day. Ælnoth on the other hand is an Englishman comitted to St Cnut, who gives what I am tempted to call the real motives for his English expeditions, and these again rather tell against the idea of a consciously planned North Sea kingdom, though they do not, of course, affect its potentiality. It seems unlikely that Cnut or his father Svein could ever have believed that Svein had a claim on the English throne as a nephew of Edward or son of Hardacnut. They at least must have known, whatever Norman chronicles thought, that he was not either of these things, being a cousin of Hardacnut and no relation at all to Edward, a child of Emma's first marriage before her second to Cnut. Nor does it seem likely that Ordericus made up a false claim; he is just as (pardonably) confused about the intricacies of the progeny of Canute the Great. Ælnod, at St. Cnut's court is naturally better informed; interestingly, he is equally well informed about the deception techniques prepared by William against St Cnut's 1085 invasion of England. As that never sailed, the knowledge and his political intelligence about native English compliance suggest he had a special interest and sources of information in this field. I think it likely that he had himself met many of the numerous emissaries from England he refers to.

After this review of the source material it is time to present a brief calendar of the relevant entries.

865

The great army (A) landed in East Anglia, took twelve months to consolidate there before moving, and then campaigned for 10 years without any use of ships. In both these features it differs from all preceding and succeeding Scandinavian forces in England. The contemporary title "Great Army" might well be connected with this difference.

878

Viking fleet (B), 23 ships from S. Wales lost 800 men in defeat at Countisbury Hill, Devon. Leader "brother of Ingvar and Ubbe". Viking fleet C at Fulham, thence to Ghent.

884

Fleet C returns to Rochester, then to Benfleet, thence to Louvain. Assisted by ships from A from E. Anglia. 16 ships of A captured off R. Stour. Cuerdale hoard of Cnut coins coined in York and Quentowic.

892

Army D shipped from Boulogne. 250 ships Appledore, 80 Milton. Junction prevented by Alfred until synchronised diversionary attacks on North and South coast of Devon by ships from A.

894
At conclusion of campaign D follows circuitous route from N. Wales to Essex, keeping within area settled by A.

897
Beach battle with well known chronicle description of Alfred's new ships.

914
Fleet E Brittany to Wales in spring, on to Ireland in summer.

927
Guthfrith unsuccessfully besieges York.

937
His son Olaf brings large fleet from Dublin, defeated at Brunanburh. Harald Harfagre sends gift of ship to Æthelstan in York.

947
Erik Bloodaxe, expelled from Norway, takes York.

980-990
Raids on South and West coasts *not* North and East.

991
Olaf Tryggvason treaty with Ethelred after Maldon. "Any merchant ship of any country, even if wrecked, is immune from pillage in English estuary. English ship and cargo immune in foreign waters if afloat or beached and sheeted. Cargo *not* protected in foreign warehouse".

994
Olaf Tryggvason and Svein Haraldson 94 ships (Fleet F)

997-1002
South and West coasts raided again.

1003-1008
Danish raids mainly South and South East. 20 English ships going (Fleet G) pirating pursued by 80 which were driven ashore, subsequently burnt.

1012
Thorkell Havi defects to Ethelred with 45 ships (Fleet H).

1013
Sweyn. Denmark – Sandwich – Gainsborough, where ships left. Harries only across Watling St.

1014
Cnut. Gainsborough – Sandwich – Denmark.

1015
Thorkell Havi redefects with 9 ships to Cnut. Cnut. Denmark – Sandwich – Poole. Thorkell Havi's remaining 40 ships join Danes. Cnut accepted as king 1016.

1018
Viking fleet 30 ships (Fleet I) defeated by Cnut's royal fleet of 40 ships, which were reduced to 16 by end of reign.

1019
Cnut goes to take over Denmark on Harald's death, leaving Thorkell as regent in England.

1021
Thorkell outlawed.

1023
Thorkell regent of Denmark.

1028
Cnut takes 50 ships (Fleet J) of English, conquers Norway.

1040
Hardacnut takes England with 62 ships (Fleet K).

1042
After Hardacnut's death Magnus of Norway claims England as well as Denmark.

1045 and 6
35 English ships (Fleet L) at Sandwich on guard against Magnus.

1047 and 8
Sweyn of Denmark requests (Fleet M) 50 ships from England against Magnus. Declined on both occasions as too risky.

Viking fleet 25 ships (Fleet N) raid Isle of Wight and South. Sell booty in Flanders.

1049
Edward's Royal fleet reduced to 14 ships then to none.

1066

May
Tostig takes Sandwich. Joined by 17 ships (Fleet O) from Orkney.

June
Tostig with 60 ships enters Humber, defeated on South and North banks. After losses 12 ships continue to Scotland.

August
Steady Northerly winds delay William in Normandy. August 12 – September 27.

Sept. 8
English ships moved from South Coast to London (weather losses on way). Harald Hardrada 300 ships (Fleet P) Orkney, Cleveland, Scarborough, Humber, English ships withdraw up Ouse, then Wharfe to Tadcaster, so Norwegian fleet stops at Riccal below Wharfe-Ouse confluence.

Sept. 25
Battle of Stamford Bridge.

Sept. 27
William sails at night, loses touch with fleet, anchors until daylight, fleet rejoins.

1069
In response to prayers for help, and payment, Sven Estridson dispatches 240 ships (Fleet Q) of Danes and English. Sandwich – Ipswich – Norwich. Entered Humber between August 15 and September 8. One ship foraging in North Lincs, surprised by Lincoln garrison, all but 3 captured, abandoned ship broken up. York sacked September 20. Valthjof cuts Norman heads off one by one.

Danes on William's arrival retire to ships, cross to Lincolnshire. On William's arrival at Axholm, re-cross to Yorkshire bank. William goes South, leaving Robert. Danes emerged from marshes to share the feasts of the country people. Normans attacked whilst they were at table, pursued them to ships. At Christmas Danes return to York. William hastening there delayed at Pontefract river crossing. When William arrives at York the Danes have gone. William posts forces along the banks of the Humber to resist Danes. Danes allowed to remain in Humber over winter, paid to desist.

1070
Danish Vikings at the Tees. Svein from Denmark to Humber. Danish housecarls to Ely. Outlaws in many boats to Peterborough. By the time Normans arrived all afloat. Peace between William and Svein, who sailed from Humber to Thames, waited 2 days then sailed to Denmark.

1075
Earls Roger and Ralph send to Denmark for a pirate host. 200 (Fleet Q) ships under Cnut Svein's son and Earl Hakon entered Humber. Raided York minster losing all men involved including Hakon's son.

English ask Cnut to avenge his kinsman, Harald's death at William's hands and restore their ancient liberties, sending him many messengers. Cnut moved by both reasons and by a desire to restore the glory of Danish arms and recover the Danish kingships in England. Cnut seeks Olaf's help for expedition against England which Olaf can lead. Olaf declines as Danes have done well in England but Norwegians haven't, but offers 60 ships (Fleet R) for venture.

1085
Cnut collects fleet in Limfjord. William removes supplies from English coast, imports troops, (perhaps starts Doomsday survey to feed them) and orders English to shave beards and assimilate their appearance to Norman, to delude the adversary, but few did. Cnut's fleet dispenses after long delays. S Cnut martyred.

This very cursory compilation of the annals of maritime interest I hope gives a conspectus brief enough to be grasped as a development, and must suggest a couple of dozen speculations about the role of the ships and the men on board them. The 878 entry suggests that the ships had appreciably more than forty men each, as it does not claim they were annihilated. Once we assume a crew of fifty or sixty men it seems that we are well into the range of size represented by the Gokstad ship. Any leader in South Wales able to muster more than twenty such ships would have been of considerable standing in Norway or Denmark. Fleet E is 36 years later, but one wonders whether it had any units in common with B. Or were some the children of B and if so had they never been "home" to the east side of the North Sea? It must seem to us that fleets B, C and E were at best tangential to the concerns of A, and yet A or its descendants usually turned out to assist them. But was that part of a grand design, as some have thought, or simply fellow-feeling?

Fleet N in 1048 does not act like the vanguard of any invasion from Norway, and we cannot know what sort of ships composed it. One wonders what they bought with the proceeds of the sale of the booty in Flanders, and where they went with it. Home? It seems slightly reminiscent of the infamous eighteenth century triangular trade of goods to Africa, slaves from there to America, colonial produce from there home so that a single voyage produced a tripled profit. Such triangular routes seem at least as likely for the Viking age, in part because of the restricted navigational techniques available, as well as commercial, considerations. My impression is that "there and back" almost "liner" routes are essentially a nineteenth century phenomenon, and that earlier seafarers were essentially engaged upon a venture rather than a return trip from A to B. The circulation round the periphery of the North Sea, rather than direct crossings over the Dogger Bank which the sources depict, is not to be attributed to timidity or

incompetence. These ships also crossed the open Atlantic to Greenland, at this period, but we never hear of a fighting fleet or even a single warship getting as far as Iceland!

The sizes of the fleets do not seem as hard to believe as some recent historians have asserted.

865 A unknown
878 B 23
878, 884 C unknown
892 D 250, 310, 80.
914 E unknown
994 F 94
1003 G 20
1012 H 45
1018 I 30
1028 J 50
1040 K 62
1046 L 35
1047 M 50
1047 N 25
1066 O 17 - 60 - 12 P 300
1075 Q 200

It is apparent that in two centuries there were four major fleets, two in the first twenty years, two in the last twenty. 994AD Olaf Tryggvason and Svein Haraldson looks more like a large small fleet than a small large one and its movements support this. The rest, "normal" Viking fleets run from 20 to 60 ships, and there is no obvious reason to regard these figures as some historians have done as incredible or conventional.

Does a suggestion of at least two different ship types emerge? 20 Gokstads, 1500 men seems a very large minimum unit, whilst 50 vessels much smaller (2500?) seems scarcely adequate to conquer Norway.

These figures bring out well that the early and late periods of intense N. Sea Viking activity were at any rate from the point of view of chroniclers here, separated by one of very little, the tenth century. But of course the tenth century is the period of Dublin-York activity, which may well have impinged a good deal less on communications of other N. Sea kingdoms.

We see east Anglians (ex A) co-operating with C, and 16 Viking ships captured in a sea battle 13 years before Alfred's "new" ships are recorded in the Chronicle. What sort of English ships captured them at the mouth of the Stour? English "old" ships or hired Viking ships? One might compare the continental practice of hiring Viking fleets, or Thorkell Hávi's? Æthelweard is clear that "a fleet was sent by Alfred, sixteen ships met them, were cleared by force of arms and the officers killed. The rest of the pirate fleet came on its way, they plied their oars, put aside thole-pins, the waves shone with clashing arms".

What sort of ships made up the 310 for D? Surely not all Gokstads from Denmark; the army involved had long been fighting away from its ships. The O.E. Chron. says *wurdon gescipode* perhaps "were shipped". Æthelweard says *construunt classem, primnas dant ventis volant rostra ad Anglicas partes*. The diversionary attacks on the North and South coasts of Devon from E. Anglia and Northumbria suggest excellent staffwork and communications, but this is the only occasion on which the army is said to cross in one lift with horses and all, and it must on the face of it seem that some of the ships at least were not of the Ladby or Gokstad type.

D's route in 894 suggests the A area was regarded as "home ground", in which they would be safe from attack. The embassy from Harald suggests that Norse and English kings had common interest against the Irish Sea Vikings, and his son Erik Bloodaxe's move to York suggests it was regarded as alternative kingdom, part of the same world.

The distribution of places raided in England 980–990 and 997–1002 markedly avoids A areas; it also suggests a normal route coasting down the Frisian islands, not crossing direct. The importance of Sandwich 1013, 1014, 1015, 1046 confirms this. If this was so firmly so in eleventh century, is it at all likely that the situation earlier was different?

The English fleet going Viking in Fleet G was probably not unique. Thorkell Hávi's fleet of Jomsborg Vikings were obviously professional mercenaries quite devoid of nationalist prejudice, and their fates reflect this. Some, e.g. Hemming changed sides once too often, some e.g. Eilaf were saved by an English mistress.

In the early eleventh century both Cnut and Edward ran down their fleets, Cnut from 40 to 16, Edward first to 14 then to none. This is scarcely consistent with the idea that Viking fleets of forty ships were any longer likely to erupt at any time but suggests a fairly peaceful period at sea outside large dynastic wars. One would suppose it could too imply an increase of seagoing merchant ships available to charter.

Had the warships become so large and specialised as to be expensive, shortlived and of limited utility? Or was the nature of sea warfare changing in some way? The numbers involved in the early eleventh century seem very small by comparison with the previous century and increase again in 1066. Tostig's fleet O illustrates the fluidity of a Viking fleet as we can follow its changes in the records. The original number on arrival at Sandwich is not recorded, 20–30 seems most likely. At Sandwich it was increased by 17 from Orkney (presumably with Harald Hardrada's consent) and some (13??) local ships. By the time it appeared in the Humber it had 60 ships (perhaps of three different types?) and there some deserted (Orkney 17, Sandwich 13?) and some were lost, leaving 12 to continue North.

It seems that the English ships opposing Harald may have regarded their main role as being to ensure that essential land reinforcements from the South could reach York (and they therefore protected the

Tadcaster crossing) whilst the Norse ships were unwilling to risk being bottled up in the Ouse if they went past the Wharfe confluence, or to risk allowing the English ships to move out into the estuary behind them.

The implications of all Norse accounts of the Stamford Bridge campaign are of foreboding, and disappointed hopes of local solidarity. The well-known saga account of the refusal of a local carter to let the shivering Styrkar, in flight after the defeat, have his sheepskin coat is emblematic. If the episode ever took place it certainly cannot be used as evidence that Anglo-Saxon and Old Norse were still mutually intelligible at this date, the whole point is that the carter was one of those local Scandinavians who had shown no readiness to rally to the support of a Norwegian king they by this date regarded as an invader.

The account of the archaic-looking random adventures on the Humber in 1069 shows the loose organisation of a Viking fleet. The most important English ally, Edgar the Atheling is one of three men to escape when a solitary ship looking for provisions (down the Trent?) is surprised. This (mainly from Ordericus) is the best close record I know of a very professional exploitation of the ship's advantages which reduced the best general and best army of Europe to sulky helplessness. William's hasty departure South leaving Robert in charge has somewhat the air of a general preserving his image, and it is striking that his victory there is described as easy; by comparison presumably with events on the Humber. The difficulties at Pontefract on his return, by comparison with Harold's rapid transit at Tadcaster, show what he lost by not having the ships to command a better river-crossing.

Svein's arrival in 1070 suggests that the base remaining in England was solid enough to make a re-conquest worth considering on the spot. He evidently decided that it was not attractive. Harald Hardrada had been disappointed of support locally,

and one consequence of St Cnut's adroit exploitation of the fleet's mobility was that William's vengeance had been concentrated on the local population. After two devastations Scandinavian England was probably no longer much richer than Denmark or Norway, and much more difficult to hold against William, who had been skilfully eluded rather than defeated. On the return the 2 day wait at the Thames (for stragglers to catch up?) as well as indicating the southern route suggests what a large area a Viking fleet or army on the move was dispersed over.

The last two entries are based on Cnytlinga and Ælnod. One wonders whether Cnut was really bothered about the Wends, or whether he was coming round to Svein's opinion? The conversation between Olaf and Cnut in Cnytlinga is no more historic than that between Harald and Tostig in Heimskringla (why should, how could, an Icelander 200 years later know of it?) but it is a shrewd assessment, which could just as well have been formed in 1080 as 1250, of what the situation then was.

Conclusion

This selection (and it is admittedly only a selection) suggests that those in the best position to judge, Harald Hardrada, Tostig, Svein Estridson, St Cnut, all concluded that attempts to establish a North Sea kingdom were not rewarding. The Norway of Harald Hardrada, the Denmark of Svein Estridson were not capable of defeating the England of Harald Godwinsson or William. *If* Harald Hardrada had won at Stamford Bridge he might have been able to fight, with superior ships, the sort of campaign against William fought by St Cnut. But would he have defeated him at Hastings? Stenton makes the point that William advancing inland probably did not know which Harald he would have to fight. But he did know it would not be both, and it seems to me that the really decisive period is not 1066 and after with its large fleets and armies, but the time thirty years earlier, of Canute the Great's death, when his own lack of interest in any unification of the three countries led him to treat them as a family estate to be divided between the sons.

About the ships I'm happy to be more positive. It would quite simply have been impossible for the recorded history of these two centuries to have taken the course it did without a large number of intelligent and skilful shipbuilders, navigators and fleet leaders whose ingenuity produced improved ships, techniques and tactics which are as important as, and more attractive than, the castles, cavalry and cathedrals developed outside the North Sea area.

Appendix I

Wendover
Cnut attacks Mercia, London (unsuccessfully) & Northumbria
Ethelred dies, and all English except Londoners choose Cnut as king.
Londoners choose Edmund. First battle between Cnut & Edmund at Pen
2nd & 3rd battle in Worcestershire
Edmund fights in van. Eadric holds up dead head, saying it is Edmund's. Some English flee, others, knowing the king is alive, fight on, then flee

4th battle at Brcinford
5th battle at Ottefort
6th battle at Essendon
Edmund penetrates the Danish ranks and confronts Cnut. They have "conflictus gravissimus". Eadric once again behaves treacherously

Formal single combat at Deerhurst between Cnut & Edmund

Agreement between Cnut & Edmund to divide kingdom

Edmund killed by Eadric, who sent his son to kill him at night in the privy

Family of Edmund banished

Cnut marries Emma
Various benefactions of Cnut
Cnut's expedition to Sweden & Norway

Cnut goes to Rome with great magnificence

Cnut conquers Scots

Cnut crowns his sons, Swein son of Alfgifu over Norway, Hardecnut son of Emma over Denmark

Cnut dies Idus Novembris "in urbe Wintoniensi in veteri monasterio, more regio, cujus anima gloria perfruatur æterna".

Cnut once rebuked the waves (and his courtiers)

Knytlinga
Cnut attacks Lindsey, Northumbria, then goes south
Ethelred dies, Emma intends to go to Normandy, is detained by Cnut who marries her

Battle between Edmund and Cnut at Skorstein (= OE Sceorstan, second battle)
Edmund rides into Danish army, attacks Cnut in person, but is then forced to retreat.
Some of his men thought him dead and thus fled, some saw him retreating and thus retreated themselves, though he called them back

The Ulfr jarl battle

Battle at Brentford

Battle at Assatun

Battle at Norwich

Unsuccessful attack on London, joined by Jarl Erik

The Erikr jarl passage

Agreement between Cnut & Edmund to to divide kingdom

Heithrick Strjona kills Edmund "meth morthvigi"

Family of Edmund banished

Cnut at first receives Olaf from Norway, but later invades Norway

Cnut crowns Swein son of Alfifu king of Norway, Horthaknut his son king of Denmark
Cnut has a great part of Scotland, puts it under Harald.
Cnut goes to Rome with great magnificence.
On his return dies Idus Novembris "var i borg, theirri er heitir i Morstr"

Appendix II

Chronicon Æthelweardi, Cap IV
Porro Anglia vetus sita est inter Saxones et Giotos, habens oppidum capitale quod sermone Saxonico Slesuuic nuncupatur, secundum vero Danos Haithaby... Præfati enim duces eorum inde venerunt Brittaniam primi: hoc est Hengest et Horsa filii Vuyhtelsi, auus eorum Vuicta, et proauus eorum Vuithar, atauus quidem eorum Vuothen, qui et rex multitudinis barbarorum. In tanta etenim seductione oppressi aquilonales increduli ut deum colunt usque in hodiernam diem, viz. Dani, Northmanni quoque et Sueui. De quibus Lucanus: Fundit ab extremo flavos aquilone Sueuos.

This is mainly from Bede, but it is the only reference to O.N. Vidarr in England, Æthelweard is obviously well-informed about Scandinavian matters and regards them as interesting (Schleswig = Haithaby, Woden still worshipped).

Bk IV cap II
Iam apparatu æquestri quem natura negarat obliti classe aut certe explorationis ritu tam celeres aut æterni numinis per arua silvasque feruntur.
"Now provided with equestrian equipment (formerly) denied by nature, having put their fleet from their mind they are born through woods and fields swift as exploratory scouts or the divine spirit." The O.E. Chronicle texts surviving simply say "They rode"!

Bk IV cap III
Denique classes eorum elevant vela, dant vento carinas, procella ingruit tristis, mergitur pars non minima, centum numero carinæ supremæ, iuxta rupem quæ Suuanauuic nuncupatur.
Then their squadrons raised sails, entrusted their ships to the wind, but a sad squall attacked, a large part to the number of 100 first-rate (or excellent?) ships was lost near the rock of Swanage.
Ibique lurido motu partitur socia manus, quidem manent, quidam petunt ultra partes marinas. Itaque classem mittit in eodem anno in orientales partes Anglorum rex prefatus, etiam Ælfred, statimque aductu in eorum occursum fuere in loco Stufemudan sexdecim scilicet numero karinæ; vastantur quidem armis, ferro truncantur magistri. Cætera classis piratica cursu obvia vehit illis; insistunt remis; deponunt scarmos; unda coacta rutilant arma; post gradum barbari victoriæ scandunt.
There the band was divided by bloody quarrel, some remaining some going overseas. And in the same year the aforesaid king, that is Alfred, sent a fleet to East Anglia, where immediately on their arrival sixteen ships confronted them at the Stour

entrance. These were overcome by arms, their officers put to the sword. The rest of the pirate fleet met on opposing course, they plied their oars, laid aside thole-pins, the waves shone with clashing steel.

Appendix III

As the following extract shows, one possible reason why not much use has been made of the reference to ships in such writers as Æthelweard, Ælnod and the author of Encomium Emmæ, is that their Latin is so complex that it is rarely possible to be quite confident what they are trying to say; occasionally it is tempting to give two versions, one of their text translated as far as possible, and one in which what they must have meant is allowed to depart from what they actually wrote. The English version below puts such guesswork in brackets; it is based on great help from my colleague Mrs. P.M. Simcock, whose ability to make sense of medieval Latin is far superior to my own, but she is not to blame for the guesswork. Ælnodi Historia S Canuti Regis, Cap. V.

Transactis littoreis remigiis, & adjacentium regionum intuitu jam satiatis obtutibus, ad altum pelagus tendentes, ratis nostræ rimas solerti industria obstruamus, ne qua vena insidiantis æquoris navigantes intercipiat & erecto crucis dominicæ ligno, vela virtutum in altum resurgant; quo Sirenarum canta auribus obtusis, veloci Euro perflante, discurrentes, Herois nostri meritis ad sinum optati portus delatis, anchoram spei nostræ divinæ affigamus clementiæ: ne spiritualium mercium navim scopolorum adversitas includat, & littorea gaudia, gazis porro vectis, jam sparsim unda nantibus, fletuum planctibus admisceat.

"Oars being got ready for sea, & eyes having seen enough of neighbouring regions, let us, making for the high seas, skilfully caulk the leaks in our ship, lest an inrush of the hostile and deceptive sea carry off the voyagers prematurely, and the beam of the cross of the Lord having been raised, let the sails of brave deeds rise aloft; so that running speedily before a south-east wind, we may carry the merits of our hero to the bay with our wished for port, and by divine mercy affix the anchor of our hope (fixing the anchor of our hope in the divine mercy), our ears deaf to the songs of sirens, lest disaster on the rocks destroy the cargo of spiritual wares, (leaving luxuries brought from afar scattered floating on the waves in which we mix our tears).

It is tempting to speculate that the first period, ending with the raising of the mast, was intended to begin with a coasting under oars until eyes were sufficiently satisfied (i.e. point of departure identified and reached) when washboards and tarpaulins etc are rigged after the mast has been raised. (Vena, insidiantis, intercipiat might suggest pirates are also in his mind.) Gazis is extremely rare, probably from Persian, and for an English cleric working in Denmark in the eleventh century to select it for the cargo of his metaphorical ship is certainly not without significance.

Appendix IV

Sources are in three languages, Latin, Old English, Old Norse. The first, once dominant, has received less attention recently than the other two, and I therefore include modern editions (with English translations) where they exist. There are already exhaustive bibliographies, and there seems to me no point in repeating references to such well-known collections as Mon. Germ. Hist. Script. or Mon. Hist. Britt. Texts have been selected as a basis for a brief calendar to illuminate the two questions treated in this paper; for many other purposes a different selection would have been preferable.

Latin

Chronicon Æthelweardi, ed. and transl. A. Campbell, Nelson Medieval Texts 1962, *Florentii Wigorniensis Chronicon ex Chronicis* ed. B. Thorpe 1848 *Encomium Emmæ,* ed. A. Campbell, Royal Hist Soc Camden Ser III No. 72. *Ordericus Vitalis,* ed. and transl. M. Chibnall, Oxford 1969. *Ælnd Hist. Sct. Canuti Regis* in Script. Rer. Dan. Med. Æv., Langebek.

Old English

The O.E. Chronicle, parallel text version in modern English, G.M. Garmonsway, Everyman's Library
English and Norse Documents . . . M. Ashdown.

Old Norse

Heimskringla, ed. B. Adalbjarnarson I.F. 1951
Knytlinga saga, ed. C af Petersen SUGNL 1919
Hemings thattr ed. G. Fellows-Jensen Ed. Arnamagnæanæ 1962
Egils saga, ed. S. Nordal I.F. (English transl. C. Fell, Everyman's Library).

Such a small selection does not of course provide a sufficient basis for a discussion of the historical reliability of hagiography or Old Norse saga.

The Clinker-built Boats of the North Sea, 300 – 1000 A.D.

ANGELA EVANS

The seven centuries that span the maritime history of Northern Europe between 300 AD when Britain, Germany and Gaul were provinces of the sprawling Roman Empire and 1000 AD by which time the nations of Europe had coalesced into recognisable political entities are characterised by a general lack of evidence relevant to archaeologists involved in the development of ships and boats. It is clear from archaeological finds and contemporary documentary sources that well before the fall of Rome in 410 AD both the southern part of the North Sea and the English Channel were alive with boats engaged in raiding and trading and in carrying migrating groups from the North European plain westwards to Britain.

From the first century the Romans maintained a fleet, the Classis Britannica, based at Dover in the English Channel. This was designed both as a logistic support to the occupying army and as a unit to protect the web of trade routes that developed rapidly between the Province of Britain and those of Gaul and Germany. Later, at the end of the third century, the network of forts and signal stations, known as the Saxon Shore defences, was established by Constantine, as a measure to protect the east-facing coast of Britain from attacks by raiders of Frankish and Saxon origin. After the fall of Rome, the eastern and south-eastern seaboards of Britain were intensively settled by migrants from the North German plains, the primary groups being the Angles, Saxons and Jutes, according to the historian Bede, writing in the eighth century.

It is clear that sea crossings between the European mainland and Britain were common, but the problem that faces any nautical archaeologist working in this period is that remarkably few finds have been made either in Britain or maritime Europe that represent typical everyday craft and, as so very few hulls survive, particularly from the earlier centuries, a rational assessment of sea-going ability is difficult to make. For the archaeologist, interested in the pattern of trade and population movement between the maritime nations of northern Europe, evidence in the shape of place-names, pottery and personal possessions in a variety of metals is abundant and the negative evidence contained in the archaeology of the period is that boats are necessarily pre-supposed in any archaeological report that, for example, includes material of continental origin found as part of the material culture of Britain. But if the question of what these boats were like is asked, then it must be accepted that the evidence is thinly spread over several centuries and conclusions of form and possible development must be drawn that would be open to criticism if applied to any other type of artefact. With this proviso, but supported by the knowledge that of all objects found during the period 300–1000 AD boats are the most conservative, with a fundamental shape that changes little over the centuries before the appearance of the cog, the pattern of boats in an archaeological context may be considered.

The number of finds that represent ships and boats in the last years of the Roman Empire and the Dark Ages is remarkably few but includes a range of small objects representing or portraying boat shapes, fragments of boats and one or two complete hulls. Boat portraits, showing simplified hull outlines survive rarely and in rather later, e.g. seventh century, contexts. There is for example a series of seventh-century Anglo-Saxon *sceattas* which show featureless hull shapes. The stem and stern-posts are crowned by knobs and the hull is semi-circular, perhaps reflecting the overall shape of the coin. The faint outline of a hull is engraved on a seventh century strap-end found at St. Germain-en-Laye, in Merovingian Gaul (Schaeffer 1939). This, apart from oars and a steering paddle, shows a central mast with stays fore and aft and a fitting of some sort at its head. A sword pommel (from c. 700 AD) in the form of a stylised boat shape was found at Sibertswold in Kent, but this provides no details of type, and drawn freehand on an early seventh century Anglian urn found at Caistor-by-Norwich that dates from the early seventh century is a scene showing a wolf-like animal barking after a boat with a high prow and a steering paddle. From the fifth century at least one ship's figurehead survives. This was found in the river Scheldt at Appels in Belgium and is a tall post with a basal tenon and a straight neck decorated with ribbon interlace. It has a rounded head with a gaping mouth full of gnashing teeth. A second, slightly smaller head of much the same date was found nearby at Moerzeke/Mariekirke and this too was perhaps the finial of a stem- or stern-post (Bruce-Mitford 1967).

Figure 1. Representation of boats on a) an Anglian urn from Caistor-by-Norwich; b) a Merovingian strap end from St. Germain-en-Laye and c) on a coin of Louis the Pious (814–840 A.D.) from Quentovic.

Fragments of boats occasionally survive, for example a second century find from Halsnøy, south of Bergen in Norway, gives an indication of the early clinker-built boats of the North Sea area. Only parts of this boat were recovered, but they included bits of sewn clinker planking, one sturdy frame and a well-formed rowlock (Christensen 1966). These fragments show that this boat was rowed rather than paddled – the style of propulsion that is followed in all the craft in this period. A similar fragmentary boat find, dating from the late sixth century – almost five hundred years after the Halsnøy find – was made at Gredstedbro in Denmark. This consisted of part of a stem-post with a horizontal scarf that had been fastened to the keel-plank with iron bolts. This was recovered together with an incomplete frame that had been secured to the planking with wooden pegs (Crumlin-Pedersen 1967). The underside of this frame was shaped to lie snugly against the overlapping timber of the hull, a feature that is rare and apparently not typical of the mainstream of boat construction, although it occurs on the Sutton Hoo ship that is of similar date.

All these examples, with the exception of the Halsnøy find, fall after the end of the Migration period and, although they add details to the patchwork of maritime development, they do not necessarily represent craft typical of the earlier period. Fortunately maritime history is not dependent on this skimpy evidence that is so inadequate in detail. At crucial stages throughout the centuries under review single boats survive like beacons to illustrate the kind of vessels that were being built. The earliest complete hull to survive in this period is that of the Nydam oak boat which has been dated to c. 350–400 AD (Åkerlund 1963). Two boats, one of oak and one of fir, were ritually deposited in the bog at Nydam, Schleswig, north Germany. They were recovered in 1864. Both were rowing boats with an open, shallow midships section and low raking stem- and stern-posts with deep cutwaters. The fir

boat was destroyed in the nineteenth century, although plans still survive, but the oak boat, 82 feet long, provides many details of a developed open rowing boat that lies well along the path from planked dug-out to the Viking boats, which were the finest achievement of the clinker tradition. Despite her size, the large Nydam boat was built using only fifteen pieces of timber. She has five strakes a side and these were fashioned from massive single lengths of oak, 20 inches broad, which ran the full length of the hull. These overlapped each other and were held by iron rivets. Inside, the hull was braced by sturdy frames of grown timber which were lashed to cleats that had been carved out of the solid oak of the strakes. The spine of the boat was a thick broad plank with only a slight projection into the water. The stem- and stern-posts rising from the keel-plank were massive timbers. These end-posts were fastened to the keel-plank with a short horizontal scarf that was held by two wooden pegs.

The boat was steered by a heavy paddle, but no evidence of how it was secured to the boat survived. However it seems likely that it was lashed to the hull, unlike the later boats which have a wooden boss outside the hull to which the steering oar is fastened. Grown forks of oak were lashed to the gunwale to give thirty rowing positions. No decking was found when the boat was excavated, but thwarts ran across the hull at the rowing positions. The hull shape is long and narrow, not suitable for sailing, and no fittings were recovered from the

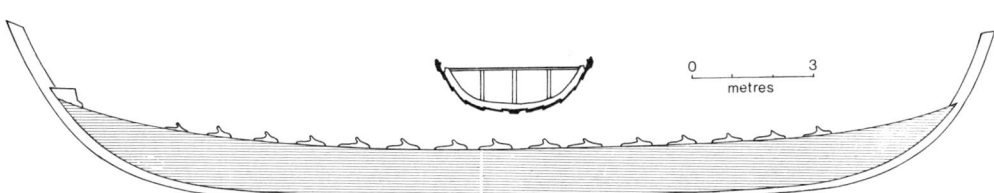

Figure 2. The Nydam boat, showing the low rake of the end-posts, and the narrow, shallow midships section.

Figure 3. The remains of the Sutton Hoo ghost-ship looking aft as she survived in 1939. The remains of the strake-lines are clearly seen. (Copyright: British Museum.)

excavation to suggest the Nydam boat ever sailed.

Despite its open cross-section and low freeboard, the Nydam boat is a sturdy vessel and one capable of making short sea journeys, either as a fighting ship or as a boat engaged in trade. Boats of the Nydam class were probably typical of those active in ferrying people from the north German plain across the English Channel during the Migration period, but towards the end of the sixth century new boat-building techniques appear and the Nydam type with its long single-plank construction is apparently abandoned in favour of composite strakes, although other details remain essentially the same.

In East Anglia by the end of the sixth century there is evidence of boat-building activity, perhaps centred on the area of Rendlesham, said by Bede to have been the site of the palace of Raedwald (d. 624/5), who was king of East Anglia and High King of the English at the time of his death. Three boats are known from East Anglia, and fragments of others have been found in the Anglian cemetery at Caistor-by-Norwich, where lengths of timbers were laid over cremation urns (Myres and Green 1973).

Of the surviving boats, all of which are funerary vessels, one at Snape was discovered in 1862 and is poorly recorded, but seems to have been about 30 m long with nine strakes a side (Davidson 1863, Bruce-Mitford 1974). A second, found in mound 2 at Sutton Hoo (Brown 1974, Bruce-Mitford 1975, fig. 59 and 86), was ransacked and survived only as a shape in the sand with few rivets remaining in position, but the third, one of the most famous ships in archaeology, the Sutton Hoo ship, survived more or less intact in the deep burial trench where she lay (Evans 1975). This vessel demonstrated a ship-building ability in East Anglia that was not to be exceeded until the upsurge of Viking boat-building which culminated in the superb Gokstad boat in the ninth century. Although built in the same tradition as the Nydam boat, the Sutton Hoo ship differs in certain details from the majority of Scandinavian boat-finds – although an example of the same construction is known in Denmark from the fragments of the Gredstedbro boat. The type seems to be isolated by the method of shaping the underside of the fames so that they fit snugly against the overlapping clinkers to which they are fastened with wooden pegs.

The Sutton Hoo ship lay beneath a large circular mound that was 3 m high and 30 m in diameter. She had been placed in a ship-shaped trench that hugged her timbers. This was then filled with sand so that when the wood disintegrated in the damp and highly acid soil, the outline of the hull, with all the iron rivets in position, was held in the sand and capable of excavation. Despite the fact that no wood survived, details of her former substance were preserved as dark shadows in the bright yellow sand and show, for example, something approaching the original shape of the plank-keel and the stem- and stern-posts. Apart from these shadows, the original wood of the timbers survived where it had been in contact with the corroding iron of the rivets, and thus on the shanks of the rivets and spikes that originally held the timbers together, the phantom outlines of

individual planks and carpentry joins can be detected. By piecing these tiny, and often ephemeral, fragments together a very complete picture of the structure of the ship was recovered, and by adding these details to the lines of the ship, surveyed *in situ* in 1939, an overall picture emerges that is deficient in only a few details. Thirty metres long, with a maximum beam of 4.8 m, the Sutton Hoo ship represents a considerable advance on the rather simple structure of the Nydam boat, although the hull profile is similar and the same skeleton of plank-keel, stem- and stern-posts is evident. However, unlike the Nydam boat, the strakes of the Sutton Hoo ship are composite, each consisting of several lengths of planking fastened at their overlap with three iron rivets, 5 cm long, that lie across the face of the plank. Forward and aft where the planks narrow, only one rivet is used. On many of these little rivets a distinct line in the wood-grain, running at 45° to the shank, shows the simple oblique scarf between the butting plank ends.

The ship's spine was a long plank-keel with a small squared lower profile and a broad, flat hog giving a stumpy T-shaped cross-section. The outline of the cross-section of the plank-keel survived as a dark shadow in the sand as did the shape of the stem- and stern-posts – long, low raking posts with a deep and thrusting cut-water. These posts could have risen perhaps as

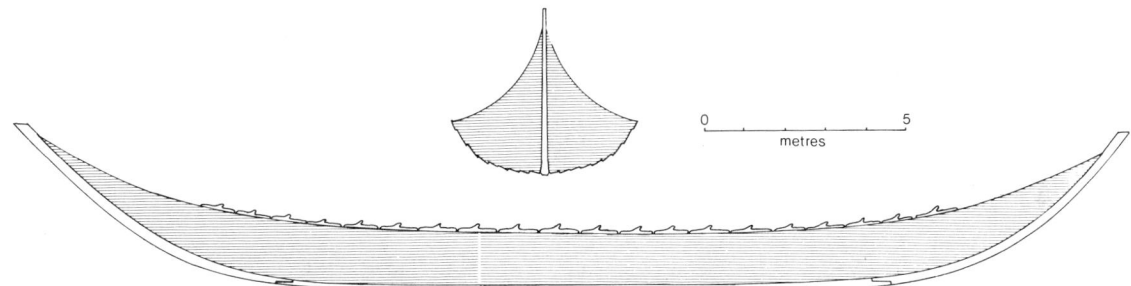

Figure 4. The hull shape and midships section of the Sutton Hoo ship, showing similar end-posts as the Nydam boat.

much as 4 m above the keel, but the terminals did not survive. When the ship was buried, the stern-post was attached to the keel-plank by a short horizontal half-scarf which was held by three massive iron bolts, but no evidence of the forward scarf was recovered, either in 1939 or during the re-excavations of the ship in 1965/67. As the stern scarf is associated with a patched repair to the garboard strake it is possible that the end-posts were originally tre-nailed to the keel (like the Nydam boat) and damage to the hull in the stern resulted in the replacement of the wooden pegs with iron bolts. The ship had nine strakes a side made up of several lengths of timber joined by small rivets. Inside and strengthening the hull were twenty-six heavy oak frames with a rectangular cross-section. These were joggled over the planking to lie tightly against the skin of the ship. They were held in place by one long iron bolt at gunwale level and trenails elsewhere.

The ship was rowed by forty oarsmen and faint traces of the grown timber forks that acted as rowlocks survived as dark shadows along the top of the gunwale strake. The tholes had long bases which were fastened down onto the gunwale by pairs of heavy iron spikes. A steering-oar would have hung to starboard associated with frames 24 and 25, which had greatly expanded heads strengthening the hull at this point. However no trace of the paddle survived and it is not possible to say whether it was lashed to the hull like the Nydam steering-oar, or whether it pivoted on a boss of wood outside the hull like the steering paddles of the later Scandinavian boats.

No evidence for the use of sail was recovered from the Sutton Hoo ship. The amidships area, where a keelson and mast partner would have been was occupied by the burial chamber, but although it is probable that any fittings would have been stripped from the ship before burial – probably before she was hauled overland to her final place of burial – there is no firm reason to suppose that the Sutton Hoo ship was a sailing ship.

The Sutton Hoo ship was possibly a royal barge like the Oseberg ship and represents, in the adoption of composite planking which would make the hull more flexible, a further stage of achievement by the boat-builders of the Dark Ages. She is an exceptionally large vessel and would not be typical of everyday craft that traded around the coasts facing the North Sea. The slightly smaller boat from Snape, 20 m long, perhaps approaches these more closely.

By the early century there is evidence in England and Denmark of a series of double-ended rowing boats, following the Nydam tradition with plank-keels and low-raking plank-on-edge stem- and stern-posts. The survival of this form is possibly

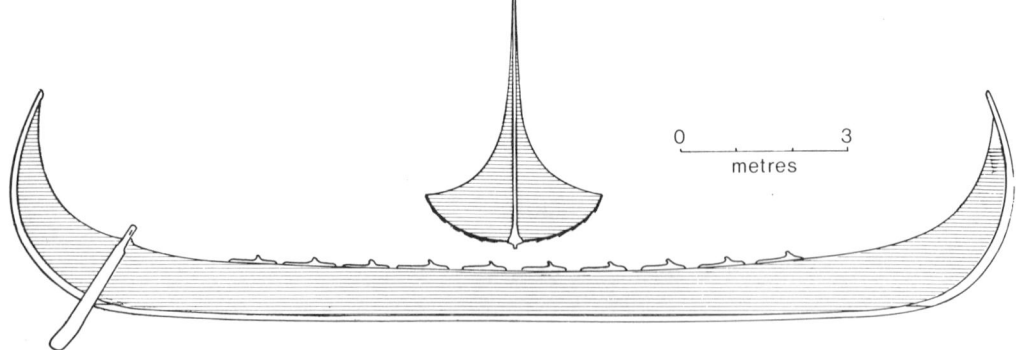

Figure 5. The larger of the two Kvalsund boats, showing the tight curve of the end-posts and the deepening keel-section.

reflected in the tenth-century Graveney boat, which still shares the low rake of the end-posts, but in this case with a heeled lower profile. However by the end of the seventh century, boat finds in Norway already show a move away from this distinctive profile and examples with tightly curving stem- and stern-posts appear in the archaeological record with lines that survive until the twentieth century. They clearly developed alongside the boats of a low-raking type and some distinction can perhaps be made either in terms of function or more simply in cultural background between the boats of Jutland, North Germany and East Anglia and those of the more northerly waters of Norway and Sweden.

The Vikings themselves are justly renowned for their ships and their remarkable open sea voyages to Iceland, Greenland and the northernmost fringe of the east American coast. In their boats they also ranged through the riverine routes of Europe, reaching the Mediterranean areas. They established a reputation not only as sailors, navigators and adventurers but as traders working out of entrepôts like Hedeby and Birka. But what of the development of their ships? Before the recovery of the five late Viking vessels which formed a deliberate blockade of the Roskilde fjord in Denmark, the ships of the Viking era were known only from a handful of burial and ritual sites where the wood had been preserved by waterlogged conditions in the same way as the oak and fir boats from Nydam. One or two small boats have been found, like the Årby boat, buried in a late Viking grave in Uppland, Sweden, and pieces of other Viking period craft have also been found. A large number of buried boats also survive as ghostly shapes with jumbled strake alignments, and these point to a variety of boats, large and small. All the finds emphasise the fact that movement by sea, especially in Norway, where the land is so unsuitable for overland transport, was the norm as it has been up until the twentieth century.

In western Norway a pre-Viking find that was a votive offering like the Nydam boats was made at Kvalsund, Herøy (Shetelig and Johannessen 1929). Here a 20 m long ship had been placed in the mud together with a small 4-oared boat. No accompanying finds were recovered except for a number of pointed sticks, perhaps symbolising weapons. A date in the late seventh or early eighth centuries has been put forward for these two vessels. The larger of the two craft is clinker-built of oak with pine frames. She has a broad keel-plank which has a T-shaped cross-section that is deeper than the plank-keels of the Nydam and Sutton Hoo ships and approaches the true keel of the Viking ships. The keel-plank scarfs horizontally with the stem- and stern-posts and these scarfs are held by two vertical iron rivets, just as those on the Nydam boat are held by two trenails.

However, the distinctive feature of the large Kvalsund boat is the tight curve of the stem- and stern-posts. These rise high above the keel-plank and completely change the profile of the boat, giving her a far more elegant appearance compared with the Nydam boat. The pine frames of the Kvalsund ship are held to the hull by both lashings and trenails, reflecting the traditions seen at Nydam and Gredstedbro. One of the after frames is specially shaped and supports the steering oar, which on this boat pivots against an oak boss that is attached to the outside of the planking by nails. The oar, which is lashed to the boss, is additionally supported at gunwale level, and the elasticity of this system enables it to be readily manoeuvred. The boat is undecked and has twenty rowing positions which, like the earlier boats, are grown forks lashed to the gunwales. No trace of any form of mast fitting survives, and although the broad hull shape with its deepened keel and fixed steering oar would be capable of being sail-assisted, it seems unlikely that even unsophisticated sailing equipment would have vanished leaving no trace on the hull. Thus the large Kvalsund boat was probably

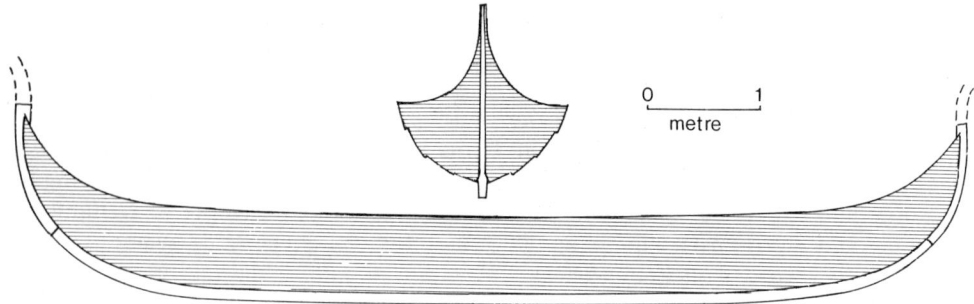

Figure 6. The boat from Valsgärde 7.

a rowing boat. The small Kvalsund boat is of similar construction but has fewer strakes a side and frames that are trenailed to the hull throughout. The end-posts do not curve back on themselves in quite the elegant manner of the large boat but reflect the shallower lines of the Nydam style. This small boat has four rowing positions and a fixed steering-oar.

The two Kvalsund boats represent the only complete examples of what is probably the mainstream of boat-building in northern waters during the seventh and eight centuries, the period that runs up to the Viking era. Occasionally pieces of timber from other similar boats are found, but by far the largest number of examples are known only as ghost ships beneath burial mounds. The best known of these lie in the wealthy grave-fields of Vendel and Valsgärde in Sweden. Here, shallow boat shapes with confused rivet alignments have been excavated over many years. One of these, the boat from Valsgärde 7, was 10 m long and had five strakes a side and must be typical of the smaller boats from the pre-Viking era (Arvidsson 1977).

The Kvalsund boats and their contemporaries are characterised by light, highly flexible hulls with an inner framework of widely spaced frames that brace the boat from gunwale to gunwale. The development of a keel, as opposed to the plank-keels of the earlier boats, gives greater longitudinal strength to the hull and as the keel deepens, so the scarfs with the stem-

and stern-posts turn through ninety degrees and become vertical with horizontal fastenings. With these changes the evolution of the sailing hull is virtually complete, but the date when the sail was actually adopted remains uncertain. Boats with sails, often with elaborate rigging, are depicted on some of the finest picture stones of Gotland in Sweden, for example the stone from Örebro, but these are notoriously difficult to date and the earliest extant sailing equipment is the short keelson, mast-fish and mast of the Oseberg ship that dates from c. 800 AD.

However this sailing equipment is sophisticated, the result of a long adopted tradition, which suggests that the sail must have become established during the previous century or so. Also, between the building of the large Kvalsund boat and the beginning of the ninth-century innovations in structure took place that are seen fully evolved in the two most famous Viking survivals, the Oseberg and Gokstad ships (Brøgger, Falk and Shetelig, 1917; Nicholaysen 1882), as well as on more fragmentary finds like the boat from Äskekärr, Sweden (Humbla 1934).

The Oseberg and Gokstad ships, and a third ship found at Tune (Shetelig 1917, pl. 1), were all burial ships and owe their remarkable survival to the conditions in which they lay. They were placed in trenches cut deep in the blue clay deposits that occur in the outer Oslo fjord and the qualities of the clay preserved the timbers in

Figure 7. The remaining of the Oseberg ship during excavation.

extremely good condition. The Oseberg ship was additionally protected by a carefully built mound of turf sods and most of the upper planking and her magnificently carved stem- and stern-posts were recovered. The decoration on these posts can be dated on stylistic grounds to c. 800 AD. The Gokstad and Tune ships were probably built a little later in the last half of the ninth century. The extravagantly furnished Oseberg burial is that of a woman, and the ship, which was richly carved, may have been a royal barge, like the ship found at Sutton Hoo two hundred years earlier, and used similarly for river and short coastal voyages. The Gokstad ship, with a higher freeboard, is more seaworthy and capable of long sea-voyages as was shown when her replica was sailed across the Atlantic in 1893.

Both the Oseberg and Gokstad ships are large and beamy. The Oseberg ship is

21.44 m long with a beam of 5.10 m. She was rowed by 30 oars. The Gokstad ship is 23 m long and 5.20 m in beam, with thirty-two rowing positions. The boat from Tune is badly damaged but was originally approximately 20 m long. All three have steering oars held against bosses on the outside of the hull in the same manner as the Kvalsund ship. But in structural detail the three ships represent a great advance on the earlier examples. Although the same foundation of keel-plank and end-posts is common to all, in the Oseberg and Gokstad ships the keel-plank is now a true keel with a deep T-shaped cross-section and vertical scarfs. In addition, a length of wood is placed between the long flat keel-plank and the heavy, curving stem- and stern-post.

Inside, the frames no longer span the clinker-built hull from gunwale to gunwale, but lie as floor timbers, lashed to cleats in the planks. The ends of the floor timbers rest at the level of a thickened strake – the *meginhufr* – that lies on the water line. Running across the hull and bracing it at the level of the *meginhufr* are a series of cross-beams, one for each floor frame. Over the cross-beams lies the planking of the deck. The strakes above the *meginhufr* are supported by knees which are nailed to the cross-beams and trenailed to the hull. Oar-ports, running the length of the ships, replace the tholes of the earlier ships – although they remain in use on small boats as the three Gokstad ship's boats demonstrate. On the Oseberg ship the oar-ports are cut through the gun-

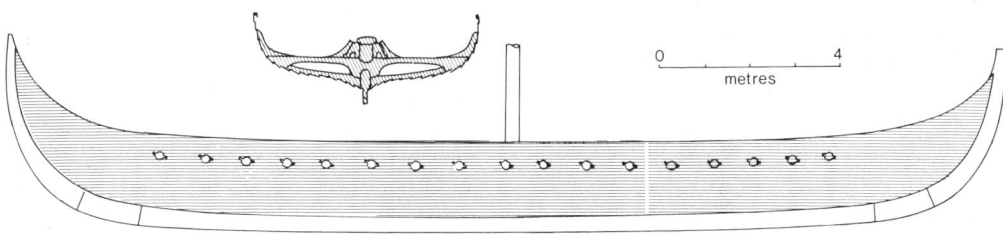

Figure 8. The Gokstad ship.

wale strake, but on the slightly later Gokstad ship two strakes are added above the one carrying the oar-holes, giving the ship an increased freeboard. In addition, the oar-ports have wooden covers that drop down over the holes when the oars are not in use.

These three ships stand apart from their predecessors because they are sailing ships. They are all fitted amidships with heavy keelsons that lie on the floor-frames and into which the mast is stepped. Straddling the cross-timbers, giving support to the mast, is a mast-partner which, in the Gokstad and Tune ships, is braced by knees that are nailed to the cross-timbers.

Few details of sails or rigging survive from the three ships, but complex representations on the Gotlandic picture stones suggest that the square-sails were highly evolved, and occasional descriptions in the later sagas describe sails as being coloured and striped. The combination of the deep keeled, highly flexible hull and the square-sail was formidable and led to the Viking domination of the northern seas and the English Channel for generations during which time the historical reputation of the Vikings as raiders, invaders and colonists, navigators and traders was established.

The Gokstad ship, belonging to the second half of the ninth century, symbolises for the modern world perhaps the highest achievement of the Viking boatbuilders. Yet, magnificent as this vessel is, she would have been only one of a great variety of ships and boats that thronged the coastal waters of Scandinavia during the high Viking period. Small craft, like the Gokstad ship's boats or the Årby boat, must have been a familiar sight to the independent farming communities that formed the backbone of Viking society.

The Viking fleets contained several classes of fighting ship including the "snake" ships, so named because of their narrow, flexible hulls, of which the ship buried at Ladby, Funen, Denmark, is thought to be a typical example (Thorvildsen 1957). The Ladby ship, like the Sutton Hoo and Valsgärde craft, survived only as a shadow in the sand, her hull shape preserved and filled out by undisturbed strake alignments of iron rivets. She was 22 m long and 3 m in maximum beam and was clinker-built with eight strakes a side. The keel-plank had a T-shaped cross-section and four shroud rings are now the only evidence that she was worked with a sail. Her stem-post was decorated with iron spirals, perhaps the mane of a wooden figurehead that had vanished together with the rest of the ship's timbers. The burial was ransacked in antiquity but surviving fragments of dog-harness with characteristic Jellying-style decoration suggest a date in the middle of the tenth century for the boat and its contents.

The Sagas contain a wealth of information about the classes of ship that were current during the Viking period, but few of these are known from archaeological finds; thus the discovery in Denmark of five late Viking ships blocking a narrow channel in the Roskilde fjord, at Skuldelev (Olsen and Crumlin-Pedersen 1967), is vitally important to the nautical archaeologist, particularly as one of the wrecked ships represents a type that was the backbone of the Viking trade – the *knarr*. The hulls had been filled with stones to sink them and the wood of the damaged timbers was badly degraded and extremely fragile. Because of this, the wrecks were recovered by building a coffer-dam around them and treating the site as a land excavation. When the site was drained of water, the timbers were recorded photogrammetrically before the pieces were lifted and packed for storage. To avoid damaging the friable wood, each fragment was lifted on a piece of hardboard to which it was tied for support before being put in an airtight polythene tube – exactly the same system was later used with great success on the timbers of the Graveney boat, with the addition, in this case, of small chocks of wood to preserve the curvature of the planking.

72

When the lifting of all the fragments was complete, the work of conservation began: the timbers were cleaned, fitted together where possible and then placed in tanks containing a solution of polyethylene glycol 4000 to preserve them. After a period of immersion that varied between six months and two years, depending on both the degradation and thickness of the wood, work on reconstructing the five boats began. The distorted and damaged remains of the five boats were found to represent warships, two merchant ships and a smaller vessel, perhaps a ferry or a fishing boat.

All five hulls show variety in shape and construction but clearly belong to the same boat-building tradition. All are sailing ships, with light and flexible clinker-built hulls, with T-shaped keel-planks that scarf vertically with typical and elegantly curved stem- and stern-posts. One additional feature that they all share is the stem- and stern-piece. Unlike the Gokstad ship, for example, where the stem- and stern-posts have simple grooves to house the hood-ends of the planks, the Skuldelev ships have stepped wings carved in one with the posts and the hoods are attached to them, rather than to the edge of the post itself.

The Skuldelev find gives the ship archaeologist the first opportunity in northern waters to examine contemporary ships that lie within the same ship-building tradition but which were constructed for quite different purposes. Although similar in basic form, the proportions of the merchantmen and the warships are significantly different: the hull of the larger merchantman for example, which has amidships accommodation for cargo, is "short, squat and relatively tall" in comparison to the long, narrow and low lines of the warship. It has provision for only a few oars fore and aft of the cargo hold, in contrast to the long ships, which have oar-ports running the length of the gunwale, providing for maximum speed and manoeuvrability in the swift attack and withdraw

tactics for which the Viking fleets were renowned. The merchantmen, on the other hand, with a greater dependence on sail, would ply stolidly between ports and across open seas with great reliability but with no great speed.

The five ships, although falling into two categories, represent different types within those categories. The warships are different in size. The smaller, no. 5, probably represents the typical Danish Viking longship, similar to the ghost ship of Ladby. It is 18 m long and 2.6 m in maximum beam, with twelve pairs of oars – the same kind of warship that can be seen, for example, in the Bayeux tapestry and one which is known from practical experience of working with the Imme Gram, a full scale replica of the Ladby ship, to be capable of quick manoeuvring, easy beaching, and of carrying and landing horses. A useful and handy craft, this would have been the basic fleet vessel, used no doubt in the Danish/English skirmishes of the ninth and tenth centuries. However, the Sagas tell of massive ships, symbols of personal power and prestige, and the larger warship, no. 2, must surely be one of these. Unfortunately this ship lay at the top of the blockade and is consequently the most damaged with only one half of the hull surviving. It seems to have been a "snake" ship, of at least 30 m long, similar in length to the great ship at Sutton Hoo, with provision for twenty-six pairs of oars. Such a vessel would be capable of moving with great speed, and would carry fighting troops, perhaps as many as fifty or sixty, as well as a basic crew to man the sweeps. This would have been a fearsome craft, and possibly represents the type upon which the late Danish maritime defence was built and thus would have been a type well known to the English in the tenth and eleventh centuries.

The merchantmen stand aside from these swift men-of-war. The small merchantman, no. 3, built of oak, was 13.5 m long and had a beam of 3.2 m – giving a length to breadth ratio of 4.2:1, which can

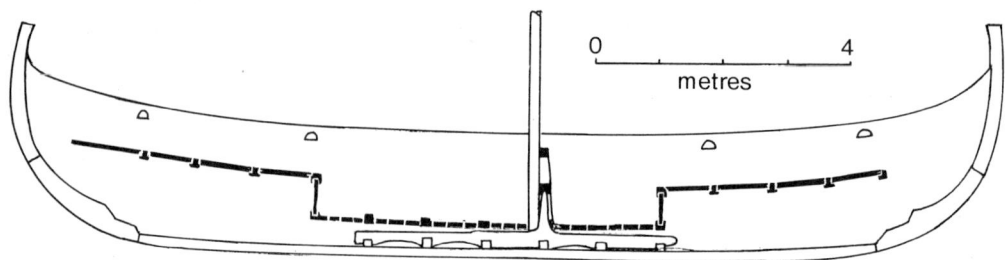

Figure 9. The larger trading ship from the Roskilde fjord – Skuldelev 1. The open area amidships designed for cargo stowage. The ship was presumably used with sail, although manoeuvering would have been undertaken with oars fore and aft.

be contrasted with the ratios of 6:1 and 7:1 for the warships. Amidships lay an open hold in which the mast was stepped and cargo stowed. She had five oarholes forward of the cargo space and two aft. This small ship was probably a coastal trader and would have been familiar on the North Sea and Baltic routes. She is small enough to use even the lesser riverine routes, and stripped of her contents, would be capable of short portages. In contrast to this flexible little trader, the larger ship, 16.5 m long with a beam of 4.8 m, is of a far sturdier build with end-posts and keel of oak and planking of pine, with fourteen heavy oak frames. She was decked fore and aft with an open hold amidships. Unlike the other surviving Viking ships which were designed for flexible handling, even portage, this merchantman is designed to withstand heavy open seas. Perhaps built in Norway, the tough, rugged hull suggests that it was this kind of ship that was used on the long North Atlantic crossings from Norway to Iceland, Greenland and North America. The Sagas tell us that the type of ship used in these voyages was known as a *knarr*, broad beamed, utterly reliable craft that carried the questing Vikings over such inhospitable seas.

The fifth boat in the Skuldelev find is very different from its contemporaries. Smaller, with a length of about 12 m and a beam of only 2.5 m, she is undecked with large, broad thwarts that are too low to be rowing positions. She is tentatively thought of as a ferry or perhaps a small fishing boat.

The diversity of the Skuldelev finds throws a narrow shaft of light over the principal kinds of vessel that would have been familiar to any Viking child in the tenth and eleventh centuries, and also to the people of northern Europe outside Scandinavia, the Baltic, central riverine Europe – even the Mediterranean. The Viking ranged wherever their boats could carry them, both as raiders and colonists, and equally important as traders working out of the great Viking centres of Hedeby, Helgø and Birka.

In the British Isles the three centuries that separate the Sutton Hoo ship and the Graveney boat are empty of boat finds with the exception of the burial at Balladoole on the Isle of Man, where a scattering of iron rivets beneath a stone cairn is all that survives of a Viking boat (Bersu and Wilson 1966). In Scandinavia, as we have seen, it is possible to follow the slow progress of the clinker hull from Nydam to Skuldelev, but until the discovery of the Graveney boat, nothing was known of the different kinds of craft that might have been used around the coast of England in the late Saxon period.

Remains of a boat were found during work to improve the drainage of the Graveney marshes in Kent in 1970 (Evans and Fenwick 1978). A narrow watercourse was being widened and deepened when some timbers were grabbed up and recognised as belonging to a boat of some kind. When the hull was emptied of mud, it was realised that her shape suggested a pre-Conquest vessel and because of her potential value to archaeology the Kent River Authority held back their schedule to allow ten days for the timbers to be lifted and recorded.

It was clear when the boat was uncovered that she belonged to a slightly different class of vessel than that found at Sutton Hoo. Although the hull was clinker-built in the same way and the lines, though slightly flattened, were similar, the frames were quite different as they were composite and exceptionally heavy. Apart from this, when the stern-posts was lifted, it became immediately clear that the boat represented a new type as the post, although super-

Figure 10. The Graveney boat: the closely-spaced, exceptionally heavy frames distinguish this boat from the light flexible Viking vessels.

ficially similar to the low-raking Nydam and Sutton Hoo end-posts revealed a curious lower profile – instead of having a gentle curve beyond the horizontal scarf with the broad plank-keel, the stern-post was distinctly angular. Thus the Graveney boat stood to one side of the known pattern of contemporary hull forms and pointed to an alternative design, suspected from occasional graffiti and illustrations, but never before encountered.

The timbers of the Graveney boat were badly damaged: the forward end was missing altogether and her upper strakes had been systematically robbed from the time of her abandonment in a narrow creek, but in essentials, she is not different from her predecessors or contemporaries. Her original length is estimated as being approximately 14 m with a beam of 3 m and this gives a ratio of length to breadth similar to that of the merchantmen from Skudelev.

The Graveney boat is clinker-built of oak and her hull is made up of lengths of planking, joined end to end by a simple tapering scarf fastened with iron rivets across the face of the plank – exactly the same method used from the sixth century onwards. The strakes themselves were riveted together and between them caught in the overlap of the planks was a luting of wool that had been soaked in a vegetable based tar to ensure watertight joints. A curious feature of the fastenings is that wooden pegs seem to have been placed in the rivet holes before the iron shanks were driven through – a method which can be found in the Baltic but not elsewhere.

The boat had a broad, flat and heavy plank-keel with a stubby projection underneath that had been worn and rubbed by beaching. A short horizontal scarf, held by five iron rivets, joined this plank to the stern-post, whose lower edge projected forwards and upwards with a sharp angle or heel at the point where the upward rise begins. The stern-post was pierced by three holes and in one of these fragments of a rope survived. A series of extremely heavy rectangular sectioned frames ran, often sinuously, across the hull. Ten of these massive timbers survived, and they lay tightly against the planks and were held to the hull by large willow trenails. These had knobbed heads that lay on the outside of the planking and around their necks, sealing the hull, were strips of tar-soaked wool. Inside the hull, the ends of the trenails were cut off flush with the upper surface of the frames, and little wedges of oak were driven into them to prevent them from slipping out of position. The frames were composite with side timbers rabbeted to the floor frames.

Because of systematic robbing none of the side frames survive and, as the upper strakes had also gone, no details of the gunwale strake are known. It is thus not possible to say how many oars were used to work the boat, or what kind of steering system she possessed. It seems possible that the Graveney boat may have been used with a sail during her life as three of the central frames have shallow rebates in them which could have accommodated a form of mast step, however these rebates had been filled at some stage in her life and the tops of the frames levelled off for cargo stowage.

The Graveney boat was abandoned, not wrecked, and practically no evidence of her role as a load-bearing cargo ship survives. Two clues found in the rubbish accumulated within the boat suggest two possible areas of activity. Hop seeds were found in the debris trapped beneath some of the floor frames and also low down in the strake-lands. Pollen analysis however revealed no evidence of pollen from hops and the presence of seeds could suggest that the boat carried a cargo that included hops.

But it is clear from her reconstruction that the Graveney boat was essentially a load-bearing vessel, and thus the discovery in the bottom of the boat of a few fragments of basalt lava of Middle Rhine origin from unfinished querns together with pieces of Kentish rag-stone and fragments of Roman tile may indicate that the boat was engaged in trading across the English Channel, even perhaps sailing into the Viking trading town of Hedeby, where both hops and unfinished querns have been found amidst a mass of other material. The alternative is that these fragments are the remains of ballast only and that the Graveney boat's trading pattern was less adventurous, and that she was essentially a riverine and coastal craft that plyed up and down the local water systems, carrying a range of heavy cargo.

Whatever the use and potential of the Graveney boat, it is clear that she belongs to a different tradition of boat-building to that of the light, flexible clinker-built boats of Scandinavia. She appears to have been a more pedestrian vessel, designed primarily for small scale trading. Sturdy, slow and reliable she was perhaps able to make the difficult, though short, crossing of the English Channel and thus reach the trading depots of northern Europe. She would have stayed mostly in coastal waters, not venturing on long sea journeys as did the merchant ships found in the Roskilde fjord. Her main interest for the archaeologist lies not so much in her capabilities as in her different design, representing as she does a class of boat existing alongside those of Scandinavia, but belonging to a different tradition.

One other major find that, like Graveney, belongs to a quite different tradition, is the boat found at Utrecht in 1930. She is characterised by an extraordinary banana-shaped hull which has no stem- or stern-post – the planks simply converge at either end. The hull is 56 ft, 6 in long and 12 ft wide, with a huge plank-keel that is 6 ft 6 in at its widest. A mast step is placed forward of amidships and the boat is strengthened by heavy closely-set floor frames.

The ship is dated by radio-carbon analysis to 790 ± 45AD, and bears a strong resemblance to the ships depicted on a series of *denarii*, struck at Dorestadt and

Quentowic between 815 and 840AD (fig. 1). She is thought to have been suited primarily for river work as the forward mast position would have been adequate for towing but unbalanced for carrying a sail. It has been suggested that the Utrecht boat is a possible ancestor for the medieval *hulk,* but her importance in this early period is that her hull shape demonstrates the variety of traditions existing outside the clinker-built series that dominates boat-building history from the Nydam ship until the development of the cog, best seen in the example from Bremen.

Bibliography

Arwidsson 1977, G. Arwidsson, *Valsgärde 7,* 95–99.

Bersu and Wilson 1966. G. Bersu and D. M. Wilson, "Three Viking Graves in the Isle of Man", *Society of Medieval Archaeology Monograph Series,* no. 1

Brøgger, Falk and Shetelig, 1917. A. W. Brøgger, H. Falk and H. Shetelig, *Osebergfundet,* Vol. 1. 283 ff. pls. XIX,XX

Brøgger and Shetelig 1951, A. W. Brøgger and H. Shetelig, *The Viking Ships, their Ancestry and Evolution*

Brown 1974, Basil Brown in Bruce-Mitford 1974, 147 ff-

Bruce-Mitford, 1967, R.L.S. Bruce Mitford "A new wooden ship's figure-head found in the Scheldt", *Acta Archaeologica,* XXXVIII, 119–209

Bruce-Mitford 1974, Rupert Bruce-Mitford, *Aspects of Anglo-Saxon Archaeology,* 114–40, fig. 17

Bruce-Mitford 1975. Rupert Bruce-Mitford, *The Sutton Hoo Ship Burial* Vol. 1, 104–7, 110–11, 127–30, figs. 59 & 86

Christensen 1966. A.E. Christensen "Scandinavian ships from earliest times to the Vikings", in G.F. Bass (ed.), *A History of Seafaring based on Underwater Archaeology,* 159–80

Crumlin-Pedersen 1967. Ole Crumlin-Pedersen, "Gredstedbroskibet", *Mark og Montre fra Sydvestjyske Museum,* 1967, 11–15

Davidson 1863. Septimus Davidson, Excavations at Snape, *Proceedings of the Society of Antiquaries of London,* Second Series, Vol. II, January 8th 1863, 177–82

Ellmers 1972. Detlev Ellmers, *Frühmittelalterliche Handels-shiffarht in Mittel- und Nordeuropa,* Offa-bücher 28

Evans 1975. Angela Care Evans "The Ship" in Bruce-Mitford 1975, Ch. V

Evans and Fenwick 1971. Angela Care Evans and Valerie Fenwick, "The Graveney Boat", *Antiquity,* XLV, 89–96

Fenwick 1978. Valerie Fenwick, "The Graveney Boat", *BAR British Series 53,* 1978

Humbla 1934. P. Humbla, "Båtfyndet vid Äskekärr", *Göteborgs och Bohusläns Fornminnensföreningstidsskrift,* 1934, 1–21

Marsden 1972. Peter Marsden. "Ships of the Roman Period and After" in G.F. Bass (Ed.), *A History of Seafaring based on Underwater Archaeology,* 113–32

Myres and Green 1973. J.N.L. Myres and Barbara Green, *The Anglo-Saxon Cemeteries of Caistor-by-Norwich and Markshall, Norfolk.* Society of Antiquaries of London 1973, 118, text fig. 5

Nicholaysen 1882. N. Nicolaysen *The Viking Ship discovered at Gokstad in Norway, 1882,* pl. I, II

Olsen & Crumlin-Pedersen 1967. Olaf Olsen and Ole Crumlin-Pedersen. "The Skuldelev Ships", *Acta Archaeologica,* XXXVIII, 73–174

Schaeffer 1939. C.F.A. Schaeffer *Un voilier de l'époque Mérovingienne du Nord de la France, Revue Archéologique,* 6th series, 13, 181–7

Shetelig 1917. Haakon Shetelig, *Norske Oldfund II Tuneskibet,* fig. 1, pl. 6

Shetelig and Johannessen 1929. H. Shetelig and F. Johannessen "Kvalsundfundet og andre Norske myrfund av fartøier" *Bergens Museum Skrifter, Ny Rekke, Bind II,* no. 2

Thorvildsen 1957. K. Thorvildsen, *Ladbyskibet 1961.*

Åkerlund 1963, H. Åkerlund, *Nydamskeppet.* En studie i tidlig Skandinavisk skeppsbyggnadskonst, Gothenburg 1963

Frisian and Hanseatic Merchants Sailed the Cog

DETLEV ELLMERS

The Development of the Cog

In 1863 the Danish archaeologist C. Engelhardt by his pioneering excavation of the Nydam-ship opened the way for research into the Anglo-Scandinavian shipbuilding tradition, of which the Viking ships are the most famous vessels. One hundred years later, in 1962/65 a nearly complete wreck of a Hanseatic Cog (fig. 1) was excavated in silt deposits of the river Weser some kilometres downstream of the mediaeval centre of Bremen. This ship find turned out to be the key to another hitherto unknown chapter in European nautical history: that of the Continental shipbuilding traditions.

Let us take a short look at the construction of the cog and see how this new key works. When the forest workers in the Weser mountains in 1378 cut some huge oak-trees, which they dispatched as a raft to Bremen, and when the cog-makers of Bremen after a short time sawed these trees into planks of 60 cm breadth and 5 cm thickness, they could hardly know that they were working on one of the last ships of that type. Some twenty years later the hulc pushed the cog out of traffic at all Hanseatic towns. Thus the Bremer Cog is the most developed vessel within her shipbuilding tradition. The experience and the knowledge collected by generations of shipwrights had been invested in her construction and is now to be deciphered from it.

Compared with the Viking ships the cog appears somewhat clumsy. She is bigger though, with 23.20 m in length she is not longer, than those much older Scandinavian ships from Nydam and Gokstad. The main differences are the width of ca. 7.60 m and the height above keel of ca. 4.20 m, which enabled the cog to carry a cargo of about 80 t. or 40 lasts as the medieval measurement was called. The sides of the cog are so high that in contrast to Viking ships she could not be rowed. Her only propulsion was one square rigged sail stretched out by one mast 1.60 m afore the middle of the keel (fig. 2).

The main features of the cog are a very shallow but broad keel at which stem- and stern-post meet with definite angles. At midship the bottom is flat and carvel built and the steep sides are constructed in a specific clinker-technique, which differs so much from the clinker-technique of Viking ships that any relationship (which formerly had been claimed) is to be excluded. Not only have the strakes more than double the thickness (5 cm = 2 inches) and three or more times the width (more than 60 cm = 2 foot) of Viking, thus giving the cog a very stiff appearance and a corresponding behaviour in the sea in contrast to the elastical

Figure 1. Model of the cog of Bremen (1380), L. 23.50 m. Washstrake and sides of the after-castle are missing to show the substruction.

construction of a Viking ship, but also the clinker seams of the cog are not riveted like those of Viking ships but nailed with iron nails, the points of which are rebent into the timber inside the hull (fig. 3). As we do find these bent nails also under ribbs, we are sure that these ribbs were inserted into the hull when the shell was built up. These ribbs are fastened to the strakes by treenails hammered in from the outside through holes, drilled by spoon-shaped auger.

Into one of the upper edges of each strake a fase had been planed to be filled with moss for caulking, kept in position by a lath of willow which was secured by iron clamps. Each of these clamps, which look like butterflies, is hammered out of small iron lumps and placed so close together that more than 8000 were necessary for one ship while the number of nails is about 3000. As both, nails and clamps differ so much from the rivets of Viking ships,

archaeologists are enabled to separate the two different shipbuilding traditions not only when they find small fragments of planking but also when all timber is gone and nothing but nails and clamps or rivets are left. Thus let us take the nails with the rebent point as a "guiding fossile" and see which types of craft we find were built by means of them.

First we find a greater variety of recent small boats along the Dutch, German and

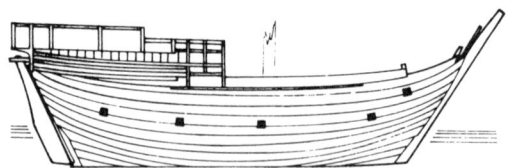

Figure 2. Sideview of the cog of Bremen with washstrake and sides of the after-castle (drawing W. Lahn).

Danish shores of the North Sea and the western Baltic and as far upstream as Berlin. They all have flat, carvel built bottoms and pointed stems, most of them also pointed sterns, but the variation with transom stern is not infrequent. Both stem and stern meet in definite angles with the bottom, and the sides – so far they do not consist of only one strake – are clinker built with the well known nails, but the small craft usually do not use clamps for keeping the caulking in position. We learn from these observations that the predicted nails are up till now part of a technical system that always produced everytime the same pattern of hullshape in a very limited range of variation under which the Bremer Cog is by far the most developed example.

Looking for the roots of this special technical system we find all its elements completely developed already in Roman times. But so far we do not know one ship of that period with the complete combination of all the elements. The seagoing vessel of Blackfriars, London, has the shape of a cog with a flat, carvel built bottom, stem- and stern-posts and steep sides. But in contrast to the cog her sides are carvel as well and the characteristic nails with their rebent points are used for a connection of strakes and ribbs. The inland watercraft of Zwammerdam at the Rhine, Netherlands, look like little cogs as far as the cross-section is regarded: they have the carvel built bottom and steep clinker built sides, the strakes of which are fastened one to the other by the typical cog-nails, and the ribbs are fastened by treenails to the strakes. But unfortunately with these long boats the stem- and stern-posts are missing; instead of these they have a special sort of transom like a punt. A third type of ship is represented by a ceramic bowl shaped like a cog from Beckeln at the river Weser in Lower Saxony. We see the flat bottom and the steep sides with stem- and stern-posts, but are not sure of the clinker construction and the use of cog-nails with real ships of that shape, as the bowl does not give these

details. From this evidence we are able to judge that all elements of the technical system of the cog are to be found in the coastal regions between Rhine and Weser already in Roman times. That is just the region in which we find the first evidence of the complete system from the 7th century onward. But we are not able to give a definite date for the invention of this system.

The first evidence for a real cog is the 7th century slip-way of a ship yard for cogs at Hessens in Wilhelmshaven, Lower Saxony. This timber-construction was designed for flat bottomed ships of at least 2 m width at the bottom. No parts of the ship itself have been uncovered, with the exception of fragments of an oar and of a rudder. And this rudder is of a type we only find with early cogs and its small relatives.

In order to understand the function of this rudder we have to look at a series of coins struck at Hedeby, Schleswig-Holstein, after a prefiguration, issued by Charlemagne (768–814) and Louis the Pious (814–840) at Quentowic (northern France) and Dorestad near Utrecht, Netherlands.

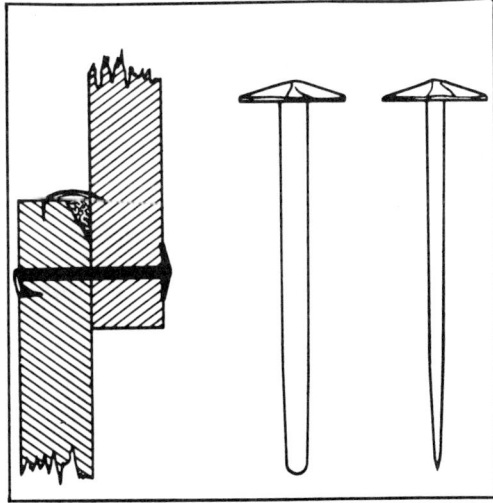

Figure 3. Clinker seam of the cog with nails, the point of which is rebent into the timber (drawing W. Lahn).

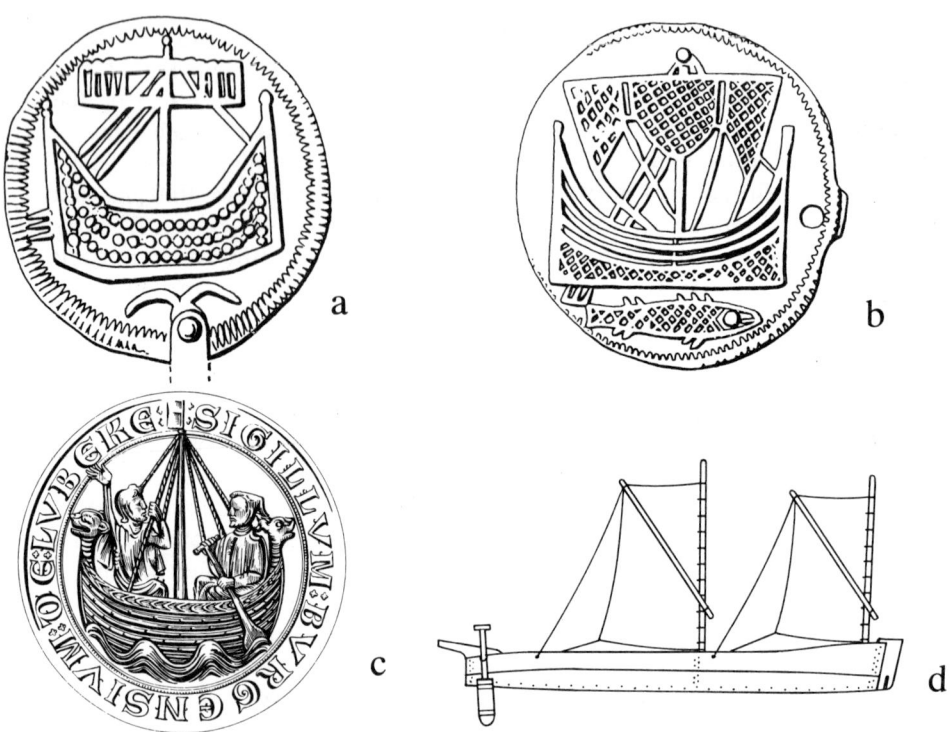

Figure 4. The side-rudders of early cogs worked like lee-boards.
4a,b. Cogs on Hedeby-coins of early 9th century.
4c. Town-seal of Lübeck, 1281.
4d. Kahn from Steinhuder Meer near Hannover, 1970. (Drawings B. Malner, H. Ewe, G. Salemke.)

These Carolingian coins show a banana shaped sailing vessel, which could be identified as a hulc, the outstanding ship type in traffic between the Continent and England. At Hedeby they altered the elegantly rounded shape of the hulc into a chest-like shape of another sailing vessel with stem- and stern-posts (fig. 4). The horizontal bottom-line of this ship appears to be broken and bent upwards a little bit at both ends on some coins. This means that the real ship depicted here had a flat bottom bent upwards at both ends as is typical for coastal vessels on the shallow flats of the Wattenmeer, allowing the vessel to fall dry at low tide and to get afloat again with high tide. Without the bent up ends of the flat bottom the ship would stick to the ground even at high tide. The flat and broad keel of the Bremer cog in spite of being ca. 550 years younger is contructed from three pieces of timber forming just that broken line we saw on the coins. So we are quite sure that these coins show early versions of the cog.

One of these coins even shows three horizontal rows of nail-heads to demonstrate the clinker seams, with which four side-strakes are fastened one to the other; and two vertical lines of nail-heads show how these four strakes are nailed to the stem- and stern-posts. Other coins just have horizontal lines instead of rows of nail-heads. Most of the issues – and just the most accurate ones – in that way demonstrate a flat-bottomed vessel with four side strakes set up in clinker technique. In contrast to these early cogs the Bremer cog has eight side-strakes and one additional washstrake on top of the flat bottom. On top of the fourth side strake some big cross beams protrude from the side as a new element of construction typical of late medieval times. This late cog is so to speak one early cog on top of another, with the cross beams in between to give latitudinal strength to that odd construction. Compared with the Bremer cog the sides of the early cogs on the Hedeby coins with only four strakes may have been 1.80 m high as a maximum amidships. That is the midship height of the 9th century Viking ship from Gokstad from keel to dollboard! This figure may just give an idea of the size of early cogs of which so far no example has been found. And we may keep in mind that these early cogs could easily be rowed like the Gokstad ship.

The most confusing detail on these coins is the rudder. Sometimes it appears like a stern rudder, sometimes it looks like a side-rudder on the port side protruding underneath the ship. We have to compare these details with cog seals of the early 13th century, depicting something like side-rudders on the port side in another scale so that more details are to be seen (fig. 4c). These rudders differ very much from Viking side-rudders. They lack the tiller, instead of which they have T-shaped handles. And we see them in two different positions: in a vertical position with the blade deep down in the water or in a diagonal position with the blade nearly out of the water so that it is to be seen behind the ship when looking from the other side. Thus the seals show just the same two positions we found at the Hedeby coins. If we did not have a recent cog-like sailing boat in the Steinhuder Meer near Hannover (fig. 4d) with a rudder working just the same way as the rudders on the coins and seals, we would hardly be able to find out the function of that rudder. This type of rudder works after the principles of a lee-board. Essential is a rigg laid out to turn the bow of the boat into the wind, when the rudder is outside the water. If the rudder is put deep into the water it forms a sort of obstacle, which turns the bow out of the wind. Keeping the rudder at medium depth makes the ship sail straight ahead. Ships with this sort of "lee-board" used as a rudder are mere sailing vessels. For propulsion by oars another steering equipment had to be installed.

This rudder does not work without a lateral pressure in the sail. That means, a wind from behind has to be cut by the sail into one component for sailing ahead and another component for lateral pressure. Consequently the broad rectangular sail depicted on the coins could not be used like a common square sail but must have been set into the wind like a lug-sail. Indeed we find the best drawings show the yard not being fastened in its middle to the mast but so that most part of the yard is aft of the mast and only a short part afore the mast. Further on there is only a yard from which the sail hangs down, but there is a boom as well all along the foot of the sail as is clearly to be seen on one of the coins marking not only both yard-arms by a point but both arms of the boom as well. Being stretched out between yard and boom the rectangular sail could be used like a lug-sail with the largest part of its area aft of the mast.

This type of sail is already to be seen on a mosaic and a tombstone of Roman times in the Rhineland in connection with ships of a construction that includes a lot of those constructional elements we find again with the cog some centuries later. On the other hand looking to Gotlandic and other Scandinavian tombstones depicting Viking ships we again find the broad rectangular sail with a yard on top and a boom along the foot. As these sails do not occur before the 7th century in Scandinavian ships, the early cogs seem to have been the intermediary, delivering a type of sail from the Roman Rhineland to Scandinavia and thus enabling the Vikings to sail their long range voyages.

For reconstruction of Viking sails scientists always looked at north Norwegian boats of the 19th century and at the tapestry of Bayeux, which indeed shows sails with loose feet. But the tapestry is not of Viking age but marks the end of that age. For reconstruction of Viking age sail we have to follow the pictorial evidence of that age.

When people of Hedeby imitated the coins of Dorestad but changed the type of ship depicted on them from hulc to cog, the hulc obviously played no role in the traffic from the Rhine estuary to Hedeby. Vice versa up till 1200 there is no evidence of a cog in England or along the French coasts. But there is evidence of cogs in the 9th and 10th century written sources for the Netherlands and in archaeological sources not only for 7th century Wilhelmshaven but also for Hamburg from late the 9th century onward in all layers up till the end of Middle Ages. All these places are within the area of the shallow tidal waters of the Wattenmeer. This observation fits in very well with the design of the cog, which enable her to fall dry at low tide. So we have good reasons to believe the early cog to be a ship of the Wattenmeer, sailing the relatively calm waters behind the islands and dunes and upstream the coastal rivers as far as the tide reached. In Schleswig-Holstein she sailed as far as Hollingstedt, the North-Sea harbour of Hedeby, from where normally the merchandise had to be carried by carts to Hedeby at the Baltic, a distance of only 16 km across the dry land. But sometimes they even dragged some cogs across that small ridge between both seas.

Perhaps some skilled ship-wrights from the Frisian coast settled at Hedeby and built the sort of cogs they had learnt to build at home. At any rate we see that people at Hedeby struck coins with pictures of cogs. And they would not have done

so if the cog had not been one of the most important ship types in that harbour. Of course, the cog was not the only type of ship on these coins. They struck Viking ships as well. But as Hedeby was a town under Danish and Swedish government in the 9th and early 10th century, nobody is astonished to find Viking ships on coins of this town. But to find cogs as well means that their role in trade must have been not too small in a Baltic harbour like Hedeby. Indeed there is archaeological evidence of another cog as far east in the Baltic as Birka near Stockholm in the 10th century. What has been found are about 60 typical cog-nails among thousands of rivets from Viking ships, demonstrating the cog to have been a foreigner in those days at Birka. But there is no doubt that the good trading connection between Hedeby and Birka was at least to a certain extent maintained by cogs.

In all we get a picture of consequent expansion of traffic with cogs from the Rhine to the east, at first along the southern shores of the North Sea and its tidal rivers, and then at least in the 9th century cogs reached the Baltic at Hedeby and from this bridgehead started to sail along the Baltic coasts.

When, about 1200, harbour towns started to show ships on their town seals, they of course depicted the type of ship that was the main type produced or owned by inhabitants of the town. So these town seals give an impressive survey not of the total distribution, but of home ports for ship types: In England and along the opposite Continental coast we find the types of hulc and keel as far east as Munikendam near Amsterdam in the 13th and the 14th century. The westernmost seal with a cog is that of Damme near Bruges in Belgium and from the Ijsselmeer to the Baltic there is no other type than the cog, if we exclude Scandinavia with their own Scandinavian ships. The distribution of home ports for cogs along the North Sea coast in the 13th and the 14th century is surprisingly the same as in the 9th century, whereas in the Baltic the picture had changed completely. Instead of Hedeby forming one small bridgehead there is a long series of harbour towns founded between ca. 1150 and 1250 from Kiel in the west to Elbing (now Elblag) in the east which in their seals presented themselves as homeports for cogs. With these towns the base for traffic with cogs had been remarkably enlarged. The reasons for and the consequences of this enormous enlargement will be discussed later. Let us first take a brief look at the constructional development of the cog in the 13th and the 14th century.

We left the cog as a flat bottomed ship with four side strakes on top of the bottom, equiped with a special side rudder, working like a lee-bord and with a broad rectangular sail working as lug-sail, as depicted on 9th century coins (fig. 4 ab). The next good picture of a cog we find on the seal of Lübeck from 1226. But as the ships presented there and on the later seals from 1256 (fig. 5a) and 1281 have gently curved stem- and stern-posts with animal heads on top, which look like the dragonheads of Viking ships, these seals caused a lot of confusion to scientists. Contemporary written sources say these seals depict cogs. And so scientists thought the cog had been developed from Viking ships. But the seals themselves give three details which are never found with Viking ships but are typical for cogs. So they surely show cogs, which in their construction differ completely from Viking ships:

1. The oldest seal shows clearly reversed clinker-construction, that is the underneath strake overlaps the upper one. With Viking ships this is always vice versa, with cogs the reversed clinker-construction is not the rule, but several times found.

2. The strakes overlap completely both stem- and stern-posts, so that nothing of them is visible but the heads. All old cog seals show this detail. The Bremer cog shows this construction in reality but with one specific addition: outside the stem-and stern-posts, which are

a
b

Figure 5. Hanseatic town-seals depicting the cog.
5a. Early cog with side-rudder, but without castle-construction. Seal of Lübeck 1256.
5b. Later cog with stern-rudder, castle constructions and additional outside stem- and stern-posts. Seal of Stralsund 1329 (drawing H. Ewe).

overlapped by the strakes, second stem- and stern-posts had been put to close the scarf between strakes meeting in front of the inside posts. Thus the Bremer cog has two stem-posts and two stern-posts. This construction is an invention of the 13th century. The oldest town seal with additional outside stem- and stern-posts is that of Staveren in the Netherlands from 1243; in the Baltic it is that of Wismar from 1256, whereas the seals of Lübeck from 1256 and even that of Neustadt in Holstein from 1351 with a rather small version of a cog lack this new invention, which made the cog more seaworthy.

3. All three Lübeck seals show cogs with that special type of side-rudder, which operates like a lee-board. Even in this detail we see no alteration to the cogs of the 9th century. But in the course of the 13th century this very sophisticated steering equipment was altered, too, in favour of the stern-rudder, for the first time to be seen on the seals of Elbing 1242 and Staveren 1246. Lübeck seemed to distrust the new invention for a long time, as the cog on its seal from 1281, in spite of having adopted the newly invented additional stem- and stern-posts at the outside, sticks to the old fashioned side-rudder. The small cog on the seal of Neustadt in Holstein even in 1351 had not altered the side-rudder.

Unfortunately no cog-seal of the 13th century shows the sail. So there is no possibility to find out in which way the sail was changed corresponding to the altered rudder. We just find a last reflection of the broad rectangular lug-sail of 9th century cogs with the cog on the seal of Kiel from 1365. Though this cog already has a stern-rudder, the sail is hoisted like a lug-sail with the yard not being set horizontally and not fastened in the middle, but with the short part before the mast far down and the long part behind the mast rising to

a considerable height. In contrast to the 9th century sails, the Kiel sail of 1365 has already a loose foot and no longer a boom along the foot. In consequence of this alteration we see the foot flaccid in the wind. The Vlaardingen seal from 1312 shows a cog with the yard hoisted down, but like the predicted sail of Kiel the short end before the mast is kept deeper than the long end aft of the mast. Both seals seem to mark the last phase of lug-sails with cogs, whereas the Stralsund seal from 1329 shows the first real squaresail hoisted at a cog.

The oldest wreck of a cog, found at the Juttish coast near Cap Skagen and dated to the 13th century, gives another hint to the construction of the rigging, though hardly more than the bottom has been excavated. But in this bottom the position of the mast was so far before the centre of the ship, that she could not be sailed with an ordinary square-sail. Nothing but a lug-sail could manoeuvre a ship with the mast in this position round Cap Skagen.

For the voyage round Cap Skagen the cogs could no longer be those small, flat bottomed "mud-gliders", which in the 9th century sailed the Wattenmeer behind the islands and dunes from the Rhine to Hedeby and were just able to sail from Hedeby along the Baltic shores. In the above mentioned wreck we can see, how cogs gained more seaworthiness: The bottom no longer meets in a definite chine with the steep sides, but there is a rounded transition between both, allowing the hull to make smooth movements in the waves instead of hard rockings caused by an angled chine in rough water.

By adding more strakes to the ship her sides were increased until 8 strakes and an additional washstrake built one side of the cog on top of the bottom, as can be seen at the Bremer cog (fig. 2). This process started some time before 1200, as the early seals show cogs with 5 or 6 strakes above the waves. The result was not only more seaworthiness and in consequence the expansion of voyages but also an increasing cargo capacity. Whereas cogs of the 9th century are thought to have had a cargo capacity of about 40 t., in 1241 there is mentioned a cog carrying about 240 t.

Designed for mere trading purposes these highboarded vessels still in the 13th century had open decks without any protection against rain and wind for the crew. But towards the end of the 13th century even on board of cogs high fighting-towers were installed, from which archers could shoot their arrows much more effectively than from the low deck.

English ship-seals show these towers already one century earlier. The first cog with such a tower appears in 1299 on the seal of Danzig, the second on the seal of Damme 1309. But already on the seal of Stralsund from 1329 the aft tower was no longer a single addition on board of the ship but had become part of it, giving not only a high vantage point to the archers but also a sort of protected room or cabin underneath its platform, which formed a sort of roof, to the height of which the sides of the ship were built up by additional timbers (fig. 5b). This is the state of development we find in the Bremer cog of 1380 with nicely done benches inside along the walls of the cabins and – to make comfort complete – a real toilet at the aft end of the castle, where it protrudes beyond the sides of the ship.

In all we have been able to trace back the continuous development of an ever increasing ship-type, which became more seaworthy, got more and more cargo capacity, better rigging and steering gear, became more effective for military purposes and at least became more comfortable for the crew or just the officers. Of course this development was not an automatic one, but had been pushed forward by men who wanted to do something with this particular type of ship. So let us have a look at these men and what they wanted to do with the cog.

The Socio-economic Background

The first people we meet with a cog are Frisian peasants living in a lonely farm on top of an artificial hill in the amphibious coastal region of the North Sea, where today Wilhelmshaven in Lower Saxony is situated. But in the 7th century there was flat land not yet protected against the sea by dikes, so that every high tide the saltwater flooded deep into the land. Arable land was rare and all timber for buildings, ships, carts and whatever had to be bought from people further south. The Frisians bred cattle and raised sheep in at least two different breeds, and their women and girls specialised in making woollen cloths of high quality. So they had something to sell for all those things they had to import. They were not only able to produce special merchandise; on their farms they also produced the ship, that is the cog, by which they were able to sail along the calm waters behind the islands and dunes to foreign markets where they got good prices for their products. This Frisian trade from a rural startingpoint and with rural products of high quality in the 7th century reached a high frequency with England, and contacts with Scandinavia were so intensive that Scandinavian ships adopted the sail of the Frisian cogs. Frisian activity along the river Rhine is reflected not in the Rhineland itself but by Rhenish pottery of late 7th century date at Scandinavian trading centres such as Kaupang at the entrance to the Oslofjord, being brought there from the Rhineland by Frisian merchants.

Of course the Frisians were not the only shipowning merchants in the 7th century. There is evidence for English, Frankish, Gotlandic and other merchants as well. But the Frisians sailed the longest distance of all of them. To understand their situation we have to keep in mind that sailing in those days was carried out in close contact with the shores. Sailors did not dare to cross the open sea out of sight of land, with the exception of narrow passages which could be covered in one day's sailing, for example from Lowestoft Ness in England to the estuary of the Rhine or from Gotland to Grobin in Lettland. Thus the main lines of pre-Viking traffic in the North Sea can easily be reconstructed.

There are coastal trading routes along the English and Frankish shores and a close network of sailing routes to link England to the Continent. The easternmost of these routes led from Humber and Thames to Maas and Rhine, the estuaries of the latter lieing within the western wing of the Frisian sphere in those days. All along the shores of the Scandinavian peninsula we find a second system of coastal sailing routes, including the waterways around the Danish islands. The Frisians made contact with the Scandinavian routes via their bridge-head Hedeby in Schleswig-Holstein at the eastern wing of their sphere. The only navigable connection between both traffic-systems, the English-Continental and the Scandinavian one, led through Frisian coastal waters. Thus Frisian shipowning merchants found themselves in a very favoured geographical position, which enabled them to hold the monopoly in long distance trade between Scandinavia on the one hand and Rhineland and England on the other hand. And at least in the 7th century they had learned how to use this position. They no longer waited for merchandise to be carried to Frisia by Scandinavian, English and Rhenish ships and just transmitted by themselves through Frisia to the consumers outside the other end of their region. They penetrated into the Scandinavian, English and Rhenish routes to get to the sources of those products which they could sell for a good price at one of the opposite ends of their trade routes. The Frisians kept their monopoly until the Vikings in the late 8th century opened an alternative route from Norway via Shetland to England. Thus from 700 to the second half of the 11th century the southern parts of the North Sea were known as the Frisian ocean.

The market-places visited by the Frisians with their ships (hulcs for England, cogs for the east, both for the Rhine) had to lie on the banks of navigable waters with good conditions for landing of ships. As the ships had drafts of 60 cm or less, even shallow waters or tidal streams were navigable and landing facilities were given at every sandy strand or bank where ships could be beached or cogs could fall dry. The ships could be loaded and unloaded as if they were land vehicles. No quay construction nor other harbour installations were necessary. The merchants just preferred the calm water of dead arms or small tributaries of great streams, to avoid the danger of their currents. The market-places had a special topography: As all merchants arriving there by ship had to beach their vessels, all these vessels stood in one long row along the border line of water and dry land. During market time the merchants lived and sold their merchandise in tents, which they erected on the dry land as near to their ships as possible in order to keep an eye on their ships. All those customers who travelled by road had their tents close to those of the Frisians and the other shipowning merchants. The result was a second row of tents running parallel to the row of ships and tents along the bank, but further into the dry land, leaving just a broad street in between both rows of tents to enable intensive interchange.

Of course good landing facilities were not the only requirement for a well frequented market-place. Quite a number of people had to live in the neighbourhood of the site, which had to be in easy reach of them. So in the 7th and 8th centuries we often hear of market-places in between the river-side walls of former Roman towns, with the rivers themselves giving easy approach for ships very near to settlements of populous. In regions without towns even ramparts or other fortifications were the starting points for establishing market-places, promising a certain amount of security to the visitors and at least their precious merchandise. Other favoured points for the meeting of people of two different political units in those days were market-places at the border of both units.

The main step in the development of these far-stretch market-places along riversides and beaches was from the late 7th century onwards the tendency to establish dwelling-places for the merchants, who converted their temporary tents into permanent houses to live in with their families and servants. They built store houses for merchandise and landing places for their own ships and those of their business friends just behind their back-doors. Without boats there was no access to the waterside of these merchants' houses, the front-doors of which opened to a street running parallel to the water. By this street pedestrians, peasants with carts, Jews with their cross-country caravans and so on could easily enter the houses of the shipowing merchants, which served for transshipment from cross-country trade to trade carried out by ships and vice versa. And as pedestrians and land vehicles could carry only small fractions of the cargo of one ship, there was a high frequency of people with small amounts of goods in the street, while ships did not land so often but brought and took away large quantities of cargo, the warehouses of the shipowning merchants serving as intermediary stores for collecting the products of the surrounding country to be carried away by ship and for distributing in the surrounding country the goods brought by ship. No wonder that along the other side of the street Jews and other cross-country merchants started to settle.

These market settlements have been termed by scientists one-street-settle-ments. But in spite of the vivid market life along that one street, it was not the street itself that was the starting point of the settlement, but the riverbank or shore serving as landing place for a lot of ships. So the best term might be "embankment-settlement". All "grown" harbour towns of early medieval date round the North Sea and along the rivers flowing into it had this special topography. Some of them have it up to our time, like Trondheim in Norway or Otterndorf on the lower Elbe. In many of these towns in the course of time the harbour had moved away from its old site as the water there was no longer deep enough for the enlarged ships. But the houses of the shipowning merchants stayed there and so the oldest port quarter is to be identified in maps of the towns. Most of these harbour towns had not only the long row of merchant houses along the waterfront but also one public market without houses where foreign ships might land even when the foreigners had no relationships to any merchant of the town. The more the trade concentrated to the houses of the merchants, the more this function of the market became superfluous and so most of these market-places lost their connection to navigable water, being converted into markets for local trade only.

Let me make 3 essential points regarding this development.

1. Harbour settlements of this special type were not only the first medieval addition to former Roman towns but became the first towns in the hitherto purely agricultural regions outside the former Roman Empire round the North Sea.

2. Not only in topography but also in all other manifestations of urban life shipowning merchants, became the decisive element of these first towns. So the spirit of merchants including the will to make profit by investment of money even at the risk of life, became the

motor of a new way of life in medieval society.

3. Craftsmen followed the merchants into the originating towns, and worked for export but remained more or less dependent on the merchants in spite of their greater numbers. In the course of medieval time both groups of people united and formed the civil society of free townsfolk in contrast to the hierarchic society of rural districts.

The Frisian shipowning merchants of course took part in this development. In their own country they settled at small market-centres on top of artificial long hills along navigable waters (instead of round hills for rural settlements). Most of these trading settlements remained relatively small. Only border markets such as Dorestad near Utrecht developed into big trading towns. But the main impulse Frisian merchants gave to long distance trade around the North-Sea outside their own country. Wherever they had started good trading connections in foreign countries in the 7th century they established *trading colonies*. Frisian merchants with their families in the 8th and 9th centuries settled at York in England as well as at Birka in Sweden or at a lot of Rhenish towns as far upstream as Straßburg, to mark just their utmost stations. The importance of Frisian trade is highlighted by a statement of A.D. 886 saying the best part of Mainz was thought to be not the quarter round the cathedral but the Frisian quarter along the riverbank. From as far as St. Gallen in Switzerland people travelled to Mainz to buy Frisian cloth. Obviously the function of Frisian trading colonies in foreign countries was to distribute Frisian products in those regions and to collect products of those regions to be brought there or carried to other countries respectively by the fellow-countrymen of the colonists. As has previously been stated the type of "embankment-settlement" suited this purpose very well.

Frisian merchants did not invent trading colonies. They as well as Anglo-Saxon merchants had only learned from Syrian and Jewish merchants in the Merovingian Empire how to organize effective trade by these colonies. While Anglo-Saxon merchants founded colonies along their way to the Mediterranean for example at Marseille, Frisian merchants transferred the idea to Scandinavia, where for instance Gotlandic merchants not only adopted the cog-sail for their ships but in the late 7th century already started to found Gotlandic trading colonies at the south-eastern coast of the Baltic opposite to Gotland.

A second item of Frisian trade organization is *travelling fellowhip*. As times were always dangerous, especially for foreign merchants travelling far away from their country, they gathered in groups to defend and support one another. They did not sail alone but in fleets of several ships and gained privileges not as single merchants but as groups on the basis of fellow-countrymen. How strictly the fellowship was limited to countrymen we do not know. In the late 11th century we find a Frisian guild at Sigtuna north of Stockholm including people with German and Scandinavian names as well, perhaps a result of Scandinavian activity in Viking times.

The third element of Frisian trade organization is the desire for special *trade-privileges* which had been granted to them – as far as we know – only in the Carolingian Empire. These privileges included special protection by the king for personal security and against robbery as well as exemption from certain customs and other duties.

Until the end of the 8th century the Frisian merchants remained the most active sailors in the North Sea and enjoyed their monopoly. Then suddenly the centre of activity turned to the Vikings, who for some centuries were able to dictate, events in North-Sea shipping. With violence they opened the way for themselves, and Continental merchants feared them as pirates or plunderers but welcomed them as peaceful traders, who gave a lot of impulses to trade. The most outstanding impulse was the widening of the horizon. They no longer stuck to coastal navigation but crossed the high sea without seeing land for much more than only one day: The Vikings had developed new methods of deep-sea navigation and used their know how with emphasis: the Viking time just started with the opening of an alternative sailing route to western Europe for Norwegian ships, which previously had to sail along the Danish and Frisian shores towards England or the Continent but since 793 just sailed from western Norway via Shetland to the British Isles. They discovered Iceland, Greenland and even America, opened the cross-country routes along the Russian rivers, where they established intensive trade with the world of Islam and they extended their activities into the Mediterranean via Gibraltar.

Though the Vikings acted as pirates and plundered a lot of Frisian ships, the latter were not pushed out of traffic. But in spite of the explosion of the sailing area the Frisians in the 9th century, as far as is known to us, did not sail much beyond their traditional routes marked by the towns of York, Birka and Straßburg. Only in the 10th century the Frisians seem to have completely vanished from the scene. What had happened? We had left the Frisians as inhabitants of Rhenish and other harbour towns, where in the 9th century they lived in the best quarters. About 900 A.D. the development of citizenship had reached the stage of communities being separated from the law of the surrounding countries. For the merchants and their privileges their Frisian origin no longer proved to be decisive; they now were privileged as inhabitants of special towns and consequently were named as "mercatores de Mogontiaco" (merchants of Mainz) and so on. And as the most developed towns with merchants of Frisian origin lay outside Frisia, these merchants in total were named men of the emperor or just Saxons, as the North Sea ports of the German Empire belonged to the dukedom of Lower Saxony.

These 10th century Saxons still sailed the cog along the traditional Frisian routes and lived in trading colonies abroad, the first of which is mentioned at Hedeby in 934. Like the Frisians the Saxons were organized in fellowships, of which the Frisian guild of Sigtuna even in the 11th century conserved the old name from the time of the Frisian trade.

In newly founded trading centres such as Lund there is evidence of proper Saxon guilds. And at about 1000 A.D. there is the first evidence of special privileges in favour of German merchants abroad. For example at London in the course of time especially merchants of Cologne gained a very favourable position. Altogether trade on German ships was carried out after the same pattern as before the Viking era. Though the Vikings were the masters of the sea both in peace and in war they did not push other merchants off the stage. On the contrary we can observe an ever growing number of people being engaged in trade as merchants or as craftsmen, settling in an ever increasing number of trading towns.

New impulses are to be noted in the 11th and the 12th century: German merchants for the first time entered the Viking routes beyond the traditional Frisian terminals. They are to be found at Trondheim or in Iceland, along the southern shores of the Baltic, and towards the end of 11th century they entered the Mediterranean to participate in the crusades. That means, German merchants had learned from the Vikings, how to cross the open sea. Trade relations still remained much more reciprocal than in the 13th century and later. We do not only find German merchants in Norway but Norwegian ones at Utrecht or among the inhabitants of Cologne. In 1191 Bergen harbour is said to have been visited by Icelanders and Greenlanders, by Englishmen and Germans, by Danes, Swedes and Gotlanders. The pottery excavated at Bergen reflects this internationality of trade as it originated from England, from the Maas- and Rhine valley and from the Weser valley, from where it was brought to Bergen by Bremen merchants. Sleswig, the successor of Hedeby, was visited by Saxons, Flemings and Icelanders, Russians and Gotlanders.

They had all become Christians in the meantime and that made trade less complicated. They all founded trading colonies in foreign harbour towns, most of them with a special church in the neighbourhood for service and for a burial in consecrated earth in case of death abroad, but not least as a storehouse in which the merchandise was protected more by the fear of God than by locked doors. At Sigtuna near Stockholm the ruins of five of such merchant churches are still to be seen. Bardowick near Lüneburg has had nine churches, Sleswig even about a dozen. Merchants in those days had a very constant relation to the church; they had their own priests on board not only for sermons but also for writing lists of merchandises and consequently in the course of time learned how to trade no longer by travelling with their merchandise but by directing it with the help of trade-letters, wherever they wanted.

In spite of the fact that all merchants seemed to have had access to all the harbours they wanted, 11th and 12th century trade was far from beeing free-trade. Many groups of merchants had special privileges, but their privileges differed very much: At London about 1130 the Lorraines were allowed to stay not more than forty days, the men of the Emperor, i.e. especially those of Cologne, might live as guests at London without restriction, but those of Tiel, Bremen and Anvers were not allowed to pass London bridge, the Norwegians might live there for one year without permission to go outside the town, and the Danes were not only allowed to live at London all the year but even to travel outside the town through all England. This is just one example out of a real jungle of privileges granted to different groups of merchants.

A new chapter in North-Sea trade had been initiated by an event not in the North Sea but in the Baltic: This event was the foundation of Lübeck as the first purely German town and bridgehead in the south west corner of the Baltic in 1143/59 as is generally accepted. But if we ask what really was new in this foundation we get a lot of answers, some of which we cannot accept: The cog is said to have been introduced into the Baltic via Lübeck, but we know it had already been sailed from Hedeby to Birka by Frisian merchants in the 9th century. German merchants are said to have started to sail in travelling fellowships (the so-called hanses), to have founded trading colonies with merchant churches as centres and to have gained special trade privileges. But all these things were far from being new. Frisian and Saxon merchants even in the Baltic did all the same things long before.

Nevertheless something new did start with the foundation of Lübeck. We observe a new way of making use of all those old arrangements, ships and so on. And we find a number of reasons enabling people to do so. One of these was a surplus population in Germany which led to a penetration of German farmers and townspeople into the countries east of the river Elbe, where before only a thin Slavian population was living. The result of this development was in the course of the 13th century an enormous growth of markets with masses of new consumers as well as producers of surplus production as for example of grain. Lübeck itself had been founded in the Slavonic area and participated as the first new city very much in this development, being pushed forward by the spirit of pioneers.

The most important group of merchants who started to settle at Lübeck were cross-country merchants (!) from all over Westfalia. Their relatives still remained in the very productive Westfalian trading centres, and as the merchants at Lübeck during the Hanseatic period kept in close contact with them, they all the time had intimate knowledge of the market situation in Westfalia.

The second important group of merchants settling at Lübeck were those well known shipowning merchants who since the time of Frisian trade sailed the cog from Hedeby/Sleswig into the Baltic. With their own town seals the Lübeckians themselves tell us what they about two generations after the foundation of their town thought to be the main point of this new start: They depicted a ship of cog type with two persons on board; one of them wearing sailor's clothes and acting as the helmsman of the ship represents the group of shipowning merchants, the other with the common clothes of rich people all over the country is swearing an oath to represent the cross-country merchants who were organized in sworn confederations (fig. 5a).

Both groups of merchants at Lübeck for the first time established a close unit or "hanse", named the union of German merchants visiting Gotland. Thus the cross-country merchants at Lübeck were enabled to enter a ship to travel with their merchandise across the Baltic to Gotland, the turntable of Baltic traffic, from where the merchants organized their markets. Especially at Nowgorod in Russia they established a commercial agency. On the other hand the shipowning merchants were provided with a hinterland of hitherto unknown dimensions. Instead of sailing from one harbour to the other, where they had to wait for customers or cross-country merchants to come and see them, they now

were able to direct their merchandise to customers or merchants living up till 500 km in the inland.

Into this "marriage" the Westfalian merchants brought a lot of new ideas. They already started the new port with a hitherto unknown topography. Instead of the old schema of the embankment-settlement with the market-place at the harbour and one row of houses along the riverside, providing the merchants with landing facilities for their ships behind their back-doors, they now divided the different functions of this one settlement and separated them into different areas. They did not find it necessary any longer to have the local market-place for interchange between townspeople and surrounding peasants at the harbour and thus established the market-place in the centre of the town. For reasons of defence the landing places of the ships were separated from the merchants' houses, the city-wall being built inbetween ships and houses to protect the latter against hostile actions. Consequently there was no longer any necessity to build the merchants' houses in one long row along the riverside. The best situation for these houses now was along the streets that led down from the centre of the town to the harbour gates in the city wall. By this new arrangement many more long-distance merchants were enabled to live in favourably situated houses.

Long distance trade concentrated on these houses, but nevertheless during the first century of the town the merchants had to travel with their merchandise as the townseal shows (fig. 5a). In the second half of the 13th century the merchants more and more learned how to make use of writing. Thus they remained in their houses and directed their business affairs by trade-letters, which made trade much more effective.

From their hometowns the Westfalians had brought with them the most developed city law of middle and northern Europe.

But as Lübeck was a newly founded town nobody had to pay heed to old arrangements, and thus the Westfalian city law at Lübeck was developed into the most modern constitution of a city in those days, with a very flexible selfgovernment in the hands of a municipal council recruiting its members from the families of long-distance merchants.

With the expansion of trade other members of these families started to settle where trade concentrated along the shores of the Baltic. Within one century after the foundation of Lübeck the Baltic was surronded by a chain of newly founded towns and markets, into which the Lübeckian merchants not only had imported German products but also their own municipal constitution and the new harbour topography. Many of these towns like Lübeck showed cogs in their seals (fig. 5b). All these towns became very effective trading centres for their special hinterlands. All these merchants remained members of the initiative unit of German merchants acting via Lübeck in the Baltic as a private co-operating society, which later on was known as Hanseatic League. In the hinterland of the newly founded towns the Hanseatic merchants with their capital organized surplus production of raw material, the consumers of which were at hand in Westfalia and other areas of Middle-Europe: In central Sweden they started copper mining, south of the Baltic they organized grain trade and in Danish Scania they organized herring trade and thus made it possible for an ever growing population of Scandinavians, Slavonians and immigrated Germans to earn their livings. But the other side of the medal was the monopoly of Baltic trade in the hands of the Hanseatic merchants.

This monopoly in Baltic trade was not without severe consequences for North Sea trade. The Flemings for example, who up till the early 13th century sailed with their cloth as far as at least Sleswig-Holstein, were completely pushed out of traffic.

Lübeckian merchants had made arrangements with their colleagues at Hamburg and thus had got their North-Sea harbour from which they sailed to Bruges in Flandres, where they established their second commercial agency (Nowgorod was the first). The Flemings could now buy all Baltic raw material in their own towns and needed no longer to sail to the Baltic themselves. At London the Osterlings, as the Hanseatic merchants from the Baltic were named, found themselves in competition with merchants from Cologne and other Rhenish towns which had old and good trade connections with England. But in late the 13th century the Rhenish merchants made arrangements with the Osterlings, their old privileges for England were expanded for all Hanseatic merchants, and the Cologne Guildhall in London together with the neighbouring Stealjard was turned over into the third Hanseatic agency.

Norway was not able to harvest enough grain for its growing population. England up till the early 13th century had a surplus production of wheat and English merchants sailed it to Norway. But then England needed her grain for her own population. The Hanseatic merchants filled in the gap with Baltic rye and initiated mass production of Norwegian stockfish, for which they opened new markets among the Catholics of Continental Europe. Thus many Norwegians were enabled to earn a good living, but depended on the Hanseatics, who at Bergen established their fourth commercial agency. In the late 13th century the Norwegians tried to become more independent. But the Hanseatics stopped grain transport and opened an economic war by blockading Norway's shipping connections. This was the first economic war and, though Bremen refused to participate because of her good and old relations with Bergen, the Norwegians after a short time had to accept the Hanseatic privileges. Their monopoly was heavier than before, but the Norwegians got as much grain as they wanted and earned much money by selling stockfish. The Norwegian war was not without consequences for the Hanse. Hanseatic merchants had learned the value of castles on board of their cogs giving high vantage points for archers. From that war on their cogs were fitted with these tower-like constructions, which already one century before had been very common on English ships. But in contrast to English-men within only some decades Hanseatic merchants closed the room underneath the platforms, connected the castle to the hull, and thus got the first cabins on board of seagoing vessels in the North Sea and Baltic on the one hand and on the other hand got a cargoship which could be used in war without much alteration (fig. 5b).

The Norwegian war was the first step from mere trade towards politics in favour of this trade. Consequently in the 14th century the private unit of Hanseatic merchants step by step was turned over into a political confederation of trading towns which knew how to use their economic power and if necessary even to arm their trading vessels. Thus they proved to be able to defend their privileges even against centralised kingdoms for some centuries to come.

Towards the end of the 15th century the Hanseatic League was no longer flexible enough to get along with new tendencies. More and more English and Dutch ships sailed into the Baltic to break the Hanseatic monopoly even in the original Hanseatic area, where in 1496 the commercial agency at Nowgorod was closed by czar Iwan III.

So Hanseatic merchants found themselves being pushed into a defensive situation, when Columbus in 1492 discovered America and the Spaniards and Portugueses started to establish their colonial empires. English and Dutch and even Scandinavian shipowners succesfully tried to participate in the new development. But Hanseatic merchants just tried to keep a reasonable position in European coastal trade to provide their own hinterland with adequate supplies until in 17th century the Hanseatic League came to an end.

Bibliography

A. v. Brandt and others, *Die Deutsche Hanse als Mittler zwischen Ost und West,* Köln (1963)

Ph. Dollinger, *Die Hanse,* Stuttgart (1966)

D. Ellmers, *Frühmittelalterliche Handelsschiffahrt in Mittel- und Nordeuropa,* Neumünster (1972)

D. Ellmers, "The Cog of Bremen and related boats", in: S. McGrail (ed.), *The Archaeology of Medieval Ships and Harbours in Northern Europe,* BAR International Series 66, (Oxford 1979), p. 1–15

H. Ewe, *Schiffe auf Siegeln,* Bielefeld/Berlin (1972)

S. Fliedner, *Die Bremer Kogge,* 4th ed., Bremen (1974)

P. Heinsius, *Das Schiff der hansischen Frühzeit,* Weimar (1956)

B. Scheper, Kaufmann, Stadherr, Ratsgewalt. "Über die norddeutsche Städtelandschaft im 12. und 13. Jahrhundert", in: *Stader Jahrbuch 1979,* p. 18–38.

U. Schnall, *Navigation der Wikinger. Schriften des Deutschen Schiffahrtsmuseums,* vol. 6, Oldenburg (1975)

W. Vogel. *Geschichte der deutschen Seefahrt,* Vol. 1, Berling (1915)

Hanse in Europa. Brücke zwischen den Märkten. 12.–17. Jahrhundert. Ausstellung im Kölnischen Stadtmuseum 9. 6.–9. 9. 1973 (Köln 1973)

"… except through the Agency and Intermediary of the Aforementioned Sea …"

Some Observations on the Development of Dutch Sea Power and the Diffusion of Dutch Influence in North-Western Europe

PHILIPPUS MEESSE BOSSCHER

It seems appropriate to begin this paper with an attempt to present a point of view regarding the causes of the rise of Dutch sea power and its subsequent development through the eighteenth century (for various reasons, some of them quite down-to-earth, I will not venture beyond the Napoleonic period). For this I consider the best point of departure the concept of the elements of sea power developed by Alfred Thayer Mahan. As many of my readers will know, in the introductory chapter to his most famous book the Patriarch of modern maritime strategy sums up these elements as follows:

geographical position;
physical conformation;
extent of territory;
number of population;
character of the people;
character of the government.[1]

One glance at a map of Western Europe suffices to understand why the territory of the present-day Kingdom of the Netherlands so early became and since stayed an important hub of trade. As Charles Wilson puts it in an admirable little book: "The wealth of the United Provinces derived largely from their geographical position". He goes on to point out that they stretched across the estuaries of the rivers Scheldt, Maas and Rhine, which connected them with the "great hinterland of Germany", and that they looked westward to England and the Atlantic. He rightly rates "more immediately significant" though their position "midway between the great corn and timber areas of the Baltic and the markets of southern Europe".[2] Wilson is writing of the period of the Republic.[3] However, already long before the same geographical factors had been at work with basically the same effect. They had been the primary cause of the commercial prosperity of, to mention just some instances, Dorestad on the Lower Rhine in the Carolingian period, of the Frisian Zuyderzee port of Stavoren in the 10th and 11th centuries, and of Kampen near the mouth of the river Yssel during the later Middle Ages.

It should be pointed out here that a geographical position that left little to be desired from a commercial point of view was not without grave strategical disadvantages. This soon becomes clear to everybody who studies the campaigns of what we in the Netherlands use to call the English Wars and certain other people the Dutch Wars. Whilst they were being waged it was usually quite risky for Dutch merchantmen to enter or leave unescorted the North Sea by way of the so-called English Channel.[4] Also quite often the battle fleets of the States-General were prevented from leaving harbour as

Figure 1. Bird's-eye view of Amsterdam, 1544. Woodcut by Cornelis Anthoniszoon. At the time Amsterdam was already the most important commercial port in the Northern Netherlands. Note the "industrial estate" outside the city wall, at the left. It was called the "Lastage": a number of the Hanseatic Ports on the Baltic used to have a "Lastadienstrasse".

geration that during the 15th and 16th centuries a ship could from the sea reach almost any town in Holland, Zeeland, Groningen and Friesland without encountering obstacles that were really troublesome for all but the largest vessels of those times.

Subsequently this began to change, though it is for instance still possible for ships up to a certain tonnage to proceed from the Zuyderzee (or Ysselmeer, as it should be called now[7]) to the Rhine delta and vice versa – and to do this along a route "inside the dunes" which is fairly identical with one of those used during the Middle Ages. The change just mentioned is not mainly due to neglect – which is after all quite a recent phenomenon – or to the increasing size of ships. It is one of the ironies of history that it chiefly came about as a consequence of the successful performance of the Dutch at sea. The improvement of dikes and other defences against floods in quite a number of cases had the effect of barring waterways by means of weirs and the like or causing them to silt up; the same holds true for land reclamation. More often than not these operations were paid for entirely or in part with money earned at sea by Dutch freighters and fishing vessels.[8]

I should also mention here that in the seventeenth century a number of the main arteries of the Low Countries' system of inland waterways became the stage for what has been termed "an organizational innovation" in transport that was "unique for its time": the "dependable, convenient and cheap" transportation of passengers by means of horse-drawn barges over relatively long, interconnected route networks.[9]

Seen from a sailor's point of view the physical conformation of the country is not without disadvantage either. As many mariners have discovered to their cost, the Dutch North Sea coast can certainly not be described as particularly hospitable: it is no accident that one finds so few important harbours actually *on* that coast.[10] It seems to me though that this peculiarity has not only

soon as they were ready to confront the enemy by the westerly winds which blow so frequently over the North Sea.

As regards physical conformation one of the main characteristics of the country is that it possesses what is arguably the world's most narrow-meshed system of inland waterways. During the last decades this system has to a certain extent undergone decline: a number of canals and rivers have suffered rather badly from insufficient maintenance; others, notably in the North and East, have even been filled up.[5] Nevertheless even today the situation is such as to allow a remarkable number of the more important centres of population, especially in the region north of the "great rivers",[6] to be accessible by water. Some four or five centuries ago this was the case with far more of them. It can be stated with little exag-

hampered but also fostered the rise of Dutch sea power. From about the beginning of the 14th century one could witness among "Easterlings" (the traders from the Hansa towns of Northern Germany) a trend to avoid the ports of Flanders and let their ships end their southbound journeys in Amsterdam and other Zuyderzee ports. This shift no doubt was largely due to political and economic developments in Flanders.[11] Yet it seems likely that the Hanseatics would have proved less keen to divert their vessels to the Zuyderzee if this had not enabled them to give the North Sea coast of Holland and Zeeland a wide berth. After all to the South there were not only waiting for them the Flemish ports but also those of Zeeland, like Middelburg and Zieriksee, and of Brabant, like Antwerp and Bergen-op-Zoom, where the political and economic climate was far less disturbed.

To come back for a moment to the subject of land reclamation, this was the main – but not the only[12] – cause why in the late Middle Ages the name "Low Countries" became even more appropriate than it had been before. The acreage of that portion of the available agricultural land which could only be drained sufficiently to be used for either pasturing or haymaking increased almost continuously. Hence there soon arose a situation in which considerable quantities of dairy produce became available for marketing in other regions. Not much later the relative abundance of good grassland combined with the demand for meat to feed an increasing population spurred another development which offered golden opportunities to Dutch shipowners. People started to import into the Low Countries and particularly into Holland for fattening-up and subsequent slaughtering large numbers of "lean" oxen bought in Denmark, sometimes as far away as Skåne.[13]

Once I heard an eminent political scientist – who, incidentally, was born in Germany and educated in France – declare emphatically that there is no such thing as national character. I am still inclined to believe that he was overstating his case. None the less I have to admit that I do consider the concept of national character a most awkward one

Figure 2. Passenger barges of the "night-service", from one of the celebrated series of etchings by Reynier Nooms, alias Zeeman ("the Sailor", abt. 1623–1664). These barges were normally drawn by horses, but they also used their sails when the wind was favourable.

to use even under the most favourable circumstances. It certainly involves special difficulties if one tries to use it with reference to the population of the Low Countries.

Already in 1566 William the Silent had good reasons to write about "a country not only bounded by neighbours but also interwoven with peoples".[14] It is worthy of our attention that this was before between, say, 1590 and 1690 the prosperity of the United Provinces together with political and religious upheavals in neighbouring countries[15] caused immigration to assume what I take to have been record proportions. During that period Amsterdam – but also, albeit perhaps more intermittently, towns like Leyden, Rotterdam and Middelburg – were functioning as veritable "melting-pots". After about 1700 the number of immigrants to the Low Countries started to dwindle but it remained significant until far into the 19th century.[16]

So one cannot but conclude that it is, to say the least, not beyond doubt whether one can speak of a character of the Dutch nation in the sense of a peculiar set of innate characteristics. It appears in fact that we have to do with a clear case of human beings of quite varied descent being moulded into one nation through living in the same environment and being confronted with the same challenges and opportunities.[17]

In this conglomeration of "peoples" those with the longest record of continuous residence on Dutch soil are the Frisians. From archeological and geological evidence, but also from written sources – notably a famous passage by Pliny the Elder [18] – we know enough about the conditions they had to face during the first centuries after their settling in these parts to be able to state categorically that from the very moment of their arrival they must have devoted considerable mental and physical effort towards solving the problems connected with staying alive – if possible in some degree of comfort. We also know that quite soon they did not remain content any longer with waiting for foreigners to come to their ports and markets. They ventured abroad – and in particular overseas – themselves in search of opportunities to do business, or other means to improve their fortunes. In this connection we may refer to the Frisian merchant who in 679 bought a slave in London and for that reason has been immortalised by the Venerable Bede, to the Frisian traders making their appearance in the Trondelag before the end of the first millennium A.D., but also to the "Ubbo Dux Fresonum" who in 868 joined a Viking raid to the British Isles and to the Frisian sailors who are mentioned as having served in the Navy of King Alfred the Great.[19]

A pronounced interest in what makes life safe and comfortable and a tendency to try one's luck at sea as evinced by these ancient Frisians have remained very clearly discernible ever since among their descendants and among the population of the Low Countries in general.[20]

So much so that I for one do not hesitate to pronounce them essential features of the character of the Dutch nation. Why they have been so clearly in evidence here for so long a time – in fact as long as we can look back – perhaps can be explained as follows. This part of the world has always – or at least until quite recently – remained rather a "hard country" in the sense Toynbee has employed the term.[21] To make a living from tilling its soil meant really hard work for most who tried to do so. Only after the beginning of this century has it been discovered that it possessed other mineral resources than the, not particularly rich and accessible, coal and lignite deposits in the extreme South, the exploitation of which goes back to medieval times. The part situated below sea level can only be kept fit for human habitation by dint of continuous vigilance and considerable financial sacrifices.

So it is understandable that the sea is often regarded as the great enemy, whose

Figure 3. A "mud-mill" and three mud-barges, etching by Zeeman. A mud-mill was an early form of dredger, with "scooping-boards" in stead of buckets. Motive power was supplied by horses.

voice – to quote one of our most esteemed modern poets – "is listened to with fear".[22] It is, however, also easy to understand why the official who in 1488 drew up the oldest surviving instruction for the High Admiral of the Netherlands wrote that the country was "unable to acquire anything good, profitable or useful except through the agency and intermediary of the aforementioned sea".[23] Although I am inclined to side with those who doubt whether there can ever be sufficient reason to call the sea generous, I sometimes feel tempted to use that adjective when discussing the role of the sea in Dutch history. This temptation becomes particularly strong when I am looking at a development which should perhaps already have been mentioned when I was discussing the element of geographical position. I am referring to what Charles Wilson has called "the mysterious change in the habits of the Gulf Stream", which in the beginning of the 15th century brought the herring shoals from the Baltic to the southern basin of the North Sea – a change which ought to be ranked among the main causes of the rise of Dutch sea power.[24] Generous or not generous, the sea for countless people in the Low Countries

has been the obvious choice when they just needed a job, when they were looking for a way to escape the consequence of foolish or criminal actions, when they were feeling the urge to venture beyond the horizon to better themselves or just to satisfy their curiosity.[25]

As regards the number of people who found employment on board seagoing vessels flying the flag of the Seven Provinces, an estimate has been published recently by Professor Bruijn. He puts it at about 55 000 in 1680, and at about 60 000 both in 1725 and in 1770. It appears safe to assume that in 1680 about half of these "sailors"[26] were foreigners by birth; the percentage of born Dutchmen among them during the first half of the 18th century is thought to have been considerably higher, getting lower again afterwards.[27] In order to be able to put these figures into proper perspective we should be aware that the total population of the United Provinces about 1680 must have been in the region of 1 900 000 souls and that afterwards there was hardly an increase until the second half of the 18th century.[28] I do not think it is possible to give a similar estimate of the number of those for whom the sea indirect-

101

ly provided employment. We can rest assured, however, that this must have been quite large. In this connection it is worthy of note that in the 17th and 18th centuries the Dockyards of the Navy and the East India Company were in all probability the largest industrial establishments in the Northern Netherlands.[29]

It seems hardly necessary to point out that even when the Seven Provinces were at the peak of their prosperity, life for the great majority of their seafaring population proved to have nothing more in store than a precarious existence and a nameless grave – the latter more often than not on a foreign shore or somewhere in the vastness of the ocean: Professor Bruijn tells us that about one in every three people who left Europe as servants of the East India Company ever came back.[30] It is far more remarkable that some of those who tried their luck at sea with nothing, or all but nothing, to their credit except their deserts of mind and body succeeded in acquiring impressive fortunes. Michiel Adriaenszoon de Ruyter is a case in point but in this paper I want to deal with him in another context. Here I would like to dwell for a moment on an example which could perhaps be called more typical. In the first half of the 18th century a boy was born of humble parents at Langenhorn in Holstein. As Soenke Ingwersen he emigrated to the Low Countries and took service with the East India Company as a barber's apprentice. Having "made his pile" he retired to his native region, where in 1758 he bought the castle and domain of Gelting. It is still possible to enjoy the exquisite stucco decorations, with a strong "oriental" flavour, which Seneca Inggersen, Baron of the Holy Roman Empire, commissioned to embellish his residence.[31]

The pronounced concern with certain aspects of life which I have deemed an essential characteristic of the Dutch nation put its mark quite strongly upon its contribution towards the scientific and cultural development of Europe – notably during what is not without justification called the Golden Age of Dutch History. When I state that these contributions are very often distinguished by a practical, businesslike approach to matters, I believe I have on my side no less eminent authorities than Professor J.H. Plumb and the late Lord Clark. The former, in his introduction to the fine book of Charles Boxer on "The Dutch Seaborne Empire", calls the Dutch of the 17th century "superb realists" and states emphatically that "the real world was the Dutch world".[32] Lord Clark in his masterly survey of the development of Western civilisation characterises the Dutch Republic as the first society which profited from "the revolution that replaced Divine Authority by experience, experiment and observation", where people without feeling embarassed asked "does it work?" and even "does it pay?" instead of confining themselves to the question "is it God's will?" After this he regales us with lucid comments on the work of quite a number of Dutch painters of the seventeenth century and with his appreciation of Dutch architecture of the period which he likes because it is "dignified, comfortable and harmonious".[33] He also mentions two men whose main interests lay in the field of abstract, speculative philosophy. But they are Descartes, who when already at a mature age came to the Low Countries from his native France "to escape interference",[34] and Spinoza, an Israelite born into the community of Portuguese Jews which had been established in Amsterdam only a short time before, and whose main source of inspiration is assumed to have been the philosophy of the East.

The questions "does it work?" and "does it pay?" must of course have been very often foremost in the minds of those who played leading roles in a process which was instrumental in providing the indispensable economic foundation for the Dutch Golden Age – what Lord Clark has called with a most felicitous phrase "the fluid capital ... which ... is one of the chief

Figure 4. Herring-busses fishing off a rocky coast (the Shetlands or the Far-Oer?). The fluyt in the foreground is perhaps a "herring-chaser" which transported the herring from the busses to the ports where it was brought to market. Etching by Zeeman.

causes of civilisation".[35] The process I have in mind has been called the Dutch industrial revolution. Elsewhere I have tried to demonstrate that there is indeed a striking similarity between this process and what we usually, but in my opinion wrongly, call "the" industrial revolution – both in nature and in effects.[36] Here I will limit myself to pointing out that one of the main features of both was the application of new technology to manufacture and that the Dutch Republic of the 17th century like the Britain of the 18th and 19th centuries was an important "exporter" of engineering and managerial skill.

Of the technological innovations which originated there certainly the most momentous as regards their economic effect were the introduction of a new type of merchant vessel, the "fluyt" – about which more anon – and developments in the art of the millwright. The introduction of the "molengang" – a series of windmills built on different levels and connected by what I call, taking my cue from L.T.C. Rolt, "rises"[37] – made it possible to pump water to a much greater height than had been practicable before. The replacement of the waterwheel by the spiral screw – first recorded about 1634 – made it possible to achieve the same result with one mill. The introduction of other innovations provided the main impetus for the building of hundreds of "industrial windmills" which up to the end of last century made up the bulk of the equipment of Dutch industry.[38] To the export of engineering and managerial talent from the Netherlands I will also come back later.

Most of us know that the Dutch Republic is the product of the Eighty Years' War. There has been a time that this conflict was usually interpreted as mainly, or even exclusively, a religious struggle. By now it is generally agreed that it has been as much, or even more, a contest between two currents of thought concerning secular politics, represented by a King who wanted to convert his dominions into one "modern" centralised state run by a bureaucracy which was really responsible only to him, and by his "conservative" subjects who wanted to hold on to their traditional communal privileges and freedoms.[39] Therefore we need not wonder that the Dutch Republic emerged as a rather loose confederacy.[40]

"Political theory attributed to each of the Provinces the fulness of sovereignty".[41] In practice they enjoyed a high degree of independence – even with respect to matters which had been declared in the "Union of Utrecht", the Covenant drawn up in 1579 which formed the kernel of the Republic's "constitution", the business of the Republic as a whole: foreign affairs, defence, overseas plantations and the common treasury. Quite often as regards these topics the Provinces did not see eye to eye. About naval and military affairs for instance – and more specifically about the amount of money to be spent on either branch of the armed forces – the "sea-provinces" tended to cherish opinions quite different from those of the "land-provinces", which, with the exception of Utrecht, were all directly adjoining foreign territory.[42] These differences of view notwithstanding the Republic during the 17th century performed on the European scene with conspicuous success and subsequently it survived in quite a decent manner until the Napoleonic period. This clearly would have been impossible if dissenting "regents"[43] had not quite often proved amenable to the negotiation and persuasion which were perhaps the most essential elements in the machinery of Dutch politics.

A factor which greatly enhanced the stability and efficiency of the system of government was the preponderance of Holland. From the beginning of the 17th century to the eve of the Napoleonic period that province regularly paid 58 per cent of the sum levied annually to defray the expenses of the "Generaliteit" (the central government). Its "Pensionary" – one might call him the provincial Prime Minister – soon became the most influential and powerful civil servant in the Republic, with the exception of the Statholders.[44] This made for a state of affairs where – in the words of one of today's leading Dutch historians – "in actual practice Holland played the leading role, something which reflected quite well the real economic and social power situation within the Republic".[45] Holland being what it was, and given the dominant situation of the great emporium of Amsterdam within the province, we may safely say that the Republic enjoyed a system of government which ensured that due attention was given to the affairs of the sea and where the "maritime" interest – needless to say this comprised many more than just merchants and shipowners[46] – could make its voice heard and listened to. Perhaps the most striking demonstration of the government's deep concern with maritime affairs has been given by the great Pensionary Johan de Witt – he has been called the best Navy Minister the Netherlands ever had – when he in 1665, shortly after the Second Dutch War had "officially" begun, passed several months on board De Ruyter's flagship as the battlefleet of the United Provinces was cruising in the North Sea.

Figure 5. Whaling-vessel with whaling utensils, 18th-century engraving by A. de Blois after C. Mo(o)y. The vessel depicted is of the "bootship" type which was more suitable for whaling than the fluyt because its main deck offered more working-space.

During the time she would be considered one of the major European powers the Dutch Republic always was the smallest among them as regards extent of territory – smaller even than "metropolitan" Denmark after the Peace of Oliva or than the dominions of the Elector of Brandenburg. During the Eighty Years' War the Republic – and more specifically the "sea-provinces" – experienced the last phase of what has been termed a "population explosion". As we have already seen, this brought the total number of inhabitants to an estimated 1.9 million in the middle of the 17th century. During the next hundred years the population of some regions continued to increase but this was set off completely by a decline elsewhere, the North of Holland furnishing a case of "spectacular depopulation".[47] Yet the Republic remained one of the most densely populated and most highly urbanised parts of Europe.[48] However, comprising only a relatively small area she was surpassed as to the absolute size of the population by quite a number of European countries – notably her two most dangerous competitors on the high seas, England and France, who both could boast millions of inhabitants more.[49]

When discussing "extent of territory" and "number of population" Mahan understandably shows himself most interested in their possible significance in a maritime war.[50] I would like to follow a different line of approach. What has been stated before about the size, the density of population and the number of inhabitants of the Republic implies that she was a relatively small market with little or no prospects of expansion. This was one of the factors which made her particularly vulnerable to big competitors who adopted mercantilist politics towards her. This vulnerability forms an important element in the background of some of the main trends in her economic development during the 18th century: the decline of important industries, the decline – relative or absolute[51] – of maritime trade, the increasing tendency of Dutch capitalists to invest in foreign instead of domestic enterprises.[52]

Perhaps some of my readers are of the opinion that until now too much emphasis has been put upon the economic history of the Low Countries. To them I can only point out that all people who have studied the subject seriously appear to agree that Dutch sea power was essentially commercial power, based on the fisheries and on maritime trade. Notwithstanding this the Republic, as long as it was in existence maintained naval forces, often of considerable strength. The second theme I would like to deal with is the organisation of these forces and the way they have been employed.

The first "navies" in the Low Countries appear to have been municipal. We know that for instance early in the seventies of the 14th century the town of Deventer on the Yssel owned a small man-of-war. Under the Burgundian Dukes and their Habsburg successors an attempt was made to create a unified maritime defence organisation for the entire territory of the Netherlands. The office of High Admiral was instituted – I have already quoted from the oldest surviving instruction for this dignitary. Before the end of the 15th century there was operating in Veere – at that time an important port and also the main residence of the family which produced most of the Admirals[53] – a Court or Council of Admiralty. Incidentally this was quite a long period before Henry VIII created the Navy Board in England.[54] Before 1540 Veere could boast a naval arsenal, or at least a storehouse for guns and other naval equipment, and not long afterwards the stage was reached in which the Veere Admiralty had permanently at its disposal a number of vessels which it could equip, and use, for warlike purposes.[55] However, the attempt to put this organisation in control of the entire maritime defence of the

Figure 6. The launching of a ship from the old shipyard of the Amsterdam Chamber of the East-India Company. Until the 19th century ships in the Netherlands were usually launched bows-first because in that position they developed less speed during their launching. This was important because most shipyards were situated along relatively narrow waterways. Etching by Zeeman.

Low Countries failed, and soon after the beginning of the Eighty Years' War all units of its small fleet had been either destroyed or taken by the rebels.

The Seven Provinces never have achieved the same degree of centralisation of the navy as the old regime. In 1597 a long-standing issue was settled by the decision that the five "Colleges of Admiralty" which had meanwhile come into existence would all be retained. Each of them would continue to remain responsible for providing part of the warships that were needed, for manning and equipping this contingent. To enable them to meet the expenses involved they were empowered to levy taxes on imports and exports, according to a rate fixed by the "Generaliteit". It was expected that in this way they would receive enough money to finance their operations during "normal" periods, when no large battle fleets needed to be commissioned.[56] For the financing of such extra efforts recourse could be had to the "Generaliteit", and the States-General,

the assembly of representatives of the provinces which constituted the supreme governing body, might decide to award the Colleges subsidies from the general treasury.

In theory the Admiralties formed branches of the "Generaliteit"; on their boards there were always represented some other provinces besides the one where the College in question had its headquarters (there was one Admiralty in Zeeland, three in Holland and one in Friesland[57]). In practice, however, the provinces where the Admiralty in question had its seat usually more or less laid down the law.[58] It is no exaggeration if one states that there were in fact five separate logistic organisations, each with its own dockyard or dockyards, its own storehouses, its own administration, its own exchequer, its own military and civilian personnel. Usually they were not working in very close contact with each other and mutual jealousy, or worse, was often strongly in evidence.

The only aspect of naval affairs about

106

which it could truthfully be said that it was being taken care of by one central authority was the laying down of the broad outlines of naval strategy. This was the special responsibility of the Admiral-General, an office which always has been held together with the Statholdership of Holland.[59] During the two periods this charge has been in abeyance the Pensionary of Holland more or less replaced the Statholder as the key figure where the working out of naval strategy was concerned. None the less we know of at least one instance of a College mounting a major naval operation at the behest of solely its "home-province".[60]

The disadvantages of this extreme decentralisation are obvious and have been pointed out quite often, both when the system was still in operation and afterwards.[61] As a matter of fact one continues to wonder how it was possible it came into being and even more how it was possible it survived to the very end of the Republic. Its origin surely is bound up with the circumstance that the Eighty Years' War was, among other things, a struggle for the maintenance of local and regional privileges.[62] The only explanation that can be offered for its retention until 1795 lies therein that certain vested interests would have suffered from its abolition. To have the headquarters or another establishment of a College within its walls entailed obvious advantages for the city or town concerned. Centralisation inevitably would have meant the closing down or reduction in size of a number of these establishments, with the attendant loss of jobs. Tragically this was militating most strongly against reform of the naval shore organisation during the 18th century, when notably the towns on the West bank of the Zuyderzee, where the establishments of the North Holland Admiralty were located, were suffering from a bad slump, but when on the other hand the reduction in strength of the navy of the Republic made a reduction of overheads an even more sensible operation than it had been before.

Also it must have been realised in the "sea-provinces" that if one lost one's "own" Admiralty one lost a measure of control over the navy and a means to ensure that there were warships available when one needed them. To be able to assess the significance of this one should be aware that the "sea-provinces" did not always agree on even the basic issues in foreign politics; also there was a certain amount of "specialisation" among them as regards the branches of maritime trade in which they were most interested and the protection of which they had consequently most at heart.[63] This last statement leads us to a fact of primary importance in the naval history of the Republic. As perhaps has already been surmised from what has been stated before regarding the nature of Dutch sea power,[64] the navy of the Republic has nearly always been used first and foremost as an instrument for the protection of seaborne trade and the fisheries, both "Great" and "Small".[65]

The idea of the "Dominium Maris" as something to be sought after for its own sake or as a right to be vindicated by the

Figure 7. The "Vergulde Sonne", grisaille by William van de Velde the Elder (1611?–1693), a good example of his art. The ship depicted, which supposedly belonged to the Dunkirk Admiralty, is of the same type as contemporary Dutch frigates. It has been painted twice, to show both the figure-head and the "tafferel" (stern-decoration), like on many early "ship's portraits".

107

Figure 8. A fluyt, painting by Jan Theunisz. Blanckerhoff (1628–1669). This was the most successful product of the 17th-century Dutch shipbuilding industry. Its length-beam ratio made it into a relatively fast vessel; it could, owing to its uncomplicated rig, be handled by a minimum-sized crew; it was endowed with ample cargo-carrying capacity.

naval forces of the State – as has been subscribed to by many people in Britain from the time of Adam de Moleyns (or earlier?) to the 19th century (or later?) – has had hardly any adherents in the Republic and – at least as far as I know – none among its rulers. They always regarded control of the sea as strictly a means to an end, to safeguard the country against attack or to protect its merchant and fishing fleets. As luck would have it the Republic has only seldom experienced a serious threat of seaborne attack. Perhaps there have only been two occasions when this was really present. One was in 1588, after Philip II had sent the Invincible Armada on its way.[66] The other was in 1672/1673 when an Anglo-French fleet was cruising intermittently off the Dutch coast and once or twice was not very far from the point of landing an army.

So the naval forces of the Republic have mostly been used to protect its seaborne trade and fisheries. It should be stressed though that this has quite often entailed

much more than just providing some men-of-war to escort convoys or individual ships and to ward off small numbers of pirate vessels or other commerce raiders. Especially during the second half of the 17th century it has often meant mounting naval campaigns on a truly grand scale and of a character often quite different from what one is inclined to regard as "normal" operations for the protection of trade. It could entail armed intervention in conflicts between other powers, witness the famous expedition of 1658/1659, first under Van Wassenaer-Obdam and then under De Ruyter, which resulted in the defeat of the Swedish battle fleet off Kronborg Castle, the relief of Copenhagen and the restitution of Fyn to the Danish crown. Perhaps it should be added that this deservedly famous campaign was only one among several mounted for basically the same purpose: to prevent that the Sound came under the exclusive control of one too powerful monarch. Given the main reasons why the Dutch Republic and Britain went to war in 1652 and 1665, there is certainly a case for bringing all actions of the navy of the Republic during the First and Second English Wars under the heading of commerce protection.

To the student of naval tactics the performance of the Dutch navy during these two wars and the subsequent conflict of 1672/1673 – which one had better not call the "Third Dutch War"[67] – presents a most interesting phenomenon. The war of 1652–1654 set the pattern which has been so ably described by Michael Lewis: "The Dutch stood up, every time, and fought the thing out. So did we. Doubtless the phenomenon was, in part, a matter of national psychology. The protagonists were near enough to each other in blood and habit of mind to react in a very similar way to the grim circumstances of a naval clash: they both possessed in a marked degree that national characteristic known as "taking it": and even if they did not possess it originally, it certainly became an acquired characteristic. It is indeed instructive to notice how, on those few later occasions when they met,[68] the same fighting conditions have always recurred: the same dour fights, the same reluctance to give the other best. In all ages, given a Dutch-British battle, there was the same fight to the death, with little evasion and long casualty lists".[69]

There is, however, no doubt that during this first Anglo-Dutch maritime conflict the tactical performance of the Dutch did not compare very favourably with that of their opponents. The latter, especially after the famous "Instructions for the better ordering of the fleet in fighting" had been issued to Cromwell's navy in March, 1653, showed themselves adept at the new manner of fighting seabattles in a well-ordered line formation, preferably in line ahead, and using this formation to outmanoeuvre one's enemy and to take maximum advantage of one's gunpower.[70] The Dutch, except perhaps during the last battle of the war, still kept to the traditional group tactics.[71] These were quite suitable if one wanted to bring about what Nelson has called a "pell-mell battle" and the attendant opportunities of boarding the enemy. But they left far less scope to the gun, which was becoming more and more the dominant weapon at sea, and

Figure 9. "Catships" in a roadstead, painting by Jan Claeszoon Rietschoof (1652–1719). These long, box-shaped vessels with very simple rig were mainly used to carry timber from Norway and the Baltic.

they offered excellent chances to isolate and destroy portions of the enemy fleet to those who used the "new" tactics with determination and skill.

The Second Dutch War opened with the battle of Lowestoft, in which the proud battle-fleet of the States-General was completely outmanoeuvered and badly beaten.[72] The next year the Dutch more than held their own in the Four Days' Battle. But it was mainly the encounter on St. James's Day in the same year when the Dutch van and centre managed to extricate themselves from a seemingly hopeless situation which showed that the gap between the English and them was narrowing as far as tactical prowess was concerned. Narrowing, not yet closed: most students of the Second Dutch War appear to agree that during this conflict the English have on the average shown themselves to be the better tacticians.[73]

There is ample evidence that during the war of 1672/1673 the gap just mentioned was a thing of the past. A French naval captain who saw the Dutch battle-fleet manoeuvre during the first encounter on Schooneveldt – June 7, (N.S.) 1673 – recorded his impression as follows: "il fust un bon horloge comme en un peloton".[74] During the four main battles of this war the Dutch fleet always was numerically far weaker than the combined forces of its English and French adversaries, and yet in all four engagements the Dutch achieved what they had set out to do and barred their opponents from achieving their aim – notably from launching the invasion which would have presented the land forces of the Republic with an impossible task.

Of the last of these great sea-fights Mahan has written: "The battle of the Texel, closing the long series of wars in which the Dutch and English contended on equal terms for the mastery of the seas, saw the Dutch navy in its highest efficiency and its greatest ornament, De Ruyter, at the summit of his glory."[75] He might have added that the efficiency of the Dutch fleet

Figure 10. An East-Indiaman and a West-Indiaman. For understandable reasons the ships used in these trades were usually rather heavily armed. Up to the time of the "Second Dutch War" East-Indiamen sometimes fought with the battle-fleet. Etching by Zeeman.

was to a considerable degree the personal achievement of De Ruyter. Almost all who have ever recorded their opinion of this extraordinary man have done so in laudatory terms. And it is easy to understand why. He was a charismatic leader of men, a brilliant tactician and a superb seaman. Possessed of these qualities he was indeed very well fitted to play the leading role in the transformation of the Dutch battle-fleet from a rather unwieldy force into an "admirably tempered instrument".[76] The fact that this was achieved within the space of less than a decade – between 1665, when he was appointed Commander-in-Chief, and the beginning of the "War of 1672" – together with his brilliant victories in the North Sea immediately afterwards make a strong case for dubbing him the greatest admiral of all time.[77]

The Dutch battle-fleet did not remain such a redoubtable force for very long. De Ruyter's death in action, already in 1676, was a crippling blow, least because he had mainly taught by example and had never set great store by putting his ideas on tactics in writing.[78] However, the chief cause

of the decline in naval strength of the Republic must be considered the Anglo-Dutch *rapprochement* which occurred after the second Peace of Westminster (1674). As early as 1678 the States-General and King Charles II concluded a Treaty of Defense, which entailed that if one of them was attacked the other would provide succour in the shape of land troops and men-of-war. As long as this treaty remained in force it would not be necessary for the Republic to possess a battle-fleet equal in strength to that to the King of France, because if one were fighting the French at sea one would be doing so almost certainly with the English as allies. On the other hand, 1672/1673 had shown that, the prospect of English military support notwithstanding, to fight the French on land would be a very tough proposition for the Republic.

No wonder that under these circumstances there became perceptible among Dutch politicians a tendency towards a significant rundown of the navy. But for the time being several factors were at work effectively to keep this tendency in check. William III had always wanted the Dutch navy to be kept at a goodly strength and had been at great pains to ensure it was. When during the Nine Years' War the French for the first time adopted the "guerre de course", it soon became clear that one almost could not have too many ships to be able to protect adequately one's merchant and fishing fleets against their privateers. The same held true during the War of the Spanish Succession.

Yet during the last-named conflict the Dutch tended more and more to leave the war at sea to their English allies and there set in a really steep decline of their navy's strength. After March, 1702, there was no William III any more to spur on the States-General and the Admiralties to keep their naval forces up to the mark. Also this war appears to have affected the economy of the Republic much worse than the preceding conflict. The consequent loss of revenue was the more serious because the finances of the Provinces, and more particularly those of Holland, were already in a precarious condition at the beginning of the war: to be a Great Power for so long had proved to be a most expensive busi-

Figure 11. The dockyard of the Amsterdam Admiralty, anonymous painting in the manner of Abraham Storck. To the left a "mud-mill", in the centre large men-of-war, one of them in the process of being careened, to the right the Great Storehouse, built 1655–1657, now the home of the Nederlands Scheepvaartmuseum.

ness. How much all this affected the rate of shipbuilding for the Dutch navy is shown by the fact that between 1682 and 1700 173 new vessels were added to the naval forces of the States-General, between 1700 and 1713 only 36.[79].

After the Peace of Utrecht the curve went down even more steeply. The foreign policy of the Seven Provinces became largely guided by the desire to keep aloof from crises and to avoid military and naval commitments as much as possible. This being the case the Admiralties could not expect to receive much aid in the form of subsidies to enable them to lay down new keels. Their own coffers were empty and likely to remain so for some time: they were in debt to the extent that during the first years after 1713 they were unable to repay to the captains in their service all the money these had spent during the war to buy victuals for their ships' crews.[80] At first when the Colleges needed to equip ships in order to discharge their normal peace-time duties, like providing escort for the herring-fleet and for returning East-Indiamen, they could just take them out of the stock left over from the wars. However, as the art of keeping laid-up ships in good condition was still in its infancy, this stock soon began to deteriorate in quality and diminish in quantity. For the Amsterdam College this presented no problem as it continued to build new ships in significant numbers. The four other Colleges, which enjoyed far smaller revenue, only started to lay down keels again in the seventeen-twenties – at a much slower rate than Amsterdam. The Friesland Admiralty sold (!) its last vessel, a frigate, in 1721 and waited until 1728 before it started building a new ship.[81]

The decay of the *matériel* was accompanied by a deterioration of spirit and skill in officers and men. One of its main causes certainly was that the service offered far fewer opportunities than before to acquire practical experience in handling ships and their weapons. In this connection it is significant that the Amsterdam Admiralty, which kept its servants most regularly employed, seems to have suffered the least damage through incompetence of its personnel afloat. Another important cause of the decay was that it had become more difficult to recruit in the Netherlands good seamen or those who were likely to become in time good seamen.[82] Thirdly the nepotism and corruption that had become a conspicuous feature of all branches of the public service have played their part.[83] The nadir appears to have been reached in 1744 when the Republic had to send an auxiliary squadron to Britain, the Treaty of Defense still being in force. Of officers, men and ships it had to be admitted that they all were of a rather low average quality. The Admiral in command had perhaps once been a promising officer but he had meanwhile reached a condition of senility.

During the second half of the 18th century the navy of the Republic went through a process of regeneration.[84] It never again reached the numerical strength in ships and men it had been able to deploy during the War of the Spanish Succession, but its officers and men soon did not compare badly any more with their colleagues in the front-rank navies of the time. For that matter even during the "lean years" before 1750 it could boast a number of officers of outstanding ability. One of them was Louis Count of Bylandt, who later, in 1767, produced a revision of Bigot de Morogues' book on naval tactics, the first work on the subject ever to appear in the Dutch language.[85] Perhaps even more important has been his share in the nautical and military education of Jan Hendrik van Kinsbergen (1735–1819). Van Kinsbergen is one of the great naval figures of the second half of the 18th century. During the War against the Turks of 1768–1772 he served with great distinction as a "Kapitan 2. Ranga" in the navy of Catherine II. By the way he led his small flotilla in several sharp engagements he showed himself to be an excellent tactician, of a dashing and origi-

Figure 12. Michiel Adriaenszoon de Ruyter, Lieutenant-Admiral-General (1607–1676). Painting by Karel Dujardin (1622–1678). This portrait is not so much intended to produce an exact likeness as to show the great admiral as "the hero, the right hand of the State", as he was called in a poem by his biographer Gerard Brandt.

nal turn of mind.[86] For the Netherlands navy he has been mainly important as a refomer – in fact the reformer of this period – and as the acknowledged and wielloved head of a "school" of officers who have spread his influence well into the 19th century. By a narrow margin he failed to play a role of importance in the history of yet another navy. In 1795 he was invited to become Commander-in-Chief of the naval forces of the Danish Crown; he even accepted this appointment but owing to various circumstances he never actually assumed the duties that went with it.

Of one of those who considered themselves Van Kinsbergen's "followers" – to use an expression current in the British Royal Navy at the time – one at least has

112

achieved international renown. This was Louis Sigismund Gustave Count of Heiden (1772–1850). Like Van Kinsbergen, after having served in the Netherlands navy he entered the Russian naval service as a relatively young officer. But in his case this was not the beginning of a relatively brief interlude. After having become famous as Commander-in-Chief of the Russian Mediterranean squadron in the battle of Navarino, he ended his career as Admiral in command at Reval, where he was buried in the Cathedral.[87]

The careers of Van Kinsbergen and Count Heiden have some bearing on the last theme I want to touch in this paper: the influence of the Dutch abroad. This is in many ways a daunting subject. Even if one confines oneself to the period of the Republic and the region of Northern and North-Western Europe, already after superficial scrutiny it proves to be of somewhat alarming scope. Also one soon discovers that it has been in part intensively studied,[88] in part hardly at all. Next there are problems connected with the selection and interpretation of evidence. I have once been gently upbraided for mentioning the achievement of Louis de Geer (1587–1652) as evidence of Dutch influence in Sweden. Indeed this great merchant prince and industrialist was born in present-day Belgium. On the other hand he lived in Dordrecht and Amsterdam, in the last-named city for twelve years at a stretch, and his remains were not buried somewhere on the vast estates he had acquired in Sweden (part of them still owned by his descendants[89]) but in the family vault at Dordrecht. There are quite a number of similar cases – similar too in this respect that the people concerned were figures of no mean importance.[90]

An interesting problem of interpretation is presented by the 1771 edition of the regulations for the Imperial Russian Navy, a copy of which one finds in the rich library of the Scheepvaartmuseum in Amsterdam.[91] Like a number of the preceding editions it is printed in Russian and in Dutch. Does this indicate that even in 1771 still a sizeable proportion of the Russian navy's personnel consisted of Dutchmen or does it just show that Dutch had become a kind of lingua franca if not among all seafaring folk in the Baltic at least in the Russian navy?

I think the above will make it understandable why I do not feel up to presenting something like a general survey of the subject – even not one which remains confined within the limits of time and region I have just suggested – but want to restrict myself to offering some remarks and suggestions.

Not surprisingly there appears to be no room for doubt that Dutch influence abroad has been strongest in the realm which Professor Plumb has called the real world and notably in maritime affairs. It is well-known that especially in the 17th century the Republic did not only export many works of art – to give just one example: the earliest known work of Jan Steen, bought in 1651 for Marshal Wrangel and still at Skokloster[92] – but that also a sizeable number of Dutch artists went abroad, often settling there permanently and sometimes exerting great influence in their new environment. Perhaps the most striking example is afforded by the Van de Veldes, father and son, who went to England in 1672 and there became the founders of a school of marine painting which continued to flourish far into the 18th century.[93] But in this connection one may also mention architects like Tylman van Gameren, who introduced the baroque style in Poland. That 17th-century Danish and Swedish architecture show so much indebtedness to the Netherlands is partly due to immigrant architects like Justus Vingboons, who worked in Sweden from 1653 to 1656 and designed the facades of Riddarhuset in Stockholm for Chancellor Oxenstierna.[94]

It is less widely known that the Republic for quite a long period of time has been an important "exporter" of engineering and scientific talent. The role abroad of the Dutch technical expert in the 17th century bears comparison with that of the Scottish engineer in the 19th. Adam Wijbe with conspicuous success applied his inventiveness to the building of new fortifications for the defence of Gdánsk. Johan Sems did important fortification work for King Christian IV. A generation later Hendrick Ruse ended a brilliant career, which had brought him to many parts of Europe, in Denmark, where he rebuilt the fortifications of Copenhagen and was ennobled as Baron Rysensteen. Cornelius Vermuyden went to England, where he made and lost a fortune in draining large areas of East Anglian fenland. Johan Kuyl worked on the locks and fortifications of Göteborg. Johan van Rodenberg served as "Engineer-General" in Livonia and Ingermanland.[95]

Of the Dutch scientists who spent a considerable part of their career abroad I mention but three: the lawyer Hugo Grotius and the philologist Isaac Vossius, who both for a time were in the service of Queen Christina of Sweden,[96] and Christiaan Huygens. The lastnamed, famous for his achievements in three fields: mathematics, physics and astronomy, may be called the Founding Father of the Paris Académie des Sciences.[97]

Mention should also be made of the Dutch "export" of expertise concerning business management and banking. Louis de Geer's activities in Sweden have already been touched upon. Roles similar to his there have been played by Joachim Irgens in Denmark and Benjamin Raule in Prussia.

Of course Dutch influence was not only spread in foreign parts by Dutchmen who went abroad. It has also been a matter of foreigners visiting the Republic. Of its universities Leyden was the most renowned; 47 per cent of the students enrolled there during the first seventy-five years of its existence (1575–1650) were foreigners,

about two per cent hailing from England, Denmark and Poland each.[98]

Particularly impressive is the number of foreigners coming to Leyden during this period to study medicine; perhaps the most famous among them was Sir Thomas Browne. The other Dutch universities also had their share of foreign students. Arguably the most distinguished among them was Carolus Linnaeus, who in the seventeen-thirties took a degree at Harderwijk.[99]

Certainly the great majority of the foreigners who from time to time have enrolled in the armed forces of the Republic did not do so with the primary object of learning the art of war. Yet it is fair to state that these forces have performed a role of significance as "teaching institutions". This applied to the army mainly during the last decade of the 16th and the first decades of the 17th century when, largely through the efforts of Prince Maurice of Orange, his cousin William Louis of Nassau and his half-brother Prince Henry Frederick (later Frederick Henry[100]) it was a paragon of modernity.[101]

So it was no mere whim that Gustavus

Figure 13. The "Hollandia" standing into the Texel, November 5, 1665. Painting by Ludolf Backhuysen (1631–1708). The new flagship of the Amsterdam Admiralty is depicted as she returns from a cruise with the fleet in the North Sea, flying Admiral De Ruyter's flag as Commander-in-Chief, and with him and Pensionary Johan de Witt on board.

Adolphus, in the words of Oxenstierna, "from the beginning modelled his outward appearance and his manners on those of Prince Maurice".[102] When one studies the career of Marshal Turenne one comes across one of the minor ironies of history. He got at least part of his training as a soldier in the army of the States-General under the command of Prince Frederick Henry, but in 1672 he returned to the Low Countries as one of the chief commanders in the invasion army with which Louis XIV tried to subdue the Republic, nearly succeeding in doing so.[103]

The Dutch fleet understandably has attracted most foreigners who came with the primary aim of getting acquainted with the arcana of naval warfare during the years between 1650 and 1680. Just after the beginning of that period Niels Juel served in it for some years, part of that time under De Ruyter.[104] The great Danish admiral never had to fight the navy in which he began his nautical apprenticeship. In that respect his career presents a striking contrast with that of his near-contemporary Jan Bart of Dunkirk, who as a youth also spent some time in the naval service of the States-General.[105]

We know of artists coming to the Netherlands and receiving there impulses which show quite clearly in their subsequent work, like Nicholas Stone, the sculptor, and Jürgen Ovens, the painter.[106] Rather less study appears to have been made of the foreigners – who must have been quite numerous – who came to the Low Countries in the 17th century to acquire first-hand experience of the working of the Amsterdam market, which, as Violet Barbour has so aptly put it, was unrivalled for "expert knowledge of market conditions the world over, skill in appraisal and classification of merchandise, informed brokerage, commission and wholesale services, credit, insurance and exchange facilities."[107]

In the field of shipbuilding people, like the unlucky Hendrick Huybertssoon, who

Figure 14. Title-page of the "Spieghel der Zeevaerdt" by Lucas Janszoon Waghenaer of Enkhuizen, printed for him at Leyden by Christoffel Plantyn, 1584. This book was produced according to an entirely new formula. It contains a treatise on the art of navigation, maps – it was in fact the first sea-atlas and sailing directions. Waghenaer published Latin, German and French translations. In 1588 there appeared a "pirated" edition in English, "The Mariner's Mirrour".

played a significant part in the "Wasa" tragedy, and the shipwrights engaged by Peter the Great, have been important too as vehicles of Dutch influence abroad. However, it may be said that much more important in this role have been the products of the Dutch shipbuilding industry, the ships themselves. In this connection one should perhaps mention the men-of-war ordered from the Netherlands by Richelieu in the sixteen-twenties, but certainly the hundreds of prizes the English took from the Dutch in the course of the wars of the third quarter of the 17th century. Ralph Davis has shown how important an addition they were to the English merchant navy, which had before been very deficient in ships that could be worked by relatively small crews and that "measured little and stowed much."[108] The ability to construct ships answering to that description had been the main forte of the Dutch shipbuilding industry at least since the time the "fluyt" was evolved in Hoorn on the Zuyderzee, the fifteen-nineties. This particular brand of medium-sized cargo carrier soon proved its worth, especially on the European trade routes, and spawned a "whole range of types for particular kinds of cargo".[109]

It stands to reason that books also have been of great importance as vehicles of Dutch influence abroad. It appears though that as yet scant research has been devoted to the diffusion outside the Republic of books like the works on engineering and the art of fortification by Simon Stevin and Menno van Coehoorn or Cornelis Allard's treatise on Dutch shipbuilding.[110] A French edition of the last-named work was published in Amsterdan in 1718/1719, so well into the 18th century. That fact leads me to the remarks with which I would like to end this paper.

Charles Boxer has stated that he does not doubt that "the land of Rembrandt, Vondel and De Ruyter was a better as well as a more stimulating place in which to live than was the land of Cornelis Troost, Bilderdijk and Zoutman".[111] I can agree with him completely. And yet we see that in the 18th century there was apparently a market for a book on shipbuilding, "tirée des meilleurs auteurs hollandois" foreign students continued to be enrolled in Dutch universities – of course Boerhaave attracted quite a number of them to Leyden – Dutchmen continued to be appointed to important positions abroad (two interesting cases are Jan Willem Ripperda and Gerard van Swieten[112]). All this indicated that Dutch influence abroad was still more than negligible. The main reason why I want to plead for more effort to be spent on the study of that phenomenon as it presented itself after the "Golden Century" is that it presents us with a most interesting question. How far did the reputation of the Republic for modernity or even excellence in various fields outlive the reality of things?

All illustrations: Copyright Vereeniging Nederlandsch Historisch Scheepvaart Museum

Notes

1 Cf. A. T. Mahan, *The Influence of Sea Power upon History, 1660-1783*, London 1890, pp. 28-29

2 Cf. Ch. Wilson, *Profit and Power, a study of England and the Dutch Wars*, The Hague 1978, p.2.

3 The Dutch Republic arguably came into being in 1579 when the document called the "Union of Utrecht" was signed by representatives of most of the regions which later became known as "the Seven Provinces" – and of the municipalities of Venlo, Antwerp and Breda – and remained in existence until 1795, when it was conquered by the French and the "Batavian Republic" was with their backing constituted in its stead.

4 For a similar reason this route was also dangerous for Dutch merchantmen during the Eighty Years' War and the wars with France of the second half of the 17th and the early 18th century. Dunkirk, the almost impregnable privateers' lair, was in Spanish hands until 1658; after a brief English intermezzo it became French in 1662.

5 A number of the canals that were filled up have been dug to make possible the transportation of peat. The Groningen coasting trade, which still occupies a very special place among Dutch maritime activities, owes its origin to the need of cheap long-distance carriers for this commodity.

6 The Dutch equivalent of this term is very often used to describe collectively the rivers Maas, Waal and Rhine, which bisect the country in an East-West direction. The southern boundary of this river-system is more or less coterminous with that between the former "sovereign" territories of the Republic and the "Generaliteitslanden" (cf. *infra*, note 20) and still constitutes an important cultural watershed.

7 When in 1932 the "Enclosing Dyke" was finished the Zuyderzee ceased to be part of the North Sea and became a lake. In the same year it was renamed "Ysselmeer" ("Yssel lake": from the river which discharges into it from an easterly direction).

8 Understandably these engineering efforts caused some rather acrimonious conflicts between agricultural and maritime interests, e.g. the one centred upon the lock in the town of Edam, the building of which met the heartfelt desire of the farming communities to the landward of that town but was very much disapproved of by its shipbuilders, who rightly feared the silting up of the town's harbours.

9 Jan de Vries, *Barges and Capitalism:* Passenger transportation in the Dutch Economy (1632-1839), Utrecht 1981, p. 24.

10 Before the North Sea Canal was opened in 1876 there were no proper harbours on the Dutch North Sea coast between Den Helder and Den Briel.

11 In the industrial towns the patricians and the guilds were competing for the hegemony in municipal government; the Counts of Flanders were attempting to emancipate themselves from the French Crown, which was allied to the aristocratic party in the towns. Several violent clashes occurred; the most spectacular of them was the Battle of the Golden Spurs (1302; near Kortrijk) where the Flemish citizens' army defeated a force of French knights and their retainers.

12 Deposits of peat which were known to have a large salt content were dug up and subsequently burned. After this the salt could be separated from the other material which was left. There is a sixteenth-century painting of this "darinc-delven" in the beautiful medieval town hall of Zierikze.

13 Some of the methods used in this trade are quite interesting. It appears for instance that when the oxen were transported on board ships during part of their journey, they were usually fed upon eggs. Enkhuizen had an important market for oxen until about 1660, when this was moved to Amsterdam. In the town of Groningen the memory of this trade is kept alive in the name of one of its main squares, where one can admire a most impressive example of the kind of town house East-Indian "nabobs" sometimes had built for themselves in the 18th century.

14 Quoted in J.A. van Hamel, *Vaderlandsche Voetsporen*, Amsterdam 1945, p. 26.

15 It seems to me that those who have tried to find an explanation for the Dutch "miracle" of the 17th century sometimes have not paid sufficient attention to the fact that the first half of the 17th century saw the devastation of a large part of the German Empire owing to the Thirty Years' War, a whole series of violent conflicts with a politico-religious background in France and the Civil War in England. On the other hand the States-General, with their army commanders, after the first decades of the Eighty Years' War were almost continously successful in trying to keep the actual military operations from the territory of the Seven Provinces proper, except for some

districts in the South-East. One may therefore say that this made the Republic into something of a haven of security in Western Europe.

16 The decline in the 19th century was connected with the growing prosperity of Germany, whence traditionally many of the immigrants had come.

17 One finds most worthwhile discussions of the characteristics of the Dutch nation in the book of G.J. Renier, *The Dutch Nation*, London, 1944, and in several of the works of J. Huizinga, arguably the greatest Dutch historian this century has produced so far, notably his *Nederlands beschaving in de zeventiende eeuw, een schets*, Haarlem 1941, and some of the essays published in *De Nederlandse natie*, Haarlem 1960.

18 In Naturalis Historia, XVI, 2-4. According to Pliny, the Chauci, who in his time were living between the Ems and the Weser, were in an even worse situation than the Frisians, who were at least able to keep cattle. The difference may well have been not as big as it appeared to him.

19 Cf. for the Frisian buying a slave in London *Bede, A History of the English Church and People*, IV, 22; for the Frisian trade with the Trondelag Gwyn Jones, *A History of the Vikings*, London 1973, p. 82; for "Ubbo Dux Fresonum" and the Frisians in King Alfred's Navy, some of whose names have been preserved in the Anglo-Saxon Chronicle, P.C.J.A. Boeles, *Friesland tot de elfde eeuw*, The Hague 1951, p. 392.

20 The term "The Low Countries" in most cases is used to indicate the area now occupied by the Kingdom of Belgium and the European part of the Kingdom of the Netherlands. The territory of the latter is more or less identical with that of the former Republic of the Seven United Netherlands, without its overseas plantations. This Republic was a federation of seven "sovereign" (see below, p. 8) Provinces: Gelderland, Holland, Zeeland, Utrecht, Overijssel, Friesland and Groningen. Its European territory comprised next to that of these provinces themselves that of one self-governing region, Drenthe, which was not represented in the States-General, the governing body of the Republic, and the so-called "Generaliteitslanden", non-self-governing territories under the direct rule of the States-General, viz. Staats-Vlaanderen (the part of the present province of Zeeland situated South of the main course of the Scheldt), Staats-Brabant (the present province of Noord-Brabant), the lands of "Outremeuse" (scattered territories in the present – Dutch – province of Limburg), Wedde and Westerwolde (two districts now part of the province of Groningen where that province already under the Republic had more of a say in the government than the States-General). The term "Holland" should only be used with reference to the province of that name, which in 1840 was divided into two,

the present provinces of Noord-Holland and Zuid-Holland. Referring to the European territory of the Republic one can also use the term "the Northern Netherlands". Although I have in this paper as a rule used the adjective "Dutch" I do prefer "Netherlands" – like many of my countrymen.

21 Cf. A.J. Toynbee, *A Study of History*, II, London 1935, p. 31 sqq.

22 The last line of the poem "Herinnering aan Holland" by Hendrik Marsman (1899-1940).

23 The French and Dutch texts of this instruction, which was issued over the signature of Maximilian of Austria, is in the Groot Placaet-Boeck (a collection of laws and government decrees published between 1658 and 1796), Vol. IV, p. 1208 sqq).

24 Cf. Ch. Wilson, o.c., p. 2.

25 The globetrotter, in the sense of the person who undertakes long and arduous journeys mainly to satisfy his curiosity, did not make his first appearance in the 19th century. An earlier example is Samuel van de Putte, scion of a patrician family from Flushing, who in the 18th century travelled in China, Tibet and India. See about him J.J.L. Duyvendak, *De Grote Chinese Muur*, Leiden 1958.

26 A large number of them were recruited, and subsequently employed, as soldiers for the East-India Company. The estimate in question has been published on p. 147 of Professor Bruijn's contribution to Volume III of the new *Maritieme Geschiedenis der Nederlanden*, Bussum 1977.

27 J.R. Bruijn, l.c., p. 151.

28 P.W. Klein, De zeventiende eeuw, in: J.H. van Stuyvenberg, *De economische geschiedenis van Nederland*, Groningen 1977, p. 86–87; J.A. Faber, De achttiende eeuw, ibidem, p. 120.

29 Cf. about the naval dockyards the article on pp. 187–213 in: P. Nijhof (ed.), *Monumenten van Bedrijf en Techniek*, Zutphen 1978.

30. J.R. Bruijn, l.c., p. 150.

31 Cf. for the delights of Gelting Castle J.H. Koch, *Schleswig-Holstein*, Köln 1979, p. 196. Seen from the outside the central part, which was rebuilt by Inggersen, looks very much like a Dutch colonial building of the period. Inggersen went first to the East Indies as a barber's apprentice (assistant-surgeon) in 1737. He ended his career as Resident of Cheribon with the rank of Principal Merchant.

32 C.R. Boxer *The Dutch Sea-borne Empire*, London 1965, p. XXI, XXIII.

33 K. Clark, *Civilisation*, London 1969, p. 193 sqq.

34 K. Clark, o.c., p. 209.

35 K. Clark, o.c., p. 197. I should add that Lord Clark makes the restriction that fluid capital is one of the chief causes of civilisation "at a certain stage of social development". Personally I doubt whether this restriction holds true.

36 Cf. The Industrial Revolution in the Northern Netherlands, in *Transactions of the Second International Congress on the Conservation of Industrial Monuments,* Bochum 1975, published Bochum 1978, p. 216-222.

37 Cf. L.T.C. Rolt, *Navigable Waterways,* London 1973, caption to plate (10).

38 A.M. v.d. Woude in his exemplary survey of the demographic and economic development of part of Northern Holland from the 15th to the 19th century *Het Noorderkwartier,* 3 Vols., Wageningen 1972, mentions some twenty different kinds of industrial windmills. Apparently the largest number of windmills was reached in the Netherlands around 1850. It is estimated at about five thousand.

39 "Particularist felling had always been especially strong in the Netherlands . . . – that was what the Dutch Revolt had been about for many people", G. Parker, *Spain and the Netherlands, 1559–1659,* Ten Studies, London 1979, p. 176 of the Fontana edition. The same author discusses the causes of the Eighty Years' War more extensively, and most lucidly, in his *The Dutch Revolt,* London 1977.

40 The best decriptions of the system of government of the Dutch Republic are to be found in: S.J. Fockema Andreae, *De Nederlandse Staat onder de Republiek,* Amsterdam 1961, Verhandelingen Koninklijke Nederlandse Academie van Wetenschappen, afdeling Letterkunde, Nieuwe Reeks, LXVIII, no. 3, and R. Fruin, *Geschiedenis der Staatsinstellingen in Nederland tot den val der Republiek* (based on lecture notes of the most outstanding Dutch historian of the 19th century edited by his pupil H. Th. Colenbrander, first edition The Hague 1901, reprint, with an introduction by I. Schöffer, The Hague 1980).

41 S.J. Fockema Andreae, o.c., p. 5.

42 Groningen is usually counted among the "land-provinces". In my opinion this is not quite correct. Its Northern boundary is the North Sea. Already in the 18th century vessels from Groningen had a significant share in the coasting trade, which later on became a prominent feature of the province's economy (cf. *supra;* note 5). Also the City of Groningen from 1622 was the seat of a "Chamber" (department) of the West India Company. How this institution affected the economic and social life of the Province is admirably analysed in: P.J. van Winter, *De Westindische Compagnie ter kamer Stad en Lande* (werken uitgegeven door de Vereeniging Het Nederlandsch Economisch-Historisch Archief, no. 15), The Hague 1978. The large profits that were, at least initially, hoped for very rarely materialised. On the other hand Groningen's stake in the West India trade directly or indirectly provided quite a numer of jobs for natives of the Province. If Groningen is counted as a "sea-province" it was the only one directly adjoining foreign territory, i.e. the country of Ostfriesland (Eastern Frisia, independent until 1744, subsequently part of Prussia).

43 All those who were members of the States-General, of the various courts of law and of the governing bodies on the provincial and municipal level, and also the higher-ranking permanent officials used to be known as "regenten". Cf. Fockema Andreae, o.c., p. 37.

44 Before 1747 Friesland, often together with Groningen, had another Statholder than Holland and the other Provinces. However, all Statholders in office after the end of the 16th century were members of the various branches of the House of Nassau.

45 I. Schöffer in *Winkler Prins Geschiedenis der Nederlanden,* II, Amsterdam 1972, p. 140.

46 To give just one example: in the 17th century most inhabitants of the village of Wormer in Northern Holland derived their livelihood from the manufacture of either ships' biscuits or sailcloth. In 1648 there were in Wormer no less tan 50 bakeries.

47 V.d. Woude o.c., I, p. 99.

48 The degree of urbanisation reached in the Southern part of Holland around 1620 (more than 60 per cent of the national population was living in urban communities) had only been reached in England and Wales shortly before 1870.

49 C. Mc Evedy and R. Jones, *Atlas of World Population History,* Harmondsworth 1978, estimate the total population of the British Isles in 1650, 1700 and 1750 at respectively 7.5, 9.25 and 10 million, that of France in the same years at 21, 22 and 24 million.

50 Cf. Mahan, o.c., p. 42-49.

51 In some branches of maritime trade, e.g. with Russia, the absolute share of the Dutch continued to increase during at least part of the 18th century, but at the same time it declined relative to that of other nations. Generally speaking the development of the maritime trade of the Republic did not conform with the significant increase in volume of international trade discernible in the 18th century.

52 "During the 18th century the Republic developed into the world's creditor nation, which not only participated in the financing of the South Sea Company and the Bank of England and that of other (sic) industrial and mining operations abroad, but also of the governmental machinery of e.g. Sweden, Prussia, Poland, Austria and the United States" (J.A. Faber, l.c., p. 150). Charles Wilson has published an interesting study of the "London Dutch merchants" in the middle of the 18th century. He calls them "the most important in commercial and political influence" among the foreign element in the City (The Anglo-Dutch

Establishment in Eighteenth Century England. Proceedings of the symposium *The Anglo-Dutch Contribution to the Civilization of Early Modern Society,* London, 27–28 June, 1974, Oxford 1976, p. 11-32).

53 The office of Admiral has been held by so many members of the same family, the Lords, later Marquesses, of Veere, that one is tempted to call it "semi-hereditary".

54 This happened on April 20, 1546 (cf. N.M. Rodger, *The Admiralty,* London 1979, p. 5).

55 It is not at all certain that these ships were actually designed as warships.

56 I.E. periods when there was no need of great naval campaigns to be mounted and the merchant navy and fishing fleets only had to be protected against more or less permanent nuisances like the depredations of the "Barbary pirates" of Northern Africa.

57 The Admiralty in Zeeland had its headquarters in Middelburg. Of the three Admiralties in Holland the Admiralty of the Maas had its headquarters in Rotterdam, the Admiralty of Amsterdam in that city. The headquarters of the third Admiralty in Holland, that of the "Northern Quarter" or West-Friesland, moved every three months from Hoorn to Enkhuizen or *vice versa.* The headquarters of the Admiralty in Friesland until 1645 were located at Dokkum, but in that year they were transferred to Harlingen because the harbours of Dokkum had silted up too much.

58 Cf. the pioneering study by J.R. Bruijn, *De Admiraliteit van Amsterdam in rustige jaren,* 1713–1751, Amsterdam 1970, especially p. 40 sqq.

59 As Admiral-General the statholder of Holland was an official of the "Generaliteit": the central government of the Republic (cf. *supra,* p. 8).

60 The expedition to the West Indies under Cornelis Evertsen, the member of the Zeeland "dynasty" of admirals who is distinguished by his nickname "Cornelis the Devil", which left Flushing in December, 1672. After joining with an "Amsterdam" squadron under Jacob Binckes Evertsen's took part in the reconquest of New York, which was, however, in 1674 given back to the English in exchange for Surinam, which had been occupied by them. At the time this was considered a very good bargain for the United Provinces.

61 Cf. e.g. H. Richmond, *Statesmen and Sea-Power,* Oxford 1947, p. 38.

62 Cf. *supra,* p. 8.

63 Zeeland for instance was specially interested in the slaving and privateering trades.

64 Cf. *supra,* p. 1–8.

65 Perhaps surprisingly the herring fisheries were called the "Great Fishery" and whaling was termed the "Small Fishery". They were, of course, classified according to their economic importance.

66 The Dutch share in the defeat of the Armada has long been neglected by our neighbours on the other side of the North Sea. As far as I know the first book in English which does justice to Justinus of Nassau and the ships under his command is G. Mattingly, *The Armada,* London 1959.

67 It was essentially not a trade war like the two previous ones. Also the English this time were members of a coalition, which was headed by the King of France and to which also belonged the Elector of Cologne and the Prince-Bishop of Münster. Perhaps the best "international" name for this war is "Guerre de Hollande" – as it was called in France at the time.

68 Like the (first) battle of Dogger Bank (1781) and the battle of Camperdown (1797).

69 M. Lewis *The Navy of Britain,* London 1948, p. 466.

70 C.f. J.S. Corbett, *Fighting Instructions,* London 1905. p. 94 sqq.

71 The evidence respecting Tromp the Elder's use or non-use of the line-ahead formation in his last battle, that of Ter Heyden, is not quite clear. The most recent study of the introduction of the line ahead as a battle formation in the Netherlands navy is a most informative article by R.E. J. Weber, "Een beschouwing over het invoeren van de linie van bataille bij de Nederlandse oorlogsvloot 1665–1666", in: *Marineblad XC (1980),* July– August, p. 331-342.

72 It might have been totally defeated if the English had not relaxed their pursuit when already off the Dutch coast. Who initiated the order to shorten sail, the Duke of York, who was Commander-in-Chief, or somebody else, has never been really cleared up.

73 Cf. e.g. H.A. van Foreest, De Vierdaagse Zeeslag *(De Vierdaagse Zeeslag en haar betekenis voor de nazaat, Engelse en Nederlandse voordrachten, gehouden in het kader van de manifestatie "1666 Nederland ter Zee 1966",* s.l., s.d., p. 43-63); H.A. can Foresst/R.E.J. Weber, *De Vierdaagse Zeeslag 11-14 Juni 1666,* Amsterdam 1984.

74 Quoted in: J.C.M. Warnsinck, *De Ruyter in den slag op Schooneveld,* 7 Juni 1673 (in: *Van Vlootvoogden en Zeeslagen,* Amsterdam 1940, p. 354-373), p. 370.

75 Mahan, o.c., p. 157.

76 Ibidem.

77 Perhaps I should add that another reason why I am of the opinion that his achievement as an admiral surpasses even that of the hero of Trafalgar lies in the fact that he had much more "to begin from scratch" and that the men-of-war of his time were on the average much more unwieldy than those of the Napoleonic period.

78 Once, when asked to give his opinion on a plan

of attack against the English, which had been submitted to Pensionary Johan de Witt, he wrote: "Not bad, if it could be practised like it can be put in writing, but there may happen so much in between which cannot all be written down".

79 These figures are culled from the history of the Netherlands navy by J.C. de Jonge, *Geschiedenis van het Nederlandsche zeewezen*, 1st edition The Hague 1833–1848; 2nd edition – added to and slightly revised by the author's son J.K.J. de Jonge – Haarlem 1858–1862, still an indispensable book on the subject.

80 Until the Napoleonic period captains in the Dutch navy, except admirals' flag captains, customarily bought the victuals for their ships' crews, being reimbursed subsequently according to a fixed rate "per man per day". Admirals did the same for their flagships' crews. Provided the officers concerned were paid in full and after not too long a delay the system was not at all unprofitable for them.

81 Cf. L. Kamminga, *Schepen van de Friese admiraliteit*, Leeuwarden 1973, p. 18-19; J.R. Bruijn, *De Admiraliteit van Amsterdam*, p. 7.

82 This is connected with the fact that adverse trends in agriculture and industry led to an increase in pauperism and to deterioration of the health and general well-being of large population groups.

83 Notwithstanding the reappraisal of this period of Dutch history which is going on at present there still appears to exist agreement that the so-called "second Statholderless period" (1702-1747) was marked by a degree of nepotism and corruption unique in the history of the Republic.

84 This may be considered as an international trend, also discernible in e.g. the French, British and Spanish navies of the time.

85 *Zeetactiek; of, Grond-regulen der krijgskunde ter zee . . . in het Franch beschreeven door Bigot de Morogues . . . vermeerdert met nuttige aanmerkingen . . .* Amsterdam 1767. A French edition had been published in Amsterdam a few years earlier, as one of the very many books in a foreign language which have been published in the Republic. It knew only a very mild form of censorship and its printing industry was already in an advanced state of development in the second half of the 16th century.

86 There is a story that during one of these engagements against the Turks he wanted a certain signal to be hoisted but discovered this to be impossible, because the spar where this particular signal ought to be hoisted had been shot away. This allegedly inspired him to devise a system where the significance of a signal was no longer dependent on the position where it was flown or displayed. What is certain is that the idea in question was born also at about the same time in the British and in the French navy.

87 It is worthy of note that "Gaiden" is one of the very few Russian admirals of foreign birth mentioned by Admiral S.G. Gorshkow in his most recent book in Russian sea power.

88 During the last decades Anglo-Dutch relations during the period of the Republic have been researched intensively, notably by the Sir Thomas Browne Institute at Leyden. E. Wrangel, *Sveriges litterära förbindelser med Holland särdeles under 1600-talet*, Lund 1897 (Dutch translation Leyden 1901) is a scholarly survey of the relations between the Dutch Republic and Sweden, with the emphasis on the 17th century. Cultural relations between the Netherlands and Denmark are the subject of L.L. Hammerich/K. Fabricius/V. Lorenzen (eds.), *Holland-Danmark, Den kulturelle Forbindelse gennem Tiderne*, København 1945.

89 Notably Lövsta Bruk with its manor house which reminds one so much of a Dutch "buitenplaats" of the 17th and 18th century.

90 An example is Willem Usselincx, who was born in Flanders and played a prominent role in the early history of the Dutch West India Company. Later he went to Sweden, where he repeatedly attempted to float similar enterprises.

91 *Zeereglement in de Russische en Hollandsche talen over alles wat betrekking heeft op een goede leiding van de vloot in zee . . .* St. Petersburg 1771. The same library holds bilingual editions from 1720 and 1746.

92 "Winter Scene", bought at an auction in The Hague, 3. July 1651, by the Swedish Resident Harald Appelboom (cf. catalogue "Jan Steen", Mauritshuis, The Hague 1958-1959, no. 1).

93 Cf. about them and their influence the important publications of M.S. Robinson and also the catalogues "The Art of the Van de Veldes" (National Maritime Museum, London1982) and "Schok der Herkenning" (Mauritshuis, The Hague/Tate Gallery, London 1970-1971).

94 Cf. W. Kuyper, *Dutch Classicist Architecture*, Delft 1980, p. 100.

95 Cf. about the activity of Dutch military engineers in Scandinavia during the 17th century Ed. Taverne, *In 't land van belofte: in de nieue stadt; Ideaal en werkelijkheid van de stadsuitleg in de Republiek 1580–1680*, Maarssen 1978, and various studies by Dr. Juliette Roding, e.g. De invloed van de Nederlandse vestingbouw in Scandinavië (in: *Vesting; Vier eeuwen vestingbouw in Nederland*, 's-Gravenhage/Zutphen 1982).

96 Cf. Wrangel, o.c. (Dutch edition), p. 190 sqq. On p. 192 the author remarks that, contrary to what is usually written, Grotius was already called to Sweden before Queen Christina came of age.

97 Cf. A. Romein (-Verschoor), Christiaen Huygens, Ontdekker der waarschijnlijkheid, in *Erflaters van onze beschaving,* Amsterdam 1956[VII], p. 395-422, p. 409 sqq.

98 Cf. catalogue "Leidse universiteit 400, Stichting en eerste bloei 1575 - ca. 1650", Rijksmuseum Amsterdam 1975, p. 46 sqq.

99 Which need not imply that he stayed there more than a few days. So it is quite possible that for him much more important was his sojourn on the "Hartenkamp" estate South of Haarlem, where from 1736 to 1738 he described the botanical collections at the behest of its owner George Clifford.

100 He was apparently baptised Henry Frederick but later on was always called Frederick Henry

101 Cf. W. Hahlweg, *Die Heeresreform der Oranier und die Antike,* Berlin 1941.

102 Cf. Wrangel, o.c., (Dutch edition), p. 7.

103 He probably would have succeeded if the fleet of the Republic under Admiral De Ruyter had not held its own against the combined fleets of England and France (cf. *supra,* p. 14–15).

104 Cf. J.H. Barfod, *Niels Juel; A Danish Admiral of the 17th Century,* s.l., s. d. (Publication No. 14 of the Marinehistorisk Selskab of Copenhagen), pp. 10–14.

105 Jan Bart was born a "Netherlander": only twelve years after his birth, in 1662, Dunkirk definitively become a part of France. Before it had belonged to the Netherlands domains of the King of Spain.

106 Nicholas Stone was a pupil, and son-in-law, of the Amsterdam architect and sculptor Hendrick de Keyser. After his return to his native England he became very much sought after as designer and sculptor of funerary monuments. Jürgen Ovens was a pupil of Rembrandt. He lived for many years in Friedrichstadt in Holstein, that remarkable Dutch "colony" which still has retained much of its 17th-century atmosphere. The altar-piece in the Lutheran church is a work of his; his masterpiece is perhaps the "Blue Madonna" in Schleswig Cathedral.

107 V. Barbour, *Capitalism in Amsterdam in the 17th Century* Ann Arbor 1963, p. 21.

108 R. Davis, *The Rise of the English Shipping Industry,* (Reprint, Greenwich, s.d.) p. 49.

109 Davis, o.c., p. 48.

110 *Nieuwe Hollandse scheeps-bouw; waar in vertoond wordt een volmaakt schip …* 1st edition Amsterdam 1695; the French edition of 1718-1719 has as its title *L'Art de bâtir les vaisseaux et d'en perfectionner la construction.*

111 Boxer, o.c., p. 294. Cornelis Troost was a painter, Vondel and Bilderdijk were poets, Jan Arnold Zoutman commanded a Dutch fleet against the British in the (first) Battle of Dogger Bank (1781).

112 The former, a pupil of Boerhaave, reorganised medical education in Austria under the Empress Maria Theresia; the latter became a grandee and Principal Minister of Spain. It is interesting to note that Van Swieten was a Catholic and therefore not eligible for public office in the Republic.

The Timber Trade

The Case of Dutch-Norwegian Relations in the 17th Century

JAAP R. BRUIJN

Some Features of Dutch Trade and Shipping

Trades and numbers

Dutch involvement in shipping during the 17th century was many-sided. One can divide all these activities into five separate branches: merchant shipping, whaling, fishing, East India shipping and the navy.[1] The first branch was by far the most important. The bulk of the merchant fleet operated in the North Sea, Baltic, White Sea and along the Atlantic coastline of France, Spain and Portugal. Dutch overseas trade was an integrated and complementary system, mainly between Western Europe and Northern plus Northeastern Europe, which consisted of buying the products of the first area and selling them in the second area and the other way around. The staple market of Amsterdam was in the middle of this network, although many ships maintained a direct link between both areas. The Mediterranean and West Indian trades gave the system more strength and widened the scope of products and commercial possibilities.

The number of ships according to the lowest estimates was approximately 2,000 around 1635 and probably about the same during the 18th century. Exact figures are not available. By and large, the average tonnage increased in the first half of the 17th century but decreased later, that is, in the 18th century. Most merchantmen were unarmed or carried only a few guns. This saved on personnel. In certain trades, the masters organized their own convoys, and, if necessary, the navy provided convoy-ships. The smaller types of ships sailed with only a few hands on board, the larger ones with ten to at the utmost twenty or twenty-five. However, the merchantman used in the Mediterranean and West Indian trades were more heavily constructed, always carried guns and had far larger crews. The size of the crews could vary widely. The Mediterranean ships had between 20 and 40 men and the West Indian ships often needed more hands. For an estimate of the total labour force in the merchant fleet a general average

Figure 1. Shipping on the IJ, the Amsterdam roadsted. Oil painting attributed to Adam Silo, c. 1725 Rijksmuseum Nederlands Scheepvaartmuseum, Amsterdam.

of 12 to 13 men per ship is an acceptable one. A high level of Dutch merchant shipping activities was maintained during the whole period in question; during the first half and the last quarter of the 17th century they were at their zenith.

Shipping to the Baltic and the White Sea (Archangel) was not possible during the winter and the early spring. A great many of the participants sailed as long as weather conditions during the generally more severe winters of the 17th century permitted them to leave and enter ports. Ships to the Mediterranean often sailed in the autumn. Ships sailed from every port in the maritime provinces of Zeeland, Holland and Friesland, but a decided tendency became visible towards a concentration on Amsterdam and to a lesser degree on Rotterdam, especially in the 18th century.

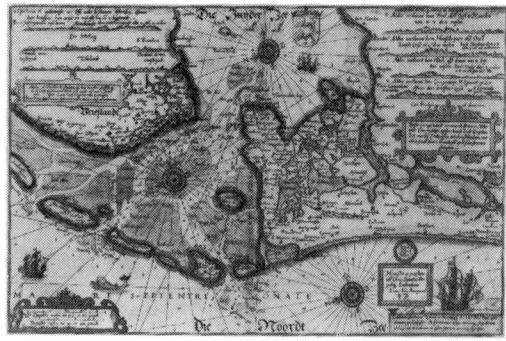

Figure 2. Map of Holland, Friesland and the Wadden Isles, by Lucas Jansz. Waghenaer in the Spieghel der Zeevaerdt, 1584, Rijksmuseum Nederlands Scheepvaartmuseum, Amsterdam.

Masters and mariners

The port to which a ship belonged can hardly be equated with the actual place from which the master and crew came. Shipowners and masters were sometimes the same persons in the 16th and earlier part of the 17th century, but more and more the master became an employee of the owners. Thus the origin of the ship was generally not the same as the origin of the master and his crew.

For the years around 1600, the origin of 735 masters mentioned in 1065 charteringcontracts submitted to Amsterdam notaries can be traced. Most of them 449 (61%), were from the northern part of the province of Holland. Only 21 lived in Amsterdam itself. Friesland was the home-province of 16% of these masters while 68 (9%) were said to be from foreign countries. The same proved to be true later, for example around 1650: only 5 masters out of 384 mentioned in documents dealing with the Norwegian timber trade came from Amsterdam. These and other examples also make clear a shift in the geographical origin of the personnel. At first the majority of the masters generally came from the northern part of the province of Holland as we have already seen. The shift

was towards the province of Friesland. This tendency was noticeable on several trades, not least in the large Baltic trade. Here the share of Frisian masters increased from 29 per cent around 1650 to 57 per cent a century later. This decline of Northern Holland's participation in shipping coincided with economic stagnation and sharp decline in the population of this part of Holland.[2]

As to the crews, we have no statistical sources about the geographic origins of the seamen in the merchant marine. Nevertheless, recent research[3] proves convincingly that the master recruited the majority of his men in his own town or village, in his own local neighbourhood. Friesland and the Dutch Wadden Islands were among the main suppliers of masters and other seamen for the merchant marine. Hardly any adequate knowledge exists about recruitment in the southern part of Holland or in Zeeland.

In a larger port town such as Amsterdam the master of a merchant ship did not look for a crew himself but left it to a so-called seamen's agent. This was a professional hirer of sailors. Also in the many smaller port towns or villages in which seamen lived, several of these agents were to be found. When the agent succeeded in arranging employment, he claimed a share of the one or two months wages paid in advance. For an ordinary seaman European merchant marine wages were usually higher than those for a colleague on a ship going to Asia: about fourteen guilders a month. In times of war the pay would be considerably higher. Merchant shipping was completely "free enterprise" and was subjected to the law of supply and demand for labour. In times of scarcity wages rose. However owing mostly to the loss of nearly all 17th (and 18th) century muster-rolls, in which the level of the wages of the different ranks was written down, we do not have systematic data at our disposal. The master had of course the highest pay. But besides this, he enjoyed some traditional benefits such as "kaplaken" (primage) and the right of "voering". Primage was the

Figure 3. A Frisian sailor. Engraving in C. and A. Allard. Dragten Boeren en Boerinnen, *Leiden c. 1700. Maritiem Museum, Rotterdam.*

premium for the safe and speedy conduct of ship and cargo, while "voering" was the privilege of carrying some merchandise of whatever kind for his own account. Part of his crew shared this privilege to a lesser extent.

Regarding the social position a seaman had in his home-society, almost nothing is known about Dutch common sailors. It is certain that they and their families could barely live through the winter on the sailor's pay. In many seafaring communities women and children of seamen had to live on charity, especially in the spring and summer. In villages and in the countryside of the province of Holland, north of Amsterdam and Haarlem, there existed a combination of two occupations: seaman and farmer, a combination which presumably also existed in other areas linked with the sea. It goes without saying that in case of disability or old age a sailor was not entitled to a pension.

The merchant masters almost always formed a rather closed group of families within a town or village. When they were not at sea, they held offices in the local government or were board members of their churches. Their business and social connections were mainly with merchants and shipowners. They often intermarried in their own circle, and many a master was born a master. Their investments were in land and diverse shares, for example of the East India Company.[4]

The foreigners in the Dutch economy
The rapidly expanding economy of the Dutch Republic during the first half of the 17th century offered employment to thousands of people. Together with a high level of wages – still rising until about 1650 – this factor attracted many foreigners. They were either seasonal labourers or they settled down permanently. Industrial and port towns were often flooded by foreigners and also by people from less prosperous parts of the Netherlands. For example in Hoorn, a small flourishing port on the Zuyderzee, 46 per cent of the 718 bridegrooms who married

for the first time in the period 1605–1610 were not born in Hoorn itself; 23 per cent came from abroad, mostly from German counties. Hoorn's population reached c. 14,000 in 1622. In 1655–60, the situation still had not changed: 188 or 23 per cent of the 871 bridegrooms were foreigners. Half of them were Germans, but amongst the others were no less than 50 Norwegians. In the same period 18 Norwegian girls found a partner in Hoorn![5]

Details about the composition of ship's crews are scarce, but they were indeed a motley mixture of nationalities. Thirty or forty per cent foreigners seems to have been normal on board those ships which relied most heavily on Amsterdam and the maritime provinces for recruitment, namely the East Indiamen and men-of-war. But foreigners on board merchantmen were a constant phenomenon too. To the end of the 18th century this situation did not essentially change.

Dutch-Norwegian Trade and Shipping

Stockfish, timber and an intensive traffic
Trade and shipping relations between Norway and the Netherlands go back as far as the Middle Ages. The main Norwegian products in this trade were stockfish (dried cod) and timber, transported mainly in Dutch ships. Exports from the Netherlands consisted of a greater variety of products: cloth, wine, salt, tobacco, cheese, bricks, tiles and spices, but the balance of trade was often negative for the Dutch, as it was for other trading partners of Norway such as England. Many a cargo was acquired by payment in cash.

Very little is known about the trade in stockfish. This trade, concentrated in Bergen, is very seldom mentioned in the literature. Its significance has always been overshadowed by that of the timber trade. Nevertheless, the well-known Amsterdam business guide of Le Moine de l'Espine (and

Le Long), published in several editions starting in 1694, mentioned stockfish as the first product imported from Norway. Import into Amsterdam during 1667–68 was more than 5,000,000 pounds. Stockfish must have been regularly consumed by Dutch families. On board weekly ration lists mentioned it almost every day. The stockfish trade probably did not decline much in the 18th century. Part of the fish was re-exported to other countries such as Germany. An increase in shipping between Rotterdam and Norway in the 1780's parallels an increase in the import of stockfish to 3,500,000 pounds a year.[6]

The stockfish as well as the timber trade required regular and frequent navigation between Norway and the Dutch Republic. As long as the harbours were not frozen over, shipping was carried on. It was a rather special Frisian business – a specialization in a trade by an area or even by a village was often one of the characteristics of Dutch merchant shipping – in which more than two-thirds of the masters declared their residence to be in Frisian towns and villages. As we have seen, this did not imply that the shipping activities also took place in this area. Quite the opposite! Amsterdam was by far the most frequented port in the Republic. The great majority of all trading and shipping was concentrated in that city. Recently discovered figures about the outgoing traffic in 1652 reveal that seagoing vessels left the harbour of Amsterdam more than 3,000 times. The year 1652 was the first year of the first Anglo-Dutch War (1652–54) and until April a temporary embargo on all shipping had been imposed so that enough sailors could be enlisted for the Dutch navy. No less than one third of the ships leaving (about 1,000) were in the Norwegian trade, the so-called "Noordsvaart". Most of the ships made several sailings a year. Later, in 1790, the total amount of shipping to Amsterdam had not declined, but the frequency of sailings to Norway had been halved: about 500, one out of every six vessels. An increase in shipping to Rotterdam at that time has already been noted.[7]

It goes without saying that Dutch relations with Norway were the most frequent of all commercial and shipping relations in Europe during the 17th century. Most Norwegian ports were regularly visited by Dutch ships, where masters could easily fill a vacancy in their crews and where many Norwegians embarked for a passage to the Netherlands in the hope of finding employment there. Many of them settled permanently in Amsterdam and in other cities.

Amsterdam was the most cosmopolitan city in the world. Its population reached c. 105,000 in 1622 and c. 200,000 in 1670. One third of the c. 240,000 men and women in Amsterdam who gave notice of their first marriage during the 17th century were foreigners. Most numerous amongst them always were Germans. But Norwegians also scored high, much higher than Danes and Swedes: 7784, i.e. 4657 grooms and 3127 brides. The greatest number of Norwegians was reached in the third quarter of the century. Most of them came from Risør-Sund Bergen and Listerlandet: 1392, 1378 and 653 respectively, from the first and third places more women than men. More than 80 per cent of the bridegrooms declared themselves to be seamen. During the 18th century one fourth of the c. 370,000 men and women who married in Amsterdam for the first time were foreigners. The number of Norwegians dropped considerably, to 4085, i.e. 2462 men and 1623 women. The decline in the Norwegian migration to the Netherlands had already started at the end of the 17th century. From Risør-Sund, Bergen and Listerlandet the numbers were not higher than 572, 513 and 388 respectively.

Scandinavians and Germans must have met comparatively few problems adapting in Amsterdam. There was almost no language-barrier. No services in Scandinavian languages had to be held in the Lutheran churches. The migration of Norwegians was heavily concentrated on Amsterdam, but the already quoted example of Hoorn proves that other parts of Holland also took a share in it, although on a much smaller scale.[8]

Settlement of Dutchmen in Norway also took place, although it was more incidental. Dutch merchants used to send their relatives as factors abroad, to places from which they drew the commodities. A good example is Crijn Crijnszoon Hooft, who moved from Amsterdam to Bergen in 1609. His uncle and cousin were involved in the Bergen trade. In 1611 he became a citizen of Bergen. He was one of main participants in the Bergen Russia Company (1629–1638), trading in stockfish and grain. During a business trip to Amsterdam he freighted no less than five ships for a voyage to Archangel. There they had to load rye for Bergen, Copenhagen and Glückstadt (1631). In 1632 together with some Norwegians, he got a privilege for whaling and for a try-house in Northern Norway.[9]

The Timber Trade

The Dutch side

Search for employment, often resulting in a position on board Dutch ships operating in one of the five maritime branches, permanent settlement in the Republic, very frequent sailings in the "Noordsvaart" and stockfish do not make up the complete story of Dutch-Norwegian relations. One of its main components has only been alluded to: the timber trade.

Timber was the most essential raw material in the 17th century. Before iron ore could be properly handled, timber was used in almost all human activities. Timber was in particularly high demand in the Dutch Republic, a country without forests of any importance. Apart from normal uses timber was also being used for pile-driving and for the construction and maintenance of dikes. The population was rapidly growing from 1,3 million in 1550 to 1,9 million in 1650. Several so-called "polders" were being drained during the 17th

Figure 4. Shipyard. Engraving in C. van Ijk, De Nederlandsche Scheepbouw-kunst opengestelt (Amsterdam 1697). Rijksmuseum Nederlands Scheepvaartmuseum, Amsterdam.

century. Moreover, the shipping industries and fisheries required all sorts of timber. Each year hundreds of ships were being built, from the smallest fisherman to the biggest East Indiaman or man-of-war. Shipyards did repair work on a massive number of ships. Each year thousands of staves were needed for making new casks for the storage of herring and blubber. More examples could be given to emphasize the importance of timber to the Dutch economy and in daily life. The Republic constantly depended on a great supply from abroad.

That supply of timber, however, was not a problem most of the time. Purchase, transport, sawing and sale of timber, all these activities belonged to the pattern of the Dutch cargo-carrying trade and staple market. In addition there was the high demand for timber abroad, e.g. in France, England, the Southern Netherlands and the Iberian Peninsula. Dutch merchants and masters fulfilled a great part of this demand, and for a long time they were indispensable to those countries. Their

position was strong, because they were never dependent on one area of supply.

There were no less than four of these areas: the interior parts of Germany along the river Rhine, the northern parts of Germany along the rivers Weser and Elbe, the Baltic area and Norway. Oak came from Germany. Bremen and Hamburg were the ports from which North German oak was shipped to the Republic. Rhine oak drifted in log booms to Dordrecht and Amsterdam. In the Baltic Poland and the Baltic dependencies were the main suppliers of oak and spruce. The Sound Toll Registers show that up to the second half of the 18th century Dutch vessels were the greatest transporters of this Baltic timber. The Republic could never be wholly cut off from these three areas of supply at the same time. This also never happened with the fourth area: Norway, the supplier of the soft woods fir and spruce. While war could not have a lasting influence on this trade, Danish measures of protection and foreign competition did. No timber was imported from Asia and the Western hemisphere.

The national and international demand for timber, the carrying trade, the staple market and the dependence on four areas of supply do not fully account for the leading role of the Dutch in the timber trade, especially in the first half of the 17th century. The timber trade is a highly capitalized one with long term investments: the seasoning of wood takes time, credit has to be given to the suppliers and freight charges have to be paid before the timber can be sold to consumers. The required capital was available in the Republic. Moreover, the invention of the wind-powered saw-mill in 1591 and the subsequent construction of many of these mills – run by four or five men – made possible cheap sawing and guaranteed a high quality of sawn timber. Public auctions brought sellers and buyers in almost permanent contact with each other. Auctions were being held in Amsterdam once and often twice a week and

Figure 5. Underwater photo of planks stowed in the hold of a wreck at Dalarö near Stockholm, Sweden. Photo, Sjöhistoriska Museum, Stockholm.

Timber export extended from the southern to the northern parts of Norway. The bulk of the trade, however, was carried on from the south, from the area east of Lindesnes through Oslofjord to the Swedish border. This area was responsible for about 85 per cent of the 17th century-export. Drammen (Koperwijk in Dutch) and Christiania were by far the most important export-cities. The two cities together were responsible for almost half of the total export of deals. The yields of a tithe levied on timber export clearly illustrate this. Ports such as Langesund, Arendal, Fredrikstad and Kristiansand in the south still had greater exports than Bergen and Trondheim in the western parts of Norway. Apart from most of these places,

next to this main auction local auctions took place in the Zaanstreek (north of Amsterdam) and in Dordrecht. Oak and soft-wood were auctioned separately.[10]

The Norwegian side
Timber export from Norway had begun to increase from the beginning of the 16th century. Demand was growing and the introduction of the water-powered saw-mill made greater production possible. Timber soon became *the* Norwegian export product. The trade raised the living standard in rural areas and it was the economic foundation of many a Norwegian town. The exported timber consisted of soft wood: fir and spruce. There were hundreds of kinds and qualities – e.g., the port of Drammen in 1668 listed more than 160 – but in general one can say that deals and balks were of the greatest importance, not masts. In the Republic, the demand was for balks, so-called "kapbalken", butts in the round, in England for deals. Deals were 6 to 9 inches wide. Balks also became more or less standardized products, at least 8 inches across at the top. The different varieties were often named after the town or area from where they were shipped.

Figure 6. Timber saw-mill, invented last decade of the 16th century. "De Gekroonde Poelenburg", "De Zaanse Schans", Zaandam. Photo, Ver. Zaansche molen, Zaandijk.

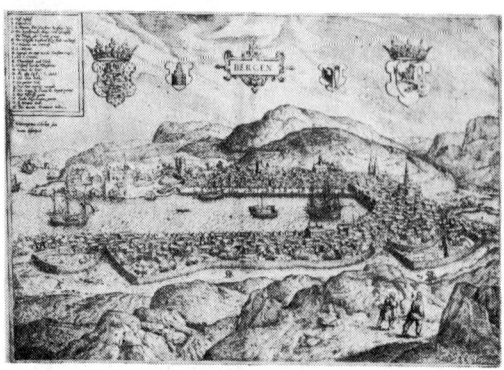

Figure 7. Bergen c. 1580. Hieronymus Scholeus, copperplate engraving.

also Flekkerø and Mandal were well-known names amongst Dutch merchants and seamen.

Ports were preferably situated at the mouths of large rivers or at least at points to which timber might be easily transported from the forests. This explains the importance of Trondheim: it had a large hinterland of valleys, while in the rest of western Norway forests were small and scattered, growing on narrow strips between mountains and fjords. When forests became exhausted or less accessible, a port lost its significance, for exampel Krokstad and Kragerø.

The weather was of great importance for timber production. Snow was needed for transporting logs to the riverside and deals from saw-mill to the port. Mild winters or a shortage of snow put a stop to deliveries. In spring there could be difficulties in floating the logs downstream. When saw-mills were short of water-power, production could be seriously hindered. Too much rain or snow, on the other hand, put the saw-mill out of action, and slowed the cutting and transporting of logs. A millowner was obliged to have sizeable stocks to be able to meet a sudden increase in demand or a stoppage in delivery. Normally two to three years were required to process a load from the stump in the forest to the timber yard at the loading place.[11]

The special position of Dutch masters

Dutch masters played a prominent part in the Norwegian timber ports. Although, as we have seen, merchants sometimes sent relatives as factors or agents to Norway and in spring so-called "Schotsmen" took passage from Amsterdam to operate as sutlers in Norway, still most masters seem to have bought their own load of timber. They were familiar with local circumstances: they often sailed to the same place year after year. They acquired their cargoes through barter or through cash-payment. Notarial records tell about bags full of silver stored in master's cabins. They could make several journeys a year; three to five were not exceptional. Under favorable conditions a return voyage could be made in six to eight weeks. Two weeks in port in Norway was normal. Master Broer Markes of Koudum (Friesland) of the "Groene Leeuw" made four trips between Amsterdam and Southern Norway between March and October, 1668. Each time he was paid 2050 guilders.[12] The master acting independently sharply contrasted with the general tendency in other trades towards a master being only a navigator. But the timber trade was different from other trades in many ways. Timber merchants were mostly involved in shipping. They owned their own ships – of course in accordance with the system of part-ownership – and freighted their own ships. Trade, management and ownership were not divided. It explains why masters could maintain their independence. They often failed to submit books. It even went to the point that nearly forty Amsterdam timber traders who were also shipowners joined forces in 1680 to try to compel their masters to submit their accounts regularly.[13]

Although it is a well-known story that even old and leaky ships could be used in the timber trade – the cargo supplying buoyancy – it is nevertheless more interesting that a special type of ship was being developed in the beginning of the 17th century. Masters and shipowner merchants in the Norwegian timber trade were a specialized group of people who had ships with special equipment. The so-called "houtvaarders" or "noordsvaarders", belonging to the category of fluyt-ships, had two feet draught more than the normal fluyt, and were equipped with gates at the sides and at the stern and stem for loading the long pieces of wood. Later in the 17th century a new type of ship was being developed perhaps in Hoorn that could be cheaply used for the transport of light, bulky cargoes. It was mainly built from fir. These "katschepen" had a steep stem and stern and could completely fill their holds. Norwegian masters who played a leading part in the rapidly expanding Anglo-Norwegian timber trade during the second half of the 17th century also had specialized ships. Many of these ships must have been bought in the Republic. Dutch ships were cheap and

Figure 9. Fluytship on a Dutch roadstead, c. 1650. Oil-painting monogrammed "BH" (Jan Theunisz, Blankerhoff?) Rijksmuseum Nederlands Scheepvaartmuseum, Amsterdam.

Norwegians such as Barent Goendersz of Bergen knew that. In 1674 Barent Goendersz ordered Dirksz de Vreyer, shipbuilder and member of town-council of De Rijp (north of the Zaanstreek) to build him a fluyt.[14]

Not many indications of a weakening of the Dutch position

That Dutch-Norwegian shipping was very frequent, has been mentioned before. It is however, not possible to compile any sort of statistical survey based on Dutch sources. Only a single source about the extent of Dutch shipping is available. Freight contracts, recorded by notaries, have no quantitative value. The number of Dutch ships involved in the Norwegian trade has been estimated at 350 in 1635. Twelve years later 387 ships of more than 100 tons and trading to Norway were included in a list of ships that were eligible for a reduction in taxes. In 1697 no less than 300 ships of more than 100 tons would have been operating to Norway. These figures do not indicate a decline in Dutch-Norwegian relations. The destination in the Republic in most cases was Amsterdam, but the ports of Hoorn, Medemblik, Dord-

Figure 8. Dutch timber traders acquired their cargoes through barter or through cash payment. These late 16th and 17th Century European coins were found at a farm in the timber district of Ryfylke, in Skjold near Haugesund, Norway.
Photo: Universitetets myntkabinett, Oslo/ Karmsund Folkemuseum, Haugesund.

Figure 10. Katships on the roadstead of Hoorn. These ships were often used for timber transport. Painting by Jan Claesz. Rietschoof (1652–1719), c. 1700, Rijksmuseum Nederlands Scheepvaartmuseum, Amsterdam.

recht, Rotterdam and Harlingen also got a share, though a minor one, in this traffic.[15]

Next to the system of the staple market another characteristic of the Dutch cargo-carrying trade was the direct transport of commodities from producer to consumer. This took also place in the Norwegian timber trade. Schreiner discovered 959 freight contracts, recorded in Amsterdam between 1625–1649. About two-thirds of these contracts for carrying Norwegian timber were for direct transport to foreign countries, mostly to France (442). This figure does not tell much about the extent of direct trading, but does prove that its importance should not be minimized.[16]

Thanks to the Navigation Law of 1651 and its later refinements the Dutch lost the English market for their foreign commodities. Protectionistic legislation was being introduced by other governments too, but none hurt the Dutch as severely as the English. There is, however, no ground for the assumption that the loss of the English market particularly hit the Dutch direct trade from Norway to England. Few freight contracts deal with this transport (46 in the example quoted from Schreiner). The re-export of timber from the Republic was a greater victim.

Norwegian timber to England:
a different story
The rise of the English economy in the second half of the 17th century caused a change in the pattern of the Norwegian timber export. All sorts of timber were in great demand in England. The navy almost had to start from scratch. The merchant marine began to grow in numbers and tonnage. Coal-mining at Newcastle and elsewhere depended on supplies of pit-wood from Norway. The house-building industry used much Norwegian timber.

Figure 11. Timberships on the Norwegian or Swedish coast: the timber enters the ship through special portholes. Painter unknown. 17th century. Rijksmuseum Nederlands Scheepvaartmuseum, Amsterdam.

The great fire of London in 1666 certainly caused a boom in demand: "the Norwegians warmed themselves at the Great Fire"! The navy contracted mostly for deals. English forests were shrinking. For all these reasons, the import of timber into England increased enormously, but proportionally the Norwegian part increased most. Around 1700 no less than 43 per cent of all imported timber came from Norway. It dominated the English market. The increased English demand ousted the Dutch from their prominent position in the Norwegian timber trade.

However, it was not the English, who took over the trade, but the Norwegians themselves. Before 1650 Norwegian masters already had a stake in the then still small Anglo-Norwegian trade, but from that time on they completely dominated the transport of timber. Perhaps Barent Goendersz in January, 1674 brought his new Dutch fluyt for the transport of timber to England! During the Third Anglo-Dutch War (1672–74) the entire English timber trade from Norway depended on Norwegian and Danish ships. Not before the end of the War of the Spanish Succession (1713) did English masters seize a considerable share in this transport.[17]

Norwegian masters often acted as selling agents in English ports on behalf of Norwegian merchants. But especially after the 1666-fire Norwegians and also Danes established themselves as commission agents in London and sold timber on behalf of Norwegian merchants. In the 1680's and later they handled the major portion of London's timber trade. They were a close-knit group, with their own Lutheran church. This very active part played by Norwegians in the Anglo-Norwegian timber trade is in sharp contrast with the Dutch-Norwegian trade, in which the Dutch were the actors. Both, the Anglo- as well as the Dutch-Norwegian trade showed a positive balance of payments for Norway. The deficit was covered by both countries by exporting coin and bullion, but from 1660 bills of exchange superseded cash as the chief means of payment.[18]

Tveite wants us to believe that in the second half of the 17th century the Dutch had lost their leading position in the Norwegian timber market and had to content themselves with all but the left-overs. The first point he has convincingly proved. Dutch trade and shipping were at their peak around 1650, with a second, though lower peak in the 1680's. Not any figure nor any contemporary suggests a growth in Dutch-Norwegian trade and shipping but neither does anything suggest a serious decline in the late 17th century. Therefore the Dutch position was only relatively weakened. The volume of timber exported from Norway expanded throughout the 17th century. But there is no reason to accept Tveite's figure for the volume in 1699 as completely reliable or representative. It is the figure upon which Tveite based his conclusion that only 23 per cent of timber exports were going to the Continent south of Denmark and that total exports diminished by 30 per cent after 1688. Kjaerheim has since demonstrated that figures entered in the customs records at that time could not be allowed to exceed lawful production quotas (set in 1688). The manipulations which ensued remained unknown to authorities, and customs officials had to conceal the real amount of timber that went overseas. Fraudulent practices amongst merchants were fairly common around 1700. Just one example proves the unreliability of the 1699-figure. Seven merchants kept a secret stock of deals that was equal to one-ninth of the officially registered exports.[19]

Moreover Tveite based his assertion only on figures dealing with the export of deals. Important as deals were (two-thirds of exports) one should not forget that one-fifth of exports consisted of balks. And balks, as has been mentioned were *the* Norwegian timber imported into Holland.

Notes

1 For the most concise and modern information see the chapters on shipping trade, seafarers, merchant shipping in and outside of Europe, North Sea fishing, whaling and the navy, written by different authors, together with the most updated bibliographies, in vols. II and III of the *Maritieme Geschiedenis der Nederlanden*, Bussum, 1977. No further specific references to this publication will be made. I would like to thank Mrs. E.S. van Eyck van Heslinga, A.C.J. Vermeulen (both University of Leiden), the late Dr. S. Hart (Amsterdam), and Prof. R.W. Unger (University of British Columbia) for their help and advice.

2 For the examples see also A.M. van der Woude, *Het Noorderkwartier*, Wageningen 1972, (AAG-Bijdragen 16), 390 and 804; also J.A. Faber, *Drie Eeuwen Friesland*, Wageningen 1972, (AAG-Bijdragen 17), 646.

3 This is currently done by P.C. van Royen in his Ph.D. thesis on the crew aboard Dutch merchantmen around 1700.

4 J.R. Bruijn, Seamen in Dutch ports: c. 1700–c. 1914, *Mariner's Mirror*, 65 (1979), 327–337; J.R. Bruijn and E.S. van Eyck van Heslinga, Seamen's Employment in the Netherlands (c. 1600–c. 1800), *Mariner's Mirror* 70 (1984), 7–20; P. Boon, De sociale en economische positie van schippers in het Westfriese dorp Schellinkhout rond 1700, *Mededelingen Ned. Ver. voor Zeegeschiedenis* 39 (1979), 5–14.

5 The figures on Hoorn are available in an unpublished report written by C.F.L. Paul, dealing with the results of a seminar on the maritime communities of Enkhuizen, Hoorn and Medemblik at the University of Leiden in 1975/6. For seasonal labour in the Republic see also the pioneering book J.M.W.G. Lucassen, *Naar de kusten van de Noordzee. Trekarbeid in Europees perspektief, 1600–1900* (Gouda 1984).

6 Examples quoted in J.R. Bruijn, Scheepvaart in de Noordelijke Nederlanden (1650–1800), 209–238, esp. 224–225, in *Algemene Geschiedenis der Nederlanden* vol. 8, Haarlem 1979.

7 The Hague, State Archives, Archief Directiën ter equipering van oorlogsschepen, 10. W.F.H. Oldewelt, De scheepvaartstatistiek van Amsterdam in de 17e en 18e eeuw, *Jaarboek Amstelodamum*, 45 (1953), 114–151.

8 S. Hart, Zeelieden te Amsterdam in de zeventiende eeuw. Een historisch-demografisch onderzoek, *Mededelingen Nederlandse Vereniging voor Zeegeschiedenis*, 17 (1968), 5–20. S. Hart, Geschrift en Getal. Onderzoek naar de samenstelling van de bevolking van Amsterdam in de 17e en 18e eeuw, op grond van gegevens over migratie, huwelijk, beroep en alfabetisme, in: *Geschrift en Getal*, Dordrecht, 1976, 115–182.

9 J.W. Veluwenkamp collected this information during a seminar on the Dutch whaling trade around 1640–50 at the University of Leiden in 1973/4. For Pieter Crijnsz. Hooft, see J. Schreiner, *Nederland og Norge 1625–1650. Trelastutførsel og handelspolitik*, Oslo, 1933, 40.

10 For a short survey of the development of saw-mills and the timber trade, together with up to date references, see Van der Woude, *Noorderkwartier*, 472–484 and also P.J. Middelhoven, De Amsterdamse veilingen van Noord-Europees naaldhout 1717–1808, *Economisch-Sociaal Historisch Jaarboek* 41 (1978), 86–114. See also R.W. Unger, *Dutch Shipbuilding before 1800*, Assen, 1978.

11 S. Tveite, *Engelsk-Norsk trelasthandel 1640–1710*, Bergen/Oslo 1961. The detailed summary in English has mostly been used. See also Middelhoven, De Amsterdamse veilingen, 87 and 94.

12 J. Schreiner, Die Niederländer und die Norwegische Holzausfuhr im 17. Jahrhundert, *Tijdschrift voor Geschiedenis* 49 (1934), 303–328. More detailed information in J. Schreiner, *Nederland og Norge*. Further S. Hart, Een bijdrage tot de geschiedenis van de houthandel, in: *Geschrift en Getal*, Dordrecht, 1976, 71–92, esp. 78, note 23.

13 See *Maritieme Geschiedenis der Nederlanden* vol II, 112.

14 Haarlem, State Archive in North-Holland, notarial records of De Rijp no. 4460, 31.1.1674. J. van Beylen, *Schepen van de Nederlanden*, Amsterdam, 1970, 106–115. An earlier type of ship is referred to by A.B. Andersen, Et vrakfunn på Tau fra 1500-tallet, in: *Stavanger Museums Årbok 1974*, 25–43.

15 Figures quoted in *Maritieme Geschiedenis der Nederlanden* vol. II, 220 and 223.

16 Schreiner, *Nederland og Norge*, 112–161 and the same, Die Niederländer, 322.

17 On 18th-century Anglo-Norwegian trade, see R. Davis, *The Rise of the English Shipping Industry*, Newton Abbot 1972[2] and H.S.K. Kent, *War and Trade in Northern Seas*, Cambridge 1973.

18 Tveite, *Engelsk-Norsk trelasthandel*, 568–569 and 571.

19 See S. Kjaerheim's review of Tveite's book in *The Scandinavian Economic History Review 12* (1964), 91–95.

North Sea Warfare in the 17th and 18th Century

BÅRD KOLLTVEIT

Introduction

When walking past the massive belfry of Bergen Cathedral, an observant stroller may notice a black cannon ball sticking out from the wall some way up in one of the corners. It was fired from a high-aiming English gun on August 2, 1665, during the naval encounter which has been recorded in history as the Action at Bergen, involving a Dutch fleet of fifty East Indiamen and 21 English warships.

The battle was indeed dramatic, and even more so, because the gun batteries of Bergenhus joined in to support the Dutch. Both the military Supreme Commander-in-Chief in Norway and the Commanding Officer of Bergenhus were present during the action; neither of them, however, being aware that a messenger was under way from Copenhagen, with the instruction that the fortress should stay aloof from the encounter, according to an agreement between the Danish-Norwegian king and the English envoy in Copenhagen. Such an attitude would doubtless have led to an English victory, and the agreement went further on to say that the booty be divided between the English and the Dano-Norwegians.

And a rich booty it would have been indeed. The Dutch vessels were heavily laden with an extremely valuable cargo, consisting among other items of spices, chi-naware, pearls and precious stones. In order to avoid capture by the English, the fleet had sailed north of Scotland and anchored in Bergen, waiting for Dutch naval ships to escort them on the final leg to the Netherlands.

However, the outcome of the action

Figure 1. The Action at Bergen, August 2, 1665, between Dutch East Indiamen and British warships. Grisaille (detail) by Willem van de Velde (elder).

became diametrically opposite of what had been intended in Copenhagen. The active support to the Dutch from the fortress guns decided the battle. After three hours, the English had to retreat, with three damaged ships and 600 killed or wounded men, while the corresponding Dutch figure was no seriously damaged vessel and less than ten persons lost. Eight soldiers lost their lives on the fortress, while ten civilians perished from shell hits in the town itself. The damage done to town houses was, of course, considerable. After necessary repairs, the East Indiamen proceeded safely under Dutch naval escort from Bergen to Amsterdam at the end of August.

The Action at Bergen created much stir, both in peaceful Bergen and in international political circles. Nevertheless, the battle is nowadays better remembered in local than world history. One seeks vainly for the battle in Michael Sanderson's reference guide "Sea Battles", published in 1975.

Although of smaller importance than many others, the encounter can nevertheless be regarded as rather symbolic for naval warfare in the North Sea during this period.

The main opponents were the great maritime and colonial powers the Netherlands, Britain and, to some extent, France, while the Scandinavian countries were only occasionally involved in the big naval encounters in the North Sea. The Swedish as well as the Danish-Norwegian naval fleets were generally concentrated east of the Naze and the Skaw. While big battles were fought between the English and the Dutch in the North Sea and – mainly – the English Channel, most naval actions involving Scandinavian men-of-war took place in Skagerrak, the Sound and the Baltic Sea.

Strictly speaking, most Scandinavian naval affairs are thus beyond the scope of matters pertaining to the North Sea. However, it is only appropriate to have them included as well. The present survey will

therefore divide itself between the conflicts England vs. the Netherlands, and matters relevant to Scandinavian warfare, as rather separate elements. Still, the reader will probably notice how often the two fields get in contact and have influence upon each other.

Innovations in Naval Tactics

As late as the mid-17th century, the only fleet tactical manoeuvres seem to have been the old opening gambit of getting the wind and then massing fire on the weathermost ships of the enemy, in order to throw him into confusion and profit by his mistakes.

In 1653, things began to change in English naval tactics, probably as a result of generals with experience from land warfare, entering commanding positions in the Navy. They brought with them into the Navy the philosophy of systematic battle formations. That same year, a new set of Fighting Instructions was issued, stating among other things that "All ships of every squadron shall endeavour to keep in line with the chief ...", and doing away with bunching and follow-the-leader tactics. The column was established as the standard battle formation, where no broadside is barred by a friendly ship. It marked a final break with galley tactics, which implied firing in the direction of individual advance of the ship. A great deal of discipline from every ship master was required, which may account for why the column tactics had more difficulties in being successfully adapted by the Dutch than the English. Apart from less discipline among their captains, the Dutch ships were also more shallow and therefore more leewardly than the deeper and heavier British ships.

Guns first appeared on ships during the second half of the 14th century, and then only as defensive anti-personnel weapons. An important change came about 1620 in ship design, when decks were run almost horizontally from bow to stern, allowing the

Figure 2. The works of 17th century Dutch marine artists are among our most important historical sources of maritime knowledge from this period, not least due to their attention to detail as well as visual correctness. This is well demonstrated in this study by van de Velde (elder) of contemporary Dutch warships.

shifting of wheeled guns as needed. The British were the first to realize the importance of heavy gunnery as a ship-destroying weapon, also a result from the new column tactics.

Earlier warfare at sea had been based on direct contact between ships, grappling and man-to-man fighting. The first Anglo-Dutch war witnessed the beginning of fleet actions and tactical sea battles in the more modern sense. New guns had longer range, which also fostered the basis for the new trends in naval tactics.

Anglo-Dutch Warfare in the 17th and 18th Century

Until the end of the 16th century, the increasing overseas trade had been heavily dominated by the hitherto greatest colonial powers, Spain and Portugal, who in 1581 had become united under one monarch, Philip II. This hegemony, however, came to a turning point at the end of the century, partly due to the Declaration of Independence of the 7 Dutch provinces from Spain in 1581 – internationally recognized in 1609 – and partly by the disastrous defeat of the Spanish Armada by English warships and the weather gods in 1588.

Another result was, however, that England and the Netherlands, who had earlier cooperated against the common enemy, Spain, from now on became mutual competitors and antagonists.

The inner solidarity among the Seven Provinces, created by the war against Spain, was of vital importance for the Dutch in their purposeful work to expand foreign maritime trade. While England and France suffered from domestic discord caused by conflicts between king and Parliament and between king and nobility, the diligent and industrious Dutch Calvinists expanded their mercantile spheres of interest – in the Baltic, in America and in the Far East. They sent whaling expeditions to the Arctic, and developed extensive fisheries in the North Sea.

Efforts from England and France to thwart or recapture the advantageous position the Dutch had created for themselves, were met with stubborn resistance, and the more mercantilistic and protectionist ideas conquered England and France, the faster the Netherlands transformed from a troublesome competitor to a direct and threatening enemy and a real danger to the expansive plans of the two other rising powers.

The strong naval position achieved by England during the Elizabethan period, reaching a temporary climax in the battle against the Armada, had not been followed up by the Queen's successor, King James I. The naval fleet had fallen into decay, which also was the case when Charles I ascended the throne. His demand to the Parliament for "ship money" to restore the fleet was regarded as an untimely royal decree against the people, and was a contributing factor to the outbreak of civil war in 1642.

However, during the Commonwealth period, the governmental administration had become sufficiently strong to carry through a decision to grant enough funds to rebuild the Navy to its former status. In the same period, Dutch merchants and shipowners had utterly consolidated their mercantile strategic positions. As late as 1670,

Figure 3. "Aemilia", flagship of the Dutch admiral Maarten Tromp.

the total Dutch fleet was estimated at a tonnage of 900,000 or nearly double that of the English.

The English counter-measures were both of mercantile and military character. The Navigation Act, passed in 1651, did indeed aim at forcing the Dutch out of carrying trade between other countries. The Dutch realized the disastrous effects this Act might have upon their trade, and already in the following year the First Anglo-Dutch war was a reality.

Despite the few years the English navy had had to restore itself, it was already sufficiently strong and efficient to meet the however swift and easily manoeuvrable, but nevertheless, small and heterogeneous units of the Dutch fleet. On the other hand, the Dutch could master two of the most eminent naval tacticians in history, the admirals Maarten Tromp and Michael de Ruyter, while the English had to recruit new leaders from the ranks of the Army, partly because Cromwell had some doubts about where loyalty actually lay among higher Naval officials. Nevertheless, the "Generals-at-Sea", as the new naval leaders were called, fostered amongst themselves several eminent naval tacticians, like Robert Blake and George Monk, thus bringing new ideas into traditional tactics of sea battles.

The first year of the first Anglo-Dutch war saw no final decision, but during the next,

Figure 4. *Scene from the third day of the Four Days' Battle in the Channel, 1–4 June 1666.*

the English Navy and the maritime generals succeeded in achieving peace on their conditions. This was due in great part to two decisive battles, of which the Three-Day-Battle at Portland, February 18–20, is regarded as the actual turning point.

A squadron of 80 English men-of-war, led by Robert Blake, intercepted a Dutch fleet of equal size, commandeered by Tromp, heading up the Channel with a convoy of 150 merchantmen. Tromp had a very difficult task, in trying to combine fighting against the English fleet and giving protection to the convoy. Due to Tromp's superb seamanship, the Dutch fleet succeeded in proceeding up the Channel, although with the loss of eight large warships and at least 30 merchant vessels.

As the Netherlands no longer had sufficient naval resources to break the ensuing English blockade of Dutch seaports, the country was forced to surrender. The peace treaty included war damages, besides equal rights for English and Dutch vessels in the East Indian trade.

Still, England and the Netherlands were on collision course in mercantile policy. The rivalry in colonial trade and maritime hegemony continued, despite the treaty of 1654.

In 1660, the English monarchy was restored, when Charles II ascended the throne. During his reign the title Royal Navy was instituted. Five years later the conflicting interests of England and the Netherlands again flared up in open war. The Second Anglo-Dutch war lasted between 1665 and 1667, and it was during this period of strife that the Action at Bergen, mentioned in the introduction, took place.

While that encounter lasted but three hours, the same war also saw the so-called Four Days' Battle, regarded as one of the most prolonged and intensive naval battles in history. It took place in the Channel between North Foreland and Dunkirk, from June 1 to June 4, 1666.

In the erring belief that the French had sent a squadron to assist the Dutch, the English fleet was split in two. One squadron, commanded by Prince Rupert, was ordered to continue down the Channel to meet the French, while Monk was alone with only sixty ships to encounter the entire Dutch fleet. Despite vigorous fighting, Monk was forced to retreat, while several of the best units of the English navy were either captured or burnt. Prince Rupert returned from his fruitless mission just in time to save Monk from total destruction. The fourth day, all formal battle columns had broken up, the battle having developed into a total mêlée, with vessel fighting against vessel. That same evening, de Ruyter decided to withdraw from the scene. The battle had inflicted a serious defeat on the English, who lost 17 ships and 8,000 men.

Barely a month and a half later, however, the English had their revenge when the Dutch and the English fleet met between North Foreland and Orfordness, July 25. The Dutch van was forced to retreat, and after intense cannonade between the two centre divisions, where de Ruyter's flagship had two masts shot off, his division had to make a retreat. The rear divisions continued their fighting further west. Tromp personally took his ship out of the column to engage with the English rear division, but eventually had to head for the Dutch coast. Having lost a total of 7,000 men and 20 ships, the Dutch fleet sought refuge in the shallow waters off Flushing, while Prince Rupert and Monk freely raided the coast of the Netherlands. In Vlie alone, more than 160 Dutch merchant ships were destroyed. Again, the Netherlands had to ask for peace negotiations.

King Charles felt so utterly reassured, that he prolonged the negotiations, while at the same time he laid up most of the naval vessels and paid off the crew, despite vigorous opposition and warnings from Monk. The result was one of the most humiliating defeats in English naval annals.

In June 1667 a Dutch naval squadron, led by de Ruyter, sailed up the Thames estuary without meeting any resistance. In Sheerness, they captured vast amounts of English naval equipment, whereupon they bombarded Chatham, set fire to several large men-of-war in lay-up, and took with them the flagship of the Navy, the *Royal Charles*. According to tradition, de Ruyter on this occasion mounted a broom on the fore truck, indicating that the Channel now had been swept free of British vessels.

The ensuing Dutch blockade of English merchant shipping proved so effective, that only a couple of weeks later, serious peace negotiations were in progress. These led to concessions on both sides. England relinquished all demands in the East Indies and made some modifications to the Navigation Act, while the Dutch recognized the West Indies as an English sphere of influence. At the same time, the Hudson Valley was ceded to England, together with the small coastal colony Nieuw Amsterdam, immediately renamed New York.

But further antagonism between the two countries was yet in store. Only seven years later, the Third Anglo-Dutch war broke out. However, this time, the third big European power, France, was the triggering factor.

Louis XIV, now well established as the absolute Soleil Royal of France, wished to annex the Netherlands to his kingdom. Building up a blockading chain around the seven provinces, he also obtained support from Charles II, who was still eager to thwart as much as possible of further Dutch mercantile expansion.

But King Charles' plans had only small support in his own kingdom, and the Netherlands, led by Stadtholder William of Orange, succeeded in breaking up French policy. He stopped a French invasion by opening the dikes and flooding the country, while de Ruyter without serious effort managed to keep the English navy at bay. Peace between England and the Netherlands was restored in 1674, and the friendly relations were utterly confirmed by the marriage between William of Orange and Mary, daughter of the Duke of York, and later the election of William and Mary as the English sovereigns. Louis XIV made peace with the Netherlands in 1678, without having gained a square inch of Dutch territory.

With the end of the Third Anglo-Dutch War, the naval rivalry between the two countries had been brought to an end. In the

Figure 5. Model of the Danish-Norwegian warship "Den Norske Løve". This exceptionally beautiful and detailed contemporary model (1654) is made of ivory, apart from the silver guns and rigging. Displayed at Rosenborg Castle, Copenhagen.

following century, England and France became the main antagonists in European warfare on land and sea. However, the naval actions between the two countries took place in waters outside the North Sea.

Scandinavian Naval Warfare in the 17th and 18th Century

As in England and the Netherlands, the 17th century was a period of growth in Scandinavia as well. Although Sweden and Denmark-Norway did not join actively in the great encounters between the first-mentioned, the Scandinavian countries were nevertheless of such mercantile and strategic importance, that they were constantly flirted with or threatened by other European powers, as pieces in the international political chess game, particularly in the aim to secure a political balance in the Baltic area. At the same time, the Scandinavian countries were almost constantly involved in conflicts between themselves. This was certainly the main reason why both Sweden and Denmark-Norway built up naval fleets of considerable size.

In Denmark-Norway, King Christian IV (1588-1648) is regarded as the nation's first real naval king. Although the navy was formally led by a State Admiral, the king was for long periods the real and personally engaged head of the fleet. His interest went further than the vessels themselves. He built a new naval arsenal, and also living quarters on land for both naval officers and ratings. The houses for the latter, called Nyboder, today forms one of the most picturesque quarters of Copenhagen.

Christian IV used his expanding naval fleet to secure a bigger foothold in international mercantile affairs. In 1618 four Danish naval ships sailed to India to establish Danish colonial factories. Several unsuccessful attempts were made to find a seaway to the East Indies via the Northwest Passage. Most famous of the expeditions was the one led by Jens Munk in 1619–20, who left Copenhagen with two ships, and eventually returned to Norway the following autumn with only two men, the rest having perished in the Arctic frost. The expedition had reached as far as the inner part of Hudson Bay. Naval ships were also sent to other waters to open Danish trade routes, e.g. the Mediterranean, the Arctic and the Atlantic.

After having seen a period of great expansion during the reign of King Gustav Vasa (1523–1560), the Swedish naval fleet suffered a long period of stagnation and neglect until the second decade of the 17th century. Only smaller ships were built, for coastal defence. They were sufficient to serve Swedish naval purposes during the feuds on the Swedish borders with Poland and Russia, but the expanding Danish-Norwegian naval fleet under Christian IV, gave reason for growing Swedish concern. Although superior in number, the smaller Swedish ships could not be compared to the bigger and more offensive units which were added to the Danish-Norwegian fleet.

In 1611 Gustav II Adolf became King of Sweden. In the same year, Denmark-Norway declared war upon Sweden, King Christian hoping that his superior fleet would help him to restore the Danish hegemony in Scandinavia of a century ago. The superiority of his navy was also demonstrated during the sieges of various Swedish fortified ports, and a successful raid in the Stockholm archipelago.

Without pressure from outside, the result might have been successful from a Danish point of view. But neither England nor the Netherlands wanted a shift in the local balance of power in the Baltic either in Danish or Swedish favour, and after diplomatic pressure from them, this so-called Kalmar War was ended in 1613. Sweden had to pay heavy war damages, but retained her integrity.

The contact between the strongly Protestant Swedish king and the likeminded Dutch led to a Swedish-Dutch defensive alliance. This was perhaps more of economic than strategic importance, as it gave Sweden access to the Dutch capital market.

However, the amicable relations cooled off considerably when, after successful conquests during the first stage of the Thirty Years' War, Sweden introduced heavy duties on trade in ports of the Eastern Baltic in 1629. But Dutch sympathy towards Sweden was again restored when Denmark on her part put heavy increases on duties to be paid by vessels passing Glückstadt on the Elbe, and the Sound, in an effort to compensate for the heavy expenditure caused by King Christian's unsuccessful attempts to join the war.

Spurred by the antagonism from England and the Netherlands against Denmark-Norway, caused by the heavy duties, Sweden felt safe to declare war upon Denmark in 1643. In the meantime, the Swedish naval fleet had been considerably increased, partly by a long-range newbuilding plan, and partly by the fact that Sweden had captured

Wallenstein's fleet at Wismar in 1632. In 1644 Sweden also chartered 22 fully equipped Dutch naval ships.

In October that year, the numerically superior Swedish-Dutch fleet defeated a Danish squadron at Fehmarn. Of 15 Danish men-of-war, only two managed to get away. In the following spring, the Netherlands dispatched a squadron of 47 warships to the Sound to demand a reduction in the duties, and in the same year Denmark had to sign a peace treaty with Sweden in Brömsebro.

The Dutch regard for the balance of power in the Baltic prevented even further Danish concessions to Sweden. Nevertheless, Denmark-Norway was forced to cede considerable land areas.

The friendly Swedish-Dutch connections

Figure 6. Danish-Norwegian ship-of-the-line "Sophia Amalia", built at Oslo in 1651. Of 165 feet in length, she exceeded the British "Sovereign of the Seas" (1637) by 3 feet. Reconstruction model at Norwegian Maritime Museum, Oslo.

were again seriously strained as a result of the Peace of Westphalia in 1648. Sweden had received large tracts of land in Pomerania and Brandenburg, and also the dioceses of Bremen and Verden. The two latter were of extremely great importance to Dutch shipping, and the Swedish supremacy in these areas caused considerable annoyance.

After England and the Netherlands entered into hostilities from 1652 onwards, Sweden seized the opportunity to make a treaty of friendship with England. The relations between Sweden and Denmark were constantly marred by bitterness, especially from the Danish side, after the, in their opinion, most humiliating Peace Treaty of Brömsebro.

The Peace of Westphalia had not created a final solution to the disputes on the Eastern Swedish border. Fearing an increase in the pressure from Russia in Poland, Sweden in 1655 decided to declare war on Poland, in order to secure her own foothold in this area. Sweden met heavier resistance than expected in Poland and therefore had to send reinforcements eastwards. Denmark-Norway saw the weakened Swedish position in the West as an appropriate opportunity to take revenge for Brömsebro, and therefore declared war on Sweden in 1657.

At this time, Denmark-Norway had made a defensive alliance with the Netherlands, but being the offending party, did not receive any Dutch support on this occasion. The war was, however, a most welcome excuse for the Swedish king, Carl X Gustav, to shift his operations from the deadlock in Poland to Denmark.

The Danish-Norwegian fleet proved sufficiently strong to prevent the Swedish fleet from breaking the Danish blockade of the Western Baltic, but instead the forces of nature gave the Swedes the aid needed. The winter 1657–58 was exceptionally long and cold, making it possible for the well-trained Swedish soldiers to cross the Sound and the Belts by foot on the ice. Denmark-Norway on her part, was poorly prepared for the war declared by herself, and in January 1658 had

to sign another peace treaty at Roskilde, which was even more humiliating than that at Brömsebro. To secure their position even further, Swedish troops again invaded Denmark that same autumn, besieging Copenhagen.

This time, however, the Danish-Dutch defence treaty was brought into action. Besides, the Dutch had certainly every reason to bar a Swedish demand that the Sound should be closed to all foreign traffic. 49 Dutch support ships were hastily fitted out and dispatched the Baltic, commanded by Admiral Jakob van Opdam.

On October 29, 1658, the Dutch fleet passed Elsinore and encountered a numerically superior Swedish squadron, led by Admiral Wrangel. A prolonged and ferocious battle followed, but eventually the Dutch proved the victorious. Late in the afternoon Opdam continued on his way down the Sound, receiving an ovation as he entered the roads of heavily beleaguered Copenhagen.

The Swedish main attack on Copenhagen took place on 10–11 February 1659. The city withstood the assault, but again the war was brought to an end more by diplomatic than military action. Fearing that Denmark, in getting the upper hand, might put forth claims to have Skåne re-ceded from Sweden and thus again upset the balance of power in the area, the Netherlands remained cautious.

At the same time, the English put their foot in, fearing Dutch dominance. In the summer of 1659, a fleet of 40 English men-of-war entered Danish waters, and in response, the Netherlands sent another squadron of 39 ships, commandeered by de Ruyter, to Denmark. The mobilization of naval vessels around Denmark in 1659 was thus quite formidable. Political unrest at home forced the English squadron to leave in August, while Opdam was ordered back to Amsterdam with his fleet in October. De Ruyter remained, and assisted the Danes in shipping 11,000 troops to Funen, which was then recaptured for Denmark.

Parallel to these events, the Netherlands, England and France had negotiated in order to re-establish peace and political balance in Danish waters. Neither Denmark-Norway nor Sweden was willing to accept this kind of big-power intervention, and not until the death of King Carl X Gustav in 1660 was the general atmosphere sufficiently calmed down to allow for further negotiations.

These were held in Copenhagen, and ended in a limited recession of Swedish land areas to Denmark-Norway. From 1660 onwards, the borders between Denmark, Sweden and Norway have remained unchanged. The balance of power in the area had been achieved not so much through Scandinavian warfare, as by political and diplomatic action from other powers, eager to secure as smooth access as possible between trading areas around the North Sea and the Baltic, and also fearing that the Baltic might be transformed into an all-Swedish inland sea.

Political balance, however, was not synonymous with peaceful relations between the Scandinavian countries. The Third Anglo-Dutch War, set off by French expansionism, again brought Denmark-Norway and Sweden into war with each other. The Netherlands wished to bring Denmark-Norway into the conflict on their side, offering generous financial support, after Louis XIV's successful attempt to blockade the Dutch, assisted by England and Sweden. Despite heavy domestic political moves to prevent a severing of the present fairly amicable Dano-Swedish relations, King Christian V in 1674 nevertheless formed an alliance with the Netherlands, who promised to dispatch a well armed naval squadron to the Baltic to aid Danish naval operations against the Swedes.

The Skåne War, seen from a Danish-Norwegian angle, was a highlight in naval history, and especially so because of the battle at Køge Bay July 1, 1677. Admiral Niels Juel, with a squadron of 24 ships managed to split up and defeat a considerably larger Swedish naval force, led by Admiral Horn. Seven Swedish ships-of-the-line were captured, while another was destroyed by fire.

Again, European diplomacy brought about peace. France opened individual negotiations with the various opposing powers, even acting as negotiators for her ally, Sweden, when conditions for peace were discussed with Denmark-Norway. This was a severe blow to Swedish national sentiment, but probably led to better terms for Sweden than might otherwise have been obtained. Denmark-Norway again demanded land areas from Sweden, but France succeeded in confirming the borders decided upon in 1660.

Among the last Royal decisions made by King Christian V before his death in 1699, was to join a triple alliance with Russia and Sachsen-Poland against Sweden. In 1698, King Carl XII, one of history's most eminent army leaders, ascended the Swedish throne. Two years later the Saxons attacked the Swedish Baltic provinces, which eventually led to the conflict called the Great Nordic War (1700–1721).

The first part of the war was mainly fought on land, and was generally marked by continued Swedish progress, with the victory at Narva in November 1700 as a spectacular climax. In the same year, peace was re-established between Sweden and Denmark-Norway. Gradually, however, the Swedish stronghold in the East was weakened, and in 1709, Denmark-Norway again declared war on Sweden.

The war period between 1709 and 1721 was even more meaningless than most other conflicts, but some of the naval actions in that period are held in particularly high esteem in Denmark and Norway even today. This is especially due to the daring, sometimes even brilliantly unconventional forays carried out by Peter Wessel Tordenskiold, who advanced to the rank of Vice Admiral at the age of 29.

Probably his greatest feat was the action

Figure 7. Battle of Køge Bay, July 1, 1677. Oil on canvas by Norwegian marine artist Ants Lepson, 1979.

at the narrow inlet of Dynekilen on the Swedish coast, near the Norwegian border in 1716. With a daring manoeuvre he was able to take almost by complete surprise, a large Swedish fleet carrying supplies to King Carl XII and his troops, then beleaguering Fredriksten fortress, a major gateway for an invasion in Norway. The action at Dynekilen forced the Swedes to lift the siege for the time being.

When peace was finally restored in 1721, Sweden had to cede her Baltic provinces to Russia, Hanover and Prussia. This led to a more equal state of affairs in Scandinavia, with less need for international support on either side to keep the balance in position. Denmark-Norway once and for all relinquished any thought of recapturing areas formerly ceded to Sweden. Sweden herself was later again afflicted by conflicts in the east, but in inter-Scandinavian affairs, the period from 1720 to 1801 is known to posterity as "The Long Period of Peace".

Sovereigns and Sea Power

The growth rate of the naval fleets of various nations strongly reflects the attitude taken by different monarchs and state leaders towards the importance of military sea power.

In England, as already mentioned, the navy had remained in the doldrums during the reign of James I. Due to parliamentary resistance, Charles I did not succeed in raising sufficient funds to seriously alter this state of affairs, although some of the most spectacular warships in English history, among these the *Sovereign of the Seas,* were built in this period (1637).

During the Commonwealth period, however, the English navy entered a stage of rapid expansion, which was continued after the accession of Charles II in 1660. His brother, later King James II, was appointed Lord High Admiral, for which he was well qualified both by education and intellectual bent. Under his leadership, and assisted by the eminent Naval Secretary, Samuel Pepys, the Royal Navy was reorganised from bottom to top. Among other innovations, a permanent corps replaced the hitherto temporarily appointed naval officers.

Although British warships of this period did not greatly advance the art of naval architecture, England built some of the largest naval vessels of the 17th century, most of them bearing the mark of the Pett family (Phineas and Peter), ship designers and shipbuilders.

It has later been said that the single useful legacy that James II left behind when he fled England in 1688, was a fleet, big, strong, and efficient enough to bar his return. It was further increased when the accession of William and Mary brought the Dutch and English fleets into combination. In the same period another major power, France, had built the world's most powerful navy, with Louis XIV's great Minister of Finance, Jean Colbert, as the chief architect.

France was the first country to develop ship construction into a field of scientific research, and by the end of the century, French warships were reputedly the best in the world. In 1689, the French fleet equalled the combined Dutch and English navies. A main drawback for the French,

Figure 8. French 18th century ships-of-the-line. Watercolour by French marine artist Albert Sébille.

however, was the necessity to split the navy in two, to protect the two separate coastlines facing the Atlantic and the Mediterranean. A most definite aim of the English was to keep the two French squadrons as completely separated as possible.

Since the War of Independence, the Dutch had realized the importance of a powerful navy. Unlike England, France and other monarchies, the republican Netherlands did not suffer from fluctuating monarchial naval interest. But the shallow and tricky waters along the Dutch coast forced them to rely on rather small and shallow craft, as opposed to the heavier units of other rising sea powers.

It should be noted that the thrifty and economical Dutch produced the naval hermaphrodite called the armed merchantman – also called "defension ship" – the forerunner of the auxiliary cruiser of the late 19th and 20th century. A considerable number of merchant ships were given extra gunnery and enjoyed certain privileges in times of peace, on the condition that they were put at the disposal of the navy in case of war. This system was also adapted by other countries, e.g. Denmark-Norway and also Sweden, although in the latter case they were referred to as "company ships", serving various overseas trading companies.

The skill of the Dutch shipwrights was widely recognized. A Dutch shipbuilder was summoned to Stockholm to construct the *Wasa*. Tsar Peter the Great in his youth travelled all the way from Russia to Zaandam to get some insight into Dutch shipbuilding methods. The shipbuilding science in France also stems from the Netherlands. When Richelieu came to power as Chancellor in 1624, he immediately ordered five 60-gun vessels in the Netherlands, partly in order to rebuild the navy, but also to have them as study objects for future French shipbuilders.

While King Christian IV of Denmark-Norway showed a keen personal interest in naval matters, his successor, Frederik III, was equally disinterested. Even a Swedish envoy was pained by the sight of the once so impressive Danish-Norwegian fleet in 1662: "It is, so help me God, indeed a pity to see how these ships fall into neglect and are rotting away".

Some of the King's counsellors, however, realized that this state of affairs could not continue, and were able at least to stabilize the situation. One of these counsellors was Cort Adeler, who had won much honour while serving in the Venetian navy from 1646 to 1661, where he had realized the possibilities for an efficient coastal defense system by extensive use of

Figure 10. "Friedrichsstadt". Danish-Norwegian coastal defence galley. Reconstruction model at Norwegian Maritime Museum, Oslo.

galleys. But it was not until the accession of Christian V in 1670, that the Danish-Norwegian navy again came into a period of rapid expansion.

The 18th century was in Scandinavia dominated by the "Long Period of Peace", followed by the "Armed Neutrality", and the fighting power of the Danish-Norwegian fleet remained fairly stable, although new vessels were constantly built to replace obsolescent units. In this period, the Danish-Norwegian navy fostered its master shipwright, Henrik Gerner. His designs were in use for a considerable time after his death in 1787.

The strategic importance of the Danish-Norwegian fleet became evident during the British action at Copenhagen in August 1807. In order to prevent the fleet from being used by hostile powers, the British captured and took with them the entire fleet – 17 ships-of-the-line, 16 frigates, 9 brigs and schooners, 23 gunboats and mortar vessels, 4 floating batteries and some smaller units. A sad end to a great era in Danish-Norwegian naval history.

The growth and decline of the Swedish navy also coincided with the varying interest in naval affairs shown by various heads of state.

Figure 9. "Staden Christiania". Danish-Norwegian "defension ship", built at Oslo in 1694. Reconstruction model at Norwegian Maritime Museum, Oslo.

When Gustav II Adolf died in 1632, the Swedish navy was the most powerful in Scandinavia. Chancellor Axel Oxenstierna fully realized the importance of a strong naval force, and the successive monarchs Queen Kristina and King Carl X Gustav supported this view.

By a Royal Decree from 1650, the size of the navy had been determined as 50 large and small vessels in top condition; ageing ships continuously to be replaced by new units. However, after the Peace of 1660, the navy was so worn-down and Sweden herself in such desperate economic difficulties, that the period of Regency between 1660 and 1671, before Carl X came of age, is reckoned as perhaps the darkest years in Sweden's naval history. This was utterly confirmed by the proceedings during the War of Skåne, in which Denmark-Norway enjoyed an illustrious period.

The first three decades after the Peace of 1679, however, saw a forcible rearmament of the navy, and in the Great Nordic War, the Swedish navy again could be ranked as one of Europe's foremost fleets.

After the war, Sweden, like Denmark-Norway, sought to keep a naval equilibrium in the Baltic. The Gustavian Period, the reign of King Gustav III, from 1771 onwards, witnessed a new upsurge in the Swedish navy. This was especially so after 1780, when the newly-appointed General Admiral was given a free hand to re-strengthen the fleet, thus opening the career for that brilliant Swedish ship designer Henrik af Chapman, whose work "Architectura Navalis Mercatoria" will always rank as one of the great milestones in naval architecture.

This rapid and illustrious period of growth ended abruptly with the death of the king in 1792, and the navy again entered a period of stagnation, which lasted till after the turn of the century.

Epilogue

This survey of North Sea and Baltic warfare in the 17th and 18th century focuses on monarchs, admirals, ships and battles. Few aspects of maritime history have been more thoroughly treated and analysed than naval matters. Each nation has its own voluminous works on the subject, heavily bound in leather and gold. To make a limited survey, including all important matters, is therefore an almost impossible task.

An aspect which, nevertheless, should have been included, is a more detailed description of conditions on board; on deck as well as below. A visit to the battery decks of the *Wasa* and the *Victory* can but give a faint idea of that inferno of noise, powder, smoke, sweat, blood, filth and stink surrounding the crews of the 17th and 18th century, which nevertheless has formed the basis for more Technicoloured sea movies from Hollywood than any other period.

The "Battle" of Trafalgar at Madame Tussaud's, despite sound effects and smell of gunpowder, cannot be anything more than a pale pastiche.

The cannon ball in the Bergen Cathedral belfry will be nothing but an outward memorial. But nevertheless a memorial to give the casual passer-by reason for thought and afterthought.

Trade and Cultural Exchange in the 17th and 18th Centuries

JARLE BJØRKLUND

In times when all heavy and bulky cargoes were shipped by the sea and the waterways, the North Sea was a home basin that linked nations and people together more than it separated them. Through the development of trade, communications and industries in the 17th and 18th centuries, Northern Europe went through an evolution with consequences even for the most remote creeks of the world. A study of the North Sea culture in that era, may thus give us a key to a richer understanding of the present world and explain the feelings of mutual relationship among the coastal inhabitants of the North Sea.

The vessel was a vehicle that represented an important part of the technological basis for a Europe and a world in transition. The ships and their men brought with them not only goods but also new technology and cultural impulses. In the 17th century the shifting of the economical and cultural gravity centre from Southern to Northern Europe was finally completed. The new metropolises grew up around the estuaries of the big rivers: The Rhine, The Maas, The Schelde, The Ems, The Weser, The Elbe and The Thames. The towns expanded to such a degree that the near hinterland could no longer satisfy the demands for food, building-materials etc. A more efficient and firmly organized handicraft needed raw materials of such types and in such quantities that they had to be carried from far away.

The expansion in the urban societies was partly due to the dynamics caused by increase in population as well as the development in communications and technology. But it was also caused by a determined policy from the authorities to create prosperous centres where commerce and industries should enrich the nations, increase the self-sufficiency and the independence of other countries.

The measures were simple: commerce, shipping, handicraft and industries became privileged occupations i.e. they could only be exercised by royal permission and by citizens of a town. Non-desirable activities and trades were suppressed by prohibitions, taxes and duties.

The town and the citizen became increasingly important within the state. The medieval town was no longer adequate. The town-walls limited the expansion. Houses and streets were too small and too narrow. Many of the medieval harbours were situated too far up the rivers and waterways to allow bigger and more draughty vessels to enter. The medieval towns were also vulnerable to fire. Renewal and expansion demanded large quantities of building materials: stone, bricks, tiles and timber. The woods were, in the most expansive areas, rapidly cut down. Accordingly people from the southern and western shores of the North Sea sailed north and east for more timber.

The growing prosperity in the Nether-

151

Figure 1. "Perlen". Part of the brick-cargo. "Perlen" (The Pearl) sank in a storm while being unloaded in Trondheim harbour in 1781. Not only the cargo, but the ship's history as well, give us a vivid impression of what trading was like in those days. Her original name was probably "Delemere" of Liverpool. She was seized by the Irish/American/French privateer, Luc Ryan, and his men of the "Le Sans Peur" of Dunkerque. The ship was brought to Bergen where she was declared "a good prize". The cargo and the ship was sold to a merchantman in Trondheim. He ordered the vessel equipped with six cannons, spoons and forks. But the old and leaky ship's dinghy would still have to do for some time. The cargo consisted of: 57 000 bricks, 166 barrels of rye, malt, flour, hops, 2 barrels of French brandy, 6 half cases of tobacco, 4 barrels of coffee, 4 barrels containing fishing nets and 1 barrel of red colour powder. Photo: Odd E. Solheim.

lands and England thus had influence upon Scandinavia and the Baltic.

Materials

In the southern parts of Norway the woods bordered the sea. In almost any bay or creek available timber could be found. As the coast gradually was stripped naked, the vessels sailed deeper into the fjords and higher up the rivers, or timber was floated to the established ports of loading. These ports grew into villages and towns reflecting the prosperous communities on the other side of the sea, and were deeply dependant on their wealth and progress. When Amsterdam and London grew in size, so would Son, Drammen and Arendal. After the great fire of London (1666), the Norwegian bishop, Jens Bircherod, reportedly said that: "Many Norwegians warmed themselves by that fire".

The Norwegian timber was mainly used as building-materials and was of inferior quality. In the Netherlands soft ground was stiffened by rafts of timber. Such timber was also used in the construction of embankments, dikes and canals.

A secure and regular supply of ship-timber was a necessity for the big seafaring nations. When the German woods were cut down, the costly oak was imported from the Baltic and Scandinavia together with pine and spruce for masts and spars. The oak forests were, however, in danger of being too heavily exploited. Already at the end of the 16th century laws against exportation were passed to protect the Norwegian oak. These regulations seem to have been eluded by building vessels in Norway and selling them abroad. Fredrik II consequently prohibited the sale of ships younger than ten years. The rules became even more rigorous in 1603 when the limit was altered to twenty years. The buyers came from both Denmark and the Netherlands, but a large number seem to have been Scots. The Scots generally sailed smaller vessels, thus indicating that these Norwegian built ships were comparatively small.

The Dutch had, in the first half of the 17th century, not only carried timber for their own import. They were also the main freighters of timber for England. The Dutch engagement in the Thirty Years War, however, gave the English an opportunity to carry a larger bulk of their own import themselves. But from 1648 the Dutch tonnage returned in full force and threatened to squeeze out the English from the timber trade. The competition was once again altered in favour of the English when the Navigation Act was passed in 1651. The Dutch were excluded from British import of non-Dutch products and British export to non-Dutch possessions. The need of tonnage was to a large extent satisfied by British ships. But Swedes as well as Norwegians were in principle sailing on the same favourable terms as the British at the expense of the Dutch.

Christiania was the administrative center of Norway. The mercantile importance of the town was, however, more representative of the average coastal town in southern Norway at the time. The fluctuations in the declines and growths of its fleet therefore, show the tendencies in south-east Norwegian trade: The town had throughout the 17th century up to 1690 a fleet of 8–14 ships. The average displacement was steadily growing, but as late as 1690, the total tonnage amounted to only 1000 net. reg.t. divided among 11 ships. Three years later the corresponding figures show that the fleet consisted of 30 ships of about 4000 net. reg.t. in total, and in 1695 the fleet reached a temporary maximum of more than 40 ships, totalling some 8800 net.reg.t. This notable increase seems to have been directly caused by The War of the League of Augsburg (1688–97). The British Admiralty claims that Britain lost about 4000 ships during that war. This figure may be too high, but the losses nevertheless seem to have been heavy enough to cause a growth in the number and tonnage of neutral ships sailing on Britain.

It has frequently been discussed whether these and similar fluctuations in the ton-

Figure 2. Dutch flute, mid-seventeenth century (British Museum).

nage, are real, or, at least to some extent, due to the transfer of ships from countries at war to neutral flags. But such movements were concealed at the time and are of course even more difficult to trace 300 years later.

Of equal strategic importance to the great seapowers as timber were materials used in maintaining and equipping the ships, such as tar, glue, hemp and flax. In the early 17th century Sweden was an important manufacturer of glue and tar. Although the value of these products was later superseded by the increase in the export of iron, Sweden remained one of the major deliverers of ship's supplies.

Such products could also be bought from Archangel. The White Sea trade was opened by English merchants in 1553. Before 1703 Russia had no access to the Baltic.

Through Archangel some Asian merchandise was exported. The English were soon challenged by the Dutch, partly because the mismanagement of the trade by the Muscovy Company. The English trade prospered after the repeal of the monopoly in 1698. This almost coincided with Peter the Great's renewals and constructions of the Russian harbours and canals which after 1703 mostly favoured the recently acquired Baltic areas, but still to some extent benefited the northern ports. The Baltic towns flourished. Riga became the largest exporter of hemp. Stettin exported timber and grain, and Danzig obtained the position as Europes main purveyor of grain. Königsberg and Memel were also prosperous ports exporting flax, hemp, grain and timber. The largest quantities of flax were shipped over Narva.

The southern and western shores of the North Sea were producing and exporting all kinds of tiles. These products demanded skilled craftsmen and long tradition. A similar technology was also used in the manufacturing of all types of jars, vessels and pottery that constituted vital parts in the European household. The production of clay-pipes, originally an English innovation, but from 1615 "a typical Dutch" product, was part of the same technology.

Squares and streets were covered with cobbelstones. Large quantities were exported from Germany, particularly from the Rheinland-Pfalz area, and brought to the coast by barges over the waterways.

Grain

In addition to the bulky building materials for towns, castles, palaces and ships, there was an increasing demand for long-distance transportation of food. The towns had become too big to receive adequate supplies from the near hinterland. Grain, the most important nutrition source in Europe, was grown wherever possible. But few nations got crops big enough to be totally self-supplied.

Norway depended on import from Denmark. But in bad years, or during wars threatening the trans-Skagerrak connection these supplies would be insufficient. In Northern Norway these shortages opened up for a new trade emerging at the end of the 16th century: Grain was exchanged for Norwegian fish between Norwegian and Russian fishermen. This so called Pomor trade (pomor: at the sea, Russian fisherman/farmer) was from time to time quite considerable, depending on the variations in the supplies of grain from southern areas, but illegal up to the second half of the 18th century. It conflicted with the Bergen monopoly in the northern trade where salt and grain were exchanged for fish. The monopoly, deriving from the Hansa League, depended on the access to the Baltic for grain supplies. The Hanseatics had made the Baltic trade a cornerstone in their empire. Much of their mercantile structure outlived the league and was further developed in the 17th century, mainly by the Dutch.

154

At the beginning of the 17th century about 12 000 Dutch vessels were engaged in the grain trade on the Baltic. In 1666 75% of the active capital on the Amsterdam Exchange seemed to be engaged in the Baltic trade. And in the first half of the 17th century the Dutch vessels passing The Sound outnumbered the British by 13 to 1. The figures show that despite the ambitious efforts the different governments had made to make their countries self-supplied and independent of other economies, none of them were able to obtain such a position, and some had a very extravert economy. The statistics from The Sound show that in the grain supply the British enjoyed a more favourable position than the Dutch. In the 17th century England had a modest import of grain and in the 18th century England became a grain exporter. From the English East Coast grain was shipped to the Netherlands and in periods also to France. The legal trade to France was brought to an end in 1678, and from 1713 a customs barrier made all legal trading even more impossible. The Dutch domination in the Baltic trade was further developed by exporting Baltic products to the Mediterranean in exchange for salt, wine, spices, oil, dried fruit, cotton, cork etc. But during four years of neutrality from 1674 England secured admittance to the Baltic-Mediterranean trade. Again it is difficult to estimate the number of Dutch vessels flying the British colours in the period. What is certain is that once admitted, the British offered the Dutch more and more competition througout the 18th century.

Fisheries

Fish represented a comparatively cheap part of the European household in a period when only the most wealthy could afford a meal of meat more than once a week.

The Dutch and the British had large seagoing fishing fleets. Pieter de la Court made an estimate that some 450 000 Dutchmen were engaged in fisheries and fish processing in 1680. Although the number must be overrated, a comparison with the 200 000 in agriculture and the 650 000 in other industries nevertheless indicates the importance of the Dutch fisheries. The boats were busses or smacks numbering about 1000 of 48–60 tons. The herring fisheries were the most important, followed by cod. In 1728 200–300 Dutch vessels with a displacement of 40–60 tons were fishing on the Dogger bank. This number was nevertheless said to be lower than the corresponding figures for the second half of the 17th century. In the 18th century the Dutch fisheries were in stagnation and even decline. This was partly due to increased competition from the British, as well as from Denmark and the Austrian Netherlands (Belgium). But one of the main reasons for the Dutch setback seems to have been a lack of labourers in the fishing industries. Europe also received a greater part of its fish for consumption from Norway. Though the Norwegians were exclusively engaged in fisheries on the coast, rich herring influxes, mainly on the western coast, and the Lofoten cod fisheries in Northern Norway, created an export industry as important to western and northern Norway as was the timber trade to the southern and eastern regions. Up to 1816 the Norwegian fish was mainly shipped via Bergen.

The Salt-trade

The North Sea fisheries created a prosperous transit trade with branches to all countries on the European continent, Russia included. For the Dutch, herring was a useful source of payment in the Baltic trade. The development of the salt trade was closely connected to the export of fish. This trade had been one of the cornerstones in the mercantile superiority of the Hansa League. And one reason behind the Dutch success was their introduction of Mediterranean and Biscayan salt as an alternative to the salt from the Lüneberg mines. In the steps of the salt trade, wine and other Mediterranean products became available on the North Sea market.

In the first half of the 18th century, salt from mines in Chesire, gave the British another ace in the mercantile game.

Products of the Arctic Waters

Dutchmen and Scots were not only clever fishermen, they were also pioneers in whaling, sealing and walrus-hunting. Towards the end of the 17th century, 14 000 Dutch seamen and about 260 ships headed for Arctic waters, bringing their prey to Amsterdam for further refining, sale and distribution.

Coal and Metals, the Development of the Mining Industry

Coal was a resource of increasing importance throughout the two centuries. England had a prosperous export already in the beginning of the 17th century. In the first half of the century, however, nearly all coal delivered to the continent was carried by foreign ships, mostly Dutchmen. The Navigation Act of 1651 and the subsequent acquisition of Dutch flutes up to 1674, however, gave England full control over the coal export. The greatest consumers of coal were found on the Continent. Some coal was shipped to Scandinavia, but in smaller quantities per head – due to their use of wood for heating and cooking. Coal and malt provided the English ships with cargoes for the Baltic. From 1740, Cheshire salt was added to the export. But as late as in 1748, more than half of the English ships passed The Sound in ballast. The colliers represented an immense potential of loading capacity. It was hard to provide them with sufficient return cargo. Many of them therefore crossed the North Sea in ballast to load timber back for England. The largest quantities of import in bulk came to England with returning colliers.

Mining expanded rapidly throughout the 17th and 18th century. The greatest efforts were made in the search for precious metals, gold and silver, but the net profit was meagre. Still, copper, pewter and iron were indispensable elements in an accelerating technological development, and investments in mining for such metals proved more successful.

Sweden was the largest provider of iron, which was the country's most valuable export after timber and glue. The Swedes also had rich sources of copper. After 1730, shipments of iron also took place in St. Petersburg. Throughout the 18th century, Russian iron got an increasing share in the English market. In 1750 the import amounted to 15 000 tons. And after The Seven Years War, the English import from Russia surpassed the import from Sweden.

Iron was mostly shipped together with lighter and more bulky goods, and thus used to improve the trim of the vessel. Ballasted ships preferred rentable iron to stone and sand, which was of no value whatsoever. The rates for shipments of iron in such small quantities, however, were low. In the 18th century it became more common to sail with iron only – with a corresponding improvement in freight incomes as a consequence.

Through the expansion of the mining activities at Røros, Norway developed an important export of copper. Trondheim was the main outlet, and most of the copper went to the Danish market. Rich copper mines were also found in Cornwall and German areas. Cornwall had rich pewter-mines as well, and England became the leading manufacturer of pewter articles.

Cloth

Great Britain had a growing production of wool and cloth. Finer linen was made in German areas. Despite the growing competition, Holland, Gent and Brügge were still large manufacturers of cloth.

Overseas Trading and Transit-trades

The traffic on the North Sea was increasingly affected by the trading overseas. Larger merchantmen and men-of-war were crossing the North Sea bound for or returning from more exotic waters. As a consequence a transit-trade with goods from the West-Indies and the Far East made the loading plans of the North Sea traders more complex. Coffee, tea, spices and tobacco added some more strange scents to the ships' ceilings. Thin, transparent and richly ornamented china made domestic products in pewter, copper and clay seem dull and clumsy.

England, France and Holland founded East Indian trading companies in the beginning of the 17th century. Denmark and Sweden followed suit somewhat later in the century. The extent of the Far Eastern trade has been examined. The figures are by necessity approximate, but give an indication of the respective size of the seafaring nations in the trade, throughout the two centuries:

Portugal	1200 sailings
Spain	100
Holland	3750
England	4000
France	650
Denmark	250
Sweden	150
Ostende	100

Italian and German companies made 40 voyages all together. Concerning the English figures, it has to be taken into consideration that the Americans made 4000 sailings, though most of them took place during the latter half of the 18th century.

Through the development of ships and navigation, the basis was laid for a transformation of Europe. Spices, china, coffee and tobacco are already mentioned, and were, in addition to silk, among the more valuable and expensive goods. More bulky cargoes were cotton, sugar and new, exotic kinds of timber.

The picture of the ships' holds became more detailed. In addition to the bulky cargoes, they carried other merchandise in smaller quantities, but often of greater value, such as presents for a broker or a merchant, for their private use or consumption, or in larger quantities for sale. Some marine-archeological excavations in Norwegian waters have revealed some fragments of what was carried across the North Sea under sail 200–400 years ago. (See illustrations.)

Customs accounts and casualty reports add information where the sea and the wood terredo have demolished organic materials. The North Sea trade was constantly growing, in quantity as well as in the number of different types of goods. Despite protectionism international trade developed, making more and more countries dependent on steady supplies by the seaway.

The Sloops of the Peasants and the smaller Merchants

"The old trade", on which the new growth in seafaring and commerce was founded, still lived on. The smaller vessels and their cargo have only been of slight concern to authorities, as the trade was by nature very hard to control. There is therefore little we know about the nature and extent of this trade from the traditional historical

Figure 3. Night pot (pewter). The wreck of an English vessel was found at Bamble (Skarveset) on the south-west side of the entrance to the Oslo fjord. The ship was dated back to about 1630. Among the excavated objects were: about 450 lead seals, most of them wearing the shield of London, stamped "De Londino", showing an angel and the text "Gloria in Exelcis" on the reverse. A second type shows a crowned rose flanked by Scottish thistles and the three plumed feathers of Wales. Other seals were stamped with the Garter, the Hansa eagle adorning the reverse. A final type shows a lamb and the writing "Cloth and Flede". The seals have originally been attached to the roles of woolen cloth which have rapidly been destroyed by the sea. The seals show quantity and weight. The cargo also consisted of objects made of pewter: plates, bowls, cups and pots. Less volumious, but nevertheless giving additional knowledge of the North Sea trade, was the finding of spectacle lenses, spurs and spoons.
Photo: Norwegian Maritime Museum.

sources. We may call it a "rustic trade and seafaring". And it can either be described in very general or very detailed terms. The peasants still sailed their crops to the local market. Sometimes a smaller merchant, often combining his trading with farming, would be the buyer of local products or a negotiator in buying, freighting and selling. The bulk cargoes were fish, grain, timber and, towards the end of the 18th century, potatoes.

The vessels were mainly coasters, but many of them were seaworthy enough to cross the North Sea. Numerous small English vessels sailed to Holland and Hamburg and across the Channel. Norwegian and Danish sloops crossed the Skagerrak bringing grain from Denmark for timber in return. Tjalks and everts sailed the shallow waters of the continental shores, the rivers and the canals. Busses sailed to Norway buying live fish, lobster and eel. The Dutch town Zirickree had almost achieved a monopoly in the lobster trade. Small easy-handled rigs were developed for tacking in narrow waters. The sprit-sail and the gaff-sail were spread from Dutch areas to the other North Sea countries. Leeboards would often replace the keel for sailing in shallow waters. A flat bottom would allow them to land on the shores. They kept the medieval harbours alive, using the old docks and warehouses. And numerous smaller ports and villages were founded on this particular traffic. As they expanded, the villages as well as the local merchants, would often thwart the interests of the merchantmen in the privileged towns, who would appeal to the authorities to have their troublesome competitors supressed.

The extent of this "underground" trade can hardly be measured. It has certainly expanded with the growth in population, industrialism and centralization. Certain conditions give reason to believe that this rustic trade, at least in periods, was booming: Smaller vessels demanded low investments and were therefor available to far more than those involved in "bigger seafaring and trading".

In the 18th century Norwegian laws and regulations must have encouraged the building of smaller vessels. Vessels measuring less than 5 lasts (ca. 10 net. reg.tons) were exempted from the export duties on timber. Excluded was also the deck cargo.

This favoured small, shallow boats with a small deplacement despite the wide deck space.

"Paragraph-ships"

Public regulations also stimulated the construction of ships for special trades. It is easy to understand how weather, wind, cargo and docks have affected the shaping of rigs and hulls. But legal paragraphs, regulations, taxes and duties also contributed to the forming of the 17th and 18th century hull. After a short visit to the steamchest, the oak-planks would be adjusted to the paragraphs.

The rules were altered little by little, following the efforts of merchantmen and shipbuilders to avoid them. It nevertheless seemed to be a hopeless task to make waterproof rules and standards of measurement without establishing a far too expensive control organization.

The duties were mainly based on measurement: the length over all, the displacement and the deck area. The l.o.a. rules favoured hulls with an almost square bow giving loading-capacity in the full length of the ship. Taxations calculated on the deck area gave a minimum of beam at deck level and a maximum towards the waterline. In Norwegian timber export it is estimated that ships of "the new façon", which largely came into service after 1656, would load about 50 lasts more than the measurements indicated.

The Shipowners

The pattern in the ownership of the North Sea fleet varied. The smaller vessels and boats were often owned by only one person, a family or a corporation of farmers. Merchantmen could have one or several vessels. The Dutch were leading in forming trading- and shipping companies. Several merchantmen joined together in a partnership or as shareholders. Overseas seafaring was capital intensive and risky, but it also presented a certain prestige and attracted capital from the upper social classes. The king/queen and the royal family would often be important shareholders.

Through the organization of the owner's interests in partnerships and companies, the risks were dispersed. In a partnership each vessel was, in principle, an independent economical unit. The profit was divided between the partners according to how many parts they owned. Losses were not covered through direct transfers from a more successful ship, but through each shareholder.

Shipping implied a considerable amount of gambling. Privateering, storms, faults in navigation and low freights could give heavy losses. It was therefore generally wealthy people, secured by other incomes, who engaged themselves in shipping. The owners of the Norwegian defension ship "Christiania" were in 1673: The Governor Ulrik Fredrik Gyldenløve and his Second in Command the Viceroy Ove Juel, Judge Niels Tolder, Presiding Magistrate Jørgen Philipsen, millowner Verner Nilsen of Hafslund etc. The ship had 40 shareholders in all. Where their occupation can be documented, it is shown that all of them were high officials or wealthy merchantmen with secure incomes from other enterprises.

Captains and Crew

The captain was, on the smaller vessels in particular, often owner or shareholder. On larger ships he was in general an employee. His tasks, responsibilities and thereby his status, varied. In the British timber trade to Norway he had firm and detailed instructions for the voyage and the buying of cargo. He was, in other words, mainly a navigator. In other trades he was also the

Figure 4. Danish timber barque (Samuel Scott c. 1702–72). A hull adapted to paragraphs and regulations.

merchant responsible for the purchase, the choice of quality and negotiating the freights. Captains sailing overseas had the highest status. That goes for the crew as well – with important reservations: The high mortality due to tropical diseases, did not encourage too many to sign on ships sailing out of the North Sea. But those who came back could easily vaunt their experiences and success among their mates and neighbours.

Whereas the ordinary seaman in the central ports of Europe seems to have belonged to the proletariat, he would in more remote areas and smaller coastal towns, obtain a certain status as a link to the big world outside.

The Vessels

The building and sailing of ships were mainly based on the technology of earlier centuries. But during the 17th and 18th century this technology was further developed. The most notable tendency was the more extensive use of fore-and-aft sails. Paintings of the vessels show that the long yard of the latee'n-sail was reduced to a gaff. The bowsprit was lowered, and around 1700 the small squaresail on the jib-boom was replaced by staysails. Lug-, sprit- and gaffsails became dominant on smaller coasters. Only on boats in western and northern Norway, and some barges sailing the waterways, did the squaresail survive. The schooner rig emerged in the early 18th century.

Larger ships had throughout the late medieval age developed a high and richly decorated poop housing the officers and a more modest forecastle (or fo'c'sle) for the crew. Throughout the 18th century these quarters became lower, gradually approaching the more seaworthy construction of a flushdecker towards the 19th century.

The Dutch were the leading 17th century shipbuilders. The most frequent ship type was the flute. In the 1630-ies, about 70% of all ships passing the Sound, were flutes. In the following decade the percentage had risen to 90. In the 18th century the picture is somewhat more complex. But the brig and the frigate dominated among the bigger merchantmen.

Generally speaking, vessels grew in size during the period. In the early 17th century, merchant ships usually measure 80–150 tons net.reg. with about 100 tons as the average. Towards the Napoleonic Wars the average size of an English ship was 300–350 tons. In some trades, however, the tonnage was quite stable during the two centuries, the Dutch ships being somewhat larger than the British. The British, nevertheless, employed some very large ships in the Baltic. After 1750, British ships for Riga measured about 400–600 tons. In Onega trade, after 1760, ships of 600 and 700 tons were engaged. These were the largest British ships outside the East Indian trade.

In 1640 the average size of the crew manning a flute in the Norwegian timber trade, was 12–14 men. A minimum of four days was needed for the crossing. Loading usually took 6–10 days. Discharge of cargo and preparations for another voyage seldom took more than two months. A ship usually made five voyages a year. The Dutch would spend 7–14 days loading, while the sailing time was about the same as for the English. The ships were normally laid up from December until mid-March. Winter storms made the sailings risky and the Baltic was blocked by ice. During strong winters the Sound would freeze and so would some Norwegian ports. Some ships made a voyage to France and Norway waiting for the Sound to break up.

Navigation

In sailing the North Sea the navigational aids were few. For measuring celestial bodies the cross-staff, the astrolabe and the quadrant were available. In 1590 Davis constructed his backstaff quadrant, but it is doubtful if such instruments were used by North Sea captains. Some of these instruments could also be used in measuring the distance to visible land. But apart from the compass, the lead, telling about seabed conditions as well as the depth, was the most useful instrument.

Maps and coastal descriptions were drawn and improved. Ports and waters frequently visited are very accurately described, whereas more remote areas are drawn with less precision and richer fantasy. Not until the end of the 18th century did the maps reach an accuracy that made a sophisticated navigation possible. In the 18th century text-books in navigation became common. Klaas de Vries book, published by James Loots in 1702, was widely spread and was republished in eleven editions altogether.

Cultural Exchange

The statistics of the two centuries are incomplete, partly because of the insufficient public survey and partly because of lost public archives. Nevertheless, the remaining material, with some restrictions and careful use, give an impression of the extent of the trade in measurable values.

The cultural exchange, on the other hand, can hardly be measured. An account could be made of, for example, how many words of Dutch origin remain in modern Norwegian. But this will not by any means touch the essence of the subject.

Some reflections upon this topic can be made out of studies of domiciliation, migration and the social consequences of trading and seafaring between the nations.

Amsterdam was in the 17th century the most cosmopolitan city in Europe. Accounts for the contracted marriages in 1651–65 show that 50–60% of the grooms were foreigners.

The crew lists from the trading companies around 1700 reveal the nationalities of the seamen as follows.

Among the foreigners

38% came from German North Sea and Baltic areas.
11% from other German speaking areas.
11% from Belgium, Luxembourg and France.
27% from Scandinavia.
13% from other nations.

The fleet in total, was manned by 77% Dutchmen and 23% foreigners.

Figure 5. In March 1726 the "Ackeren-dam", a Dutch East Indian, was in the North Sea bound for the East. She was driven north in a storm and sank outside Rundø, Ålesund. In 1972, divers found large quantities of gold and silver coins. Photo: Norwegian Maritime Museum.

A corresponding tendency towards a rather high percentage of foreigners can be observed in fleets of other North Sea countries as well. Christian IV's demand for a minimum of ⅔ Danish/Norwegian crew on the defension ships, point in the same direction. During the skirmishes between Denmark and Holland about the taxations in the Sound, Christian IV threatened to withdraw all Danish/Norwegian seamen from the Dutch fleet. This was considered as an attempt to paralyze the Dutch seapower.

The national unity was probably stronger among the officers than in the fo'c'sle. But evidence show that Dutch captains were sailing English ships and Swedish officers fought for Denmark/Norway during the Great Nordic War. A parallel can be found ashore where troopers were hired from all over Europe to form the armies.

Numerous examples show that nationalism and the feeling of belonging to a national community hardly existed before the Napoleonic Wars. The seamen seemed to have shared the spirit of the mercenaries, regarding a job for what it was and feeling rather indifferent to the political issues and the national interests.

A Royal Court judge in Christiania described a voyage he made from England to France in 1757: A Dutch flute was captured by a British privateer. The Dutchman was neutral, but had resisted inspection. In the fighting that followed, many were hurt. During the interrogation in Dover it was revealed that both the old captain of the Dutch flute and the young privateer were Norwegians by birth. Being countrymen did not seem to affect them at all. Both acted according to their duties in their present position, even in court.

This story was once published by the Norwegian historian Ludvig Daae in the midst of the strong national sentiments that arose in the 19th century, and was by the author used to exemplify what he calls "denationalisation". The fo'c'sle thus became a focal point of different languages, religions and cultural heritage. Men from all around the North Sea basin had to work out a common terminology sufficiently accurate to handle a ship, eat and spend their leisure-time together. Dutch, in particular, was widely spread in maritime terminology throughout the two centuries.

The bigger mercantile enterprises, both British and Dutch, usually sent commission agents to foreign ports. These local representatives were often a younger member of the owners' family, or an able and trustworthy employee in the firm. Shipbuilders carried their tools and know-how all over Europe. In 1645, the Englishman Jan Robbin was sent to Christiania by Christian IV to build several men-of-war. The Dutchmen Henrik Hybertson and Hein Jacobsson led the building of the Wasa in the 1620-ies etc.

During the 18th century the Dutch faced severe difficulties in getting their fleet manned. Recruiting was tried in other countries during the 17th century. They continued in the 18th century but were met with obstacles from other authorities. When Russia, Sweden and Denmark attempted to build up a stronger seapower, agents from these countries went to Holland to enlist their countrymen (and others) for their navies. Holland thus functioned as an education and training centre for thousands of seamen.

Holland was also invaded by other labour seeking groups. Young girls were employed as housemaids. Many of them married and stayed. Holland tempted with high wages. The Danish girls said they went to Amsterdan "to get paid a 100 fl. per year". The immigration had a complex background. Some would escape the law or the military service, but most of them came over because the possibilities at home were limited. The immigrants tried to get assimilated as soon as possible. Their names as well as their costumes and habits were adapted to Dutch usage. They seldom brought any big treasures back, but some pieces of furniture etc. crossed the North Sea.

It was mainly in the way they talked and dressed that the "Dutch" revealed their background. Contemporary sources usually underline that "Dutch" areas in Norway imported new usages and costumes. A particular Dutch virtue imported to Norway in those years, was improved propriety and cleanliness in the homes. Families of the upper classes therefore preferred maids who had been in Holland and learned more urban behaviour. Anders Eckstorm describes the repatriated mariners and maids in the autobiography of 1792: "After some years passing, some will return entirely Dutch, wearing lots of trousers in layers, one outside the other, with golden buttons on the sleeve and the collar, quite alien to their mother tongue and always stammering their "... en". Likewise the girls, these are then called Dutchwomen and expose themselves among the simple and unexperienced girls in a strange way – by their extremely long jackets, peculiar headcovering and some by wearing small sunhats".

When the Dutch culture in particular, was so widely spread it was obviously a consequence of the dynamics of the Dutch enterprises, but also due to a general admiration of the Dutch society at the time. The suppression of the noble class and the undisputed success of the bourgeoisie in governing and developing the most flourishing nation in Europe, caused merchants all around the North Sea to look to Holland in enthusiasm. This favoured a swift spread of at least the outer characteristics of the Dutch bourgeoise culture.

England was in a more favourable position than Holland regarding the labour market and the possibilities of manning their fleet. A general lack of seamen in the leading ports of northern Europe gave rise to a number of boardingmasters and zielverkoopers making a living of recruiting seamen – not always by means and methods too partial to human values.

Throughout the 17th century the British had been buyers of Dutch know-how. In the 18th century the situation was reversed.

Figure 6. Stone for the mashing of yams and weights for measuring the rations of food. (From the Fredensborg).

The "Fredensborg" belonged to the Danish/ Norwegian West Indian Company. The ship had two legs of her triangle run from Copenhagen via West Africa, to the West Indies, delivering her cargo of African slaves. She was homeward bound with exotic timber and elephants tusks, when she was wrecked off Arendal, Norway in 1768.
Photo: Norwegian Maritime Museum.

Great Britain, as the leading seafaring nation, had a considerable influence on the North Sea seafaring and commerce. Being more or less self-supplied with seamen, the cultural influence from the British Isles was relatively smaller than the Dutch. The influence had also a somewhat different character. Young men and women were sent to England to learn business and manners, but these mainly came from the upper classes.

The buying and exchange of expertise was not limited to commerce and seafaring. A similar process took place in handicraft and industries. It has already been pointed out that the manufacturing of clay-pipes was an English invention, which by the import of English expertise became a popu-lar and widespread Dutch export article. In 1760 the import of glass to Norway/Denmark was prohibited. A few years earlier, English glassworkers had established themselves at Nøstetangen, Norway, encouraged by the Danish/Norwegian government. Because such a large part of the industries were controlled centrally, the governments played a very active role in what we nowadays call "head-hunting". Apart from the commercial benefits of such activities, the exchange of experts within different industries stimulated the development of a common taste and a common way of thinking around the North Sea Basin.

The long days of demurrage also contributed to the cultural exchange. The ships were tied up in the harbours for weeks, loading and unloading. Besides, numerous unexpected delays in foreign ports were caused by stormy weather and subsequent repairs. In sheltered ports near dangerous waters, repair yards were established. Crews of different nations worked and spent their time of leisure together. Some married local women and stayed. Cases of bigamy were frequent. One of the owners of a repair yard at Gismerøya, nearby the Naze, seems to have been a genuine son of the North Sea culture. Some of his correspondence has in recent years passed from embassy to embassy in Oslo. Everyone has been able to translate some of his writing, but none can understand it all. Dutch, German, English and Norwegian words float together in a primitive commercial terminology that nevertheless must have been good enough in the late 18th century.

The commercial language was, for obvious reasons, influenced by the leading mercantile nations.

The seamen's language is another example of how words and expressions from different languages have been spread around from a common heritage in a North Sea Culture. Scandinavia had a wide influence on the maritime terminology in the Viking period. German and Dutch became dominant in the following centuries, and

English words were adapted increasingly following the growth in the British sea-power. An illustrating example of this tendency is the word "matros". The origin of the word is found in old Norwegian "matunautr". The first syllable means "food" and the latter "man". The word meant a companion onboard with whom the food was shared. The English version became "mate", the French "matelot" and the Dutch "matroos". In the meanwhile the word went out of use in Norway and was reimported from Holland when the Dutch became dominant in the forming of the North Sea maritime culture.

When some of the old Norwegian tars were severely scolded by their wives and daughters for speaking Dutch, this was due to the fact that the use of this language was very often accompanied by a bottle of "rheumatic liniment" or vice versa. Stories from the good old days would be told, disguised from the women's ears, but the fat grins and the twinkle in their eyes would unveil the sinful old greybeards.

The hunting-falcon on the nobleman's left hand and the marten-skin over his shoulders were exchanged for Acanthus and Ionian columns for Norwegian handicraft. Flowers at Fredrikstad and Drammen kept company with herbs from more exotic areas, transplanted by the vessels' ballast. In constant wrestling with local traditions, impulses from abroad could get rooted in different environments and under varying conditions of growth. People around the North Sea, chewing and smoking tobacco, sipping tea and coffee, had one thing in common – no one stayed unaffected by the trading and seafaring of the time.

Bibliography

Asaert, G., Bosscher, Ph. M.,Bruijn, J.R., Hoboken, W.J. van, *Maritieme geschiedenis der Nederlanden De Boer Maritiem.* Bussum 1977

Boxer, C.R.,*The Dutch Seaborne Empire 1600–1800,* Hutchinson of London 1965, 1966, 1972, 1977

Brochmann, Diderik, *Fagprat mellom sjøfolk,* Oslo 1935

Daae, Ludvig, *Nordmænds Udvandringer til Holland og England,* Christiania 1880

Davies, Ralph, *The Rise of the English Shipping Industry In the 17th and 18th Centuries,* David & Charles: Newton Abbot 1962, 1972

Jørgensen, Dagny, *Danmark-Norge mellom stormaktene 1688–1697,* Oslo, Bergen, Tromsø 1976

Kent, H.S., *War and Trade in the Northern Seas. Anglo-Scandinavian economic relations in the mid-eighteenth century,* Cambridge University Press 1973

Picard, R., Kerneis, J.P., Bruneau, Y., *Les Compagnies des Indes, Route de la porcelaine.* Arthaud 1966

Schreiner, J., *Nederland og Norge 1625–1650,* Oslo 1933

Shipbuilding in the 17th and 18th Centuries

The Wasa as a Product of Dutch Shipbuilding

CARL OLOF CEDERLUND

The North Sea area has been a central area for the development of shipbuilding and seafaring since the late iron age and has had a strong influence on other areas in this respect.

Three centres of development can be discerned on the shores of the North Sea: in the North the western parts of Scandinavia played an important role, especially during the late iron age and the beginning of the medieval period; the coast of the continent, Friesland, and later the Netherlands; and the British Isles.

In the postmedieval period it was especially the Dutch and the British shipbuilding centres which dominated the scene. During long periods they also competed with each other. The shipbuilding traditions from these centres spread all over western and northern Europe as well as to other continents.

What were the reasons for and conditions favouring this dominating influence coming from the area around the North-Sea? Which economic needs, cultural forces or groups of people in these societies stood behind it and how did the cultural process in question develop?

Here a short description will be given of a few traits within one area – the Dutch – of this development, with a few examples of its influence outside the North Sea area. An extraordinary opportunity has been given to record and study one of the products of the North Sea shipbuilding tradition in detail, namely the Wasa. The Wasa, built in Stockholm on the Baltic Sea in the 1620s, will be the main illustration of this paper, and special considerations concerning the treatment of it will also be included, in order to clarify the documentation and interpretation process.

Dutch Shipbuilding and its Development

Several historians have pointed out that the development of the Dutch society of the postmedieval period was to a high degree linked to the development of shipping and export trade. And that the backbone of this economic structure was a strong technical tradition – shipbuilding.

Dutch shipbuilding started as the building of local craft in the countryside – along rivers and along the shore of the North Sea. In the 15th century a concentration of this manufacturing in the towns took place. Just as in the Hanseatic League not so much earlier, this concentration of technical and economic resources enabled the building of bigger and more advanced ships to take place. During the 16th century a competition started between the towns and the countryside for this trade. As early as about

1480 the Dutch had also founded a foreign market for their shipbuilding, in Brabant.

During the 17th century two important shipbuilding areas developed in the Netherlands. One was Amsterdam, the other one the shores of the river Zaan. At Zaanstreek were built big seagoing merchantships, which were bought by townspeople and foreigners. The other area, Amsterdam, can, as well as Rotterdam, be said to have taken the place of Zaanstreek as it began to lose its importance around 1700.

During the 17th century the VOC started their own dockyards for their own needs. The admiralties, especially in the 18th century, started to build their own ships. All the same, shipbuilding as a private enterprise predominated during the whole period. This is an essential fact in this context. So is the fact that about 50 percent of the production of ships was exported.

Dutch shipbuilding of the 15th and 16th centuries made no revolutionary changes. There were small changes, step by step, resulting in a rationalized and augmented production. The development was based on a keen observation of the development in other areas and on the borrowing of useful ideas. The important step forward was the type of freightships developed during the 16th century, which were more efficient and less expensive than others. Examples of these were the *buyscarvel,* the *bojer,* the *vlieboot* and the *fluit.*

The first innovation was the *fishingbuss* at the end of the medieval period – giving the Dutch control of the herring market in the North Sea in the 15th century. A second very important innovation was the *fluit* at the end of the 16th century. During the two following centuries very few great innovations were made. Instead the existing types were refined and modified.

The continuity and the steady technical development of Dutch shipbuilding made it a reliable and strong instrument for the shipowners and merchantmen using it, and thus strengthened their position. It also meant that the possibilities of exporting both ships and technical innovations in the ships increased. This situation also gave the builders and their products goodwill all over Europe, not only because of the low prices but also because of a technical superiority.

The high level of production meant many buyers and low building costs. Dutch ships were more lightly built than others and thus had a shorter lifetime. These conditions meant *lower prices – about 40 percent lower than others.*

From about 1610 Dutch shipbuilding declined partly because of changing trading patterns. From about 1630 the shipbuilding technique in the Netherlands slowed down in its development in relation to other countries, especially concerning big ships. Smaller types of ships, on the other hand, continued to change and develop.

For Dutch shipbuilding the small ships used for transport within the country were the testing grounds. New ideas could be tested on them and later, if successful, be transferred to bigger ships. This shipbuilding on a small scale was not so costly and allowed empirical experiments. The aim was to reach a high degree of manoeuvrability and such technical arrangement as would enable the crew to be kept to a minimum.

During the 18th century Dutch shipbuilding went through a marked decline, one of the reasons for this being the economic and technical competition from other countries. The dominance within shipbuilding development and seafaring tended to lie in England and France instead. Another reason, and the most important one, was the fact that the Dutch shipwrights did not succeed in maintaining their technical superiority, especially in relation to England (references for this part: R.W. Unger 1978 and E. Hornborg 1948).

The Spreading of Dutch Shipbuilding Tradition

The era of prosperity of Dutch shipping and shipbuilding had an immense influence on the other countries in Europe. Nearly everywhere within the realm of maritime history and marine archaeology one can discern traits or conditions which have a Dutch origin or have been influenced from the Netherlands. This vast subject has not hitherto, as far as I know, been studied systematically and as a whole, although its economic, technical and social nature is of great importance for the history of Europe.

Here a very short and very preliminary sketch will be drawn of the different kinds of cultural influence discernible in the situation mentioned. It will not be an analysis but just an attempt to throw light on the types of transference which were most prevalent. In connection with this a few examples will be given. A sketch of the said character could be drawn as follows: Dutch influence on European shipbuilding in the 17th and 18th centuries was transferred by:

A. The diffusion of ships built in the Netherlands by
A1. the selling of them to other countries or by
A2. the taking of prizes in connection with war or privateering.
B. The transferring of the shipbuilding tradition itself to other countries by
B1. the experiences brought home by shipwrights going to work at Dutch shipyards for a time or by
B2. the summoning of Dutch shipbuilders to other countries in order to use their skill in the work at the wharfs and also to spread their know-how to the local craftsmen.
B3. The distribution of manuals on the art of shipbuilding, or by the handing over of models or plans of ships' constructions to craftsmen in other countries.

All of these different kinds of influence or cultural contacts have existed, but their importance in relation to each other is not clear. As has been mentioned, a large number of ships were sold abroad (A1) from the Netherlands. These were not only used through their construction and as models. Ships were ordered by foreigners in the Netherlands or sold by the Dutch on speculation. Both merchantships and warships were exported, the former to private merchants, the latter to states. Examples of the latter were the warships ordered by the Duc de Guise in 1626 and delivered to France in 1629 (Hafström 1968, pp. 45 f). The fluit was a type of ship that was exported on a large scale. This freightship became one of the most common types in Europe in the period in question, as ships bought from the Netherlands were copied in their new home countries.

Ships were very often commandeered during the wars at sea at this period (A2). The prizes were enrolled in the navy of the commandeering country or used as merchant ships, and one could take advantage of a prize with a good construction by copying it. The same situation, but on a smaller scale, was prevalent in connection with the very common privateering activities on the coasts of Europe.

The other main way of spreading the knowledge of shipbuilding was by the experience of the shipbuilders themselves. This transference was performed partly within the Netherlands through the experience gained by foreign shipwrights at Dutch shipyards (B1). Perhaps the most famous example of this is the apprenticeship of Peter the Great at Dutch shipbuilding centres, where he studied the building technique, bought tools and equipment, and enrolled many shipwrights and master shipwrights for work in Russia. Another conspicuous journey to the Netherlands with a similar purpose was that of the Frenchman Arnould, who in 1670 studied and described Dutch and also English shipbuilding on behalf of Colbert. His report to his employer is today a very valuable historical source of information on shipbuilding in the 17th century (Hasslöf 1970, pp. 60 f).

The different seapowers, or potential seapowers, also worked actively to attract experienced shipbuilders from the Netherlands to their countries in order to establish a high technical tradition. Shipwrights also went from the Netherlands to other countries of their own accord. Both navy shipyards and private ones opened their gates to these craftsmen (Unger 1978, p. 81).

The most well-known project of transferring craftsmen from the Netherlands was probably the hiring of shipbuilders to establish a Russian navy and merchant marine at the beginning of the 18th century. The Russians had had very little access to the sea earlier and thus had had little reason to evolve a shipbuilding technique for sea-going vessels. On the other hand, they had a longstanding tradition of building vessels for transport on rivers and lakes – the main trading routes within the country. With the assistance of the specialists from Western Europe, the Russians produced a navy that became both effective and forceful during the 18th century.

The Swedish state, at the beginning of the 17th century, also took an interest in Dutch shipbuilding for its own navy. A third way of transferring the knowledge of shipbuilding must to a certain degree have been the printing and selling of books or manuals on the subject (B3). Perhaps also the contents of models and plans of Dutch ships found their way out of the country.

Learned works on the subject, still well known and used for historical reasons, were e.g. Witzen's "Aeloude en Hedendaegse Scheepsbouw en Bestier" printed for the first time in 1671 or van Ijk's "De Nederlandsche Scheeps-Bouw-Konst Open Gestelt" from 1697. Such manuals found followers in other countries e.g. in Sweden where Åke Classon Rålamb in 1691 published a treatise on Swedish shipbuilding in

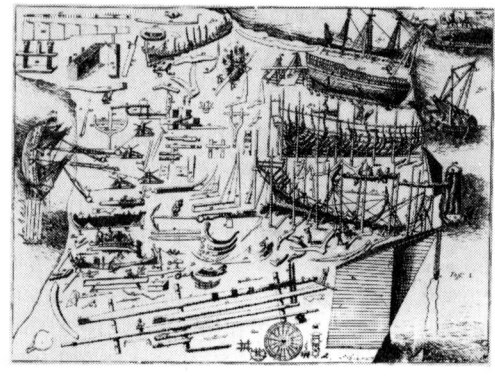

Figure 1. One illustration in the manual on shipbuilding from 1691, by Åke Clason Rålamb, the "Skeppsbyggerij eller Adelig Öfnings Tionde Tom" shows "a complete dockyard" with a large amount of working techniques and tools illustrated.

which a strong Dutch influence can easily be discerned (Rålamb 1691, e.g. Tafel I). Dutch ship types are depicted and working methods from the same country are described.

In conclusion one may say that the deciding factors for diffusion of Dutch shipbuilding in Europe were evidently not the bearers of the tradition itself but the forces engaged in trade and war. The economic and political powers had a great need of effective merchantships that were not expensive to run and of good men-of-war, products which the Netherlands could build and sell. It was to a high degree on the initiative of states and private enterprises that the knowledge of Dutch shipbuilding was in different ways brought to other countries and thus spread widely around.

170

An Example of Dutch Influence on Swedish Shipbuilding – the Warship Wasa

The process described above can be exemplified by rich historical and marine archaeological material from several countries. One such source affords an exceptionally good basis for the study of Dutch shipbuilding technique and the historical development which led to this acculturation. The case is the Wasa – the Swedish warship from the early 17th century which has been preserved nearly intact until our time.

A discussion of this find will fill the remaining pages of this paper – in order to give a detailed example – with the emphasis on the origin of the construction of the ship and also on how to record and thus collect data of the construction of the ship in question.

When the Wasa was salvaged in Stockholm harbour in 1961, it soon became a sort of symbol of the possibilities of marine archaeology in the Baltic. Because of the special conditions in this sea the ship was very well preserved after 333 years at the bottom, and she also still contained thousands of artifacts from the equipment of the ship and of the belongings of the crew.

The reason for the raising of the ship was certainly that one had located a very big, intact wreck of a Swedish man-of-war from the beginning of the 17th century. This unique find gave an extremely good opportunity for the public to look into the past. The Wasa can be said to constitute a kind of shaft down the centuries through which it is possible to study and register very interesting facets of life of that time. The ship was seen as a very rich source of historical information of different kinds. It is also probable that national feelings were involved in this find from one of the great periods in the history of Sweden.

The time since the raising has been dominated by very important, practical questions concerning the ship. Such questions are the preservation, the restoration, and the planning of a permanent museum. Several extensive scientific investigations have also been performed. Examples of these are C.O. Cederlund, *Stockholms skeppsgård 1605–1640. Personalens struktur och organisation*. Statens sjöhistoriska museum 1966; S. Bengtsson, The sails of the Wasa; unfolding, identification and preservation. *International Journal of Nautical Archaeology* 1975:1; H. Soop, *Regalskeppet Wasa. Skulpturer*. Stockholm 1978 (this publication will be followed by complete reports on the sculptural material from the ship).

All the same it is very easy to see the general aim of the project. It is primarily the exhibiting of the big ship to the general public in a preserved and restored state, and also the treatment and exhibiting of the many artifacts found on board.

If the conditions of the project had been different, the ship would probably have been treated in another way. If it had been realized at an early stage that it would have been impossible to preserve the ship and its contents for the future, it would have been necessary to make the recording and the scientific study the most important part of the work. The reason for this of course would have been to save information otherwise lost. That kind of procedure is rather common for other old wrecks – which for economic or other reasons cannot be saved in the same way.

In connection with the planning for and the establishing of the ship in a permanent museum the plans of a final, systematical recording have been worked out. In this situation, especially one important question has been discussed: what principles should be applied to the recording and the researching of such a structure as the Wasa. The answer to this question is, of course, important both for the understanding of and the presentation of the ship.

The Dutch Heritage of the Wasa

For the understanding of the construction of the Wasa two items are of primary interest: the access to the historical material giving information of the circumstances under which the ship was built and, secondly, the detailed recording of the construction.

Very little is known *in detail* about shipbuilding techniques in Sweden at the beginning of the 17th century. Only exceptionally do the archives give information that clarifies the practical methods and principles applied in this technical tradition. Some pictorial and archive evidence does exist, as well as models. Also a few, big wrecks from the period are known. But they have not been studied thoroughly in this respect.

According to the information in Swedish archives, the nationality of most of the master shipwrights and shipwrights employed in the dockyards of the Swedish navy at the end of the 16th century were, as far as their names indicate, Swedish. Of course it is not possible to say anything about the training they had received whether it had been of Swedish origin or whether they had been abroad or had learned from immigrants at home.

In the year 1600 a Dutch master shipwright was working at the naval dockyard at Stegeborg. His name was Isbrant Johansson. With him worked seven Dutch shipwrights. Between 1600 and 1605 another Dutch master shipwright was engaged by Karl IX, the Swedish king. The shipwright's name was Henrik Hybertsson. He was twenty years later to become responsible for the building of the Wasa.

Karl IX was succeeded by his son Gustav II Adolf in 1611. The efforts of the latter to strengthen the Swedish navy are evident from the records of the wages of the shipwrights and others at the naval shipyard in Stockholm during the following years. Between 1611 and 1620 their number grew steadily. At the same time the two Dutch master shipwrights just mentioned were appointed to leading positions in the shipbuilding of the Swedish navy. Most of the other master shipwrights were Swedish, according to their names, although it might be possible to discern one German and one Scot.

It is of course very difficult to say anything of the origin of the technical traditions carried on by these people. Anyway, it seems clear that the two Dutchmen in their leading positions must have been able to exert an influence on naval shipbuilding.

At the beginning of the 1620s naval shipbuilding was reorganized and strengthened. At that time Henrik Hybertsson gained a very independent position as one of the leaders of the naval dockyard in Stockholm – a few years later together with his brother Arendt de Groote, who was a merchant.

One of the results of this situation might have been that three master shipwrights were brought in from the Netherlands. One of them was Henrik Jacobsson, who a few years later was going to lead the practical work on the Wasa.

The main body of shipwrights in the 1620s were Swedish, but successively Henrik Hybertsson and Arendt de Groote hired Dutch ones. Their number is unknown, but it must have been considerable.

It is thus possible to state that the master shipwright who was responsible to the king for the building of the Wasa and who evidently projected the ship was a Dutchman, and that several Dutch shipwrights took part in the job together with the Swedish ones (Cederlund 1966). The Dutch had also had the opportunity to influence the Swedish craftsmen for about twenty years previously.

Other kinds of research confirm that. Schoerner has shown that the shape of the midship bend of the Wasa conforms entirely with Dutch practice, as does the hull form in other respects (Schoerner 1964).

It is also evident from the minutes of the investigation after the sinking of the Wasa that the building of it was influenced by a big warship that was being built for France in the Netherlands at nearly the same time. Arendt de Groote had seen this ship himself. It has been discussed how and to what extent the material he evidently brought home concerning this ship did influence the construction of the Wasa (Hafström 1968, Landström 1980 and Sandström 1984).

What we will be able to confirm in the future, in connection with the recording of the ship, is, among other things, how far this Dutch influence went as regards the Wasa, and whether it is possible to define traits in the construction which also might be of other origin, i.e. Swedish origin.

The Principles of the Recording of the Ship Construction of the Wasa

Today – in 1984 – the hull of the Wasa is restored to such a degree that few parts of the construction are unidentified. From being a wreck she has been made into a 17th century man-of-war again, by systematical restoration.

The recording of the Wasa was started quite soon after the raising. The ship is today probably more extensively recorded than any other marine archaeological find, although quite a lot of work still remains to be done. The plans that already exist number more than a thousand and the photographs several thousands.

Returning to the question put forward above, concerning the general aims of the recording of the ship as a whole, one can see that it is possible to divide it into two problems or questions: Is there any one aim concerning the recording which is more important than the others? What aims of the recording can be discerned besides such a main objective?

In the case of the Wasa one can carry out a recording for several purposes. One can

record her from the point of view of the model builder, which has already been done. One can record the shape, size, weight, etc in plans and data in order to calculate the qualities of the hull and the ship as a whole from the point of view of the ship technician; this has also been done in some essential respects. One can record the construction of the different part of the ship in order to give an interpretation of the original building principles and techniques. Such documentation will also form an important comparative material in relation to other ship finds from the same period. Some work has been done concerning this part of the job. One can, as a last example, record the ship and its sculptures from the point of view of the art historian. Here an extensive work has been done by Hans Soop (Soop 1978). All these examples imply different means of recording and different kinds of results.

The ship constitutes one of the biggest marine archaeological projects ever. A very great amount of money and work, relatively speaking, has been put into the preservation and exhibition. It is in such a situation a primary and natural reaction to protect both the historical values of this object and also the investments put into it.

The Wasa, together with a few other ship finds from earlier times, belongs to a certain kind of ship find – the well-preserved ship which is put on exhibition. It is not possible to insure such an old object and the historical value of it, so as to be able to buy an identical one if it is destroyed. What one often does instead is to reproduce the object as thoroughly as possible to preserve the knowledge of it.

The primary aim of the recording of the Wasa should then be to preserve the knowledge of it for the future, if the ship for some reason deteriorates or is destroyed. The aim of a recording to prevent serious losses in such a situation should be to collect such information as would make it possible to reproduce the ship in plans and drawings or, if necessary, *to rebuild it in full or on a smaller scale.* Such a documentation would also serve as an excellent basis for the interpretation of the ship and its construction from the historical point of view.

Some "secondary aims" of the recording have been mentioned above. There are other ones too. As has been said, they differ in character and need different kinds of recording. Some of these aims have been fulfilled. It is possibly not necessary to try to carry out all sorts of registration within the frame of a program of systematical research. The economic conditions will not permit that anyway. It will thus be necessary to evaluate and put those tasks first which are considered most important next to the primary one. Examples of such aims could be the recording from the point of view of the shipbuilding historians who want to analyse the many elements of the structure or the recording to serve the investigation of other wrecks with comparative material.

As regards the final shape or set-up of the documentation of the ship, it might be valuable to point to the construction plans for the building of ships during the 19th and 20th centuries, which have a high degree of completion and are also very logically structured. It can be very convenient to base the recording on this system of plans, from the head plans to the details, and, when it is necessary, add special documentation.

Some main Characteristics of the Construction of the Wasa

The recording of the Wasa began when she was still resting at the bottom of the Stockholm harbour. One example from 1957 shows how much information it was possible to collect in the black and muddy water with the aid of the divers and their measuring work (Fig. 2). This plan and

other similar ones sought to provide a basis for the calculations and the planning of the salvage. But it of course also gave a concept of the man-of-war from 300 years ago.

During the excavation after the salvaging in 1961 a recording started which also involved the construction of the ship. The decks were drawn in horizontal plans and perspective drawings to give the location of loose finds of different kinds (Fig. 3 and 4).

Between 1963 and 1967 the divings at the wreck-site were continued in order to take care of the loose parts of the hull remaining there. Several thousands were salvaged during these years. These and other pieces were stored and classified and then preserved. This work was one of the conditions for a successful performing of the complicated rebuilding of the hull.

During the raising of loose pieces from the wreck-site a recording was performed which aimed at the documentation of the individual pieces from the stern castle mainly. A special measuring bench was constructed in which each piece was placed and measured. The result was detailed projection plans of each piece, containing all visible elements of construction, even marks from nails. About a thousand plans

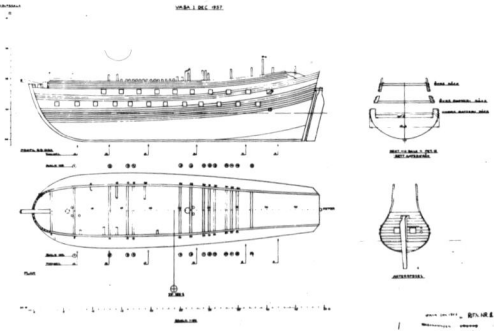

Figure 2. An underwater drawing made of the Wasa in 1957. This plan and other similar ones were made to give a basis for the calculations and the planning of the salvage.

174

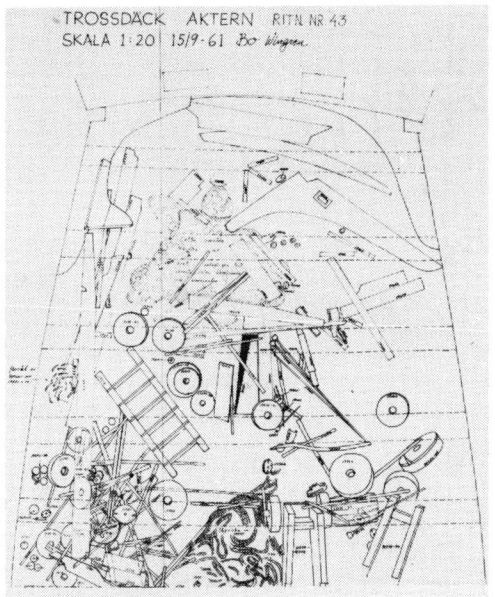

Figures 3 and 4. Examples of vertical plan and perspective drawings made to record the contents of the Wasa during the excavation and after the salvage.

were drawn and classified. They have served as a source of information concerning the restoration work on the stern and stern castle.

The rebuilding of the ship has been going on since the 1960s. The most important role in this work has been played by a group of shipwrights, who with great skill have solved the reconstruction problems and put the loose pieces back in their original places, down to the interior decoration in the cabins.

As soon as a secure system of reference for the measuring could be established within the building in which Wasa is situated, the making of plans of the ship in a systematical way was started – in the early 1960s.

Besides the evidence referred to above and in the list of literature, little work has hitherto been published on the analysis of the ship construction of the Wasa. To give a comprehensive description of the building and the structure of the ship today one may refer to the set of model building plans published by the Swedish National Museum and to Björn Landström's pub-

lication presenting his view of the building and the structure of the ship (see the list of literature). The plans of the ship enable one to study the characteristics of the ship in detail. Here a few of the plans of the Wasa will be presented with short commentaries:

The sheer (Fig. 5) shows the hull with the lower masts and the bowsprit mounted. The length from the sternpost to the outer end of the heads is 61 m and the length-breadth ratio of the hull is 1:4,28. The sternpost is straight, the stem curved. The ship has a flat stern. The draught is 4,8 m.

The hull has as many as eight wales, four under the lower gun deck, at the water line, two under the upper gun deck and upper deck, respectively.

Along each side of the stern castle two long galleries have been built in the Dutch way, which are covered with planking and have small cupolas at each end (Schoerner 1964, pp. 57 f). About half a metre above the bulwark the railing on which the waist cloth was to be fastened can be seen.

The profile (Fig. 6) illustrates the position and construction of the different decks

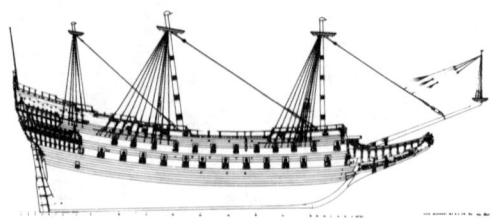

Figure 5. A perspective drawing of the Wasa with the lower masts and the bowsprit mounted.

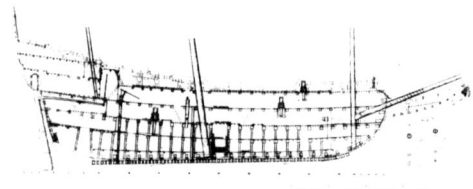

Figure 6. The profile illustrates the position and construction of the different decks as well as the position of the masts and the bowsprit.

as well as the position of the masts and bowsprit. It can also be seen that the keel has been put together in four pieces.

The ship has two gun decks below the upper deck, and below the former an orlop or between deck and the hold. On the level of the upper deck the stern castle contains the cabin and the room for the manoeuvring of the whipstaff. Above this cabin is the poop and in the top the top gallant poop. Stern galleries have been built into the cabin and the poop. On the upper gun deck, on the fore side of the bulkheads in front of the whipstaff, a pump with an aspiring tube of alder is placed, and just astern of the main mast a pump with aspiring tubes of lead is situated.

The galley has been erected in the hold just in front of the foot of the main mast. It is constructed as a brick hearth with walls of bricks to the stem and the stern. A big cauldron of cast iron, originally hanging over the hearth, was found in the galley.

On the upper deck and the two gun decks capstans are placed for the weighing of the anchors and for the manoeuvring of the sails. The bits for the anchor cable are on the lower gun deck.

In the cross-section (Fig. 7) the construction of the lower part of the hull is clearly visible. On the inner planking and the keelson rest riders. Under the thick stuff and ceiling placed about the floorheads rests the first futtock. On both sides of the deck beams one rider is fastened, which

ends at the lower gun deck. At every other beam one rider ends at the upper gun deck (which can also be seen in Fig. 6).

This ship's sides are built in carvel technique with one layer of boarding planks and one of inner planking. The lines plan (Fig. 8) gives the impression of a hull with a relatively flat bottom and a rather small volume in the lower part of the hull. The former circumstance might be compared with the flat-bottomed ships of the Dutch; the latter must have lessened the possibilities of taking ballast onboard and thus diminished the stability of the ship.

In the deck plans (Fig. 9 and 10) one can see that between the upper deck and the upper and lower gun decks there are grat-

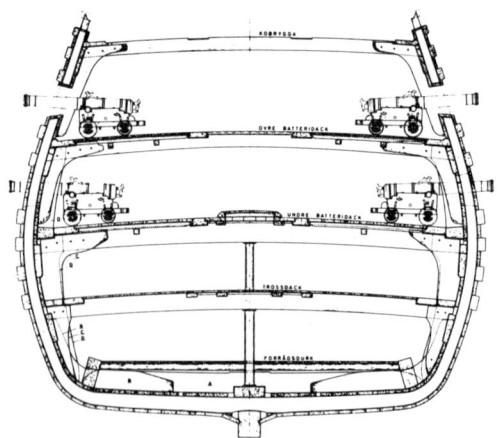

Figure 7. A cross-section.

176

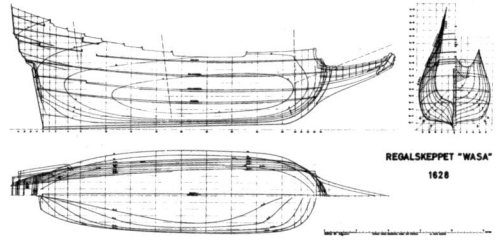

Figure 8. A lines plan.

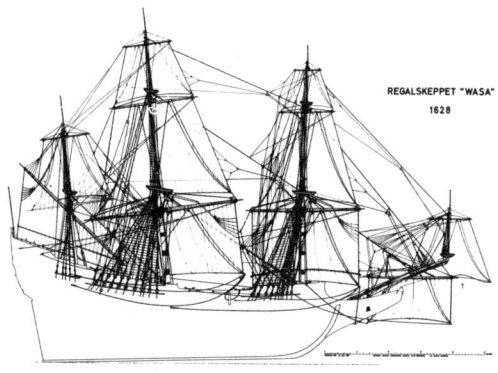

Figure 11. A profile showing the Wasa from keel to masthead.

ings for the entrance of light and fresh air. The hatchways leading to the orlop deck, on the other hand, have lids. The cross-sections of the sterncastle show that the planking on its sides was clinched, according to the Dutch manner. The total height of the hull and the main mast was, according to the reconstruction, 52,5 m (Fig. 11). The ship was fully rigged with three masts, three square sails on the main- and fore-masts, and a lateen- and a topsail on the mizzenmast. On the bowsprit have been arranged one spritsail and one sprit-topsail according to the rigging system of the time for bigger ships.

The Wasa seems to have had a relatively high rigging, at least in comparison with merchantmen of bigger size, and thus probably also a relatively large sails' area.

The heavy construction of the lower part of the stern (Fig. 12) consists of thick timbers, filling the space between the fashion-pieces and the transom. Two gun ports, leading from the orlop deck, have been placed below the transom. The connection of the stern with the shipsides has been strengthened with the help of big, horizontal knees.

A perspective drawing (Fig. 13) of the

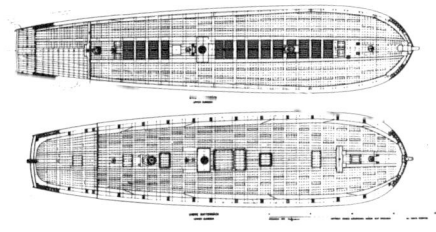

Figure 9.

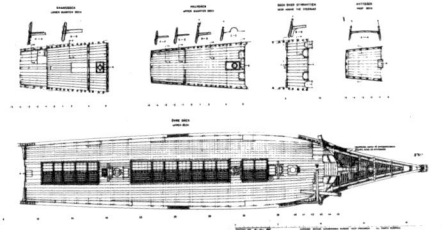

Figure 10. Deck plans.

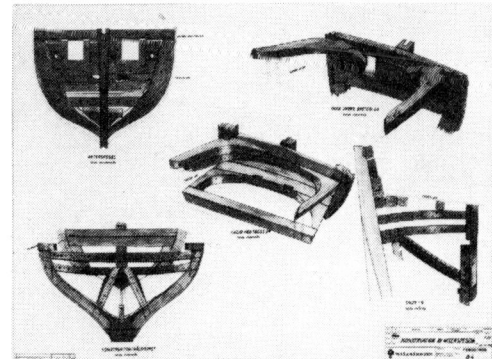

Figure 12. Details from the heavy construction of the lower part of the stern.

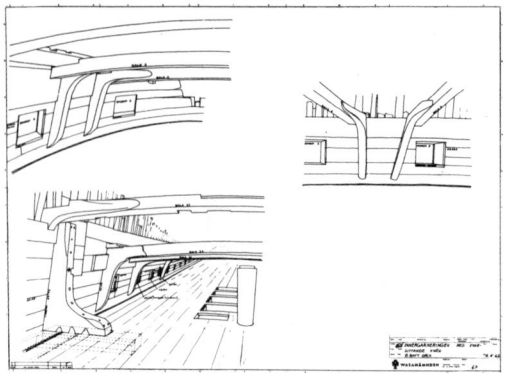

Figure 13. A perspective drawing of the upper gun deck.

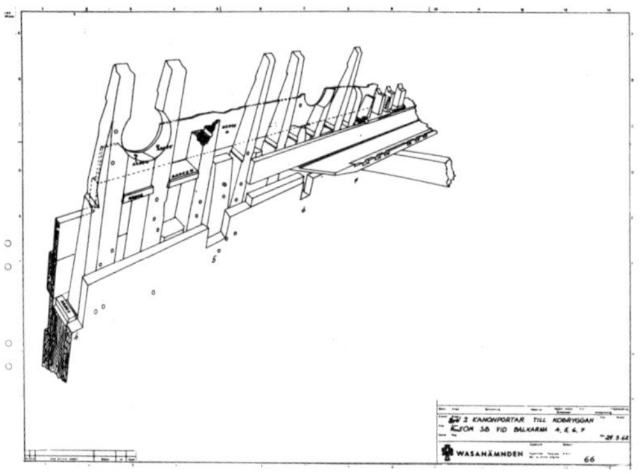

Figure 14. Details from the bulwark of the upper deck.

upper gun deck shows the beams with a distance of 1.1–1.2 m between each other. The knees are situated astern of the beams ahead of the main mast, and afore of the beams astern of the same mast. The bulwark on the upper deck on the starboard side towards the sterncastle shows the frames filling the space between the outer and inner planking, the clamps of the deckbeams, the waterways and the round gunport for the guns on this deck (Fig. 14). Figs. 15–17 show details of some of the constructions on board: the foot of the main mast seen from astern, the bits and the construction of the pump at the main mast.

The Dutch themselves mostly used smaller and lightly built men-of-war at the beginning of the 17th century – for several reasons. One reason was that such ships were well adapted to the shallow Dutch waters, especially as they were flat in the bottom and had a small draught. Also convertible merchantmen were used (Unger 1978, pp. 25 f).

The Wasa, with her large size, heavy dimensions and construction, does not belong to this category. It is then more plausible to compare her with the men-of-war that were ordered in Holland by foreign powers at the period in question. One example of these was the ships, mentioned above, which were ordered by France in Holland (Hafström 1968).

Several main characteristics and also parts of the construction in the Wasa show a close connection with the Dutch shipbuilding tradition – as has been shown above. Because of that one might say that the Wasa was built mainly in the Dutch manner. At the same time she was adapted to the type of naval warfare and the natural, hydrographic conditions which were prevalent in the waters of the Swedish navy at that time.

Concerning the relation between the natural conditions and the construction of

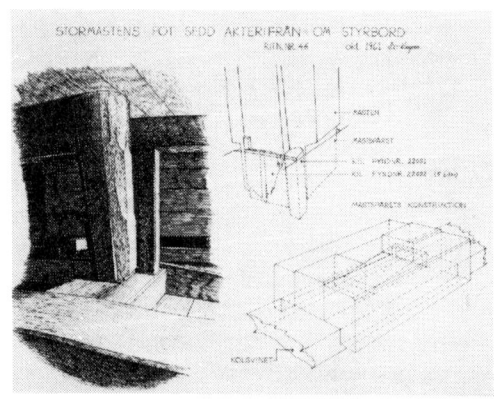

Figure 15. The foot of the main mast seen from astern.

178

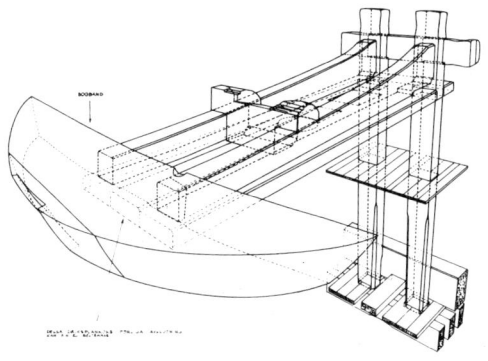

Figure 16. The bitts.

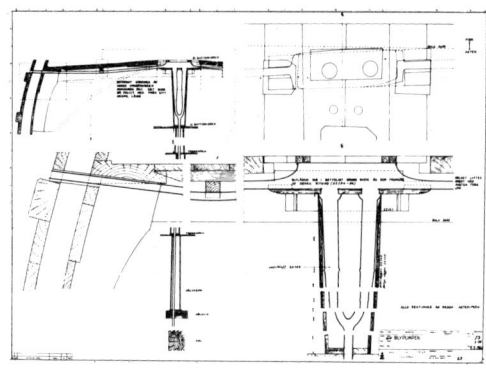

Figure 17. The construction of the pump at the main mast.

the ship, one might point out that the Swedish navy did not perform in as shallow waters as the Dutch. Accordingly it was possible to give it more draught. This gave an advantage in battle and also made the ship more durable to natural stresses in a longer time perspective.

Within the Swedish navy, during the reign of Gustav II Adolf, one can see a steady augmenting of the size of the ships (Cederlund 1966). The fleet of his father had mostly been adapted for warfare along the coasts and in the archipelagoes. With the new bigger ships one could also fight the enemy on the open sea and operate off foreign coasts. The main tasks of the Swedish fleet during the 1620s were transports over the Baltic to the south-eastern and southern coasts, the blockading of the ports there, and also convoy duty between Sweden and the other side of the Baltic.

It is quite natural to refer the size of the Wasa to this "bigships-policy" of the Swedish state and navy at the beginning of the 17th century.

Bibliography

Bengtsson, S.: "The sails of the Wasa; unfolding, identification and preservation". *Journal of Nautical Archaeology* 1975:1.

Borgenstam, C.: "Varför kantrade Wasa?" *Wasastudier* 12, 1984

Cederlund, C.O.: *Stockholms skeppsgård 1605–1640. Personalens struktur och organisation.* Statens sjöhistoriska museum 1966

Classon Rålamb, Å.: *Skeps Byggerij eller Adelig Öfnings Tionde Tom.* Stockholm 1691

Hafström, G.: "Utblickar kring tillkomsten av skeppet Wasa". Statens sjöhistoriska museum. *Meddelanden XI.* Uddevalla 1968

Hasslöf, O.: "Huvudlinjer i skeppsbyggnadskonstens teknologi". *Sömand, fisker, skib og verft. Introduktion till maritim etnologi.* Köpenhamn 1970

Hornborg, E.: *Segelsjöfartens historia.* Helsingfors 1948

Landström, B.: *Regalskeppet Vasan från början till slutet.* Stockholm 1980

Sandström, A.: "Sjöstrid på Wasas tid". *Wasastudier* nr 9, 1982

Sandström, A.: "Wasa ock kungens bestick". *Wasastudier* nr 12, 1984

Schoerner, G.: *Regalskeppet.* Stockholm 1964

Soop, H.: *Regalskeppet Wasa. Skulpturer.* Stockholm 1978

Unger, R.W.: *Dutch shipbuilding before 1800.* Assen 1978

Drawings. Wasa 1628. Statens sjöhistoriska museum. Stockholm, Sweden

Trade between Enemies

Maritime Resistance to the Continental System in the Northern Seas(1808–1812)

ANTHONY NICHOLAS RYAN

From Berlin in November 1806 and again, in apparently more propitious circumstances, from Milan in December 1807 Napoleon Bonaparte decreed the exclusion from continental Europe of the British flag and British goods and of all ships which had cleared from or touched at a British port. Between this date and the breakdown of the Franco-Russian alliance in 1812 Britain was in a state of hostility with Denmark-Norway, Prussia and Russia, and between 1810 and 1812 with Sweden also. Her response was to force trade upon the enemy through "making England the terminus *a quo* or the terminus *ad quem* of all neutral navigation of which the other term is a hostile port."[1] Trade with the enemy, especially a trade which had been formally proscribed by the enemy, was a conspiratorial business in which falsehood, forgery and fraud were practised on so vast a scale that black itself was made to look like white. Within the Scandinavian and Baltic ports the origin, destination and ownership of property on board visiting ships were disguised through the proliferation of false flags and simulated papers. There the art of deception was a way of life. At sea, although false papers were brandished, the great reality was the abiding presence of the British fleet, which imposed its protection upon all ships under any flag whatsoever except the French. Without its autocratic government of the trade routes the

games of bluff played out in the ports could never have begun.

There is abundant evidence of continuous British commercial activity in northern and eastern Europe under the continental system even when the system was most effectively enforced in 1811. There are the important admiralty records concerning the defence of trade. It is clear from these that vast convoys of merchantmen crossed and re-crossed the North Sea during the annual trading season. The Baltic trade sailed from Britain in four divisions: from the Nore, the Humber, Leith and Long Hope Sound, the rendezvous in the Orkneys for vessels from Glasgow, Liverpool and Irish ports. The Nore division was joined off the Norfolk coast with trade from Yarmouth. Convoy was provided at all these places, except the Long Hope, at fortnightly intervals between mid-April and mid-October, responsibility for the provision of which lay with the port admirals at the Nore, Yarmouth and Leith. Convoys were assembled at the Long Hope at three-weekly intervals or when a sufficient, but unspecified, number of vessels was collected there. The rendezvous across the North Sea for the convoys was Vingå Sand, near Gothenburg, where they were grouped together under the protection of the Baltic fleet, commanded during 1808–12 by Vice-Admiral Sir James Saumarez, for the voyage to their destina-

Figure 1. Capture of H.M.S. Tickler *by Danish gunboats reproduced by kind permission of the Trustees of the National Maritime Museum.*

tions within the Baltic. Convoys bound for Britain from within the Baltic rendezvoused at Karlskrona or in Hanö Bay, according to the state of Anglo-Swedish relations, sailed for Vingå Sand under the escort of ships belonging to the Baltic squadron and there joined an appropriate convoy for the crossing of the North Sea.[2]

The volume of this trade can be measured in contemporary statistical evidence, the schedule of convoys sent by the admiralty to Lloyd's for the information of underwriters who did business at this great centre of marine insurance. In 1808, between March and December, there were, according to these records, 836 clearances in 61 convoys from the United Kingdom to Scandinavia and the Baltic and 722 arrivals in 34 convoys into the United Kingdom; in 1809, between January and December, 1,643 clearances in 59 convoys and 3,181 arrivals in 49 convoys; in 1810, 2,044 clearances in 49 convoys and 3,321 arrivals in 35 convoys; in 1811, 1,206 clearances in 37 convoys and 1,618 arrivals in 23 convoys; in 1812, 1,312 clearances in 43 convoys and 1,022 arrivals in 28 convoys.[3] From these figures a picture emerges of ships swarming over the North Sea and the Baltic under British convoy, entering and leaving

the ports of the continent as if the decrees of Berlin and Milan did not exist. But this picture sheds little light on the names and origins of the ships under convoy, on the men who sailed in them and on their cargoes. It therefore leaves an enormous gap in our knowledge and understanding of the Anglo-Baltic trade during years of severe restriction.

To bridge the gap we have to go beyond the naval records, which tell us much about the battle for the defence of trade against Danish and Norwegian raiders and French privateers and little about the trade being defended. We have to rescue, from the oblivion of anonymous swarms, obscure people who have in most cases left but fleeting traces in the archives. They include merchants, shipowners, seamen, commercial and political agents who were all caught up in, and at the same time helped to shape the outcome of, great historical events. Evidence about them can be gleaned from two important sources in the Public Record Office, London: the Register of Licences to Neutral Vessels, 1809–1813, preserved by the Board of Trade, and the Privy Council Registers, 1805–1813.[3a] The first contains a brief synopsis in chronological order of applications for licences to trade with enemy states and the decisions made thereon; the second, the texts of the relevant British Orders-in-Council, copies of letters written by the Privy Council and, up to June 1811, the text, or summary of the text, of every licence issued. If we piece together sufficient of these traces we begin to form a picture of the trade. A striking feature of it is that the ships employed were foreign. The foreigners included Americans, but the vast majority was of Scandinavian and Baltic ownership and registration. In other words, though sailing under British convoy, they flew the flags of states which at one time and another during the period were formally at war with Britain.

We can discover, for example, the names of hundreds of foreign masters of ships and occasional glimpses of their activities. In August 1808 Captain C. Plorstmann of the Oldenburg ship, *Krone von Oldenburg,* was engaged by James Hill of London to sail in ballast from Britain to Riga and to return, "if necessary under Dutch colours", with hemp and flax to King's Lynn, London or another British port.[4] In December of the same year Captain Schultz of the Russian ship *Elizabeth* was engaged by Robert and John Wilson of London to sail from London to Portugal there to load a cargo of salt, to proceed with the same to St. Petersburg and, having discharged it, to take on board for London a cargo of Russian produce.[5] Captain

Figure 2. Admiral James, 1st Baron De Saumarez (1757–1836) reproduced by kind permission of the Trustees of the National Maritime Museum from a copy by Edwin Williams of the original painting by THOMAS PHILLIPS, R.A. (1770–1845).

Carsten Jensen of the Hamburg brig *Jenny* was engaged by J. Schneider of London in January 1809 to sail in ballast from London to Liverpool there to load a cargo of salt for a Baltic port, returning to the United Kingdom with a Baltic cargo.[6] In March 1810 the brig *Vrouw Catharina,* commanded by A. Matry and flying Bremen colours, was chartered by Le Mesurier & Co. of London "to sail in ballast from Plymouth to Liverpool, there to load a cargo of salt and proceed with the same to Gothenburg, there to change her colours and proceed with her said cargo, under any other colours except French, to any port in the Baltic and to import from thence."[7]

Seamen from northern Europe were also employed to disguise the nationality of British ships. In March 1809 D.H. and J.A. Ruckner, merchants of London, were granted a licence for the British ship *Kitty* to sail with a cargo from London to Riga "with permission after leaving Gravesend to assume the name of *Frau Elizabeth,* H.N. Pluss master, and to return from Riga with a cargo of goods permitted to be imported into this kingdom". Messrs. Thornton & West of London were likewise allowed to send the British ships *Sisters,* James Hill master, *Brothers,* John Muir master, and *Ann,* Henry Samuel Hook master, manned by foreign seamen and flying foreign flags, from London to Riga with cargoes of coffee and sugar, returning with Russian produce. In July 1809 the customs officer of Leith reported the arrival of two British ships, the *Richard* and the *Hope* with linseed and tallow from Riga consigned to Richard Scougall & Co. of Leith. Not only were both ships manned by foreign seamen, but the *Richard,* commanded by D. Alber, had assumed the name *Lepford* and the *Hope* commanded by G. Paulsen, the name *Magdalena.*

Foreign seamen were also employed on ships of foreign build and registration which were owned by citizens of the United Kingdom, a practice regulated by the Privy Council through the issue of permissive licences. On 16 January 1810, for example, the London house of Cox & Heisch was granted a licence on behalf of itself and others to buy thirty ships to sail in ballast from a port north of the Scheldt, or from a Baltic port, to a Russian port, there to load for the United Kingdom. In this particular case the plan was abandoned after the correspondents of the interested parties on the continent reported obstacles to the proposed purchases; and a licence to charter foreign ships was substituted.[8] Other purchases licenced in 1810 appear to have been successfully completed. In April William Etherington and P.W. Watson of Hull were permitted to own the *Helina*, a Prussian ship of 138 tons then lying in the Humber; Hilbers, James & Co. of London, the Russian-built *Carl*, Lorenz Paulsen master, then lying at Kronstadt. Leave was granted in December to Worrall & Williamson of Liverpool for the purchase of six Russian- and Swedish-built ships then in the Mersey: the *Janus*, J. Strom master, of 154 tons; the *Norbotten*, J.A. Graff master, 200 tons; the *Boreas*, E. Söderström master, 300 tons; the *Sallam Warre*, E. Hageblom master, 200 tons; the *Commercen*, G. Lindgren master, 250 tons and the *Henrica*, L. Bulin master, 250 tons. Evidence of licences to own foreign ships is less plentiful after 1810 since detailed lists have not been preserved.[9] There is no reason, however, to suppose that the practice ceased as the sale of foreign vessels continued to be advertised. An example of such in *The Leith and Edinburgh Telegraph* of 28 February 1812 aptly illustrates the nature and purpose of these transactions:

To be sold by private bargain: the fine Prussian ketch *Die Gute Hoffnung*, Jacob Poortar master, admeasuring about 160 tons; presently lying opposite Mr. Wilson's yard, Leith. This vessel is not only well found in every requisite, but sails remarkably fast and, from having a Prussian flag and real papers, may

be employed to great advantage in the Baltic under that flag; in which capacity the present master is willing to engage with the purchaser.[10]

Negotiations for the purchase and chartering of foreign ships were also conducted abroad. The best documented case of such activity is that of Edward Solly. Edward Solly was a partner resident in Prussia, usually at Memel or Königsberg, of the London house of Isaac Solly & Sons established dealers in Baltic produce, who held contracts with the Navy Board for the supply to the British fleet of hemp and timber. Edward Solly was constantly engaged in procuring foreign seamen and ships belonging both to northern Europe and the United States of America. A fleet of Solly ships can be located in April 1809. The *Uranus*, Pucke master, *Estafette*, Ticke master, *Conjunctor*, Leidke master, *Alexis*, Rhoder master, lay in the Thames ready to sail to the Baltic. The *Maria*, Martin master, *Hercules*, Paterson master, *Aufang*, Klawitter master, *Invariable*, Kermer master, were on the point of clearing from Liverpool. The *February*, Prauschriever master, was reported to have sailed under convoy from Britain to Gothenburg on a voyage to Memel. The *Satisfaction*, Patterson master, *January*, Reatall master, and the *Elbe*, Burch master, were, according to the latest accounts, at Gothenburg bound for the Baltic. The *Watzymannich*, Schultz master, was preparing to sail from St. Petersburg on the first favourable wind after the navigation of the Gulf of Finland was open. And the *Speculation*, Domeke master, *Marineuke*, Adams master, and *Superb*, Henry master, were loading at Riga.[11]

During the summer of 1809 Edward was able to arrange, through methods known only to himself, the purchase of seven ships, the transactions being reported by Isaac to the Navy Board on 8 September:

I have this day received letters from Mr.

E. Solly up to 22nd August and I take the liberty of communicating to you the information they give me relative to my contract with your honorable board. The ships that he has bought at Copenhagen are as follows:

William, D. Botcher master, 300 tons; *Margareth,* Wilcken master, 250 tons; *Europa,* 500 tons, *General Krogh,* Simelmann master, 270 tons; *Haabet,* 300 tons, *Ann,* 400 tons; *Astrea,* Witt master, 675 tons.

He has sent the following masters for the *Europa, Haabet* and *Ann,* Captains Eppert, C. Haaman and Sandberg; and, as he is in hopes of procuring more ships at Copenhagen, he has sent the Captains Streig and Kock there likewise.[12]

Further negotiations at Copenhagen resulted in the chartering or purchase of more ships, the *Louise,* 300 tons, *Margareth,* 230 tons, *Joanna Margaretha,* 300 tons, *Graf von Bernstorff,* 200 tons, *Pettra,* 300 tons, *Barbara* and *Maria,* both of 100 tons. In addition by the second half of October the *Anna Christina,* 400 tons, and the *Britannia,* 500 tons, were about to sail from Copenhagen to Russia, while three masters, M. Hentz, B. Leidke and J. Schultz were on their way to Copenhagen to take command of other ships. Edward did not confine himself to Copenhagen as a source of ships, for he chartered several at Danzig, Pillau and Riga. As a result of his efforts thirty-six ships were loading at Riga and twelve at St. Petersburg according to the information available on 7 November.[13]

Although Edward Solly's activities are less fully documented after 1809, the evidence is that they followed the same pattern. In January 1810 Isaac Solly informed the Navy Board that he was seeking licences for fifteen foreign ships, the names of some of which do not occur on the correspondence of 1809, to be employed in fulfillment of the hemp contract. In April 1811 he sent the board "a list of ships

which are the property of Mr. E. Solly and which will be employed in the course of the season in conveying goods, principally wood, such as we have contracted to deliver into H.M. stores". In the list were named forty-seven foreign ships. The abbreviated correspondence of 1812 (the contract was terminated in April following a dispute over terms) reveals the existence of a fleet of foreign-built merchantmen, owned or chartered by Edward Solly, which were either fully loaded or being loaded in the Baltic ports with hemp and timber for shipment to Britain.[14]

The business of the house of Solly, like that of other merchant houses, can also be traced from 1809 onwards in the Register of Licences for Neutral Ships. These registers, as already noted, contain applications for licences and the decisions made thereon by the Privy Council; they do not record completed voyages. It is legitimate nonetheless to use the information as evidence of the patterns of trade and to extract from it also evidence about the ships and seamen employed. The firm selected here is that of Emes, Möller and Emes of London, whose senior partners William and Philip Emes were known as chairmen of the Baltic merchants. This means that they acted as representatives of the Baltic merchants in dealings with the Admiralty and the Commander-in-Chief over arrangements for the defence of trade. The sample examined here covers March 1809 to December 1810.[14a] During this period Emes, Möller & Emes received licences for the import into the United Kingdom of 106 cargoes of Baltic and Norwegian produce and for the departure in ballast of 125 ships from the United Kingdom and six from ports north of the Scheldt to proceed to Scandinavian and Baltic ports to load cargoes for Britain.

The house also received licences, of which more detail is entered in the lists, for the export of 14 cargoes and the import of 14 in the same ships. Apart from four unnamed ships licenced to sail from Liverpool with salt, they were the Oldenburg ship *Vrou Herskinar* from London to Russia with "sugar, dye woods, etc."; the Prussian *Laufer* to Königsberg with "sugar, coffee, etc."; the Prussian *Wilhelm Gustav* from Plymouth to the Baltic with French wines; the Prussian *Oeconomia* from Hull to the Baltic; the Swedish *Gustav Adolph* from London to Liverpool in ballast and from Liverpool to the Baltic with salt; the *Louisa* to Trondheim with coffee and sugar; the Russian *Molly* from Newcastle-upon-Tyne to the Baltic with coal; the *Florigunda* from Liverpool to Norway with salt and the *Nieuwe Hoof* to the Baltic with coal. It received export only licences for a cargo to the Baltic, for two Prussian ships with wines from Bordeaux to Prussia calling at a British port to pay duties, for the Prussian *Wilhelmina* from Newcastle-upon-Tyne to Pillau with coal, the Russian *Florentina* from the same to Königsberg with coal, the Prussian *Julius Caesar* with a cargo to the Baltic, the Prussian *Phoenix* with a cargo to Gothenburg, the Prussian *Neptunus* with Dutch tiles to the Baltic, the Prussian *Wohlfarth* with colonial produce and dye wood to the Baltic, the Rostock ship *Haabet* from Newcastle-upon-Tyne to the Baltic with coal, the Russian *Albertina* from London to the Baltic with a cargo and the Bremen ship *Louisa* from London to the Baltic with 200 barrels of codfish originally imported from Norway.

Despite the interesting variety of the exports, the chief business of the Baltic merchants in the United Kingdom was the import from the forests and plains of northern Europe and Russia of grain and naval stores, of which last commodity Britain had become the biggest consumer in the western world. This trade was in the hands of a multiplicity of merchant houses. The offices of the most prominent were situated in the city of London, but well-established dealers were to be found in the east coast ports of England and Scotland and also in Glasgow and Liverpool. The conduct of business had necessarily created throughout Scandinavia and the Baltic a network of resident agents and correspondents who were merged within the general population and were equipped by experience to handle all aspects of the trade in unstable political circumstances and to keep open channels of commercial communication.

Some of these were partners in business like Edward Solly or "our partner Mr. James Hoolboom", of whom we catch a glimpse in 1808 loading the Russian ship *St. Johannis Baptist* at St. Petersburg with a cargo of "hemp and other Russian produce of great value to this country" on behalf of Oom Hoolboom & Co.[15] William Irwin, a partner in the house of William and John Irwin of London, is to be found at Gothenburg in May 1809 making arrangements for the Swedish Pomeranian vessel *Amalia,* bound from Riga to London with hemp and the *Fruchtorn*, Peter Kreuger master, from Libau to London with flax, to collect British licences at Karlskrona.[16] Mr. McLean, "the active partner" in the house of J. Simpson & Co., was reported to be making discreet and proper use of substitute licences at Danzig in June 1809 to expedite the departure of vessels for the United Kingdom.[17] Joshua Martin, described as a partner of Thomas Wilson of London, was granted a licence by the Privy Council in January 1810 to extend his residence at St. Petersburg for twelve months "without prejudice to his character as a British subject".[18]

Others who cannot be identified as partners in business have also left traces in the archives. Francis Ross of F.W. Westinghausen & Co., of London, was granted an extension of licence in June 1809 to reside in Russia on business.[19] In December 1810 James Vine, a London merhcant, obtained licences for Constantine Nicholls, "lately departed for St. Petersburg", and William Plencke, "resident in Russia for some time past", to remain abroad for twelve months for commercial purposes.[20] Captain John

Barrett, H.M.S. *Minotaur* (74), received letters in November-December 1809 from Mr. Hewletz of the house of Solly and Mr. Amburgh of the house of Schröder requesting that the departure of the last homeward convoy from Karlskrona be postponed.[21] There is also the interesting case of the enterprising W.D. Wilkinson, formerly resident at St. Petersburg, who in the difficult year of 1811 when French agents were more active in their search for colonial produce and British manufactures, established under the protection of the Royal Navy a commercial depôt on the island of Hanö to serve as a storehouse for the collection of commercial intelligence and to expedite clandestine trade.[22]

At another level the distinction between political and commercial activity was blurred. There was, for example, "Mr. Gibson of Königsberg". This was Alexander Gibson or Gibsone of the house of Solly, who performed in Prussia the functions of a business agent until his death in October 1811. Gibson, who had done service as British consul at Danzig, was also known variously as Mr. C. Booth and Mr. S. Marks.[23] As such he was an agent of the British government, forwarding to the Foreign Office commercial and political intelligence about affairs in Prussia and corresponding also with other secret agents. Isaac Solly knew of this employment in the government service and was, according to Gibson, prepared to forward letters, open credits and aid discreetly in every possible way. Also resident in Königsberg under the name of Heinrich Hahn was Louis Drusina, who had served as British consul at Memel since 1798. Drusina opened a regular correspondence with the British fleet in 1808 and through the fleet with the foreign office.[24] The correspondence was carried to and from men-of-war cruising off the coast by local fishermen who were hired at Pillau by the British agent James Fisher, who went by the name of Emmanuel Hay.[25] Drusina emerged from his correspondence with Saumarez as

a well-informed commercial agent who made a useful practical contribution to the survival of trade. He was said, however, to be indiscreet, which may have been the reason for his recall to London in 1810 and subsequent eclipse. Perhaps the most interesting of the politico-commercial agents was E.F. Schröder, a merchant and shipowner of Kolberg, where he was Danish consul. Described by Gibson as "manager of the house of Braunschweig & Co." Schröder entered the British service under the assumed name of August Schaeffer in May 1809. His recuitment had been arranged by Dublin-born John Mordaunt Johnson, a confidential agent who was regularly employed on missions to the Habsburg dominions during the suspension of diplomatic relations. Schröder became a vital link in a chain of communications between Germany and Great Britain through Kolberg, Ystad and Gothenburg facilitating the passage of agents and mail in both directions. After the war he was rewarded by the British government with a consular appointment.[26] The shadowy Patrick Cumming, "an English gentleman at Riga" who had travelled before in Russia, was mentioned shortly before his death in 1812 as forwarding military intelligence to the fleet on condition that his name would not be affixed to anything which he might communicate.[27]

With the connivance of the Swedish government, which preserved informal links with Britain even during the period of formal war between the two countries during 1810–12, British consuls with vast experience of the Baltic trade remained at or near their posts. Charles Fenwick, formerly consul at Elsinore, crossed the Sound after the outbreak of war with Denmark-Norway in 1807, and took up residence at Hälsingborg, whence he forwarded commercial and political intelligence both to Saumarez and the Foreign Office. John Smith, who had been comployed as vice-consul at Gothenburg from 1796, if not earlier, remained there as a private citizen communicating with the fleet and government, supervising arrangements for the safety of British property at Gothenburg and, through his contacts across the border, promoting the Anglo-Norwegian timber trade.[28] George Foy, an Englishman long resident in Sweden, entered the service on the recommendation of his friend Edward Thornton, a former and future British ambassador to the court of Stockholm, at the end of 1810 as unofficial representative of British commercial and political interests with the proviso that he would not be expected to take any action inimical to Sweden.[29] Finally there was the Swedish merchant John Lindegren, who was spoken of as British vice-consul at Ystad. He played a considerable if at times, according to his critics, slovenly part in the transit of commercial and political intelligence and also, perhaps more importantly, in the procurement of supplies of fresh beef for the warships of the Baltic fleet.[30]

The evidence points to the existence in the Scandinavian and Baltic ports of popular resistance to Napoleon's commercial policy. Although certainly aided by the British government through the licence and convoy systems and abetted by official and semi-official agents, this resistance was not created by government. It was a movement by producers, dealers, shippers and seamen on both sides of the North Sea to preserve a long-standing commercial way of life which was threatened by political forces. The movement's greatest asset was its multi-national character made up of a closely knit framework of active cells from Liverpool in the west to St. Petersburg in the east; from Plymouth in the south to Stockholm in the north. Without organization the trade could not have survived in a hostile political environment. Its retraction under heavy Napoleonic pressure, including military pressure, in 1811 illustrates its vulnerability. But it was not so vulnerable as to collapse, for its survival was identified throughout the Baltic region with interests which were more deeply rooted in society and more durable than the political ambitions of Napoleon.

In Europe west of the Elbe river the Continental System could be plausibly presented as favouring local industry by the increase of marketing opportunities through the exclusion of British manufacturers and colonial produce. Beyond the Elbe, however, was the Europe of forests and granaries which was heavily dependent upon the British market as the outlet for the naval stores and grain which were the chief products of its labour. The surrender of the British market could not, unless compensation were found in the territories of France and her western allies and dependents, be reconciled with the interests of Prussia, Russia and the Scandinavian states, except perhaps Denmark. It was impossible to contemplate a stoppage of traffic in the Baltic ports without contemplating at the same time the prospect of economic and social dislocation.[31] This was the Achilles heel of the Continental System in northern and eastern Europe; for no serious attempt was ever made by the French authorities to prevent the clearance of laden ships bound for the west.

Such clearances from the Baltic ports were neither clandestine nor illegal. They were officially authorised avowedly to encourage trade with France, to prevent stagnation and to raise revenue on condition that a bond to the value of each vessel and its cargo was deposited as security that the destination was a French, a friendly or a neutral port. Through this practice the agents of France, while preserving some grip on reality by pointing to the existence of abuses and the risk of capture by the British navy, created a documentary fantasy of a mass of ships bound from the Baltic to ports such as Amsterdam, Bergen, Bordeaux, Copenhagen, Emden, Rotterdam and New York. These laborious efforts to save the appearances may be consulted in the series 'Correspondance consulaire et commerciale' in the Archives des Affaires Etrangères, Paris. 338 ships were recorded as having cleared from St. Petersburg in 1809, all employed on legal business, including 78 bound for the Low Countries and 56 for North America.[32] Similar activity was reported from other Russian ports. Up to 9 November 1809, 60 clearances were reported from Libau, 12 from Narva, 14 from Pernau, 3 from Revel, 690 from Riga and 4 from Windau.[33] The shipping lists compiled in the French consular office at Memel in 1810 record the clearance of 180 ships, 30 in ballast to other Baltic ports in search of freights, the remaining 150 with cargoes of Baltic produce to French and friendly ports. In the same year, between April and September, 234 ships were returned as having cleared from Elbing, Königsberg and Pillau, both laden and in ballast, for friendly ports within and without the Baltic.[34]

However, mastery over the sea route between the Baltic and western Europe belonged to the British navy. The most important document on board the merchantmen from the enemy ports was a British licence which conferred immunity from detention by British men-of-war "notwithstanding all the documents which accompany the ship and cargo may represent the same to be destined to any other neutral or hostile port, or to whomsoever such property may belong". Licences were normally issued by the Privy Council Office on application by merchants who saw to their delivery to the ships chartered or owned by themselves. They were delivered to such ships as were chartered or purchased abroad by resident commercial agents who were said to traffic in licences in northern Germany much as pre-Lutheran preachers had trafficked there in indulgences.[35] From time to time, when delivery of regular licences from London was impeded by difficulties of communication, substitute licences were issued by Saumarez as, for example, at the request of Hahn in June 1809.[36] The immunity conferred by the licence was by no means

unconditional. No document, however carefully designed, could be made proof against abuse. Unless enforced by powerful controls the licence system was likely to become a system of licence; for, if by brandishing a document, ships could steer what courses they pleased, the British maritime system would be rendered meaningless.

The key to the success of the licence system was the convoy system. By protecting within convoy between Karlskrona or Hanö and a port of discharge within the United Kingdom those ships which had on board a British licence and by detaining those which had not, the British navy imposed its will on every flag in the Baltic trade; for outside the convoys there was no security. The system of convoy was a system of control. The protection afforded by the licence did not extend to vessels found deviating from the convoy track with the possible object of getting naval stores to the French bases. Precautions were taken in 1810 to check the practice of vessels straggling from convoys at the southern end of the Great Belt and making Kiel, whence cargoes could be transported by inland navigation to the ports of the North Sea. Even more emphatic was the provision in every licence regulating the movement in the North Sea of ships which became separated from the convoy.

It is hereby ordered in council that a licence be granted to the petitioners . . . upon condition that if any part of the cargo of any of the said vessels consists of naval stores and be destined to any port of the kingdom lying south of the port of Hull, the vessel importing the same shall, unless under protection of convoy, stop at Dundee or Leith and there obtain a fresh clearance for the port of her destination; and upon further condition that such vessel shall not sail from Dundee or Leith without convoy and shall proceed with such convoy and not desert the same till her arrival at the port of destination or as long as such convoy shall be instructed to protect her; such licence to remain in force six months from the date hereof.[37]

Isaac Solly felt the weight of this provision in May 1810 when the High Court of Admiralty ordered him to pay the expenses of the captor – £367 – and to forfeit a cargo of iron on board the ship *Europa*, which had sailed directly to London without convoy, though the ship and the rest of the cargo, consisting of hemp in fulfillment of his contract, were restored.[38]

This provision took care not only of ships coming from the Baltic but also of those coming from Norway with cargoes of timber. Here we have a striking instance of the shipping industry of a hostile state subordinating itself to the British maritime system and accepting the protection of the British fleet against its own commerce raiders. Despite the relatively conscientious adherence of the Dano-Norwegian administration to the Continental system, the same inexorable pressures as were experienced by the rural societies east of the Elbe produced a quiet revolution in Norway against the ban upon trade with Britain. The revival of the Anglo-Norwegian timber trade, which had languished in 1808, began in 1809 when 486 ships laden with timber cleared from Norway, bound ostensibly for French and neutral ports: 160 to Bordeaux, 33 to Dunkirk, 32 to Saint Martin, 13 to Saint Malo, 26 to La Rochelle, three to Teneriffe and one to Madeira. 1,625 cleared in 1810, 880 to Bordeaux, 111 to Saint Martin, 38 to Saint Malo, and five to Teneriffe; 1,412 cleared in 1811, 892 of them to Bordeaux and the rest to other French and friendly ports. Furnished with papers, including a Norwegian certificate of origin, that were perfectly in order, the ships were proof against investigation by French and allied privateers. Another important piece of documentary equipment, to be carefully concealed in the event of a search by privateers, was a British licence usually obtained through agents in Britain or through John Smith of Gothenburg, who had contacts with Danish and Norwegian commercial agents.[39]

The motives of the Norwegians are intelligible. Like the producers of naval stores in the Baltic provinces they were dependent for their livelihood upon the consumption of their goods in foreign markets. Since these goods were of such a nature that they could be profitably exported only by sea, they were subject to the direction of the power which controlled the sea. For both producers and dealers therefore it was a choice between the British market and impoverishment. The Norwegians had an additional motive. They were dependent upon the British for the import of corn from the granaries of the Danish peninsula. Even the king of Denmark-Norway, in spite of his political dependence on France, was forced reluctantly to collaborate with the British system to the extent of permitting his subjects to take British licences and subscribe to British instructions regulating the passage of corn ships from Jutland to Norway.[40]

The corn trade, like the timber trade, with which it was closely allied, directed the Norwegian mercantile marine towards the harbours of the United Kingdom, where the flag of Denmark-Norway flew alongside those of Danzig, the Duchy of Mecklenberg, the Duchy of Oldenburg, the Hanseatic cities, the kingdoms of Holland, Prussia, Russia, Sweden and the United States of America. According to the terms of an import licence the masters of these foreign ships were free, after unloading their cargoes, to take their freight charges and depart for any unblockaded port. It did not work that way. They had an interest in obtaining on behalf of the owners – in many cases the master himself might be owner or part-owner – either outward freights from the United Kingdom or a charter to go in ballast to a Scandinavian or Baltic port, there to load an import

Figure 3. Capture by H.M.S. Sappho *of a Danish brig reproduced by kind permission of the Trustees of the National Maritime Museum.*

cargo. With the British flag strictly excluded from the enemy ports, the merchant marines of northern Europe seized the chance to establish a near monopoly over the carrying trade between north-eastern and western Europe. By so doing they also became the instruments of British policy.

Foreign merchantmen, furnished with simulated certificates of origin, opened the enemy ports to the British, since only ships that were evidently non-British could enter. They might even be furnished, in the event of their having on board French wine or brandy or Biscay salt, with a genuine certificate of origin which would facilitate their entry even more. The principal risk, apart from that of capture at sea, was the discovery on board ship by hostile agents of incriminating documentary evidence. This was the undoing at Rostock in December 1809 of Captain Nicolas Jörek of Ystad, master of the *Emmanuel*, on board of which were discovered written instructions, dated 19 September 1809, from the London house of Emes, Möller & Emes.[41] The most damning piece of documentary evidence was a British licence. The instructions to the commander of a Danish privateer, taken off Wismar on 29 April 1810, by H.M. frigate *Fisgard*, Captain Francis Mason, R.N., emphasized the importance of an assiduous search for a British licence, notwithstanding the apparent regularity of a detained vessel's papers.[42] The discovery of a licence concealed in his cabin brought an abrupt end to a voyage by Captain Langhoff of the Swedish *Fredrik Wilhelm Gustav*. Detained off Danzig by the French privateer *General Pajol* in September 1811, Langhoff swore on oath during interrogation that he was bound from Riga to Wolgast. Confronted with the licence he confessed to having sailed from Britain under convoy in July 1811 with a cargo of herring to Gothenburg, where he obtained fresh papers and proceeded to Riga, taking on board there a cargo of hemp consigned to the London house of Cox & Heisch. Captain Freder of the Prussian *Johanna,* another victim of the *General Pajol,* was similarly caught out. After claiming to be bound from Arendal in Norway to Riga with a cargo of salt, he was forced to admit to having sailed in June 1811 with a cargo from Riga to Hull and there loaded the salt.[43]

The near monopoly of the Scandinavian and Baltic mercantile marines was badly dented by the French decree of 1810 that having on board colonial produce or British manufactures made a ship good prize whatever the apparent validity of its papers. The decree led to large scale confiscations towards the end of the trading season in this year and caused a decline in confidence, which was reflected in a fall in the volume of trade, especially the trade in the Prussian ports, in 1811. Another significant event was Tsar Alexander I's famous ukaze of December 1810, which imposed restrictions upon the import of French luxury goods and opened the Russian ports to neutral navigation. A leading motive of the Russian court, and in particular of the foreign minister, Nicolai Rumiantsev, was the strengthening of relations with the United States of America, whose mission to Russia was raised to ambassadorial rank.[44] The ukaze was followed in 1811 by the so-called American invasion of the Baltic.

John Quincy Adams, the American ambassador, reported on 22 July 1811 the arrival at Kronstadt of some 100 vessels flying the American flag and of 100 more at other Russian ports. Their cargoes included sugar, coffee, indigo, dyewoods. By 2 November he was able to put the total number of arrivals at Kronstadt under the American flag at 139. Adams, however, was not deceived into thinking that these arrivals indicated a boom in Russo-American commerce. Although in official exchanges, as for example with Lesseps, the French consul at St. Petersburg, he defended the arrivals as having come directly from the United States with cargoes of American origin, he was as much aware as the French agent of the deceptive quality of ships' papers. Adams knew that most of the Americans had touched *en route* at a British port, that many had been freighted and laden in Britain, had sailed under British convoy and had been chartered to load cargoes of naval stores in Russia for shipment to Britain.[45] He had an uneasy feeling that others were "cases in which everything was English but the papers": a feeling which prompted him to urge legislative provision against the sale of "real American ship's papers, whether with or without the ship in foreign ports".[46] The American flag was by no means the only flag to be found in the Russian ports in 1811. During the late summer ships cleared from elsewhere in the Baltic, especially from Prussia, shaping course in ballast for Riga and other Russian ports to load with naval stores, hemp being prominent among them, for the United Kingdom. The survival of the trade, albeit on a restricted scale, in the crisis year of 1811 underlines not only the adaptability and resourcefulness of its participants but also the strength of the organization which supported it and, perhaps above all, the in-built capacity of business activities which chimed in with so many interests to survive in times of rapid and unfavourable political change.

Popular resistance to Napoleonic imperialism is usually associated with the awakening in different parts of Europe of national consciousness and hatred of foreign government. However true this may be as an explanation of the peasant guerrilla movements in Russia and Spain and the stirrings of romantic opposition in Germany, it hardly accounts for popular resistance in the war at sea. A better explanations of the widespread refusal by the merchants, shipowners and seamen of the Scandinavian and Baltic states to support Napoleon's ban upon trade with Britain was their realization that the only trade they could have in the circumstances of the time was trade with Britain. Once convinced of Britain's will to preserve the trade and of her ability to protect it, they took shelter beneath the Baltic fleet. It proved in tempestuous times to be a durable relationship governed on both sides by a wary recognition of mutual dependence.

Notes

1 Stephen to Perceval, 13 November 1807, British Library, Add. Mss., 49177, Spencer Perceval Papers.

2 For full documentation, see A.N. Ryan, "The Defence of British Trade with the Baltic, 1808–1813", *English Historical Review* (1959).

3 Schedule of Convoy Lists sent to Lloyd's 1808–15, Public Record Office (P.R.O.), Admiralty (Adm.) 7/64.

3a P.R.O., *Board of Trade* (B.T.) 6/195–210; *Privy Council Registers* (P.C.) 2/169–194.

4 P.C. 2/177, 9 August 1808.

5 P.C. 2/179, 7 December 1808.

6 P.C. 2/179, 26 January 1809.

7 P.C. 2/185, 21 March 1810.

8 This is only one instance of many applications to own or charter foreign ships found in the Board of Trade registers.

9 One can have recourse to the often less specific evidence in the Board of Trade registers.

10 *The Leith and Edinburgh Telegraph,* 28 February 1812.

11 Isaac Solly to Thompson, 8 April 1809, A.N. Ryan (ed.). *The Saumarez Papers: Selections from the Baltic Correspondence of Vice-Admiral Sir James Saumarez, 1808–1812* (London: Navy Records Society, 1968), p. 141. Cited henceforth as *The Saumarez Papers.*

12 Isaac Solly to the Navy Board, 8 September, P.R.O. Adm. 1/4354.

13 Isaac Solly to Navy Board, 7 October, 17 October, 3 November, 2 December 1809, P.R.O., Adm. 1/4354.

14 Isaac Solly to Navy Board, 4 January 1810; 23 April 1811; 21 May, 11 July 1812. P.R.O. Adm. 106/1626. There are two references in B.T. 6/198 to Edward Solly having been granted a licence to own foreign ships.

14a The source is P.R.O. B/T 6/195–202 *passim.*

15 Oom, Hoolboom & Co. to Board of Trade, 5 October 1808, P.R.O., B.T. 1/41.

16 Irwin to Keats, 29 May 1809, Saumarez Mss., Ipswich and East Suffolk County Record Office (I.E.S.C.R.O.).

17 Hahn to Keats, 5 June 1809, Saumarez mss., I.E.S.C.R.O.

18 P.R.O., P.C. 2/184, 18 January 1810.

19 P.R.O., P.C. 2/187, 11 June 1810.

20 P.R.O., P.C. 21 December 1810.

21 Barrett to Saumarez, 7 December 1809, *The Saumarez Papers,* p. 114.

22 For Wilkinson, see *The Saumarez Papers,* pp. 184, 225, 248–9.

23 Gibson's correspondence with the Foreign Office in 1808–1809 is in P.R.O., Foreign Office (F.O.) 64/79 and F.O. 64/82; his correspondence in 1811 with the agent, George Galway Mills, in Berlin is in F.O. 64/83. The reference to Isaac Solly's readiness to collaborate is in Gibson to Smith, 7 November 1810, P.R.O., F.O. 64/82. His death is recorded in Tassaud to Bassano, 31 October 1811, Archives des Affaires Étrangères, Correspondence Consulaire et Commerciale (A.A.E.Cons.) Dantzic xii.

24 For examples of Hahn's correspondence with Saumarez, see The Saumarez Papers, pp. 66, 75, 88, 95, 105, 108–11, 115.

25 Admiral Sir Richard Vesey Hamilton (ed.), *Letters and Papers of the Admiral of the Fleet Sir Thomas Byam Martin, G.C.B.* (London: Navy Records Society, 1898), Vol. II, p. 73.

26 Gibson to Smith, 7 November 1810, P.R.O., F.O. 64/82; Keats to Martin, 8 May 1809, P.R.O., Adm. 80/146. For the documentation of Schröder's activities, see *The Saumarez Papers,* pp. 65, 83–4, 96, 111, 115, 137, 140–141, 145–6, 171, 192–4, 199.

27 Saumarez to Martin, 10 July 1812, *The Saumarez Papers,* pp. 234, 236; Martin to Saumarez, 2 July 1812, R.V. Hamilton, *op.cit.,* pp. 199 ff.

28 F. Scheel & J.S. Worm-Müller, *Den Norske Sjøfarts Historie* (Oslo, 1935), vol. II. part I, pp. 71 ff.

29 Foy to C.C. Smith, 23, 27 November 1810, P.R.O., F.O. 73/65.

30 *The Saumarez Papers,* pp. 92, 140, 176–7, 225.

31 R. Hoeniger, *Die Kontinentalsperre und ihre Einwirkung auf Deutschland* (Berlin, 1905), pp. 25 ff. See also C. Meltig, *Geschichte der Stadt Riga* (Riga, 1897), p. 424; B. de Jouvenel, *Napoleon et l'Économie Dirigée; le Blocus Continental* (Paris, 1942), pp. 269 ff.; Adams to Monroe, 16 October 1811, W.C. Ford (ed.), *The Writings of John Quincy Adams* (New York, 7 vols., 1913–17), iv, p. 251.

32 Tables in Lesseps to Champagny, 8 March 1810, A.A.E. Cons., Petersburg x.

33 État général des importations et exportations de la Russie en 1809, Commerce avec la Russie, 1757 à 1810, Archives Nationales (A.N.), F. 12. 622.

34 Tables in A.A.E. Cons. Memel ii, *passim;* Clérambault to Champagny, 15 July, 4 November 1810, A.A.E. Cons., Koenigsberg ii.

35 Framery d'Ambreux to Champagny, 14 February 1810, A.A.E. Cons., Memel ii.

36 Hahn to Saumarez, 27 June 1809, *The Saumarez Papers,* p. 92.

37 Extracted from a licence granted on 11 july 1808, P.R.O., P.C. 2/177.

38 Toller to Solly, 15 May 1810, P.R.O., Adm. 106/1626; Solly to Navy Board, 14 February 1812, *ibid.*

39 Scheel & Worm-Müller, *op.cit.,* p. 72.

40 *Ibid.,* pp. 74 and 94 ff. Examples of "corn licences" in 1809–10 abound in the Privy Council Registers. For British resolve to prevent evasion of the terms of these licences, see Fawkener to Croker, 6 July 1810, P.R.O., P.C. 2/188.

41 Désbordes to Champagny (with enclosures), 28 May 1810, A.A.E. Cons., Rostock ii.

42 Instructions to the commander of a Danish privateer enclosed in Mason to Saumarez, 30 April 1810, *The Saumarez Papers,* pp. 125 ff.

43 Tassaud to Bassano, 7 December 1811, A.A.E. Cons., Dantzic xii.

44 Patricia K. Grimsted, *The Foreign Ministers of Alexander I: Political Attitudes and the Conduct of Russian Diplomacy, 1801–1825* (Berkeley and Los Angeles, 1969), p. 176.

45 John Quincy Adams to Thomas Boylston Adams, 10 July 1811, W.C. Ford, *op.cit.,* p. 137; John Quincy Adams to Monroe, 22 July 1811, *ibid.,* p. 148 ff.

46 John Quincy Adams to Monroe, 3 October 1811, *ibid.,* p. 235.

Steam enters the North Sea

ALAN PEARSALL

By the end of the long wars, the power of steam, which had already revolutionised industries ranging from mines to mills, had already been applied to water transport, and the pioneering work of inventors from Jonathan Hulls to Henry Bell had enabled steamships to provide reasonably reliable services in rivers and estuaries. The opportunity given by the advent of peace co-incided with an increasing need for improved transport as trade revived and extended. Steamships were quickly brought into use on coastal voyages and shorter cross-channel passages, where they were found particularly advantageous in improving the transit of mails. By the early 1820s the traveller to France and to Ireland consequently enjoyed a far more reliable service than the sailing packets could provide. By the mid-1820s, an extensive network of services around the British Isles showed that steam had made its first notable contribution to transport.

The lead thus taken by British engineers and entrepreneurs meant that the next step, the development of longer sea crossings, would also take place in the seas adjacent to the British Isles, and the important economic links already existing ensured that the North Sea would take a prominent part in this progress. The problems of running a regular, and particularly a profitable, service over long distances of stormy open sea were considerable.

The early steamers were all paddle-driven, with engines working at very low steam pressures and thus they were inevitably extravagant. Such vessels were quite satisfactory for sheltered waters with frequent calls where fuel could be obtained, and where good passenger patronage might be expected, as also in cross-channel voyages of 20 to 60 miles. To go further afield, however, meant a more seaworthy vessel, hence one which was stronger and larger and thus naturally requiring more powerful engines, which in their turn added to the problems of design, particularly with wooden construction, which was all that was then available.

There were also traffic problems, as few long routes at that time could expect a large passenger flow, whereas plenty of cargo was often to be found. But paddle steamers' engines occupied much of the best space in the ship and made bulk cargo-carrying difficult, while the fuel also occupied valuable space.[1] Thus while routes across the narrower southern part of the North Sea began in the mid-20s, between London and Rotterdam, Ostend, Calais and so on, beyond that only Hamburg seemed to offer good possibilities and achievement of this 350 mile voyage in 1826, as a regular proposition, became a notable step forward. Even so, many routes were suspended in winter. Financial problems also bore heavily upon the steamer, apart

Figure 1. The ORLANDO was built by Earle's of Hull for Thomas Wilson, Sons & Co. in 1869. She was lengthened in 1878. Most of her service was from Hull to Gothenburg. Her tonnage was 1581.

from technical ones. The first coast of steamers was considerable compared with that of a sailing vessel, whilst the engine room complement was additional and fuel, unnecessary in a vessel relying upon wind, was a further expense, so that running costs as a whole were higher. All these factors therefore retarded rapid development and for this early period kept the paddle steamer as a passenger, mail and high class cargo carrier. The bulk cargoes continued much as they had always done. The impact of steam for a generation was thus limited.

In practice, there were two approaches to the problem, both proving successful in the early years. In London, centre of much of the nation's trade and finance, a number of shipowners and others combined to form a large "General Steam Navigation Company", which opened numerous routes, both local, coastal and sea-going.

Well managed, its resources and backing were sufficient for it soon to become well established. It was this company which began in 1826 the first route to Hamburg, with weekly sailings, and taking freight by special arrangement.[2] At Hull, however, the other great port which took a lead in steam navigation, acting as the outlet for the industrial areas of Yorkshire and Lancashire, a different tendency showed itself in the ownership. The owners of the regular sailing traders were able themselves to raise money to invest in a steamer, so that while routes from London remained largely in the company's hands, those from Hull came to belong to a number of smaller ownerships, often at first with just one vessel. Weddle, Brownlow & Co., began the first Hull service, once again to Hamburg, in 1828. Oddly enough, their steamer was named LONDON.[3]

While both these routes, once started,

196

Figure 2. The ANGELO, another Wilson vessel, was built by Humphrey & Pearson of Hull in 1874. Of 1541 tons, she established a good reputation on the Hull to Christiania service.

prospered, others were slow in following. Indeed, the problem was that new owners seemed anxious to add to the facilities in the existing Hamburg and Rotterdam services rather than venture into new and perilous ground. In 1830, for example, a Dutch owner began another London-Rotterdam service, which was to become the once well-known Batavier Line. Then two other firms entered the Hull-Hamburg route, where one of the former smack-owners, Joseph Gee, acquired a steamer, and another large organisation, the St George Steam Packet Company, based in the Irish Sea with Liverpool, Dublin and Cork capital, saw fit to put its vessels on the same route, but it did also open a Hull to Rotterdam service. In both cases, after a bout of competition, agreements were reached so that sailings were shared.[4]

Rotterdam and Hamburg remained, however, the only ports to the northward with regular steam communication, apart from a few sailings to St Petersburg, which usually called at Copenhagen. Norway and

Sweden remained without a service except for one effort in 1834 to run a Hull-Gothenburg service. Even routes from Hull to Amsterdam and Antwerp did not at once succeed (Antwerp was only re-opened as a port in 1839), nor did any other port on the British side enter the running. When compared with the well-developed services round the British coasts at that time, these conditions indicate something of the economics of the early steamers over distances.

All these steamers were very much of their time. Although small by present standards, most were big vessels for their period and had to take the consequences of poor harbours. They had to sail as the tide permitted, and arrive as it permitted. Some were lucky enough to lie alongside wharves to load and unload, so that passengers could also get on board easily enough, but often and particularly in the Thames, they lay in the stream, and cargo went in barges and passengers had to employ a boat.[5] (The width of dock entran-

197

ces was one of the factors affecting the design of paddle steamers with their wide paddle-boxes.) However, they lay generally in fairly accessible places such as the Pool in London, and not, as often today, in some terminal, miles from anywhere. In some ways, one might say, they were run very like their contemporary sailing vessels except that their voyages were, once begun, more certain and also that they did not, as a rule, wait for full cargoes but sailed on or soon after the day announced. In practice, the sea-going steamers were evidently quite reliable, despite the generally primitive conditions and lack of regulation. Gales and adverse winds sometimes exhausted their fuel. Occasional breakdowns occurred. Duplication of names was then quite frequent, and owners took pains to dissociate themselves when accidents such as a boiler explosion occurred to another ship of the same name. The carriage of mails was much sought after as a mark of reliability, and the employment of officers from the Navy or East Indian service was always given prominence for the same reason.

On the sunnier side, the advantages to travellers became more and more appreciated, and, with the spread of a railway network in the late '30s and in the '40s, a true transport system appeared with great advantages for both travel and trade. The '40s therefore saw further efforts to run steamers across the wider part of the sea. Another service, Hull to Gothenburg, calling at Christiansand, was begun in 1840 by the Wilson firm of future prominence, but it only lasted 3 seasons. Yet another firm, this time German, entered the Hull-Hamburg trade in 1841 and produced another round of strong competition, duplicated sailing and fare-cutting. Next year, whether as a result or merely as being a victim of its own internal troubles, the St George Co. withdrew from Hamburg and handed its Rotterdam trade over to its agent in Hull. Nevertheless, three owners still remained on the Hull-Hamburg sta-

tion, and sailings were now twice a week, as they now were between London and Hamburg. The mid-'40s were another dull period, partly at least owing to economic depression.

Travellers wishing to go to Norway or Sweden were still recommended to go to Hamburg and thence to Kiel or Lübeck, from where there were regular mail steamers to Copenhagen, Gothenburg and Christiania.[6] It was only towards the end of the decade that some new impetus came as economic conditions slowly revived. By this time, of course, the foundation of the great ocean mail services had rendered the problems of the North Sea relatively trivial, except of course that they were subsidised, whereas most North Sea vessels were not – only the G.S.N. received a quite small payment for conveying the mails from London to Hamburg. Slowly, further services were added. Sailings to St Petersburg became more frequent in the late '40s, and at last service from other British ports such as Leith and Newcastle, needless to say to Hamburg, began in 1848 and 1850 respectively, while Bremen and Harlingen were linked to Hull and London. Cattle began to be shipped from Tonning. In 1850 the Scandinavian service was revived, and some of these services were operated by screw-propelled vessels. But there were still only 168,474 tons of steamship on the U.K. register in 1850, many very small.

A sign of coming change was a fresh attempt at large-scale operation. This, the North of Europe Steam Navigation Co., was founded by railway shareholders and the Peto contracting interests, to run steamers from some of the new and rather speculative rail-connected ports coming into being in the early '50s.[7] These new factors presage the next phase of development where they may more appropriately be considered.

The beginning of the Crimean War can therefore be taken as the end of the beginning of steam navigation to the North Sea.

It was an area of small owners, of few ships, where your author could quote the individual voyages if needs be. The largest Hull owners, Brownlow Pearson and Co., had 10 ships in 1854. (also running to London and Antwerp), Gee had 5, and Ringrose 3 (to Rotterdam). The German Hanseatic Co. had 3 and Batavier had 2. However, despite the technical imperfections of their vessels and their relative fewness, the steamers had already made a mark on the economy, out of proportion to their numbers. Their more frequent voyages enabled a good deal more perishable cargo such as butter to cross the North Sea, and after a reduction of duties in 1842, a regular flow of cattle was also taking advantage of the steamer's regularity and speed. The concentration on the Hamburg routes showed that there was a steady business there.

On the passenger side, although there was nothing approaching heavy traffic by later standards, the facilities did allow more people to cross, either on business or holiday and even quite fortuitous events could start a rush, as shown by the response to reports of a destructive fire in Hamburg in 1843, when very soon so many hopefuls began arriving there seeking work, that discouraging notices were put in the Hull papers. In general, however, the scale of activity was surprisingly little greater in 1850 than in 1830 and indicated that the North Sea trade had attracted little capital, a situation which probably reflects the inadequacies of the paddle steamer as well as the rival investment attraction of the railways, a situation which technical development and economic opportunity were soon to change.

Expansion

The years from 1855 to 1857 were the period when the steamship ceased to be unusual and instead bid fair to supplant the

Table 1. *Volume of Trade*

Average Annual Imports and Exports of British Produce

Years	Imports from (£ m)			Exports (British Produce)		
	Russia	Germany	Holland	Russia	Germany	Holland
1860–4	14	15	9	3	13	6
1880–4	18	25	25	6	18	9
1900–4	26	33	34	9	24	9

Re-exports not included – these could amount to 50% or over.

Tonnage of shipping entered and cleared from British ports ('000 tons)

	Entered			Cleared		
1860–4	883	1566	817	600	1418	585
1890–4	2389	3803	3715	1688	3719	2079

For Sweden and Norway in the same years:

1860–4	entered	868,000	cleared	792,000
1890–4		3042,000		2900,000

sailing ship not only in the passenger and valuable cargo trades but also in the bulk cargoes too.

These were years of great economic development in all the Northern European countries, as production increased and industrialisation spread, bringing concurrent increases in trade between the nations, illustrated in Table I.[8] Many new demands on transport were made, and these could more readily be met by the greatly improved vessels whose existence in turn provided new facilities which fostered the general advance. That advance also provided opportunity for many new entrepreneurs to enter the steamship business. The booms of 1856–7, 1864–6 and the early 70s drew in capital. Some survived, others went under eventually, but there was proliferation of routes and competitive sailings. No longer can one easily follow the activities of all the steamers and all owners. It was an era of individual enterprise, mushroom growth and all too often, collapse.

Technological improvement, however, contributed considerably to this rapid progress of steam navigation. Steam engines and boilers themselves were being steadily improved in economy, while iron hulls and the screw propeller combined to produce a much more practical vessel than the pad-dler both for the North Sea and general conditions. Iron hulls had been in use since the '40s and were stronger and were structurally less complicated, left clearer holds and allowed the inclusion of water-tight bulkheads, all advantages when the size of ships was already reaching the largest conveniently feasible for timber. The screw propeller had also come into use in the 40s, particularly after the celebrated RAT-TLER and ALECTO tug-of-war. It was certainly a more efficient agent of propulsion, but it was also less vulnerable to the sea and could be arranged so that it occupied less of the best space in a ship, to name two of its great advantages. The combination of the two, however, does not seem to have produced really satisfactory results until the mid-50s, when the screw colliers began to show their utility and economy in the East Coast coal trade and then in long trips to the Crimea with stores for the army. From then on, the screw steamer made very rapid strides and was the basis in shipping of the increased activity fuelled also by economic growth of the 50s and 60s. They were far more suited to routes where cargo could provide a basic traffic, with a small passenger holding as well, a very common situation in the North Sea. Steamship construction shot ahead, as shown in Table II.[9] Paddle steamers,

Table 2. *Numbers of Steamships*

Steamships on the British Register in certain years

Year	Number	Tonnage	Average
1815	8	638	91
1839	720	79,240	110
1860	1907	424,980	222
1870	3178	1,112,934	350
1890	7381	5,037,666	682
1910	12000	10,442,719	870

The basis of calculating tonnage was changed at various times, so that the figures are not strictly comparable.

Figure 3. The NORTHENDEN, of 843 tons, was built in 1886 by Swan & Hunter of Newcastle for the Manchester, Sheffield and Lincolnshire Railway, to run on their routes from Grimsby to Hamburg, Rotterdam and Antwerp.

however, for many years retained their popularity for fast and powerful vessels, particularly where shallow draft was essential, as was frequently the case on cross-Channel routes.

The results of the economic and technical advances could be seen in more routes, more sailings and more ports. Capital was readily available and the screw steamer was simple and workable. Though expensive, their earning power was also great and the ordinary owner was prepared to take the plunge, and many new men too, went in for them, not only in liner trades, but also for general bulk cargoes. The old system sought the new marvels, but then they began to impose their own terms.

A rush of new services sprang up and the old owners tried to defend their position. The attractive routes between the big ports drew the attention of others so that one frequently finds three or four owners on routes like London to Hamburg and Rotterdam.[10] The G.S.N.C. was constantly complaining of competitors attempting to undercut the establishment, who increased the number of their sailings or reduced rates further.[11] Particularly from the British side, where speculation in new ports had

gone hand in hand with general expansion, new ports opened sailings to the well-established ports in Europe, and some additional ports on the Continent also succeeded in reaching the steamer's map. Places such as Goole, West Hartlepool and Grimsby, Lowestoft and Harwich were all opened for Continental services in the 50s, while the use of Bergen, Harburg, Dordrecht, Kampen, Harlingen, Amsterdam on the eastern side relieved the previous concentration on Hamburg and Rotterdam, while the St Petersburg route received much attention. Liverpool and Glasgow began steamer services to Europe, and there were routes along the continental shore such as Antwerp-Hamburg and northwards to Norway.[12]

The advance to prosperity was not, however, smooth. Although business as a whole went forward over the period, there were hectic booms and collapses which took their toll. It was still a time of small owners, the old shipping methods were still in vogue and were not yet fully adapted to new conditions. Even in the boom of the mid-sixties, we find plenty of ships, but many half full.[13] Elsewhere traffic was scarce, as Wilson found, still struggling to build a reliable service to Norway and Sweden.[14] So there were casualties. Some new routes failed or took a considerable time to become established – Grimsby and Harwich both fall in this category – or some of the rivals quietly dropped out, like one of the Scandinavian services. The G.S.N. moved smartly to take over one casualty before others could step in.[15] The most notable collapse was the biggest firm, the North of Europe Company, which went out of business in 1858. It certainly suffered from bad management, it relied solely on paddle steamers, it probably took on too much in the way of new routes, and found itself serving equally divergent interests of different ports and railways.[16]

For a time therefore, the individual owners were largely left in possession, mostly operating one or two routes from

Figure 4. Richardson, Duck & Co. of Stockton built the MONTEBELLO of 1735 tons for the Wilson Line in 1890. At first she partnered the ANGELO (plate 2) on the Christiania service, and remained on it when the latter was withdrawn.

one port. A few companies of similar or slightly larger scope appeared. These, which might be called "town" companies, were usually based on local capital, but sometimes on more speculative elements. Bergen and Bremen were established ports of this kind, while West Hartlepool or Goole represented the newer world. It will be seen too that European ships were becoming plentiful, but, although some owners expanded fast, as shown in Table 2, the scale of operations of all owners was still small.

The particularist and local interests of ports and owners were challenged for the first time during this period, owing to the appearance of the railways and their increasingly revolutionary effect on internal transport. Two matters are of importance in the early days, firstly, the influence of railway practice for through fares and rates; and secondly, actual railway ownership of steamers.

Railway business methods were quite different to the piecemeal payments to the various parties involved in a long journey which were hitherto usual. The number and extent of these charges could be considerable, quite apart from the trouble and effort involved, as numerous parties charged for slight services. The railways, once goods traffic developed (goods receipts exceeded passengers for the first time in 1852), soon began to think of one through rate with "clearing-house" arrangements for easy settlement, and they began to extend the system over the sea if possible. Such rates were therefore available from an early date via Hull, which depended on traffic from Yorkshire or Lancashire, and were extended to other ports, many of which were the new ones backed heavily, if not owned by railways. Moreover, the influence of railways greatly widened the hinterland of each port and thus created alternative routes between interior places in England and interior places in Europe.[17]

The ownership of steamers was a logical extension of the railway system once fares and rates through a port were arranged. In the early days on the North Sea, however, such intervention was limited. It was not really needed, for, as we have seen, Hull was so obvious an objective on the East Coast for the first railways, already a great port with much trade from its hinterland with plenty of shipping available. To the south, London was the principal port but was itself such a great source of traffic, of its own or by transhipment, that its steamers were never much concerned with railways. To the north, the railways already had long been in use to lead coal to ports on Tyne and Wear.

On the Continent, railways were mostly planned and owned by the State, and did not go into shipping. The railways that did were the two less prosperous and more speculative British railways, which, after building their lines to and sometimes basing their futures on new ports which they hoped would bring prosperity, then found difficulty in inducing private shipowners to run services of such risky economics, and the collapse of the North of Europe Co., for example, affected both railways, which subsequently sought to run ships on the North Sea. Both tried to attract other owners, but with little success, and both, anxious to gain traffic to improve impecunious finances, decided to seek the Parliamentary powers they needed to run steamships. Despite much opposition from shipowners, both succeeded, and thus in the mid-sixties the ships of the Manchester, Sheffield and Lincolnshire Railway from Grimsby, and those of the Great Eastern from Harwich, were added to the numerous services already crossing the North Sea. Poor though both railways might be, in railway terms, their capital resources compared with those of the average shipowner, were vast. At first, however, both railways started

quietly, the M. S & L with twice weekly routes to Antwerp, Rotterdam and Hamburg, and the G.E.R. running to the first two of these ports similarly. But the shape of the future was shown when very soon the G.E.R. increased the frequency of its Rotterdam service to daily, except Sundays, and running so far as possible to a regular time, though its 3 am arrival at Harwich was rather daunting.[18]

Turning now to the other important development of this period, the screw iron steamer was also a most effective carrier of bulk cargoes, and during the '60s took a rapidly increasing share in such trades. During that decade, construction of steamers began to approach that of sailing ships and, of course, the carrying power increased much more. In 1850 there were 168,000 tons of steamships on the British Register; in 1860, 454,000; and by 1870, 1,113,000. Steamers had, it is true, somewhat increased their size, and certainly their range of operation, but nevertheless a good proportion of this tonnage found employment in the North Sea trades. Coal from Tyne and Wear ports was needed in larger and larger quantities by railways and industrial users in all the countries along the eastern side of the North Sea, and timber offered a useful return cargo. The steamer could deliver large quantities reliably, free from vagaries of wind and weather, and this was what industry needed.

This incursion into the wider aspects of shipping brought in all the same characteristics which make it so hard to describe shipping in other than general terms. Few owners and fewer ships ever came into the public eye, for they did not operate as a "service" in the same way as did the passenger and general cargo ships, but ran as cargoes and destinations offered. Almost as soon as the ink on the peace treaty was dry, in 1856, we can find screw colliers starting up the Baltic – one of them, the GEORGE HAWKINS, was lost off Reval in 1856 – and from then onwards, one cannot keep track of their ramifications as they carried the basic materials of the industrial age from port to port.

The earlier ships of this type were mostly British, and of about 500–700 gross tons. A steady increase of size gradually took place, so that by 1914 vessels for North Sea and Baltic trade ran up to about 2,000 tons. The same type of ships became the first deep-sea tramps, and the types were for some time, interchangeable; but practical reasons of port-size and depth caused two distinct types to emerge well before 1914. Norwegian, Swedish, Danish, German and Dutch shipowners soon began to acquire steamers for their trades, from the '60s onwards. Sometimes they began with second-hand British ships, but many built new; some for their special trade, (e.g. coal) others for more diverse trading. Owners in general were on a smaller scale than those in the liner trades – as one might expect.

The expansion both of liner and bulk trades led, in terms of tonnage entered at British ports, to an increase between the early '60s and the early '90s, of 868,000 tons, to 3,042,000 from Sweden and Norway; 1,566,000 to 3,803,000 from Germany; and 817,000 to 3,715,000 from Holland – and similarly in the opposite direction (i.e. a three or four-fold increase).[19]

The 20 years following the Crimean War can be seen as a rapid spell of fundamental change, bringing the steamer from a relatively untried phenomenon to what was virtually the normal method of sea transport, at least in the North Sea. Sailing ships were far from extinct, but yearly a higher proportion of the traffic went by steam – certainly in the passenger and general cargo class. The short North Sea voyages allowed the advantages of the steamer to overcome its extravagance, which was a serious handicap on ocean voyages. Thus the North Sea was perhaps the first of the principal seas of the world to have its commerce predominantly conducted by steam power.

Well before 1880, the area of specula-tion was over and the surviving owners settled down to a period of slower and steadier progress which lasted to the end of the century. When the slack economic conditions improved, early in the new century, North Sea steamers took their share in the general improvements.

Other economic trends of the time were also reflected in the North Sea traders, with a tendency to amalgamation into larger units and the appearance of new traffics and new ports to meet new requirements. Widening industrialisation and the rise of national sentiment, together with government intervention in economic affairs, led to new lines of a national rather than private character.

Technical progress was less prominently evident, as the only important developments such as the use of steel, triple expansion and turbine engines, had little outward effect on North Sea shipping, when compared with the advent of iron hulls and the screw propellor. In reality, however, these innovations formed part of much detailed improvement which was continuously going on, both to increase the fuel efficiency of ships and to improve their earning capacity. For example, the use of steel saved much weight, while improved engines both used much less fuel, and occupied less space; so that together, with improvements of structure, ships could carry more for the same speed at less cost.[20]

Looking in more detail at these points, developments in ownership and organisation began to overtake the old individualistic world of shipping. Many of these factors became influential first in the short-sea trades, where everything seemed to favour the larger unit – the need for through bookings, greater capital needs, larger organisations, the faster tempo of commerce, the anxiety of certain railways to offer a unified service, the interest of governments and of the growing number of senders and receivers of goods who were large organisations themselves – all these factors pressed hard on owners of the old

Figure 5. The Thule Line of Gothenburg built the THULE in 1892 for Wigham Richardson & Co. of Newcastle for their Gothenburg-London service. She was large for her day, 2036 tons, and is seen off Tilbury.

"personal" type, who could not offer such unified control. Together with other of the new developments, the factors began to create a separation between "high class" and more ordinary routes, which will be examined later.

Many private owners managed nevertheless to flourish, but in most cases only by a process of amalgamation among themselves and by increasing the scope of their routes; so as to broaden their business and thus place their profitability on surer ground. At Hull, that great centre of small ownerships, two of the "original" firms sold out to other local firms around 1880. The two purchasers, Wilson, and Bailey & Leetham, both greatly extended their interests far beyond the North Sea and Baltic, and eventually the former, who had struggled so hard to establish services to Scandinavia in the 40s and 50s, created a

near monopoly at Hull, even before taking over Bailey & Leetham in 1903. They thus became one of the largest shipowners in the world, and obviously had an organisation to match, but they were still a private company.[21] In Leith, Hamburg, Bremen, Sweden and Holland, private firms took a similar course. In Denmark, however, amalgamation took place relatively early to produce the large United S.S. Co., while in Norway, steamship ownership of regular trades seems to have been embodied in the "town" companies, already referred to, with a single company operating local, coastal and overseas routes from one place, and examples of similar companies also occur elsewhere, while amalgamation produced one at Newcastle.[22] The rise of such firms points again to the need to draw upon a wider field of capital and to create a larger economic force in the

Table 3. *Numbers of ships owned by certain owners*

A. Hull owners	1851	1859	1866	1876	1913
Brownlow, Lumsden	9	11	10	7	to Wilson 1878
Joseph Gee	4	7	6	8	to Bailey & L 1881
J.R. & C.L. Ringrose	1	7	7	6	5
Thos. Wilson, Sons & Co	–	6	15	39	87
Bailey & Leetham	–	2	9	22	to Wilson 1903

B. Principal owners elsewhere		
General S.N. Co	62	49
James Currie, Leith	25	36
Bergen S.S. Co	3	36
Batavier Line	4	11
United S.S. Co	11	123
Hamburg-London Line	4	22
Thule S.S. Co, Gothenburg	4	11

new and complex transport structure of the 19th century. Some of the new ventures were likewise large from the outset.

The British railway companies, while more restricted in routes owing to their need to obtain Parliamentary powers, had equally the financial resources to set a fast pace in frequency and facilities, and their attitude to providing a service was naturally that of a regular and daily one at a fixed time, in contrast with the former uncertainties of tide and cargo. They were also believed to rig their rates to attract traffic, and while this was disputed, certainly they could and did accept loss in order to foster long-term traffic, and as we have seen, railway services did not at first do well. While not responsible for new routes in this period, the railways' influence was to provide much-improved services and new facilities, as mentioned later, which consequently attracted much traffic. In the last decade before 1914 railway interest took a new form when intensifying competition led one newcomer to take over the existing Goole S.S. Co., while another took a large interest in the remaining small Hull owner, and radically

improved the service.[23] These developments thus drew together both the "amalgamation" and the "railway" factors.

The need for large resources becomes evident when the development of traffic is studied, for although the period was one of the spread of industrialisation, particularly in Germany, Holland and Belgium, trade was in no way affected by the consequent theoretical self-sufficiency, and industrialised nations happily exchanged their goods, added new products and used new raw materials on a larger scale than ever. Increased population added its stimulus to increase of trade, and so did industrial specialisation.

The traditional trans-shipment trade from London suffered from the establishment of direct shipping routes from Europe to the distant continents, but while old staples like cotton goods and yarn still flourished, largely as a result of new facilities, three important new traffics require our special attention, the trade in food and the new larger scale movements of people, particularly in tourists and emigrants. It was these changes which mainly created the distinction between the "high class"

or "fore cabin", and cargo below the lower deck, with of course the engines amidships. Paddle steamers varied little from this layout, as their engines necessarily occupied the height of the ship to the upper deck. The screw steamer however, was not thus restricted, especially as ships became larger and engines more compact, and the process of refinement already referred to produced many variations. Engines could be moved further aft, though in the end a position just aft of amidships became most popular. Instead of continuous unbroken decks, a number of layouts were tried incorporating "wells" or what were termed "raised quarter decks", and other variations of hull design, which enabled ships to make the best of their size and yet save tonnage.

It was soon realised too that, with screw ships, the stern was far from the best place for first class passengers, what with the pitching of the ship and the vibration and pounding of the propeller, and the accommodation was accordingly moved amidships, round an engine and boiler casing. The second class (forward in older ships) took the after position. The crew were always right forward. This change began in the '80s and compelled the abandonment of the old layout of a central saloon with cabins opening off it, owing to the engines occupying the central position. A further development was thus initiated, for, where ships had hitherto incorporated all the accommodation within the hull, they now began, under the impulse towards better accommodation for more people, to have structures built above the hull. In such a way appeared lounges, smoke rooms, separate dining saloons as well as more and more cabins, which moreover were often single or double rather than the old 4, 6 or even more berths. The passengers of 1914 thus found a ship larger, rather faster and certainly more comfortable than their confrères of 1870, even if she was still one of the sturdy seaworthy vessels so much associated with the North Sea rather than the sleek packets of the English Channel.[35]

The sturdiness and seaworthiness were justified in a surprisingly good safety record. There were countless collisions and strandings and a number of total losses, but the only disaster involving great loss of life was the wreck of the BERLIN at the Hook of Holland in 1907, and even that sad occasion at the end of the voyage only emphasised the reliability with which the steamers struggled through all weathers.

This reliability arose from ships strongly built to a simple design and well maintained. By present day standards, the ships would be under-used as, on most routes, a round trip per week was all that was achieved, and on the longer ones, merely a single voyage one way. But tides and weather influenced the voyage times, particularly if the ship went into docks, loading and discharging were slow, and sometimes involved changes of berth, while coaling also took time and possibly a shift of berth too. It was not, in practice, so easy to economise in time, and the weekly cycle was thus useful in having a little time in hand to cover eventualities. The ships had, of course, regular crews, whose berths were often much sought after, even if many were on special agreements involving the seamen finding his own food.

It is evident that the North Sea trade was commercially attractive, but details of its profitability are none too profuse, partly on account of so many owners having much wider interests. The General S.N. Co. paid 10% steadily, often with a bonus, until the '80s and '90s when profits declined, to revive somewhat in the new century. The railway companies provide some guidance, but in their case it is not always clear what is included in their figures. The M.S. & L. steamers made small but steady profits after the '70s, although they fell back in the 1900s. The Harwich vessels steadily improved their position and became a useful part of the G.E.R., making £25,000 a year in the late '80s – about the cost of a ship.[36]

Although no conference existed in the North Sea trade, it is clear that agreements existed between owners in the individual trades to equalise rates and arrange sailings from the early days of the Hull-Hamburg trade onwards. In the 1890s an agreement was reached between British and German lines over emigrant traffic, but this was largely between the trans-Atlantic companies. The general owners formed a conference in 1905, but this again concerned tramps rather than liners. Finally, the railway acquisition of Humber services about the same time resulted in a virtual railway monopoly in that area, which would consequently be subject to understandings between the railways such as the traffic agreements which were made in 1909.[37]

What do we see therefore when we survey North Sea shipping in 1914? Larger, faster and more comfortable ships than before, using only a quarter of the fuel of a ship of the 1840s, were sailing more frequently but at much the same cost to the traveller. The table shows comparatively the situation in the '70s and 1914. Even those routes where frequency remained the same were now mostly operated by much finer vessels. The services conveyed over a quarter of a million people each way, compared with the few thousand of the 1840s, and the tonnage of cargo must also have been many times greater.

There were few signs of weakness. Some lesser routes still ran at low frequency with aging ships, victims of the more prosperous routes, or perhaps of the increasingly stringent legal requirements for passenger ships. "Cargo only" sailings, by the same token, were increasing, but nevertheless few routes other than purely competitive ones went under.

Taken all in all, the North Sea shipping in 1914 had reached a peak of achievement it was not to re-attain for years. What was their achievement must be judged according to one's view of the development of modern life. To compare the relatively static world of the 1830s with the large-scale movements of people and goods in the years before 1914 is to realise the opportunities which steam ships and steam railways gave to men and women of the countries bordering the North Sea to see and appreciate other lands. The North Sea, we at the conference know, was never the barrier it is sometimes thought to be, but the steamship made it a highway of universal communication.

Table 4. *Comparison of Services across the North Sea, 1876 and 1914*

The principal routes from the U.K. to each of the countries on the eastern coast of the North Sea have been selected. In some cases, a new route appeared between the two dates, and these are also shown.

To Norway	Frequency sailings per week	Hours on voyage	Fare 1st/2nd	Average tonnage of ships
Hull-Christiania 1876	1	over 48	80/–;63/4	1,000-1,500
« « 1913	1	39	95/–;65/–	4,000
Newcastle-Bergen 1913	3	44*	80/–;	1,200
To Sweden				
Hull-Göteborg 1876	1	48*	63/–;42/–	1,400
« « 1913	1	36	80/–;55/–	4,500
London-Göteborg 1876	1	48*	60/–;20/–(dk)	1,000
« « 1913	1	40	63/–;	1,600-2,800
To Denmark				
Leith-København 1876	1	60	63/–;31/6	750
« « 1913	1	54	63/–;31/6	1,300
Harwich-Esbjerg 1913	4	25	30/–;15/–	1,500
To Germany				
Hull-Hamburg 1876	4	36*	30/–;20/–	800-1,000
Grimsby-Hamburg 1876	2	36*	30/–;	500-1,000
« « 1913	6	30	30/–;10/–	1,600
To the Netherlands				
London-Rotterdam 1876	6		20/–;15/–	500–700
« « 1913	6	7½*	17/–;11/–	1,500
« « via Harwich 1876	6	14	26/–;15/–	600–900
« « « « 1913	6	10		2,400
« « via Flushing 1913	14	11	31/6;20/–	1,900–2,900

* = time at sea

Note that Germany was largely served via Harwich, Queenborough or the short sea routes rather than by direct sailings.

Notes

1 The problems of early steamship management are best expounded in Palmer.
2 Cope Cornford.
3 Pearson; Duckworth and Langmuir.
4 Statements about number and extent of sailing are based on use of local newspapers, directories and "Lloyd's List".
5 The development of ports and their facilities is usefully summarised in Bird.
6 e.g. in Milford, John, *Norway and her Laplanders,* London 1842.
7 For the North of Europe Co. see Gordon; Dow.
8 For the economic development of Europe see Clapham; Henderson.
9 The early development of the screw steamship is not yet satisfactorily described. Harley is useful.
10 The extension of sailings has been noted from similar series to note 4.
11 Annual Reports of G.S.N. Co., N.M.M. GSN 7/5.
12 The new ports have had their own historians – for Goole, Duckham and Grimsby, Dow Lowestoft and Harwich, Gordon, Allen.
13 See evidence of A.G. Robinson to P.P. 1864.
14 See evidence of C.H. Wilson to P.P. 1901.
15 N.M.M. GSN 7/5–6.
16 The collapse is outlined in the Company's meetings reported in *The Times.*
17 The two approaches are outlined in the evidence in P.P. 64.
18 Railway Steamers are dealt with generally by Duckworth and Langmuir; those of the MS & LR by Dow; and the GER by Allen, Gordon.
19 The detailed development of the cargo steamer remains to be outlined. These general remarks are based on Harley.
20 Developments in machinery are summarised in the *Marine Engineer* in 1914.

21 The history of the Wilson Line is still to be written. The details given are taken from Taylor, 1976.
22 For the United S.S. Co., see Normann the Bergen S.S. Co., see Keilhau and the Newcastle case, Northway.
23 Duckham, 1968.
24 The rise of foreign travel may be traced in Behrend. An example of a return from Scandinavia via Calais is E.L.L. Arnold's, *A Summer Holiday in Scandinavia,* London 1877.
25 Duckworth and Langmuir.
26 Rush; O'Dell.
27 Duckworth and Langmuir; Allen; Normann; Rambosch.
28 Gordon; Allen; Duckworth and Langmuir.
29 Keilhau.
30 Evidence of C.H. Wilson in P.P. 1901.
31 For emigration and general see Taylor, 1971. Detailed information derived from P.P. 1882, 1894, 1896 and 1903; Return of Transit Aliens.
32 The cruising information comes from the newspaper sources. The reference to number of tourists comes from the *Trade Report* (Norway) for 1895.
33 P.P. 1884, 1890, 1895; *Trade Reports.*
34 *Trade Reports;* Lists of Refrigerated Ships in Lloyd's Register of Shipping.
35 These notes are based on examination of photographs and plans, mostly in N.M.M. A profile of a typical vessel is Plate …
36 The financial details come from the Annual or Half-Yearly Reports of the companies mentioned. Those of the G.S.N. Co., are in N.M.M. (GSN 7/5–6) of the MS & L (later Great Central) and GER Co., in the Public Record Office (Rail 1110).
37 P.P. 1909 for the general conference, P.P. 1911 and Duckham 1968 for railway agreement.

Bibliography

Allen, C.J. *The Great Eastern Railway,* London 1967

Behrend, G., *Grand European Expresses,* London 1962

Bird, J., *The Major Seaports of the United Kingdom,* London 1963

Burtt, F., *Cross-Channel and Coastal Paddle-Steamers,* London 1934

Clapham, Sir J.H. *The Economic Development of France and Germany,* 4th Edition, Cambridge 1951

Cope Cornford, L., *A Century of Sea Trading 1824–1924,* London 1924

Duckham, B.F. *The Yorkshire Ouse,* Newton Abbot 1967

Duckham, B.F., *Railway Steamship Enterprise: The Lancashire and Yorkshire Railway East Coast Fleet, 1904–14* in *Business History,* Vol. 10 (1968)

Dow, G., *Great Central,* 3 Vols., London 1959–65

Duckworth, C.L.D., Langmuir, G.E. *Railway and Other Steamers,* Glasgow 1948, 2nd Edition, Prescot 1968

Gordon, D.I., *A Regional History of the Railways of Great Britain,* Newton Abbot 1968 2nd Edition 1977. Volume 5. *The Eastern Counties*

Harley, C.K., *The shift from Sailing Ships to Steam ships 1850-1890: A Study in Technological Change and its Diffusion* in *Essays on a Mature Economy, Britain after 1840,* ed. McCloskey D.N., London 1971

Henderson, W.O. *The Industrial Revolution on the Continent,* London 1961

Keilhau, W., *Norway and the Bergen Line,* Bergen 1953

Mathias, P. *The First Industrial Nation* London 1969

Mitchell, B.R. and Deane, P., *Abstract of British Historical Statistics,* Cambridge 1962

Normann, L.V., *Det Forenede Dampskibs Selskab A/S 1866–1926,* København 1926

Northway, A.M., *The Tyne Steamship Company: A late Nineteenth Century Shipping Line* in *Maritime History,* Vol. 2. (1973)

O'Dell, A.C., *The Scandinavian World,* London 1957

Palmer, S., *Experience, Experiment and Economics: Factors in the Construction of Early Merchant Steam ships* in *Ships and Shipbuilding in the North Atlantic Region.* Ed. Matthews, K. and Panting, G., Newfoundland 1978

Pearson, F.H., *Early History of Hull Steam Shipping* in *Transaction of Hull and District Institution of Engineers and Naval Architects,* 1894

Rambusch, S., *Esbjerg Havn 1868-1968,* Esbjerg 1968

Rush, F.A., *Denmark Farms On,* London 1970

Taylor, J., *Ellermans,* London 1976

Taylor, P., *The Distant Magnet,* London 1971

Tomlinson, W.W., *The North Eastern Railway: Its Rise and Development,* Newcastle 1914, reprinted Newton Abbot 1967

Periodicals and Reference Works

Bradshaw's Railway Guide
Directory of Shipowners
The Marine Engineer
Lloyd's Register of Shipping
Merchant Ships of the World
Sea Breezes
Shipping World

Parliamentary Papers: referred to in the notes as P.P. with dates. The full titles of the individual papers are, using the normal references of the volumes of official bound set:

1864 XI
Select Committee on Powers of Railway Companies

1882 LXII
Reports received by the Board of Trade and the Local Government Board as to the Transit of Scandinavian Emigrants through the port of Hull

1884 LXXXV
Statistical Tables as to Home and Foreign Animals prepared by the Agricultural Department of the Privy Council Office, 1883

1888 XI
Select Committee on Emigration and Immigration (Foreign)

1890 LXVI
Return of ships arriving at ports in the United Kingdom from Foreign ports in 1888 and 1889 with live cattle

1894 LXVIII
Reports on the volume and effects of recent immigration from Eastern Europe into the United Kingdom

1895 XC
Annual Report for 1894 of Proceedings under the Contagious Diseases (Animal) Act

1896 LXVII
Reports made by Theodore Thomson concerning Arrival of Immigrants and Transmigrants in England as to measures taken by certain Port Sanitary Autho-

rities with a view to prevent the importation of Cholera and other infectious diseases into this Country

1896 LXXXIV
Correspondence between the Board of Trade and Wilson, Sons & Co

1901 VIII
1902 IX
Select Committee on Steamship Subsidies

1903 IX
Royal Commission on Alien Immigration

1909 XLVIII
Royal Commission on Shipping Rings

1911
Departmental Committee on Railway Agreements and Amalgamations

1913 XL
Reports on Bounties and Subsidies for Shipbuilding and Shipping and Navigation in Foreign Countries

Sundry references have also been made to the following series of reports, all published each year in the Parliamentary Papers:

Trade and Navigation Accounts
Trade Reports from overseas countries
Returns of Alien Passengers (begun in 1900)
Reports on Veterinary Department of Board of Agriculture

The Triumph of Deep Sea Fishing in the North Sea

ALAN HJORTH RASMUSSEN

The development of a real sea-going fishery for all sorts of fish in the North Sea was a feature of the nineteenth century, after a highly specialised bulk fishery for herring, had dominated it almost without interruption since the fifteenth century.

Dutchmen, who had established themselves as the experts in the catching and processing of herring, followed the herring every year along the traditional path from the Shetlands to the Channel, but other fishermen as well took part in this drift net fishery, particularly as the Dutch lost ground during the eighteenth century. In the nineteenth, Norwegian, Scottish and English fishermen quite took over the place previously held by the Dutch as the main catchers and exporters of herring.

Whilst the herring, a pelagic fish, can be taken in a net when it is at suitable depths, the bottom-feeding fish had to be caught with the long line. Line fishing was the traditional method for cod above all, until, in the course of the nineteenth century the trawl, largely as a result of English influence became widespread in sea fishing.

The beam trawl had been known and used in coastal fishery in the northern North Sea and English Channel for many years. On the mainland of Europe it was known to coast dwellers as far north as Fanø and Graadyb.

It was however first in conjunction with the Brixham fishermen's search for new grounds in the English Channel in the first decades of the nineteenth century that the beam trawl was adopted in a significant way. In 1833 Brixham fishermen based themselves at Yarmouth, evidently with good results as many settled there. In 1843 the Brixham men reached Hull, and shortly afterwards one of their vessels brought in a miraculous catch from a place about 60 miles off the Humber. The place, still a well-known fishing mark, got its name Silver Pit according to tradition from the silvery fish scales still shining on the vessel's side when it came into harbour with the catch.

Though Yarmouth and Lowestoft enjoyed expansion in their fishery it was not to be compared with that on the Humber. The discovery of Silver Pit and the improved distribution made possible by an extended railway network provided the basis for a "colonialisation" of the sea bed in the whole Dogger Bank area, and thus fell to the Grimsby and Hull fishermen. The population of the towns increased by 500 per cent in 30 years. In 1863 there were 270 smacks in Hull and by 1880 420. At the same period Grimsby had about 500.[1]

In the course of the 1860's two types of English trawl fishery developed in the North Sea, the single boating and the fleeting. At Lowestoft and other places where dual owners were dominant the single boat was preferred, whereas at Hull and Grimsby where large capital interests outside fishing families were concerned, the fleeting system soon ruled.

In the 1870's single boating involved one week voyages, as the vessel brought home its own catch, but in fleeting special carriers collected the catch to bring it to market and the sailing smacks stayed at sea fishing intensively often as much as 6 or 8 weeks. At the head of the fishery was an admiral who decided where to fish and when to shoot and haul the trawl. Before steam was adopted in the 1880's it was usual to have three tows a day, each lasting about 5 hours. Hauling usually took several hours.

The coincidence of various factors, many deriving from the Industrial Revolution, favoured fishery development in the Humber, but there were soon complaints of failing returns because of over-fishing on the Dogger. This once more compelled the fishermen to seek new banks. In the mid 1860's the expansion of English beam trawl fishermen had reached North German coastal waters, and in 1869 they reached Denmark in significant numbers. The use of the beam trawl by seagoing vessels was not unfamiliar in Denmark as fishing everts from Blankenese and Finkenwerder had already been fishing south of Horns Rev. But it was only with the English expansion that beam trawl fishing came to be felt as a threat to previous traditions. An eyewitness from a west Jutland newspaper in August 1869: "Foreign fishing vessels are now seen every day in hundreds, close in against the coast. Their catch is carried by special steamers to some English harbour. Fear of the foreign fishermen is already so great that our own dare scarcely set their long lines for fear of having them destroyed and carried away. Only rarely is the offender decent enough to invite his victim on board to reclaim his damaged gear in its sorry state. Unless there is some change soon in these desperate circumstances, our coastal population will be compelled to abandon their means of livelihood, from time immemorial their only sustenance, and poverty and distress will be their lot."[2]

Traditional long lines could not coexist with trawling in the same area, which gave rise to many conflicts. The coastal fishermen were alarmed by the fleeting system which gave them no chance. On the 9th of June 1871 237 English smacks could be counted from Holmslands Klit outside Ringkøbing Fjord.

The interests in the same sea areas of the various North Sea fishing nations made possible a certain interchange of maritime culture between those engaged. It happened for instance when the foreign vessels anchored close inshore when the wind was too weak to move ship and trawl. Danish coastal fishermen were invited on board the smacks, which led some of them to take an interest in English fishing and later, jobs on board the sailing smacks. One young man from Holmslands Klit started his fishing career on board an English smack which was anchored off the coast.

Coastal fishermen can recall both good and evil from their contact with the foreign fishermen. English trawlermen on trips ashore killed sheep and horses, and use was made of this to create popular support for Danish fishing interests. The Board of Trade found good causes to issue against this background a notice in 1871 to "British Firshermen fishing off the coasts of Jutland or other possessions of the Danish crown" warning them that similar offences in future would be prosecuted, not only under Danish law but also under the Merchant Shipping Act 1854 section 267. The notice states that "complaints have been made to Her Majesty's Government that the crews of certain British Fishing Boats have landed on the Danish Coast and Misconducted themselves there by the commission of outrages which are a Discredit to the British Flag and Name."[3]

A combination of the influence of example, competition, and property feelings about the fishing immediately off their own

Figure 1. English smacks close against the coast, painted by Kr. Fjord, Holmslands Klit, Denmark.
Photo: Fiskeri- og Søfartsmuseet. Saltvands-akvariet, Esbjerg.

Figure 2. Running out the long line dinghy, around the change of the century. Painted as recollected by J. Thomsen.
Photo: Fiskeri- og Søfartsmuseet. Saltvands-akvariet, Esbjerg.

coast was the driving force not only in Danish North Sea fishing but also that of Germany.

In 1866 in the call for the establishment of the first German sea fishing company we find: "If one enquires into the earnings of the Hull smacks which exploit the fishing between Sylt and Borkum one finds ample confirmation of the estimates formed from our present inadequate fishery. The price of a smack is from 6000 to 6600 Thaler, and in a good year the value of its catch will nearly equal this. The captain, mate and two AB's who together with two boys constitute the crew receive no wages but a share of the catch: the first $1\frac{3}{8}$, each of the others $1\frac{1}{8}$ of the eight parts into which it is divided. Thus it is not unusual for a seaman to attain to a hundred pounds a year. The saving from a few trips often enables the captain to buy the vessel from the owner or builder and continue the profitable venture entirely on his own account. Our duty is clearly to follow the method which has given the English such success in our waters. We have the advantage over them of the shorter distance to our harbours than to Hull, Yarmouth or London. The voyage to the grounds and return to

deliver the catch, take ice and provisions, would be at most a third of the time taken to England. Moreover the market in the interior of Germany is scarcely touched, though that means we have largely to create a taste for those gifts of the sea which are in England so indispensible."[4]

In the same source we find a contemporary view of the state of the fisheries of other lands. "We allow the French, English, Norwegians and Americans to monopolise the supply to the whole Catholic world of its favourite stockfish. We allow the Norwegians, Scots and Dutch to supply Northern and Eastern Europe with the herring which is a common dish far into the interior of Germany. We do not even claim for our own table the fish which swarm along the German coast or just off the Frisian islands. Hundreds of English ships cast their nets here all the year round to provision Billingsgate, the great English fishmarket, with its fresh fish, nor do the Dutch fail to profit from the easy and rewarding fishery in German waters east of Rottum."

The company suffered the same fate as other German initiatives in open sea fishery, namely liquidation and collapse in the

Figure 3. Esbjerg fishermen 1890.
Photo: Fiskeri- og Søfartsmuseet. Saltvandsakvariet, Esbjerg.

course of the 1870's. Its leaders greatly underestimated the fact that experienced fishermen cannot be created overnight, and the market for seafish does not create itself. Not even purchasing the fish on the actual banks and then bringing it home by carrier, which another Hamburg-based company attempted at this time, was able to establish itself in the pattern of the German fisheries. Their future lay in the use of steam trawlers, of which the first was employed by the Geestemunde fish-merchant Friedrich Busse in 1885. The steam trawler "Sagitta" had clearly English models, and though like so many other initiatives its returns were at first disappointing, it had many successors. In 1889 there were 10 German steam fishing vessels whose crews totalled 109, in 1897 there were 103 with 1044 men on board.[5]

The origins and the heartland of steam trawling remained English. Steamships were first used as carriers, but from the first half of the 1880's were also used to trawl. The main development took place in the 1890's not least because of the North Sea development of the other trawl which was well suited to great towing power. In 1909 it was reported that Hull and Grimsby had more steam trawlers than the other North Sea countries put together. 1,336 trawlers were then registered in England and Wales: the nearest rival was Germany with 290, and the other countries had 143 between them. It was the steam trawler that produced the development of the intensive English-German long-distance fishery off Iceland, the Faeroes, and Greenland.

Just as it was the presence of English and Dutch vessels in German coastal waters which opened German eyes to their own under-developed fishery, foreign vessels brought about a realisation in Denmark

that traditional fishing did not extend beyond long lining along the coast. Plaice-
fishing had more or less been given up
since the Middle Ages. A West Jutland
newsaper observed sarcastically on April
25 1874 "The treasure which we do not
bother to pick up is carried off by English,
Germans and Swedes, and if you come to
Fanø and see a fleet of singlemasters you
mustn't think that they are Danish. No,
our fishermen haven't got as far as decked
boats yet. Those lying there so comfortably
are from Blankenese."[6]

Some years earlier it was complained
that Danish fishermen could not be persua-
ded to meet the demand for plaice, but
that it had to be purchased from the
numerous German fishing everts which fished up to Horns Rev. "It is infuriating as
one hears of the foreigners' good fortune
to see our own fishermen either sitting peacefully at home or at most going out in a
little rowing boat and bringing back half a
dozen fish. When on earth will it occur to
them that they could just as well enjoy the
wealth of the sea as the German and
English fishermen? Evidently it is more
attractive to sit at home and now and then,
when the weather is good or pockets

Figure 4. Blankenese fishing everts off
Esbjerg 1900. German everts habitually
sought shelter under the lee of the peninsula
Skallingen.
Photo: Fiskeri- og Søfartsmuseet. Saltvands-
akvariet, Esbjerg.

Figure 5. Frozen (iced) fish was transported
in willow baskets by rail to the German market. View from Esbjerg Harbour ca 1890.
Photo: Fiskeri- og Søfartsmuseet. Saltvandsakvariet, Esbjerg.

empty, go out for an hour or two for some
amateur fishing."[7]

The conflict between line fishing and
trawling referred to above produced a
popular feeling of support for Danish fishermen, that they should share like the
large nations around the North Sea in its
wealth. One can understand that neither
the Germans, to whom Denmark in 1864
lost one-third of its population, nor the
English, whose taking of the Danish fleet
in 1807 was still remembered, were popular, particularly when they now took fish
from under the nose of the Danes, or
almost literally from their feet. We are told
in a review of the activity of English trawlers in 1883 off the west coast of Jutland
among other places, that "the best fishing,
principally for soles and turbot, is close
under the land, and some of the vessels
work so near shore that a stone could
almost be thrown on board from the
beach."[8] Contemporary newspapers and
other sources include much about differences between Danish and foreign interests
about the exploitation of the sea's
resources. It was the beam trawl (and after
1893 the Granton trawl or other trawl in
which the mouth is kept open by the water
acting on the doors and not by a beam)

Figure 6. The beam trawl was used by English, German and Dutch fishermen. In Denmark this fishing tackle was used, in diminished form, up to Esbjerg – Fanø only. Painted as recollected by J. Thomsen.
Photo: Fiskeri- og Søfartsmuseet. Saltvandsakvariet, Esbjerg.

which triumphed over stationary devices such as long lines and fixed nets.

The fishing war of those days did not differ in essence from that of the 1970's. In the 1970's the battle was about mesh size and the relative importance of particular fish species and proteins. The background, which formed attitudes and negotiations, then as now, was the desire to preserve living standards and existing values rather than to maximise them.

Many fishermen evidently formed a view of how the foreigners were removing the resources, which compelled them to enter trawling themselves if they were to survive. One phase in the process of transition, if you cannot beat them join them, was however to declare that the unwanted method was harmful to the stock. Subjective evaluations of this sort were, then as now, in spite of the intervention of biologists and fisheries researchers an active element in forming opposed groups among fishermen both internationally and within those of one country.

There is indisputable documentary evidence that beam and other trawls were being bought in England for use by Danish

fishermen, but popular tradition is silent on the subject of Danish trawling at the end of the nineteenth century. It is certain that those in the Graadyb area on the west coast of Jutland knew small beam trawls of German type, but they were not used in the traditional fishery. Nor did the English trawls so hopefully ordered prove successful, as a want of experience and expertise led to them being dismissed as useless.

On the other hand those Danish fishermen who had emigrated to England knew how a trawl should be used, and they appear to have been relatively numerous. In September 1890 there were in the Hull fishery 15 Danish captains and about 20 second and third hands.[9] In the same year the Danish Steam Trawling Company was established, which was registered in Copenhagen but fished from England. The captains and crews of the Dania and Hafnia were Danes or other Scandinavians who had learnt trawling on English ships. Later Danish attempts to imitate English and German fishing by introducing steam trawlers were a failure.

One may ask whether the expanding English and German trawl fishery really influenced the development of fishing in

Figure 7. The dory is assumed to have been introduced into the Esbjerg–Hjerting area by Danish fishermen taking part in the bank fisheries, among others the line fisherman Lambert Sørensen. Hjerting ca 1910.
Photo: Fiskeri- og Søfartsmuseet. Saltvandsakvariet, Esbjerg.

Figure 8. Typical long line cutter, E 81 "Huitfeldt", in Esbjerg Harbour 1910. Note the dinghy used to run out the long line.
Photo: Fiskeri- og Søfartsmuseet. Saltvandsakvariet, Esbjerg.

Denmark. The foreign large-scale fishery was of the greatest importance, but more as an indirect encouraging factor than a direct impulse. The effectiveness of the foreign trawl fishery was every day apparent to Danish fishermen either on the grounds or just off the coast. But the Danes did not go in for trawling. One of the factors which prevented a change to the foreign method was the spread of Danish seining which in the 1880's and 90's came into use in the west Jutland plaice fishery and appeared to render the trawl superfluous.

The effects of English and German trawling on the Danish coasts were to demonstrate the existence of resources at Denmark's door which had been previously ignored, and to provoke a resultant reaction that the trawlers were removing something felt to be Danish property.

From that moment began the development of Danish sea fishing. Up to then example had been wanting of how large a scale fishing could assume. A powerful motive also was that in order to survive, the fishery, gear and vessels had to be developed.

It is worth noting that in spite of the contact both practical and cultural between Danish and English fishermen there was in the long term no significant result as far as adoption of fishery methods was concerned. Only what was absolutely essential and useful was taken over. Trawling in the North Sea was first seriously started by Danish fishermen at the end of the 1930's and the innovation came from Danish inland waters.

Particular pieces of technology were on the other hand more easily taken over. The use of steam power to haul the seine in Denmark has quite clear English models,

223

Figure 9. The first Danish decked vessels for line fishing were exported from Norway in the 1870's. Danish fishermen bought pilot boats from southern Norway. They were subsequently copied by a ship builder in Esbjerg. The Danish adaptation of the Norwegian specimen is seen in the foreground.
Photo: Fiskeri- og Søfartsmuseet. Saltvandsakvariet, Esbjerg.

and the introduction of decked boats in Danish North Sea fishery can be ascribed to contacts between south Norway and the fishery innovator Lambert Sørensen in Hjerting near Esbjerg. Worn out English smacks passed a peaceful old age in Danish long-lining.

The present situation in fishing is basically a further development of the methods used at the end of the nineteenth century. Fish finding and communications are facilitated by improved technology and materials improved in strength and durability: hard manual labour has been replaced by technical hydraulic aids.

The beam trawl is still used in the coastal fishery, mainly for shrimps but has had a renaissance, particularly among German,

Dutch and Belgian fishermen in the open sea. Drift netting has been replaced by mid-water trawling or ringnetting of pelagic fish, and many nations have developed industrial fishing with the trawl, where fish protein from a lower stage in the food chain is fed to animals on its way to man.

The use of tangle nets for demersal fish has greatly increased, among other ways by setting the nets over wrecks or the cast-offs of the oil-drillers. Long-line fishing has also survived and has recently become large-scale again for some fishermen in the northern North Sea and in the Atlantic in that it has proved possible to automate it (autoline-miniline) to an undreamt of extent. Finally Danish seining has been taken over and further developed to fly-shooting from Scottish and English harbours; a technique long used by Norwegians and Swedes.

The old fishing ways and gears thus survive in modern dress and altered technical circumstances. The total mass or living matter in the North Sea also seems unchanged since the turn of the century, though its composition by species has altered. The oil drilling industry has involved severe losses and restrictions to fishing, but the main problem of the 1980's will be the division of fishery resources between different nations and interest groups, for whilst populations earlier only felt proprietary about the fish of their own coastal waters the questions of rights to fish, among other things now extend over the whole of the North Sea.

Notes

1 Jeremy Tunstall: *The Fishermen,* third impression 1972, pp 17–44. Other sources: Edgar J. March: *Sailing Trawlers,* 1953, Edgar J. March: *Sailing Drifters,* 1952, *Sailing Fishermen in old photographs.* From the unpublished Ford Jenkins collection. Narrative By Colin Elliott, *Steam Fishermen in old photographs.* From the Ford Jenkins collection. Narrative by Colin Elliott, 1979, Thor Iversen: *Trålfiskets historie, Årsberetning vedkommende Norges Fiskerier 1937,* Nr. 3.

2 *Ribe Stifts-Tidende,* 10. august 1869.

3 Rigsarkivet, København. Udenrigsministeriet, samlesager. Fiskeriet under Danmark A 4682 a-h/ 1871.

4 Mittheilungen aus Justus Perthes' Geographischer Anstalt über wichtige neue Erforschungen aus dem Gesammtgebiete der Geographie von Dr. A. Petermann 1866, pp. 401–407.

5 German trawlfishing, historical information in: Professor Dr. W. Schnakenbech: *Die deutsche Fischerei in der Nordsee und im Nordmeer,* Hamburg 1947.

6 *Ribe Amts-Tidende* 25.4.1874.

7 *Fanø og Esbjerg Skibsfarts-, Nyheds- og Avertissements-Tidende* 1872.

8 *The Marine Engineer,* September 1, 1883, p. 148.

9 Rigsarkivet, København, *Landvæsensjournalsager* 1061/1892.

The North Sea in the Two World Wars

GEOFFREY TILL

Introduction

Twentieth Century naval warfare in the North Sea is largely the story of the maritime conflict between Britain and Germany, which lasted effectively from the late 1890's to 1945. The warfare of the period took the form it did largely because of three particular features in the strategic environment of that sea. It was, firstly, the obvious arena for conflict between maritime Britain and a continental adversary. Secondly, it was, and is, an area providing vital access to other seas and other strategic possibilities. Lastly, it was, and is, an area of considerable intrinsic value. Nevertheless the strategic environment of the North Sea cannot be seen in a vacuum. What happened there partly depended on, and partly determined, what happened elsewhere. Since this relationship with adjacent areas and seas was so important, it will be necessary to stray occasionally into the Baltic, often into the Norwegian Sea, and sometimes even further afield to understand fully the role of the North Sea in two World Wars.

The Struggle for Command

The North Sea is neither deep ocean nor coastal waters. As such it was the natural and almost inevitable scene of conflict between maritime power (as represented by Britain) and continental landpower (as represented by Germany). In the first half of the Twentieth Century it was, in short, the obvious battleground in the war between the whale and the elephant, as Mackinder put it in 1918.

Britain had a historic preference for a national strategy based on maritime power in which continental confrontation would be avoided. Instead, British strategy would take the form of economic pressure (through the institution of blockade), the support of European allies and diversionary attacks on the exposed flanks of her principal adversaries. Both to survive and to enable her to project her power into Europe, Britain needed general command of the seas but the particular control of the Channel and the North Sea. Britain's apparent success in such strategic endeavours led navalists like Mahan to argue that maritime power was a naturally superior form of national power, conferring upon its possessor the ability to dominate the world's affairs.

This comfortable Anglo-American view of the world was challenged, however, by the emergence in the early part of this century of the Geopolitical School of which Harold Mackinder, paradoxically an Englishman himself, was one of the chief exponents. Mackinder challenged Mahan

Figure 1. Some of the protagonists. Admiral Sir John Jellicoe, C-in-C Grand Fleet 1914–16, and later First Sea Lord. (Lady Latham.)

by contending that landpower had a natural superiority over seapower for a variety of reasons. One of them was that some of the huge resources of landpower in the world's Heartland could so easily be diverted into the creation of a substantial navy. "The surrender of the German fleet in the Firth of Forth," wrote Mackinder, "is a dazzling event, but in all soberness, if we would take the long view, must we not still reckon with the possibility that a large part of the Great Continent might someday be united under a single sway, and that an invincible sea-power might be based upon it?"[1]

But this process essentially had already begun by the late 1890's when Germany started to develop the resources of a great naval power, and the North Sea became for the first time in a hundred years a likely area of major naval conflict. The Anglo-German naval race forced Britain to change her strategic orientation. Her naval bases were moved from the south to the north; the disposition of her fleets around the world also altered accordingly. The Standard described it well in May 1912: "Because of that formidable and threatening Armada across the North Sea, we have almost abandoned the waters of the outer oceans. We are in the position of Imperial Rome when the Barbarians were thundering at the frontiers. The ominous word has gone forth. We have called home the legions ..."[2]

This, though, was not at all how it appeared in Berlin. In strategic priority, Germany was a land power first and a seapower second and her leaders in both wars doubted whether it would be possible to produce a Navy of a size and quality that would allow it to seek some final decision in a total encounter with the British Fleet. Instead, in World War I, the German High Seas Fleet aimed simply at a strategy of "equalisation". "Our object," read the War Order for the North Sea Area, "is to damage the British Fleet by means of offensive advances against the forces watching or blockading the German Bight, and also by means of a ruthless mining and, if possible, a submarine offensive carried as far as the British Coast. When an equalisation of forces has been attained by these measures, all our forces are to be got ready and concentrated, and an endeavour will be made to bring our Fleet into action under favourable conditions."[3]

The strategic assumption here was that the British would indeed "blockade the German Bight", but it proved ill-founded. Technology, in the shape of mine, submarine and torpedo boat had caused the British, as early as 1912, to replace the "Close Blockade" with the "Distant Blockade". In this new disposition the blockading squadrons stayed much nearer their home bases and so were nothing like as vulnerable to the "equalising" attentions of the German Navy. "For the old

Figure 2. Admiral Sir David Beatty, who commanded the British battlecruisers at Jutland and who later became C-in-C Grand Fleet and First Sea Lord.

Figure 3. Admiral Reinhardt Scheer, C-in-C High-Seas Fleet, 1915-18 (Imperial War Museum) IWM.

policy of close blockade," noted one commentator, "was substituted a new one, that of leaving the enemy a large field in which he might be tempted to manoeuvre; and it had this value, that should he yield to temptation, an opportunity must sooner or later be afforded to the British Fleet of cutting him off and bringing him to action. Meantime he was cut off from any large adventure far afield. He would have to fight for freedom ... Thus, no naval battle could be expected unless ... the weaker (fleet) wished to fight, or was cornered, or surprised".[4]

The German Fleet knew itself to be weaker, was anxious to avoid a central battle with the British in all but the most favourable circumstances, and had a desperate fear of being cut off by a superior force getting between it and its bases. When the British abandoned the close

blockade, there was really very little the German fleet could reasonably do to improve their fortunes in the North Sea. Their mistake, according to the German naval strategist Herbert Rosinski was not to think of some alternative. "In World War I," he wrote, "the German Navy had committed a fundamental mistake by keeping its gaze, as if hypnotised, upon the Grand Fleet, striving in vain to wrest from that fleet the 'command' which, in the nature of things it could not possibly hope to win."[5] Perhaps, instead, the German Navy should have concentrated on the submarine war rather earlier than they did. Or perhaps the Government of Imperial Germany had been premature in seeking to turn some of their resources of landpower into seapower, in the first place?

The British, too, were more cautious than was widely expected before the war.

Figure 4. Beatty's HMS Lion *being hit on Q Turret at the Battle of Jutland (IWM).*

They had abandoned the more positive close blockade in 1912, as we have seen. A probably exaggerated fear of submarines and torpedos also circumscribed their freedom to manoeuvre. In the Summer of 1916 it was decreed that the Grand Fleet must go no further north than the Faroe Islands and no more than 4° East, unless very strongly escorted by destroyers. It is also true that the facts of geography and the general correlation of naval forces meant that they had sufficient command of the North Sea already. They had more to lose than to gain in a decisive encounter, especially if it was recklessly pursued or fought.

In this way the weakness of the German position and the strength of the British both tended to mute the struggle for command of the sea in the First World War. It was certainly nothing like as dramatic and exciting an affair as most naval officers on both sides imagined it would be before the War. The German High Seas Fleet, especially under the command of its first two commanders, von Ingenohl and von Pohl, sought only to isolate and ambush detached parts of the British Fleet and this led to a few confused skirmishes and the Battle of the Dogger Bank in January 1915. Their movements about the North Sea were always constrained by the fear that the hunters might well become the hunted, especially in view of the apparent

unreliability of Zeppelin patrols and submarine picket lines.

To most British naval officers, waiting for the "Great Day", this was all very disappointing but they were still sure that one day the German Navy would come out and be defeated in another Trafalgar. "The continual pressure (on the High Seas Fleet) and (the) fettering of (its) initiative," wrote one in his diary in 1915, "is beginning to tell, and is shown in restless movements such as airship raids, aeroplane attacks on shipping and futile movements in the Heliogoland Bight during the day. Later, the temptation will become too great and they will push the High Seas Fleet out. The longer they wait to do so, the more overpowering our Fleet becomes . . ."[6]

In May 1916 they *did* come out and meet the British in the grand encounter of Jutland, but it was a disappointing affair from the British point of view. The Grand Fleet retained command of the sea, in fact it was strengthened, but the British *amour propre* had been wounded. The Germans, however, effectively ran down their surface Navy and mounted no further challenges for command. The British, conscious of the inferiority of their shell and distracted by the growing menace of the submarine

Figure 5. The loss of the Queen Mary *shortly afterwards. The British battlecruisers suffered very heavily in this battle (IWM).*

Figure 6. The wreckage of the Invincible. *British losses in ships and men were much higher than were those of the German fleet (IWM).*

war, were generally resigned to the situation. At the end of the War, though, Admiral Beatty was working on a solution to the problem. He planned for 1919 a full scale attack on the High Seas Fleet preceded by a mass air attack by some 200 torpedo and bomb dropping aeroplanes. The War ended too soon for this *dénouement*. The High Seas Fleet did emerge, but only to sail across the North Sea, to be interned, unkempt and run-down, at Scapa Flow. It was not the ending that British naval officers had hoped for. "There is considerable depression on the part of people who have so far taken no part in the war," wrote one young officer sadly two days before the Armistice, "because now our chance has gone and we shall have to slink home with nothing to show for our 4½ years of waiting."[7] Command had of course been safely retained but not in the glorious way the British Navy had hoped for.

In the First World War, the North Sea had been the focus of attention on both sides, but the situation was never again to be so simple. In the inter-war period British interest oscillated between the Mediterranean and the Far East and only began to recognise the naval threat emerging across the North Sea in the mid-1930's.

The Germans too began to consider possibilities further afield. In 1926 Vice-Admiral Wolfgang Wegener wrote an influential study called "The Strategy of the World War" in which he argued that the German Navy had too easily reconciled itself to a defensive role which, in the nature of the circumstances then prevailing, did nothing to reduce the inevitability of naval defeat. It had been a fatal strategic error to concentrate on the localised area of the North Sea, where the British were strong, and to ignore the oceans beyond, where they were not.

For the moment, though, these speculations were idle for the German Navy was forced to pre-occupy itself with the Baltic and with the problem of how to prevent the possible junction of the French and Russian Fleets. Only towards the end of 1938 was the possibility of naval war with Britain seriously considered. Then came the famous "Z Plan" of Admiral Raeder. The scheme was to force the British to divide their forces by making the most of Britain's dependence on foreign supplies. A large force of older German battleships should stay in the North Sea tying down a substantial proportion of the British Fleet.

Figure 7. The ultimate arbiter of naval battle – a division of battleships. These are the Orion *class, and faintly visible in the background there are the ships of the US 6th Battle Squadron, which joined the Grand Fleet in December 1917 (IWM).*

Figure 8. HMS Barham *(a fast battleship of the 5th Battle Squadron) steaming out to meet the German fleet in November 1918 (IWM).*

In the Outer Oceans British trade, and the naval forces defending it, would be stretched and assaulted by a combination of submarines, cruisers, commerce raiders and special task groups of 3 super-battleships supported by aircraft carriers.

The "Z Plan", however, could only work with a large Navy and the War came much too soon for this to be possible. Surface ship construction largely ceased and the German surface navy was forced once more to resign itself to being largely the maritime adjunct of continental landpower. German strategy was dominated by what Raeder called "continental ideas" which considerably limited the resources available to the German Navy. Its supportive and ancillary functions were well summarised by War Directive No. 6 of 9th October 1939 which read: "The Navy will do everything possible, while this offensive (in Poland) is in progress, to afford direct or indirect support to the operations of the Army and the Air Force."[8]

All this meant that the German surface Navy was quite incapable of challenging the Royal Navy, being, in Raeder's view, "so inferior in numbers and strength to ... the British Fleet that, even at full strength, they can do no more than show how to die gallantly, and thus are willing to create the foundations for later reconstruction."[9] Raeder was forced to resort to a Fleet-in-Being strategy the purpose of which was to stretch and dislocate British maritime forces as much as possible, but was anxious not to risk a confrontation with their main Fleet. "Enemy naval forces," Raeder ordered, "even if inferior in strength are only to be attacked if this should be necessary to achieve the main objective."[10] The role of the *Tirpitz,* based in the fjords of northern Norway, whose mere existence menaced the Arctic convoys and forced the British into difficult and costly countermeasures, illustrates this strategy exactly. The upshot of all this, however, was the creation of a Navy that concentrated neither on surface ships, nor on conventional naval operations in the North Sea, but on submarine warfare in the oceans beyond.

There was one exception to this, however, the Norwegian campaign of 1940, probably the nearest approach to a struggle for command in the North Sea that the Second World War produced. Even here, the German Fleet preferred rather to avoid a decisive encounter than to seek it. Raeder planned to seize Norway in a sudden *coup de main* before the British had time to react effectively. He hoped also that superior airpower would allow him to retain it. Even so, as he admitted beforehand, "the operation in itself is contrary to all principles in the theory of naval warfare

Figure 9. British sailors watching the German surrender (IWM).

Figure 10. The German fleet en route to internement, and eventual scuttling, at Scapa Flow (IWM).

Figure 12. In Operation Duck the cruiser HMS Suffolk bombarded the German airfield at Sola, Stavanger, Norway, in April 1940. She was caught by German aircraft as she returned home. The picture shows a contemporary attempt to summarise the bombs dropped in her vicinity (Admiral Torlesse).

as it would be carried out in the teeth of British naval supremacy".[11]

On the 9th April 1940 there were six simultaneous assaults on the Norwegian coast at widely separated points ranging from Narvik to Oslo. The British reacted with speed but not efficiency and made their own counter landings in central and northern Norway. At sea, wherever possible, the British successfully forced battle

on the German Navy, the one exception to this being *Operation Juno*, when the *Scharnhorst* and the *Gneisenau* fell on some of the forces evacuating Narvik and sank the carrier *Glorious*. Losses in such narrow and contested waters were high on both sides, however.

The strategic implications of what Churchill called "this ramshackle campaign"[12] were many but three stand out. Firstly, the

Figure 11. The impact of airpower. A Town class cruiser towing a blazing tanker away from the Norwegian town of Steinkjer, shortly after a German air raid. April 1940 (IWM).

Figure 13. HMS Suffolk was only hit once, but with great effect. Here she lies at anchor with her Quarterdeck awash. After Operation Duck, the vulnerability of ships to aircraft was well realised (Admiral Torlesse).

manner in which it was conducted showed that the German Navy did not seek to contest seriously command of the North Sea, and the wisdom of this self-restraint was apparently confirmed by the losses they nevertheless suffered. Secondly, the campaign demonstrated the impact that airpower could have on naval operations. Afterwards, it was clear that in order to enjoy command of the sea it was necessary to command the air above. Air bases had become at least as important as naval bases in maritime warfare in the North Sea. Finally, the main centres for naval operations after the campaign shifted out onto the convoy routes of the Atlantic, the Arctic and the Mediterranean. For all these reasons, the destiny of the North Sea now depended even more than before on events in the land masses surrounding it – and in the oceans beyond.

The Struggle for Access

Britain's geographic position meant that Germany would have to fight for access to the High Seas. In the First World War the Grand Fleet's blockade of the German High Seas Fleet, however boring to the British, was very successful in keeping the German surface navy confined to the waters of the North Sea. German warships that were in found it difficult to get out and, as the tragic and inevitable fate of von Spee at the battle of the Falkland Islands showed, ships that were out found it difficult to get in. Surface commerce raiders did wriggle through the British blockade, of course, but they were all gradually hunted down, leaving the British virtually in uncontested command of the surface of the world's major oceans.

In some ways this situation repeated itself in World War II, although the extension of the German base-line to include Norway and the western coast of France forced the British blockade line back to the Denmark Strait and the Iceland-Faroes-Scotland gap in the north and the Bay of Biscay and the South-West Approaches in the south. These extra opportunities for German seapower were, however, essentially the product of German landpower. The German Navy still operated from a position of geographic weakness and general inferiority. The pursuit and destruction of the *Bismarck* in 1941 and the whole harried and spasmodic careers of the *Scharnhorst* and *Gneisenau* well illustrate the nature of the war this strategic setting dictated.

To compensate for their weaknesses on the surface in both wars, the German Navy had recourse to the submarine as the major weapon against Britain's maritime communications. Faced with this novel threat in the First World War, the British made mines their first line of defence. The energy they devoted to this and to other means of physically blocking German U-boats into the North Sea is a measure both of their alarm at the magnitude of the threat and of their lack of faith in the traditional strategy of convoy-and-escort. Mines were laid continously in the Heliogoland Bight and in barrages from Scotland to Norway and across the Dover Straits. The industrial and naval effort required for this was enormous but the effectiveness of the strategy was, and still is, a matter of much controversy. Submarines sunk were few, but operational patrols disrupted were many. But, at best, mines were only a partial counter to the U-boat threat.

Certainly operations in support of and against the German submarine began to assume a more and more central role in the naval operations of both sides. Minefields had to be supervised by auxiliary craft and these required support against the possibility of local ambush by major surface units of the enemy fleet. The inter-dependence of all forms of naval activity was symbolised by the British forays into the Heliogoland Bight where the intention was partly to lay anti-U-boat mines and partly to lure unsuspecting German warships onto the guns of the Grand Fleet. The German surface Navy also entered into this contest for submarine access. "During the further progress of the submarine war (upon which, in my view, our whole naval policy will be compelled to concentrate)," said Scheer, "the Fleet will have to devote itself to the single task of bringing the submarine safely in and out of harbour."[13] Therefore, the survival and continued effectiveness of the High Seas Fleet in the North Sea was said by many to be essential to the success of German submarines *beyond* it. What happened in the Atlantic depended on what happened in the North Sea.

The notion of a physical blockade against German submarines reappeared in the Second World but was made more difficult by the German seizure of naval bases in Norway and France. Mainly at the behest of the First Sea Lord, Admiral Sir Dudley Pound, another northern barrage was laid, but the loss of Norway meant this was driven back to the Scotland-Faroes-Iceland line and proved to be of doubtful validity. In the south a much more effective and ultimately murderous air barrage was put across the South West Approaches and the Bay of Biscay by the Sunderlands, Hudsons, Liberators and Catalinas of Coastal Command. The British Admiralty's second line of defence was to try to switch the trade routes from the south-west to the north-west so as to increase the distance between the U-boat bases in France and their targets. "As we gradually work the trade up onto the Greenland-Iceland route," said Pound, misguidedly as it turned out, "it will be uneconomical for the Germans to base their U-boats on the Biscay ports."[14] In point of fact, the increased range of submarines and the growing role of airpower in the war on trade pushed the decisive areas of battle increasingly out onto the Atlantic convoy routes themselves. For this reason, in the Second War, events in the North Sea had much less of an influence on the submarine campaign than they had before.

Although access to the Atlantic was perhaps the most important opportunity flowing from the ability to cross the North Sea, there nevertheless remained the Arctic and the Baltic. In the Second War, the German seizure of Norway and the strategic importance of the sea route to Northern Russia focused attention on the very northern rim of the North Sea. The Germans established air and naval bases in Northern Norway and attacked the Russian convoys with aircraft and submarines and, occasionally, supported these with movements of their major units in the area, the *Tirpitz* and the *Scharnhorst*. The British responded and the consequent convoy battles and fleet actions were grim indeed in the forbidding conditions of the area.

The southernmost part of the North Sea was of interest too because this afforded entry into the Baltic Sea. A naval force here, said Admiral Fisher (the British First Sea Lord), could sever German connections with Scandinavia and, perhaps acting in conjunction with Russian forces, could pose a terrible threat to the strategic integrity of imperial Germany. An expeditionary force could be landed on the Pomeranian shore, 90 miles from Berlin, and could advance south brushing aside such auxiliary forces as they would encounter, outflanking and undermining the huge German armies enmeshed in the bitter conflict of the Western and Eastern fronts.

Such a campaign would have been the supreme achievement of British seapower and the idea attracted the interest of many naval leaders of the First World War, particularly Fisher and Churchill (the First Lord). The scheme petered out because there was such dissension over what the requirements of such a strategy were. Would bases in the area be necessary, and if so where? More fundamentally, did the British need to defeat the German Navy first or should this scheme instead be used primarily as a method of forcing battle on them? Generally the Mahanite principle prevailed: first the decisive victory, then the enjoyment of its rewards. Access to the Baltic, in other words, depended on control of the North Sea.

There was a distinct afterglow of this in the Second World War with Churchill's scheme for "Operation Catherine", one of those strategic endeavours which have led some commentators to conclude that in the Second War Churchill was mainly concerned to refight the battles of the First. In the Spring of 1939, long before he was First Lord of the Admiralty, Churchill wrote a paper on strategy in which he suggested that once the situation in the Mediterranean and the Far East was reasonably secure, the British should plan some endeavour against the Baltic. Germany, he said, must dominate that sea to maintain the ore trade and protect herself against the possibility of a Russian descent against her northern coastline. "If we had a superior fleet there now," he concluded, "one can say that Germany would not declare war."[15] Accordingly, once in office, he pushed through schemes by which a heavily armoured British squadron would force the Danish Straits, brush aside German mines and aircraft and play such havoc in the Baltic as to make it "the supreme naval offensive open to the Royal Navy".[16] Churchill's professional advisors fought a successful rearguard action against this scheme, until the fall of Norway made it finally impossible. So, once again, as Mackinder had said in 1918, "the fleets of the islanders could no more penetrate into the Baltic than they could into the Black Sea."[17]

Although such operations as *Catherine* undoubtedly catch the eye, it is certainly possible to argue that one of the Royal Navy's most positive contributions to victory was the imposition, in both wars, of a commercial blockade. In the First World War, much of Germany's import and export trade was choked by a blockade of inexorable and increasing severity. The whole of the North Sea was declared a military zone and Britain claimed the right to check for contraband all shipping entering it from north or south. The volume of German overseas trade was reduced by 1918 to one seventh of what it had been in 1913[18] and severe shortages resulted. A similar system was instituted in 1939, regulated by a northern patrol based on Kirkwall and a southern one on Weymouth and Ramsgate. In both wars, but especially in the second, commercial blockade took its place in a spectrum of activities aimed against the German economy which ranged from disruptive pre-emption of vital raw materials at one end of the scale to strategic bombing at the other.

It was the Admiralty's conviction that the quiet, undramatic, though demanding, operations of commercial blockade belied its very real effectiveness. Mahan, after all, had talked of "that noiseless pressure upon the vitals of France, that compulsion whose silence, when once noted, becomes to the observer the most striking and awful mark of sea power".[19] The Naval Staff believed that blockade was much more effective than it seemed and in fact was one of the Navy's principal contributions to victory.

This claim is hard to check because it is difficult to disentangle the effects of blockade from those of other forms of war. The shortage of food in Germany so often ascribed to the activities of the Royal Navy, for example, was due at least as much to the neglect of agriculture caused by the flow of men to the trenches. Germany also had recourse to the manufacture of home-produced substitutes for goods no longer obtainable abroad and, with the aid of neutrals, was able to circumvent at least some of the British measures. Finally, and especially in the second war, Germany had access to other areas of the European landmass with all the resources they contained, which largely compensated for shortages brought about by blockade. Nevertheless, only a tenth as many boots and shoes were

236

produced in 1917 as in 1913, and the Germans thought this mainly the product of the blockade. They remained acutely conscious of their apparent vulnerability to commercial blockade. As late as August 1942, argued Raeder, "it is urgently necessary to defeat Russia and thus create a Lebensraum which is *blockade-proof* and easy to defend. Thus we can continue to fight for years."[21] Even if these fears were in fact exaggerated, they formed a not inconsiderable part of the benefit the British gained through their ability largely to deny Germany access to the markets of the world.

Figure 14. The flight deck of the aircraft carrier Furious *off Norway. This was the first time that carriers had effectively intervened in amphibious war, and, despite poor aircraft and bad conditions, they were very successful (Capt. French).*

The Battle for Bases

In both conflicts, most professionals realised that sustained operations in seas adjacent to the North Sea required forward bases inside it. The prolonged debate in the British Admiralty in 1914–15 over the base requirements of an expedition into the Baltic is a good case in point. Heligoland, Borkum, Sylt, even Schleswig-Holstein, bases in southern Norway and Sweden were all considered though, fortunately for all concerned, no such expeditions were mounted.

The principle re-appeared in the interwar years, but this time from the German perspective. In 1926, Admiral Wegener argued that it was vital for Germany to keep open her communications with the rest of the world, despite her geographical disadvantages. Next time, he suggested, it would be necessary for Germany to take Jutland, advance to Southern Norway and break open the gaol door that way. Such a move would also guard the Baltic against the British. Just such reasons prompted the German invasion of Norway. "I am informed," wrote Hitler in February 1940, "that the English intend to land there, and I want to be there before them. The occupation of Norway by the British would be a strategic turning movement which would lead them into the Baltic, where we have neither troops nor coastal fortifications ... The enemy would find himself in a position to advance on Berlin and break the backbone of our two fronts." The invasion of Norway, however, would also "... secure our supplies of (iron) ore from Sweden, and would provide the Navy and Air Force with expanded bases for operations against England."[22]

From the British point of view, the strategic interest of Norway could be viewed from two perspectives. The first was that the Norwegian coast provided access to the Baltic and to the Scandinavian hinterland. In the early months of the war, the British were very uncertain how best to proceed over this. Their difficulties partly derived from the fact that they had three aims in Scandinavia and the military and political requirements of each were not easy to reconcile with one another. They wanted to interrupt the seaborne supply of Swedish iron-ore to Germany; they wanted to seize the Swedish iron ore fields themselves; and they wanted to help the Finns against the Russians. The exploration of the military and political implications of so many competing strategic options tended to produce indecision and muddle – and so

Figure 15. Virtually the last action of the European sea war. A British carrier air strike on a German U-boat depot ship and other vessels at Kilbotn, Norway in May 1945 (IWM).

the more single-minded Germans got there first.

Then the second of the British perspectives came into focus. A Norwegian campaign, nourished by British sea power, could be the latest manifestation of Britain's traditional maritime strategy of defeating a large continental enemy by turning and diversionary operations on his flanks. Even when the Norwegian campaign went badly there were many who thought Britain should persist with it because of its anticipated effects on *other* theatres of war. "The main remaining value of our forces in Norway," said Churchill on 20th May 1940, "is to entice and retain largely superior German forces in that area *away from the main decision ...* Norway is paying a good dividend now and must be held down to the job."[23] The Admiralty and Admiral Forbes, the C-in-C Home Fleet, generally agreed and there were angry protests when it was decided to abandon the campaign.

But the problem with such views was that the reverse of the hoped-for correlation of forces appeared to be happening. Small numbers of Germans, wrote Churchill angrily "... seem to be occupying three or four times their number ... and

(the operation is) eating up large quantities of shipping and other essential supplies,"[24] – and this was the result of general deficiencies both in the planning and in the execution of the British campaign. The Narvik operation, complained Churchill was a "... shocking example of costly over-caution and feebleness all the more lamentable in contrast to the German fortitude in defence and vigour in attack."[25]

The notion of further endeavours in Norway continued to attract the British even after the conclusion of the main campaign there – and for the same basic reasons. It was still an area where German forces could be diverted away from the Eastern Front and elsewhere; an assault on the Norwegian coast might therefore be something to offer the Americans and Russians. But the same confusions survived too. Would Allied forces landing in Norway be intended simply to divert German troops or to go south thereby, in Churchill's words, "unrolling the Nazi map of Europe from the top."[26] Either way, most professional military men were very sceptical about the whole idea and thought the arithmetic would turn out to be wrong. Allied resources would be squandered, not German ones. The bitter experience of the Narvik campaign went deep indeed.

Even so, the lure of the Scandinavian hinterland continued and produced many

Figure 16. A Russian convoy under air attack (IWM).

238

Figure 17. U 35 torpedoing a merchant ship (IWM).

The Struggle for Resources

In both wars, also the North Sea was an area of intrinsic value. The British, for example, were on both occasions considerably excited by the fate of Scandinavian merchant shipping and by the question of whether they would be able to use it for their own purposes. Such considerations played a part in their strategic deliberations. When they decided to terminate the Norwegian campaign, their plan had to accommodate delicate negotiations over the Norwegian cargo, whaling and oil tanker fleets. The fishing grounds of the North Sea were also particularly important in both wars. The British Ministry of Economic Warfare took a very lively interest in the whole question. The quantity of fish

exciting schemes. *Operation Ajax* in the autumn of 1941 was just such a one. Allied troops would go ashore at Trondheim, join forces with the Swedish army (assuming Sweden was being threatened by Germany) and cut the German hold on Norway in two. It would at least be something to do, for the "... British Home Army," said Churchill, "cannot stand idly by without unfavourable reactions at home and abroad."[27] Again, bases in northern Norway allowed the Germans to attack the strategic link between Russia and the Western allies both by attack on the Arctic convoys and through an overland lunge intended to sever Murmansk from the rest of Russia. The British considered whether this could not be stopped by offensive action, hence *Operation Jupiter* in the Summer of 1942. This was Churchill's scheme that the allies should storm ashore at Petsamo and seize northern Norway and parts of Finland. This scheme and *Operation Ajax* – and, for that matter, the German *Operation Ikarus* to take Iceland, were all rejected by professional opinion for the same basic reason. These areas were all too far forward of the main centre of strategic power for the operations to take *and retain* them to be militarily feasible. Raids were possible but expeditions were not. After the German seizure of Norway the battle for bases in the North was, therefore, effectively over.

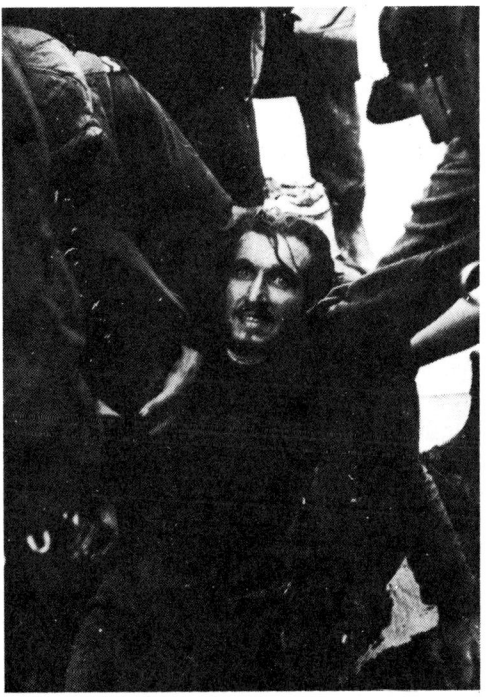

Figure 18. The submarine campaign was a bitter one for both sides. Here a shocked U-boat survivor is tended by British sailors (IWM).

Figure 19. British destroyers excercising in the North Sea (IWM).

landed by German trawlers fell by nearly four fifths of its pre-war total, much reducing Germany's sources of vitamins A and D. Such considerations led Hugh Dalton, the Minister for Economic Warfare, to propose a number of schemes such as *Operation Claymore,* the raid on the Lofoten Islands on 4th March 1941, the success of which said Churchill afterwards gave "an immense amount of innocent pleasure at home."[28]

However the fate of Swedish iron ore was undoubtedly the most important such question to enter the highest realms of allied strategy. In both wars, there could be no doubt of its vital importance to the German war effort, so the Allies naturally did their very best to interrupt the trade. In the First World War this was largely done by a policy of stockpiling, economic persuasion and strategic preemption; in the Second more positive methods were tried. In March 1940, Churchill proposed that one of two merchant ships be equipped with a ram and should "... carry merchandise and travel up the leads looking for German ore ships, or any other German merchant vessels, and then ram them by accident."[29] More orthodox, and more positive strategies included mining the iron ore routes both in the Baltic and the North Sea and even the actual seizure of the ore fields themselves. Allied strategy vacil-

lated over this point but the threat played a significant part in persuading Germany to invade Norway, so as to keep safe the iron ore. After the Spring of 1940, British operations against German interests in the area were necessarily restricted to economic persuasion and to submarine, surface ship, aircraft and mine attacks on seaborne trade, with the occasional raid on the Norwegian mainland. The most ambitious of these, if ever it had been authorised, would certainly have been *Operation Ascot,* a projected three month occupation in the Winter of 1941 of the Bodo Peninsular in order to interdict the iron ore trade. The resources of the North Sea were evidently of sufficient value to justify the taking of considerable risk, and the employment of considerable forces – by both sides.

The North Sea in the Nuclear Age

If the first half of the Twentieth Century was largely the period of naval conflict between Britain and Germany, the second seems likely to be that of maritime confrontation between East and West. The Soviet Union in some ways has fulfilled Mackinder's prophecy: it has converted some of its land power resources and has become, for the first time, a formidable naval and maritime power with a truly global reach. The extent of that reach in fact suggests that the North Sea would not be the only, or even a significant, arena for conflict between the two sides should war come. Neither of the main contestants are West Europeans and the list of their potential areas for confrontation is by no means restricted to Northern European waters.

But this does necessarily mean that the North Sea has become in the Nuclear Age a mere strategic backwater. One reason for this is its relative proximity to NATO's Northern Flank, the likely scene of considerable battles of access should maritime war ever come. The Soviet Navy's sole means of unimpeded access out onto the high seas is that from Murmansk, through the Barents and Norwegian seas and out into the North Atlantic. For this reason the Northern Fleet has become the most significant part of the Soviet Navy and there has been a startling accretion of military power in the Kola peninsula, supported by much civil and economic development in the whole of the *"Murmanskaya Oblast"*.

Assessment of the strategic significance of all this is complicated by the fact that what is the route out is also the route in. The early post-war development of the Soviet Navy seems to have concentrated on the last of these two perspectives rather than the first. The Soviet naval command were much concerned to guard the homeland against Western naval forces coming in over the top of Norway to attack Northern Russia with nuclear strike carriers and the early generations of ballistic missile-firing submarines. As a first priority it was necessary to deny the waters of the north to western forces. But then, with the growing reach of the Soviet Navy, they became more concerned to project their power outwards. And so, they now tend to see northern waters as their way out, rather than an enemy's way in.

The West has always been conscious of the Soviet naval threat to what the US calls the "sea-lines of communication" across the Atlantic, especially in a period of tension or conflict when US military reinforcements might have to be ferried over the Western Europe. Accordingly the West seems likely to contest Soviet access to the high seas by a variety of means including thorough surveillance, deep mining and blockading squadrons in the 'choke-points' of the waters north of Norway and around Iceland.

The possibility that it might have to fight for freedom has not gone unnoticed in the Soviet Navy. In his famous articles in the Soviet Naval Digest of 1972–3 Admiral Sergei Gorshkov, C-in-C of the Soviet Navy, made much of the fact that historically the occupation of vital coastal regions by ground forces had often facilitated the establishment of command in adjacent sea areas. This together with recent improvements in the Soviet amphibious capacity has led one prominent observer to remark: "Bearing in mind the significance of the Barents and Norwegian seas to Soviet SSBN (ballistic missile submarines), one's mind inevitably turns to the Norwegian coast, Svalbard and perhaps Iceland."[30] Many commentators argue that these areas would be the major arena for naval activity in the Soviet Navy's first battles for access and could well become immediate targets of amphibious assault in the event of conventional war.

A somewhat similar claim is sometimes also made of the Danish Straits and the Baltic approaches. It would certainly be of advantage for the Soviet Navy to control passage in and out of the Baltic though, on the face of it, geography would seem to make this much more difficult for them to achieve. Even so, the main focus of strategic interest would now seem to be in the Norwegian Sea and the North Atlantic rather than in the North Sea proper. While the centre of gravity has clearly shifted northwards, the North Sea, according to Admiral Rolf Steinhaus of the Federal German Navy, remains important because it links together the two main Russian outlets into the Atlantic. This importance, he claims, is not sufficiently realised. "Current force allocations are inadequate," he says, "and there is no unified command. The three major NATO commanders share responsibility for the North Sea, and this results in no consistent planning for the area as a whole."[31]

These claims are supported by the increasing intrinsic value of the area. The continuing importance of the North Sea's shipping and fishing interests and the discovery and exploitation of oil and gas have encouraged the progressive enclosure of the sea by littoral states and have substantially affected the nature of naval deployment and activity. These assets and responsibilities have now to be supervised and protected by a host of small ships on constant patrol acting in an almost constabulary role against a variety of minor threats.

Although the local functions of the North Sea's navies have accordingly altered in recent years they are still important, for the increasing intrinsic value of this area more than compensates for any decline in its strategic significance.

Conclusion

This study has attempted to show how the strategic environment of the North Sea has affected, and often determined, the nature of the naval conflict that has so far taken place there in this century. In order fully to understand particular naval events it is clearly necessary to analyse the military and political circumstances in the area as a whole, which have given rise to them. Since 1945, many of these circumstances have undergone considerable change but there still seems little reason to suppose that the North Sea will lose it's importance in the forseeable future.

Notes

1 H.J. Mackinder, *Democratic Ideals and Reality*. London: Constable, 1919. P 42.

2 *The Standard*, 29 May 1912.

3 "War Order for the North Sea Area", reprinted in *Der Krieg zur See*. Berlin, 1919, Vol 1.

4 A.H. Pollen, *The Navy in Battle*. London: Chatto & Windus, 1918. P 285.

5 B. Mitchell Simpson (Ed), *The Development of Naval Thought: Essays by Herbert Rosinski*, Newport, Rhode Island: Naval War College Press, 1977. P 66.

6 Diaries of Admiral Sir Mathew Best, entry for 17 April 1915. I am indebted to Capt O.F.M. Best, RN, for permission to quote from these diaries.

7 Diaries of Capt G.C. Harper, Churchill College Archive centre, Entry for 9 November 1918.

8 H. Trevor-Roper (Ed), *Hitler's War Directives 1939–45*. London: Sidgewick & Jackson, 1964. P 14.

9 Raeder, memo of 3 Sep 1939. Quoted in J.R.M. Butler, *Grand Strategy*, Vol II. London: H.M.S.O., 1957. P 81.

10 Quoted in Vice-Admiral Friedrich Ruge, *Der Seekrieg*. Annapolis, Maryland: U.S. Naval Institute Press, 1971. P 51–2.

11 Raeder, memo of 9 March 1940, *Führer naval Conferences*.

12 W.S. Churchill, *The Second World War*, Vol I. London: Cassell, 1948. P 480

13 Scheer, quoted in P.M. Kennedy, *The Rise and Fall of British Naval Mastery*. London: Allen Lane, 1976. P 250.

14 Pound, memo of 27 Dec 1940. Prem 328/6. London: Public Record Office (PRO)

15 Churchill, paper of 27 Mar 1939. Prem 1/345, PRO.

16 Marder, *From the Dardanelles to Oran*. London: Oxford University Press, 1974. P 140 ff.

17 Mackinder, op cit. P 140.

18 L. Guichard, *The Naval Blockade*. London: Philip Allan, 1930. P 265. Guichard gives the figures of £1180 million for 1913 and £160 million for 1918.

19 Mahan, quoted in Kennedy, op cit. P 253

20 Guichard, op cit, p 265.

21 *Führer Naval Conferences*, 26 August 1942. Emphasis supplied.

22 Hitler to Von Falkenhorst, 20 February 1940, and Directive for *Fall Weserubung* 1 March 1940. Quoted in Sir Basil Liddell Hart, *History of the Second World War*, London: Cassell, 1970, p 56 and Trevor Roper, op cit pp 22-5, respectively.

23 Churchill to First Sea Lord, 20 May 1940, Prem 328/10 (DRO), and to Halifax, 19 May 1940, quoted in Sir Llewellyn Woodward, British Foreign Policy in the Second World War, London: H.M.S.O., 1970. P 130.

24 Churchill, 20 May 1940, Prem 328/10, PRO.

25 Churchill, 14 June 1940, ibid.

26 Churchill to Chiefs of Staff, I June 1942, Prem 3 257/2, PRO.

27 Churchill, 3 Oct 1941, Prem 3 40/1, PRO.

28 Churchill to C-in-C Home Fleet, 7 March 1941, prem 328/7, PRO.

29 Churchill, 14 March 1940, Quoted Marder, op cut, p 153.

30 See, especially, M. McGwire, Soviet Naval Doctrine, a Paper prepared for a Seminar at Harvard University, Spring 1978, p 34.

31 Admiral Rolf Steinhaus, "The Northern Flank", in James L. George, *Problems of Sea Power as We Approach the Twenty-First Century*. Washington D.C.: American Enterprise Insitute for Public Policy Research, 1978. P 147.

New Trends in North Sea Shipping (1945 – 1980)

ATLE THOWSEN

Introduction

The development of North Sea shipping after 1945 may for the sake of simplicity be divided into three fairly well-defined periods:

1. The reconstruction after the Second World War (1945 – c. 1950).
2. The re-establishment of free competition (c. 1950 – c. 1960).
3. Competitive and structural changes in North Sea shipping (c. 1960 – 1980).

Before examining the development of each of these different periods, it is necessary to define North Sea shipping more precisely.

Shipping engaged in ocean transport may be divided into short sea and deep sea trades. In the first category are found, for example, the Baltic, White Sea, West-Indian and North Sea trades. Of all short sea trades the North Sea trade may be considered among the most important and representative, serving one of the world's most densely populated and industrialized areas. The definition of North Sea trade varies, although it is broadly similar. In the statistics of the Norwegian Shipowners, Association, North Sea shipping is defined as trade between Norway, Denmark and the West-Swedish ports on the one hand and the different North Sea and other Atlantic coast European ports on the other, including Icelandic, Faroese and Greenland ports. British coastal trade, trade between Great Britain and the Faroe Islands and trade between Europe (except the Mediterranean) and Greenland and Spitzbergen are also regarded as North Sea trade. Trade between Norway and Spitzbergen is, however, not defined as North Sea trade.[1]

It is impossible within a single chapter to discuss all aspects of North Sea shipping after the Second World War. Consequently, this chapter will mainly deal with the North Sea *small-ship trade,* which dominates what we may call the "real" North Sea shipping. The upper tonnage limit of what is considered to be a small merchant ship has varied from time to time, but in this context 2000 GRT has been used as an upper limit and 100 GRT as a lower limit. This corresponds fairly well with the criteria used in other works on small-ship trade.[2]

Since the Second World War, North Sea shipping has been dominated by six nations: Denmark, Norway, Sweden, the Netherlands, West Germany and Great Britain. This chapter therefore focuses on the ships and trade of these nations.

It may be appropriate at the outset to consider the importance of North Sea shipping. In terms of tonnage, the importance of North Sea shipping seems to have declined both relatively and steadily since the war. The statistics of the Norwegian Ship-

Table 1. North Sea shipping nations and their five most important trading partners in 1938, 1946, 1969 and 1979.

	1938	1946	1969	1979
Denmark	Great Britain Germany Sweden U.S.A. Norway	Great Britain Sweden U.S.A. Norway West Germany	Great Britain West Germany Sweden U.S.A. Norway	West Germany Great Britain Sweden U.S.A. Norway
Norway	Great Britain Germany Sweden U.S.A. France	Great Britain U.S.A. Sweden Denmark West Germany	Sweden Great Britain West Germany U.S.A. Denmark	Great Britain Sweden West Germany Denmark U.S.A.
Great Britain	U.S.A. Australia Canada India New Zealand	U.S.A. Canada India Australia New Zealand	U.S.A. West Germany Canada Netherlands France	West Germany U.S.A. France Netherlands Switzerland
Sweden	Germany Great Britain U.S.A. Denmark Norway	U.S.A. Great Britain Denmark Norway France	West Germany Great Britain Denmark Norway U.S.A.	West Germany Great Britain Denmark Norway U.S.A.
The Netherlands	Germany Great Britain Belgium Dutch East-Ind. U.S.A.	U.S.A. Belgium Great Britain West Germany Dutch East-Ind.	West Germany Belgium U.S.A. Great Britain U.S.S.R.	West Germany[x] Belgium[x] France[x] Great Britain[x] U.S.A.[x]
West Germany	Great Britain Netherlands U.S.A. Italy Sweden	U.S.A.[xx] Great Britain[xx] Netherlands[xx] Belgium[xx] France[xx]	France Netherlands U.S.A. Italy Belgium	France Netherlands Italy Belgium U.S.A

[x] 1978
[xx] 1948

Sources: *B.R. Mitchell, European Historical Statistics, 1750 – 1970* (Lond. 1975), *Statistisk Årbog 1980* (Denmark), *Statistisk Årbok 1980* (Norway), *Statistisk Årsbok 1980* (Sweden), *Annual Abstracts of Statistics 1981* (Great Britain), *Statistisches Jahrbuch 1980* (West Germany), *Statistical Yearbook 1979* (The Netherlands).

owners' Association, covering ships above 500 GRT, give some indication of this. In 1939 5.1% of the Norwegian merchant fleet was engaged in North Sea shipping.[3] In 1978 this figure had fallen to just 1%,[4] in spite of the fact that Norwegian tonnage engaged in North Sea shipping in the same period increased from 206,000 GRT in 1939 to 254,000 GRT in 1978. Tonnage-figures alone, however, seldom give the full picture of the importance of a trade. Looking at the number of ships employed, we find that in 1978, 75 or 9.4% of the Norwegian merchant fleet's 800 ships were employed in North Sea trade.[5] Even if Norwegian ships above 500 GRT engaged in North Sea trade in 1978 equalled the tonnage of only one Ultra Large Crude Carrier, the former gave employment to a far greater number of persons both ashore and afloat. Each of these ships has to be manned and served, so that the number of jobs a ship offers is not always in proportion to its tonnage.[6] Gross freight earnings per ton are also considerably higher in North Sea trade than in most others. Furthermore, ships employed in North Sea shipping are, more than any other vessels in the ocean-going merchant fleet, closely linked with the export and import industries of the country of registration. Table 1 shows the extent of international trading among the maritime nations of the North Sea, and demonstrates this point.

Finally, North Sea trade has an added significance, linked to a common cultural heritage shared by its participants. This has been strengthened throughout the years by maritime communications across the North Sea.

Reconstruction after the Second World War (1945 – c. 1950)

With the exception of Sweden, all the nations around the North Sea were belligerents in the Second World War. The North Sea had been one of the central theatres of war leading to a mammoth task of reconstruction after 1945. The shipping and shipbuilding industries were severely damaged; many shipyards needed extensive overhauling. The war also left its stamp on ports and inland waterways, and the merchant fleet suffered heavy losses.

To a certain degree reconstruction after the war changed the traditional economic and transport patterns of the North Sea region. However, the roots of many of the changes that took place are to be found in the inter-war period. This is especially the case with shipping. The transition from steam to motor propulsion and the growing tendency towards specialization in North Sea trade were particularly noticeable after 1945, but the process began long before the outbreak of war. War and reconstruction only helped to accelerate it.

The transition was partly a result of internal competition in North Sea shipping and partly the shipping industry's response to new competitors in the transport sector. Increasing competition and growing demands for efficiency, specialization and cost reductions, run like scarlet threads through the history of North Sea trade since the inter-war period. Shipowners engaged in North Sea shipping therefore faced a double challenge when the war ended in 1945. They had to tackle both *an acute reconstruction problem* caused by the war and *a more or less chronic structural problem* with roots going back well into the interwar period. Reconstruction proved to be the easiest to accomplish.

When the war ended the North Sea tonnage of the different nations had, with the exception of Sweden, been drastically reduced from prewar levels. The war had made it almost impossible to replace old or lost tonnage; consequently the average age of the North Sea fleet increased during the war. In addition most of the remaining ships were in a run-down condition as a result of inadequate maintenance. Thus

Figure 1. After the cease-fire in Europe the ships of the allied and neutral nations were brought under the control of United Maritime Authority (UMA). Excluded from this arrangement were ships engaged in coastal trade and regular service between adjacent countries. Thus the S/S LYRA (1508 GRT), The Bergen Steamship Company, was as early as 4 July 1945 able to resume its service between Bergen and Newcastle. (Photo: Bergen Maritime Museum.)

the armistice could not bring an immediate end to the difficulties of North Sea shipping.

During the war the North Sea tonnage had, like the merchant fleets of other nations, been under government control. As a result of the continuing war against Japan and the precarious supply situation in Europe, shipowners were not allowed unrestricted operation of their vessels from the moment of cease-fire in Europe. The ships of the allied and neutral nations were instead brought under the control of an international shipping-pool, the United Maritime Authority (UMA), which was planned to function for up to six months after Japan had agreed to an armistice. All ships engaged in coastal trade and regular service between adjacent countries were, however, excluded from this arrangement. Thus regular services across the North Sea recommenced fairly quickly after the war.

As early as 4 July 1945 the Bergen Line's S/S LYRA left Newcastle on her first post-war voyage to Bergen.[7] During the summer and autumn of 1945 a growing number of freight and passenger ships were able to resume their services as well. Finally, with the termination of the UMA period on 2 March 1946, the North Sea tramp trade could also start its adjustment to normal conditions.[8]

It was evident that, especially in the North Sea region, there would be a heavy demand for tonnage to carry the goods and tools necessary for the reconstruction of the areas devastated by the war. Europe also faced a general shortage of vital commodities, since its reserves were drained by the war. This stimulated the demand for tonnage even further. Post-war restrictions on trade, regulating the purchase and sale of goods and services, seem not to have decreased the transport demand. The transport picture was, however, to a certain extent complicated by quota and licence regulations imposed by the different governments.

It proved difficult for the shipping industry to satisfy the demand for North Sea tonnage. Germany was in ruins and occupied by the Allies. Most of the German merchant fleet either had been sunk or transferred to an allied flag as war indemnity.[9] Norway, like Denmark, the Netherlands and Great Britain, suffered heavy losses of tonnage during the war. For a time a vacuum seemed to be developing, which Sweden perhaps could have filled. The Swedes, however, seem to have deemed it more profitable to direct their efforts towards the building of ships.

The European shipbuilding industry was hampered in many ways after the war. There was a shortage of building slips and essential materials, especially steel. There was a significant uncertainty inherent in the delivery of new ships. As a consequence of a long-lasting trend towards building larger and larger ships, particularly tankers and liners, it was difficult to obtain new ships of the type traditionally used in the North Sea trade. This tendency had already become noticeable in the interwar period.[10] After the war it was exacerbated by the growing importance of oil and by the fact that most of Europe's enormous import requirements could only be satisfied by supplies from remote areas. In the first post-war years it was therefore very difficult to place orders for new ships designed for North Sea trade.

Gradually the situation in the shipbuilding industry improved. Steel supplies grew and a number of shipbuilding nations opened their shipyards to foreign orders. Toward the end of 1946 Great Britain allowed foreign shipowners to place orders at British shipyards.

The shortage of merchant tonnage in the North Sea in the immediate post-war years encouraged a search for substitutes. Shipowners cast their eyes on discarded warships which were being offered for sale from sur-

Figure 2. In order to meet the shortage of tonnage in the North Sea after the war, warships were rebuilt for civil purposes. In many cases steelbuilt escort-trawlers had their steam engines replaced with diesel engines removed from woodenbuilt minesweepers. The M/S SAMFROST (493 GRT), Ragnar Helland, Stavanger, is an example of this. The vessel was originally the escort-trawler KARI. In 1948 KARI was rebuilt, equipped with an 8 cyl. diesel engine taken from a minesweeper and renamed FANDANGO. (Photo: Per-Erik Johnsen 1968, Norwegian Maritime Museum.)

plus naval stocks. A number of such vessels were bought and rebuilt for civil purposes, with varying success, and a number of other odd, but not always economical, solutions resulted. After the war the British government disposed of a number of escort-trawlers and minesweepers. The former were steel vessels equipped with steam engincs, whereas the latter were diesel-engined wooden vessels. Neither type was ideal for cargo purposes, but by removing the steam engine and replacing it with the minesweeper's diesel engine, the trawler was converted into a serviceable cargo ship. Both the trawlers and minesweepers could be bought at reasonable prices and rebuilding costs were within shipowners' means.[11] Many of the rebuilt vessels had freezing equipment installed and were put into service carrying frozen fish to England.[12] A number of former landing crafts were also converted into cargo vessels and put into coastal and North Sea trade.

The rebuilt vessels had several weaknesses. None of them were constructed for carrying heavy loads. As a result of unfortunate experiences with some of these ships, a "heavy load clause" was imposed by the underwriters.[13] Their competitive ability was thus impaired and as building of new ships increased, these substitute ships gradually disappeared.

In the first post-war years North Sea shipping was carried on much as before. Some changes could be observed, but these mostly affected passenger and mail services. To an increasing extent the transport of mail was lost to airlines.[14] The North Sea tramp trade, however, went on more or less unchanged.

The trade was dominated by a few types of seasonal cargoes. The resulting fluctuations in the demand for tonnage meant that North Sea tramp shipping had to be supplemented with shipping from other waters.

During the first post-war years the general transport pattern of Northern Europe changed, partly as a consequence of war damage to the various ports and of the pace of their reconstruction. Before the war Rotterdam, Hamburg, Antwerp, Bremen and Amsterdam had been the dominant continental North Sea ports, but all suffered drastic declines in cargo handled in the post-war years. Exports decreased more than imports. The relative position of these ports also changed. Cargo handled by Hamburg was drastically reduced, whereas Antwerp increased its share. Bremen was quickly rebuilt and maintained its position chiefly due to the fact that the Americans used this port as a supply base for their occupation forces. Towards the end of the 1940's the rebuilding of German ports accelerated, as a result of the American reconstruction policy toward Germany. A large proportion of the cargoes transported from the USA to Europe under the Marshall plan was directed via German ports.[15] In many ways this laid the foundation of the transport pattern which became more and more characteristic of the North Sea area; namely the engagement of small ships for feeder transport and trans-shipment.

Apart from the transport of passengers and mail, certain important bulk cargoes dominated North Sea shipping in the inter-war period. This pattern was maintained in the first years following World War II. Gradually, however, significant changes took place.

In the inter-war period coal had been the largest and most important North Sea cargo. The coal trade was vital for European short sea shipping and especially for the North Sea. One could always count on a return cargo of coal from the U.K.[16]

Fish and fish products were traditional North Sea cargoes. In the interwar period the transport of fresh, cured and frozen herring dominated the fish trade, but iced and frozen fish were also of importance. Dried fish, on the other hand, mainly went to markets further south. The fish trade was seasonal, and was therefore often supplemented with tramp trade to Iceland and other places. Timber and timber products were also among the more important and bulkier cargoes in the inter-war period.

In highly industrialized Europe the coal and ore trades were closely linked. Coal remained a major cargo for the small ship fleet of the North Sea. The transport of ore, however, was at an early stage to a large extent taken over by specialized vessels designed for world-wide trade, and is therefore outside the scope of this chapter. Beside coal and ore, however, the iron and metal industries required other raw materials, producing finished and semi-finished goods and yielding useful by-products which to a large extent were sold in North-European markets. Thus in the inter-war period cargoes required or produced by the iron and metal industries gradually became important in North Sea shipping. In addition North Sea shipping in the inter-war period also included such cargoes as cement, fertilizer and sulphur.

Gradually, as European industry started production again after the war, shipping of all these cargoes was resumed. However, certain changes of a quantitative nature took place. Transport of coal declined due to a drastic fall in British coal production. In 1922 British coal exports reached an inter-war maximum with a total of 80.7 million tons. In comparison 1949, the second best post-war year, totalled only 14.1 million tons.[17] Declining production of coal and coke was a consequence of increased domestic and industrial use of oil and hydroelectricity as sources of energy. Expansion in the iron and metal industries, however, led to a rapid and strong increase in the demand for transport of aluminium and ferro-products. The fishing industry was modernized and made more efficient. Production was to a larger extent directed towards export, which slowly lost most of its previous seasonal character. Gradually products from the iron and metal industries and from the fishing industry provided a basis for year-round employment in North Sea shipping. In addition came the transport of general cargo and products like cars and agricultural machinery.

Still, coal and timber remained the most important North Sea cargoes well into the 1950's. A report from 1955, based on estimates of approximately 100 small ships of various nationalities employed in European trade, showed that the most important trades were timber from the Baltic and coal from the U.K., employing about 50% of the total number of ships. If the coal trade from Poland, Germany and other nations to Scandinavia were included, the proportion of ships engaged in these trades would have risen to 70%.[18] We must, however, bear in mind that the estimates above are not restricted to North Sea shipping only, and the selection of ships was somewhat haphazard. Thus, these estimates may not be absolutely precise. Still, it is likely that in the immediate post-war years, North Sea transport demand was dominated primarily by the same cargoes as before the war. This had an important effect upon the type of vessels chosen for North Sea shipping. The ships

Figure 3. Iced and frozen fish have for a long time been important North Sea cargoes. S/S LEDA (6670 GRT), The Bergen Steamship Company, is here seen loading iced fish for England. Compare the time consuming lift-on/lift-off technique used here with the loading and discharging technique illustrated in fig. 8. (Photo: Bergen Maritime Museum.)

operating in the North Sea in the inter-war period had not been adapted to meet the transport needs of this particular market exclusively. Seasonal fluctuations forced owners to pay attention to the requirements of adjacent markets, chiefly the Baltic and White Seas. As a result it had not been considered feasible to build up a specialized fleet for exclusive use in North Sea trade. Instead most of the ships were flexible enough to be used in various trades. This resulted in the single-decker being preferred for a long time in the tramp trade. Those with wide hatches, being practically self-trimming, were especially popular. As the trimming work was reduced to a minimum, this type was particularly well suited to the coal trade. In addition the single-decker could be easily discharged with a grab; it was versatile and could be used in other trades and waters.

Gradually, as the freight-market returned to normal, competition between the nations participating in North Sea trade became more intense. Towards the end of the 1940's the Dutch were particularly active in the North and Baltic Seas, especially in the timber trade. Due to their reasonable deep-draught and favourable cubic-capacity, the Dutch ships were well suited for carrying timber. A number of smaller cargoes ranging from 100 – 300 standards, previously carried by Scandinavian ships, were taken over by the Dutch.[19] They also made heavy inroads into the porcelain-clay trade between the ports of Fowey, Teignmouth and Par in England and various Scandinavian ports. The liberal Dutch scale of manning contributed much to their competitive ability. In addition they had the advantage of a ship particularly well suited to the North Sea, *the Groningen coaster.*

The Groningen coaster was first introduced early in the 1920's. The ship was originally a sailing-vessel, generally with a small auxiliary engine. In the course of time the sails disappeared and were replaced by a more powerful engine. Simultaneously the appearance of the vessel became more modern and the tonnage was increased: in the post-war period, some of the vessels reached about 900 DWT. There were three main types of Groningen coasters. *The raised quarterdecker* had two hatches and engine aft. The tonnage of this type varied from about 200 to 800 DWT, whereas *the shelter-decker* varied in tonnage from 350 to 900 DWT. The latter had a more powerful engine and was generally better equipped with, among other things, refrigerated and ventilated space for fruit, fish, meat, etc. *The flush-decker* was an all-round cargo vessel especially suitable for timber, coal, coke, ore and other bulk cargoes. Its tonnage ranged from about 150 to 800 DWT.[20] Compared with 1939, the Dutch coaster fleet had by 1951 increased its tonnage by 39%.[21] This success was reflected in the establishment of a number of new shipping concerns whose financing was facilitated by the frequent use of so-called "owner/skipper" companies. Additional capital came from a number of larger well-established companies which

had started to take an interest in the apparently profitable coaster trade. Rumours about vessels having covered their total investment in three years made the trade attractive. People with no previous interest in shipping started to invest in coasters.[22]

The competitive disadvantages of the Dutch single-ship ownership were more than compensated for by almost trust-like consolidations on the broker side. Under nearly any circumstances the Dutch were willing to underbid their competitors in order to oust them from the market.

Dutch coaster activity in the North Sea towards the end of the 1940's, forboded the re-establishment of competitive conditions similar to those of the inter-war period. The trade boom created by the Marshall plan and prolonged and heightened by the Korean War revitalized the economic life of Western Europe. Industrial development in particular was remarkable. The boom also affected North Sea trade. Competition intensified and made cost-cutting inevitable. As a result new and more rational ship types were introduced in order to meet the challenge.

In the period 1945 – 1950 North Sea trade was first and foremost characterized by efforts to fill the gaps caused by World War II. The main aim was to normalize trade.

To attain this, reconstruction of the merchant navy, the canals and ports had to be given priority. The time was not yet ripe for revolutionary ideas and developments. Thus the reconstructed North Sea trade bore a strong resemblance to the inter-war trade. The conversion of the North Sea fleet from steam to diesel and from singledecker to shelterdecker in the first post-war years, did not signal new trends. Both conversions were merely continuations of developments which had started in the inter-war period, as was the introduction of vessels carrying refrigerated or frozen cargo.

With the beginning of the 1950's, however, North Sea trade entered a phase in which the nations involved had to meet a number of new and decisive competitive challenges. To some of the nations it became a question of how to survive in North Sea shipping.

The Re-establishment of Free Competition (c. 1950 – c. 1960)

Towards the end of the 1940's the Dutch had prospered in North Sea trade to the detriment of the interests of Great Britain and the Scandinavian countries.[23] In the 1950's West Germany, a well-known and serious competitor, re-entered the arena. The German "Kümos" (Küsten Motorschiffe) soon became an important factor in North Sea trade. Due to the Germans having newer ships and lower crew costs the competitive ability of Great Britain and the Scandinavian countries suffered severely. Both the shipping industries and the governments of the respective countries realized that drastic measures had to be taken. The situation was thoroughly analysed and a number of unfavourable conditions were revealed. Both the age and vessel size of the small-ship fleet were unfavourable. The ships were often unprofitable because crew costs were too high, in part due to the scale of manning imposed by the authorities. In addition Norwegian owners had been hampered by the government's prohibition between 1948 and 1950 against ordering new ships unless certain very strict financial conditions were fulfilled. Great Britain was in an even more unfortunate position. In 1956 two out of five British vessels below 1000 GRT were more than 25 years old. While 90% of the Dutch and 75% of the German small-ship fleet were motorvessels in 1956, the British figure was 30%.[24] The causes of the uneven competition in the small-ship trade, including North Sea trade, were old, even in 1949 when the Norwegian Parliament appointed a committee to look into its problems.[25] In order to improve their competitive ability both the British and the Scandinavians considered it necessary to reduce costs and to make the small-ship fleet more modern and specialized. Crew costs, which represented the major part of total operating costs, depended upon the scales of pay and manning. The scale of manning varied from country to country. The intention of the Seattle-convention of 1946 had been to introduce a uniform practice in this matter. The convention had, however, not been ratified by the most important maritime nations. In spite of this, Norway and Sweden had established regulations on working hours and scale of manning in accordance with the convention. As a result a Norwegian or Swedish North Sea vessel, of just over 500 GRT, might have up to five more men in its crew than its Dutch or German equivalent.[26] Like pilotage and insurance, the scale of manning depended upon the gross register tonnage of the particular ship. In Scandinavia vessels were divided into groups in accordance with certain tonnage limits, e.g. up to 99 GRT, 199 GRT, 299 GRT etc. A similar grouping applied to the fleets of other countries taking part in North Sea trade.

To exceed a tonnage limit could mean a substantial increase in costs which was not always matched by a similar increase in profits.[27] Shipowners tried in vain to convince the authorities that it was necessary to make the manning rules less stringent. In view of the escalation of competition in North Sea trade in the early 1950's it was therefore only natural that owners and naval architects should focus their interest on the different tonnage limits and consider carefully how to construct the most profitable ships within the framework created by these limits. As a result *the paragraph ships* entered North Sea trade. Gradually it became imperative for owners taking part in North Sea shipping to have vessels whose gross register tonnage did not exceed certain limits, but whose loading capacity (i.e. deadweight tonnage and/or cubic capacity) was as great as possible.

In 1951 the first two paragraph ships for a Nowegian owner were delivered. M/V

Figure 4. In 1949 the building of the so-called paragraph ships started. In 1951 the first paragraph ship built for a Norwegian owner, M/S GLORIA (299 GRT), was delivered from C. Lühring Schiffswerft, Brake, West Germany. The owner was A/S Skandinavisk Samseiling, Arild Gerner Mathisen, Oslo. GLORIA was soon to be followed by a number of similar designs. (Photo: Norwegian Maritime Museum.)

GLORIA and M/V GRACIA, built in Germany for A. Gerner Mathisen in Oslo, measured 299 GRT with a deadweight of 450 tons.[28] Building of paragraph ships had, however, started earlier. In 1949 several shipyards had produced such vessels: three were delivered from Danish yards to A.E. Sørensen in Svendborg, all of which were just under 500 GRT, with deadweights of 725 tons and loading capacities of 35,000 cu.ft. of grain. In the same year the Swedish Kalmar Varv commenced building paragraph ships as a result of new Swedish regulations on the scale of manning. At an early stage the previously mentioned Groningen coasters were also adapted to conform with such regulations. This was not so much to comply with the demands of the Dutch owners, but rather to further export of ships, inter alia to Norway.[29]

Throughout the 1950's Dutch, French and German yards dominated the building of paragraph ships. During the summer and autumn of 1954, Norwegian owners increased their orders with French and German shipbuilders for paragraph ships significantly. Gradually domestic shipbuilders commenced to design and build them, and in 1957 the first Norwegian-built paragraph ship was delivered,[30] thus marking the beginning of a significant change in North Sea shipping. In the 1950's foreign ship-builders and maritime consulting engineers led in the designing and building of paragraph ships. In the 1960's, however, Norwegians gradually came to dominate the development of new vessel-types. Paragraph ships were constructed both as single- and as shelter-deckers, but the open/closed shelter-decker was most popular.

The introduction of paragraph ships increased competition only slightly. The Germans still had considerable advantage concerning costs. Their vessels had smaller crew, who received lower wages and less expensive food than their colleagues aboard ships of other nationalities. The Dutch, however, who earlier had been in a favourable competitive position, showed signs, due to rising costs, of stagnation towards the end of the 1950's.[31] At the same time the Danes started to expand.

In the late 1950's Northern Europe entered a stage of rapid industrial development. This affected North Sea shipping to an even greater extent than the uneven competition and the means introduced to even it out.

Competitive and Structural Changes in North Sea Shipping (c. 1960–1980)

In the inter-war period North Sea freights had represented an "open" market. This meant that ships, normally engaged in other trades and waters, in difficult periods could enter the North Sea hoping to get a cargo. At the same time ships normally engaged in North Sea trade had to accept considerable seasonal fluctuations. In some periods it would therefore be necessary for these vessels either to supplement their North Sea trade with engagements in other trades or, if times were really bad, be laid up.

By the early 1950's, however, the North Sea was becoming a "closed" market. North Sea shipping was becoming specialized, demanding special types of ships, cargo handling, and regularity which only liners or long term charters could offer. Tramps could not and were replaced. This development became especially noticeable in the 1960's. A number of factors contributed to this shift, of which the most important lay within the manufacturing industries, the shipping industry and other sectors of transport. The 1960's were the years when the idea of European economic integration became a reality. European trade was facilitated and increased as a result of the European Free Trade Association (EFTA) and especially the European Economic Community (EEC). This led to industrial expansion and increases in the demand for raw materi-

als and improved marketing for finished products. In the transport of raw materials and manufactured goods, the shipping industry played a vital, but not unchallenged part. Serious competition increasingly came from road haulage and railways, both of which could offer door-to-door service, which in many cases more than outweighed the drawback of considerably higher costs per ton/kilometre. The most significant economizing element of door-to-door transport was the avoidance of expensive and time-consuming trans-shipment.

At the same time the shipping industry was moving towards bigger, more specialized, and consequently more expensive ships. To simplify somewhat, we may say that a ship makes money when it is at sea, not when it is moored in port. As a consequence, efforts to reduce the number of ports of loading and discharging to an absolute minimum were intensified in the 1960's, as were the efforts to make the stay in port as short as possible. Shipping became more capital intensive. Especially in the seaborne trade to and from Western Europe, a new transport pattern emerged. Goods to or from other continents increasingly were carried as unitized or bulk cargo utilizing central European ports like Rotterdam, Bremerhaven, Gothenburg or Antwerp. Distribution to, and redistribution of goods from, these ports were partly based on transport over land by means of trailers and railways, partly on transport on rivers and canals by barge, and also on seaborne feeder transport by smaller ships.[32] This was the transport pattern to which North Sea shipping had to adapt throughout the 1960's.

North Sea shipping was the servant of both the manufacturing industries and of deep sea shipping. In relation to trailers and railway transport, however, North Sea shipping came to play a dual role, being both a servant and a competitor. The significant changes in transport in the 1960's resulted in the emergence of a complex transport pattern in Northern Europe, and North Sea shipping became more exposed to strong

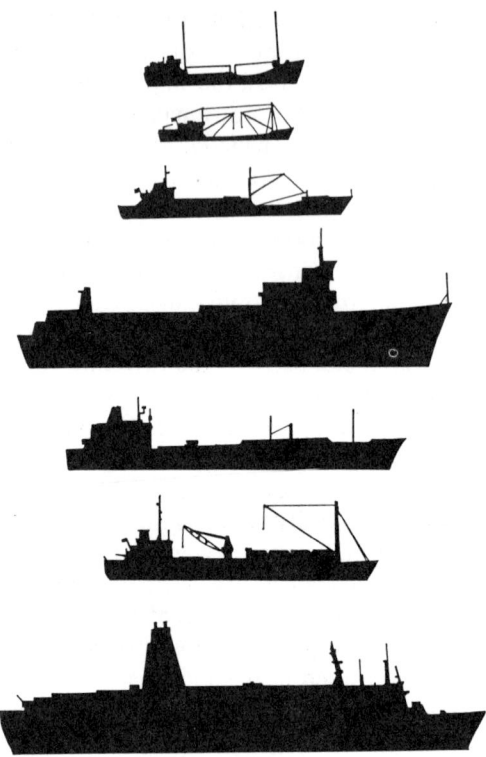

Figure 5. Stages in North Sea shipping after World War II. These silhouettes illustrate the development from the simple Groningen coaster (top) of the late 1940's to the spacious Danish North Sea ferry DANA ANGLIA (bottom) built in 1978. Between these two we find (from the top) the Norwegian paragraph ship M/S GLORIA (299 GRT), built 1951, the Swedish pallet ship M/S NERLANDIA (499 GRT), built 1964, the Norwegian ro-ro ship M/S BALDUIN (3974 GRT), built 1975, the Norwegian LPG-tanker M/S HEBE (4492 GRT), built 1975 and the Norwegian reefer M/S ATLE JARL (499 GRT), built 1976, equipped with side-ports and constructed to carry containers on three decks. (Drawings: Helge Vabø, Bergen Maritime Museum.)

competition. Because of marginal profits, operating costs became vital. Up to about 1960 the shipowners' attention was focused

mainly on crew costs, which resulted in the development of the paragraph ship. By the middle of the 1960's the advantages of the paragraph ships regarding crew costs seemed to have been fully exploited. To achieve further cost reductions, a policy of rationalization and specialization was introduced. Cargo handling held the centre of the stage, resulting in the building of vessels which were "tailor-made" for a particular type of cargo or trade.[33] Simultaneously the struggle against high crew costs continued with the introduction of the first automation and rationalization experiments on board some ships.

These post-1960 developments were reflected differently in the various countries. The Danish shipping industry enjoyed the strongest relative growth despite high domestic costs. Part of the explanation may be found in the Danish liberal scale of manning, at least compared with the Norwegian. The Danes also exploited the transport-economic advantages of EEC-membership.

But the abundant provision of capital to their small ship fleet is perhaps the most important explanation. This was mainly attributable to favourable tax allowances on the annual depreciation of ships. Also the fact that Danish shipowning was organized as partnership, joint ownership and limited partnership, offering individuals with high incomes an opportunity to reduce their income tax, contributed to the capital flow into shipping.[34] "Dentist-companies" and "panty-companies" became somewhat disparaging terms in Denmark denoting the interest of dentists and makers of ladies' underwear in shipping.[35] Towards the end of the 1970's, however, problems began to loom up for Danish small-ships owners. Costs increased, and in 1979 and the first half of 1980 the Danish small-ship fleet was reduced by about 100 vessels.[36]

In contrast to Denmark, Swedish short sea and coastal shipping had problems in manning their fleet and in battling competition from road and rail transport. The transport of such an important Swedish export product as timber was to an increasing extent taken over by railways and railway ferries.[37]

In recent years the West Germans have also faced serious problems in North Sea trade. A depressed freight market in particular affected the single-ship companies, a common form of shipowning in West Germany. In the period 1970–1975, 350 German "Kümos"-owners had to go out of business,[38] and the surviving companies have in a number of cases been merged into larger units. At the same time, though, the West German small-ship fleet has been modernized.[39] Thus West Germany has, in spite of all difficulties, succeeded in maintaining their lead in the North Sea shipping. The predominant position of West German industry in Europe has also proved to be of advantage. In contrast to the Danish and the Norwegian small-ship fleet, most of the German ships engaged in North Sea trade have been operated on the tramp market. This has, however, been compensated for by the formation of pools on the broker side.[40]

After World War II Norwegian North Sea shipping operated under highly variable conditions. In recent years, however, the government has proved more willing to give this part of Norwegian shipping better operating terms. As a consequence the trade seems to have been imbued with a new and more optimistic spirit, a spirit reflected in the editorial of a maritime trade journal in 1975:

There were times when German and Dutch small ships bid our own ships strong, almost overwhelming competition in the fight for cargo. This was not only the case on the Continent, but also in our own waters. Family-owned and family-manned vessels sailed at considerably lower costs than our own vessels, making it almost impossible for us to accept freight rates deemed satisfactory by the Germans and the Dutch. When these conditions now have changed to our benefit, it is not only due to a reduction of our costs. On the contrary, our costs have steadily been increasing. But the crew costs of the German and the Dutch have increased relatively more. In addition Norwegian owners have by means of the introduction of new methods, managed to rationalize their part of North Sea shipping to such a degree that at present we are able to compete with most other nations and to some extent we have even outstripped our previous competitors.[41]

Dutch small-ship trade, including North Sea shipping, has been through a period of stagnation in recent years. As a consequence their leading role in the North Sea trade has been taken over by the West Germans and they have also been distanced by Great Britain and Denmark. The realization of the 75-meters rule has, however, led to a reduction of costs and Dutch small-ships remain important in the North Sea.[42] Like the Germans, the Dutch to a large extent operate their vessels as tramps; likewise the brokers play important co-ordinating roles in Dutch North Sea shipping.

British statistics distinguish between "coasting and home trade ships" and "foreign-going ships" when vessels between 100 and 2000 GRT are concerned.[43] The first group is operated mainly in British waters, while the other to a large extent meets Britain's transport demands between British and foreign ports (including the North Sea). While the British coaster fleet declined in recent years, the number of "foreign-going ships" has grown significantly, especially vessels above 1000 GRT.[44] Almost half the British small-ships are operated as liners, largely because of her geographic position, which makes it necessary to have regular services with the Continent.[45] Most British lines are therefore engaged in North Sea trade and Cross-Channel services.

In order to improve competitive ability a number of pools, such as the Euro Minibulker Pool, were founded in the 1970's. Some of these cooperative projects were solely

Figure 6. In the 1960's the leading role of the Dutch in post-war North Sea shipping was taken over by the West Germans. Dutch coasters like the M/S GRETINA HOLWERDA (399 GRT) continued, however, to be a common sight in the North Sea. (Photo: Norwegian Maritime Museum.)

Figure 7. A multitude of different types of ships are involved in today's North Sea shipping. The differences are the result of a number of factors. In the case of the Norwegian M/S RHINO (499 GRT), built 1979 for Paal Wilson & Co. A/S, the designers have paid special attention to the navigation on the Rhine. The shallow waters and the low bridges of the river have to a large extent influenced the design. (Photo: Bergen Maritime Museum.)

national, but some involved international co-operation. By operating large numbers of ships in groups the expensive vessels could be utilized more effectively and a higher profit achieved.[46]

North Sea Shipping Today

Perhaps the most striking feature of North Sea shipping today is the multitude of different types of ships involved. The basic design remains, however, the paragraph ship. Many types have been constructed, each having its own characteristics and qualities. The differences are the result of a number of factors. The type, quantity and handling of cargo to be carried are of major importance in the determination of both the size and the shape of the individual vessel,[47] but other factors may also have influence. The ship may be intended for service in ports and waters with special requirements as to length, breadth and draught. Weather conditions in the region to be served may be so

severe that the ship has to be bigger and stronger than if it had been meant to operate in other waters. Additional strengthening for navigation in ice may in some cases be required. In other cases the ship may have to be able to "take the hard" at low tide, for instance in British ports, or to sail safely under the low bridges on the Rhine. All these considerations and many more have created the heterogeneous mass of ships we find operating in the North Sea today.

Huge sums are invested in the new ships. To be profitable they must be operated at the fullest possible capacity. It is not acceptable for the owners to have their ships spend more days a year in port than they spend at sea about their proper business – transporting goods – which was actually the case as recently as the late 1950's.[48] "Sea transportation, as such, is now so cheap that its costs can practically be disregarded in international trade. What costs money is the business of berthing the ship in the dock, transporting the goods overland to the quay, and loading them aboard the ship. *It is the handling stages that are expensive in practically all transport operations.*"[49] The recognition of this, together with strong demand for efficiency and integration of sea transport in the general transport pattern, have led to significant technological innovations in the handling of maritime cargoes. Keywords are inter alia *unitized cargo, improved loading and discharging gear* and the appearance of a few *giant ports* which are the entrepôts for vast regions. The number of ports to be called at by the individual ship have been reduced to a minimum. Thus "turn-around" time in North Sea ports has been steadily shortened. But bottlenecks still exist and occasional congestion may occur even at the most modern seaport. The search for efficiency is therefore perpetual.

For the sake of simplicity we may divide the different types of vessels operating in the North Sea into three main groups:

1. Dry-cargo ships
2. Tankers
3. Passenger/car/trailer/train ferries

The dry-cargo ships form the most heterogenous group. The development of the different types of dry-cargo vessels is closely related to the types of cargo to be transported, and conditions in the ports where loading and discharging take place. Previously dry-cargo was handled in accordance with the traditional and often time-consuming "lo-lo-principle" (lift on – lift off). In shape, size and weight cargo showed great variety. The integration of North Sea shipping into the general transport pattern of Northern Europe changed the situation fundamentally. In order to reduce "turn-around" time and to link maritime transport with road and rail, sophisticated loading and discharging devices ashore and aboard have been designed. To an increasing extent the piece and sack goods of former days have been unitized by being batched into larger packaging units and put onto pallets or into containers. The number of dockers handling the cargo have thus been reduced drastically, and the competitive ability of maritime transport improved.

The conventional dry-cargo ships are still numerous in North Sea trade, but they are being steadily replaced by vessels designed for special trades or cargoes. The lo-lo-principle has been supplemented with or replaced by the "ro-ro-principle" (roll on – roll off), which was introduced in the early 1950's and had a breakthrough in the late 1960's.

Limited space does not permit a detailed description of all the different types of dry-cargo ships operating in North Sea trade. Some of the main types, however, must be mentioned.

The pallet ship, which started the cargo-handling revolution in coastal and short-sea trade, may be found in a number of variations. Today we find pallet vessels specially constructed for carrying goods like newsprint, chemical pulp and fertilizers. The vessels are constructed with side and/or bow and stern ports allowing cargo to be loaded and discharged by means of forklifts. Some of the vessels are equipped with pallet elevators and holds for deep freeze.

Perhaps the most important change in maritime cargo handling came with the introduction of containers in the latter half of the 1960's. A container is a standardized "box" usually with doors in the ends. It measures 20 or 40 feet long with an 8 foot square cross section. The container is either lifted aboard ship by special cranes or rolled aboard over a ramp and through doors in the bow, stern or side of the ship. In the first case the vessel is called a *lo-lo ship* and in the latter a *ro-ro ship.* Either type may or may not be equipped with its own cargo gear.

In modern North Sea trade we find a number of dry-cargo ships which combine many different types of cargo handling. The Norwegian motor-vessel CANIS, built in 1980, is for instance a *multipurpose ship,* which can be classified as a *ro-ro/container-/lo-lo-/pallet ship.*[50] M/V CANIS sails for the Nor-Cargo line between Bergen and Rotterdam/Amsterdam. A similar vessel is the M/V

Figure 8. In order to reduce "turn-around" time in port and to link maritime transport with road and rail, ships with sophisticated loading and discharging devices have been designed. Such a ship is the multipurpose ship M/S CANIS (1999 GRT) built in 1980 for the Nor-Cargo group. The vessel is a roll-on/roll-off, container and pallet carrier purpose built to carry almost any kind of cargo. (Photo: Bergen Maritime Museum.)

Rotterdam/Amsterdam. A similar vessel is the M/V TRANS FJELL, also Bergen-owned, sailing between the Oslofjord region and Rouen/Amsterdam, usually carrying wood products to France and cars from the Netherlands to Norway as return cargo.[51] Whereas the expensive and bigger ro-ro ships are dependent on cargo handling facilities which only the great ports can offer, the multipurpose ships are able to call on smaller ports with less advanced equipment. Tanks have also been installed in some multipurpose ships enabling them to carry liquid cargo.

Bulk-cargoes still play an important role in European and North Sea trade. The five most important are coal, iron ore, cereals, phosphate and bauxite/alumina. The rising demand for regularity in the transport of these commodities has led to the establishment of a number of scheduled services. An example is the "Norge-Rhinlinjen"

operating between Norway on the one side and Germany, the Netherlands and Great Britain on the other.

M/V RHINO may serve as an example of the roughly 20 vessels operating in this particular service.[52] RHINO, a conventional dry-cargo ship with a single hatch, was built in 1979. The ship measures 499 GRT as an open and 1445 as a closed shelter-decker. The ship has been constructed with reclinable masts to ensure a safe passage under the many bridges crossing the German and the Dutch waterways. With their modest draught the vessels of the "Norge-Rhinlinjen" are able to sail up the Rhine to Duisburg and in some cases even further. The cargo from Norway to Germany consists mainly of alumina and ferrosilicon, with steel and chemical products being the most frequent return cargoes. The transport is performed on a longterm contract basis. As return cargoes from Germany are

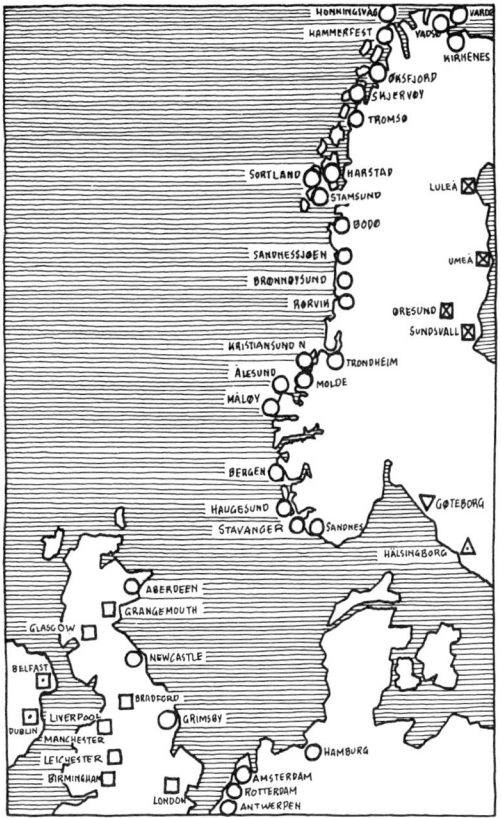

O   Port of call
△   Southbound Grimsby-line for refrigerated cargo
□   Terminals for collected cargo
⊡   Call by arrangement or transit via Grimsby or Newcastle
⊠   Transit via Trondheim
▽   Ro-ro cargo from Bergen and Stavanger and return

Figure 9. The big ro-ro ships are dependent upon cargo handling facilities which only the great ports can offer. The multi purpose ships, however, are able to call on smaller ports with less advanced equipment. The map shows the large number of ports the M/S CANIS and the other vessels of the Nor-Cargo group are able to serve. (Map drawn by Helge Vabø, Bergen Maritime Museum.)

sometime scarce, the ships often call at British or Dutch ports on their way home. The most important return cargoes from British ports are coke and steel and from Dutch ports steel and chemicals. The performance of the "Norge-Rhinlinjen" and similar shipping enterprises is essentially "door-to-door" transport of high regularity for the metallurgic industries. Other scheduled services play a similar role in relation to other industries, e.g., the forest products industries.

The energy consumption of Western Europe is great. Besides coal, hydroelectric and nuclear power, oil and gas are the most important sources of energy. Oil and gas are also raw materials for many different kinds of industry, creating a huge demand mainly supplied from outside Europe. But there is also transport of oil and gas within Europe. Large quantities are transported by means of pipelines and tankers.

In this respect the North Sea region has, both as a producer and consumer of gas and oil, come into focus during the last decade. It is estimated that oil production from the North Sea will be able to supply a third of Europe's oil needs during the 1980's.[53] This will lead to an even further increase in the transport demand within the area. Besides pipelines, three main types of tankers are employed in the transport of gas and oil from the North Sea:

1. The conventional tanker
2. The gas tanker
3. The product carrier (e.g., chemical tankers)

Conventional tankers are to a large extent engaged in the transport of crude oil from the fields to the refineries. Eighty per cent of the world's export shipments of crude oil originates from the Arabian Gulf, thus engaging most of the world's crude carriers.[54] The transport of North Sea oil employs only a few crude carriers. These are loaded at specially designed offshore terminals. The Statfjord terminal serving the Norwegian sector of the North Sea is designed for tankers like M/T POLYTRADER and M/T POLYTRAVELLER (owner, Einar Rasmussens rederier, Kristiansand, Norway). These tankers have been fitted with advanced instrumentation to ensure safe manoeuvering to the ter-

261

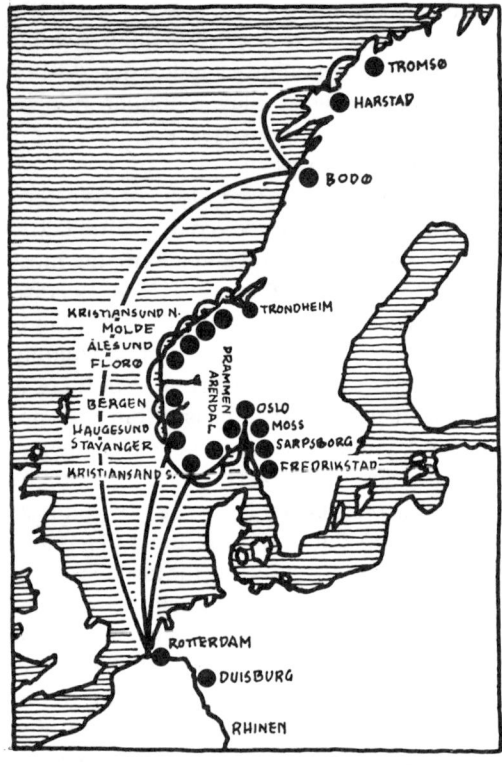

Figure 10. The Norwegian shipowners Paal Wilson & Co. A/S, Bergen are operating the Norway-Rhine Line with vessels especially designed to suit sailings between ports on the river Rhine and ports along the Norwegian coast, cf. fig. 7. The ships are able to sail the Rhine to Duisburg and in some cases even further. (Map drawn by Helge Vabø, Bergen Maritime Museum.)

minal. The terminal itself has been equipped with a crane to assist in hooking up and suspending the hose to the ship's bow manifold connection.[55]

In spite of sophisticated solutions to the problems of loading tankers under the rough weather conditions of the North Sea, pipelines seem to be preferred for the transport of gas and oil from the fields. In the redistribution and transport of refined products from the North Sea, however, a number of vessels are engaged. A product of growing importance in this context is gas.

Gas can be found alone (non-associated) or with crude oil (associated) and contains propane, butane, methane and ethane.[56] In maritime transport we deal with two major categories of gas, i.e. LPG – liquified petroleum gas mainly containing propane and butane – and LNG – liquified natural gas containing primarily methane and ethane. Before the energy crisis in the beginning of the 1970's there was little interest in the utilization of gas associated with crude oil. In most cases the gas was flared off at the well in the producing countries. LPG was expensive to recover, liquefy, store, transport and distribute. The energy crisis with escalating oil prices radically altered the world's concept of gas as a fuel and as a raw material. Thus North Sea gas became economically interesting and the accompanying technological progress made it more feasible to transport and distribute. Both LPG and LNG are transported in specialized vessels. To reduce the volume of the cargo the gas is carried under extreme refrigeration. In gaseous state the cargo would take up 300 times more space.

In 1973 the Norwegian Parliament approved plans for laying an oil pipeline from Ekofisk to Teesside in UK. As part of the agreement the Phillips Group undertook to supply the planned Rafnes petrochemical plant in Norway with 700,000 to 750,000 tons of liquid gas (ethane and propane) annually from the Teesside oil terminal.[57] On the 21st March 1979 the LPG-tanker MARCO POLO, owned by A.I. Langfeldt & Co., Kristiansand, left Teesside with the first cargo of propane for the crackers at Rafnes.[58] A new trade in North Sea shipping had been inaugurated. MARCO POLO was soon followed by four other tankers chartered on short term contracts. The Phillips Group signed a longterm contract with shipowner Helge R. Myhre, Stavanger, who undertook the future transport of gas from Teesside to Rafnes.

"The life-style of the twentieth century would grind to a halt without the mass production of industrial chemicals."[59] This is

The Oil Adventure in the North Sea seen from Norway

JAN HAGLAND

"You can see that rig from far away
It's shining clean and bright
In the early morning light . . ."

(American oil worker about Ekofisk.)

While seismic surveying vessels, semi-submersible drilling rigs, supply ships and helicopters manouevred into position in the spring of 1966 to begin the largest maritime and industrial epoch in the history of the North Sea, the authorities in Norway asked themselves if this was going to last. Whether the fairy-tale was going to come true.

Almost 20 years on – with an oil and gas production of between 50 and 60 million tons of oil equivalent (t.o.e.) – the question is the same: How long will it last? The desire for a positive answer lies within the question: The oil industry is here to stay. Naturally enough, the country and the Treasury want the oil industry to continue into the far distant future. The North Sea provides jobs, industrial contracts and billions of kroner in the Treasury, and the Storting has decided that the oil industry is to benefit the entire Norwegian society, and this has come to pass.

But as far as the North Sea is concerned, the question of duration goes deeper, since the pulse and rhythm of the North Sea are and have been constantly renewed; not only in the winds and weather which move the waters, the sea. It is just as much the marinebiological eternal wheel which turns and turns and which provides Europe's millions with food. The North Sea has the world's most productive waters for fish and they are probably the most fished, and therefore the most exposed in every respect – as regards fishing policies, environmentally and strategically.

But the guarantees of food are there from this extravagantly rich production system in the sea's inner chamber which we expect will reach from here to . . . well, eternity.

It was within this cycle that the oil explorers entwined their fates with a west coast populace for what was about to come. Some of them knew of the Stavanger poet Alexander L. Kielland's affectionate appraisal of the sea: The sea is not unfaithful, because it never promised us anything . . .

Perhaps it is different now: The North Sea's horn of overflowing bounty was to sound once more, yet with an ever so slight promise in advance which made oil explorers the world over turn exploration techniques towards a new area of confrontation between nature and technical civilization.

In 1958, Western Europe's largest gas field was found many thousands of metres below the Dutch corn fields in the province of Groningen. Oil geologists had long said that the same formations stretched out into the North Sea. Now the theory became immediately more interesting, even essen-

267

Figure 1. At 2200 hours on 22 April 1977 as the gas alarm sounded on to Bravo platform in the Ekofisk complex and 112 people had to be evacuated, Norway's first uncontrolled blow-out had become a reality. This haunting spectre of Norwegian oil debates since the outset in 1966 was suddenly alive and kicking in the form of a boiling column of oil and gas, rising from the sea 180 kilometres southwest of Stavanger.

For eight days the eyes of the world were centered on Ekofisk and our struggle to combat the nightmare side of oil production.

perienced oil explorers. They had begun carefully at a depth of 30 metres in the Gulf of Mexico just after World War II, but since then, technical marine advances were mostly made for military reasons. Among other things, submarine technology had progressed dramatically, and there, the oil explorers could learn something of moving about, navigation, communications and operating in the globe's inner chambers.

The fact that it was the Norwegian continental shelf which was to make the world's most important industry after weapon manufacture come of age, was initially viewed as David teaching Goliath: The event lacked a standard comparative measure since the reality was so overwhelming: The Norwegian continental shelf extends from a depth of 70 metres in the south to 500 metres depth in the north, and oil explorers know, together with marine technologists, that each metre down into the water costs millions and perhaps billi-

tial. There was no time to ask how unfaithful the North Sea should prove to be. The big test had to come – on the basis of more than geological conclusions alone – and the World's oil industry was anxious to throw itself off the deep end, in more ways than one, and partly because of the following situation:

Energy in all forms is the driving force in our civilization, with an emphasis on oil, and increasingly more on gas, at least for the rest of this century and well into the next. Oil is called black gold and is synonymous with power. The international oil industry has deftly used all of these advantages to keep itself and the world up-to-date with oil supplies – from ever more complex regions, both geologically and technically.

The step out into the North Sea was a big one, however, even for the most ex-

Figure 2. What's it all about? – High dimensions, enormous expense, tremedous scope.

Here the scale is clear: a supply ship, the ship's deck, some containers and a few individuals below the concrete and steel colossus of Statfjord A. Photo: Leif Berge, Statoil.

Figure 3. Supply ships, the coolies of the North Sea, our modern-day pack-horse of oil exploration, maintain the links with land. Oil platforms in the North Sea are considered to be the most isolated and hazardous workplaces of modern industry.

Though the first supply ships which came to Norway were built for the maritime conditions in the Gulf of Mexico, now their design is Norwegian, and sufficiently robust for tough service.

ons to conquer. Still, they approached the bull in 1966 – at a time when oil cost three dollars per barrel, while in the 1980's it has climbed to over 30 dollars. What was it that the oil explorers believed in?

Oil, of course. A well-used, but good comparative measure shows what the forecasters in the 1960's foresaw:

The world's total energy consumption in 1974 was converted into oil units, 6,155 million tons. Poured into a tank with a diameter of one kilometre, the tank would reach a height of 7,640 metres, or three times the height of *Galdhøpiggen,* Norway's heighest mountain. In such a tank, actual oil consumption would reach a height of 3,360 metres, almost halfway – while the remainder represents gas, coal, hydro-electric power and atomic power.

To maintain its relative share, the oil industry must discover 2,500 million tons of oil each year, which is equivalent to Norway's consumption for 400 years. This can only take place if the oil industry conquers increasingly more expensive and geologically/technically more complicated areas from which to recover oil.

The North Sea had undoubtedly been such an area: a new technological area, but also with the advantages of being at the hart of one of the world's most energy-hungry markets and in a politically stable part of the world.

Despite rough weather and great depths of water, it didn't scare the oil explorers. Just 3 years after the Gröningen find, in the autumn of 1961, the first oil explorers knocked at Norway's door: they were two representatives from the American oil company Phillips Petroleum & Co., whose head office is in Bartlesville, far inland in the state of Oklahoma. These two Phillips representatives openly asked Norway for sole rights to explore for oil and gas on the entire Norwegian continental shelf.

But Norway had no choice: Those two had to be firmly but politely refused: There was no framework of rules – and besides, territorial and boundary rights between the North Sea countries where these merged at sea, had to be clarified. Our territorial rights to the continental shelf are formalized in the so-called Geneva Agreement of 1958, which gives the coastal state sovereignty to explore and exploit natural resources down to a depth of 200 metres, or insofar as it is technically possible. This latter passage in the Oceanic Rights Treaty was called the exploitation criterium and was possibly the weak link, since it would allow the coastal states, via technological maritime developments, to subjugate the world's oceans alone, a development which the international legal society could not just sit idly by and watch.

It was remembered what a British diplomat once said: Law and order at sea has not been maintained purely for love of one's neighbour.

In the spring of 1974, the world's second conference on international law of the seas was hosted by the UN, where one guideline was that natural resources outside the 200 mile zone were to be declared as the

Figure 4. The construction labourer of the North Sea, a roughneck or drilling assistant, working on an exposed and weather-beaten drill floor. The work is tough and heavy, and only during recent years have automation and sheltering of the drill crew's workplace begun to be developed.

common inheritance of all mankind. The sea suddenly had a popular dimension beyond considerations for those who sail and work on the sea.

In 1961, however, the North Sea was divided according to the median line principle to which no international legal problems were attached. The division took place, however, before oil and gas were discovered in the area. Had the finds already been made, the division itself would have had a completely different outcome: This conclusion may be drawn by looking at the division of those 600,000 square kilometres (almost twice that of Norway's dry land area) which were available:

Great Britain received 244,000 square kilometres, Norway 131,000 sq.km, Holland 62,000, Denmark 56,000, West Germany 24,000, Belgium 4,000 and France 400 sq.km.

With oil and gas present, the outcome would have been entirely different, especially for Norway. Just off our coast, from Southern Norway to Stad, runs the Norwegian Trench, which is over 200 metres deep at all points. Far-sightedness, specially on the part of the then Deputy Under-secretay of State, Jens Evensen, of the Ministry of Foreign Affairs' legal department, made the other parties to the negotiations accept the Norwegian view that the Norwegian Trench was a chance geological fracture in the bottom of the North Sea.

With the Royal Decree of 31 May 1963, Norway proclaimed sovereignty over the seabed and its subsurface for the purposes of exploration and exploitation of its natural resources. The country had thus come one step closer to being an oil nation. The next step was to draw up rules and regulations for the activity. Without this, it could not begin – in other words: Norwegian authorities decided it should be so. The oil industry, the World's Seven Sisters among others, were prepared but had to wait: on 8 November 1963, the committee was appointed by the Government.

On 9 April 1965, regulations were laid down by Royal Decree for the exploration and recovery of petroleum on Norway's continental shelf south of the 62nd parallel i.e. the North Sea, after recommendations by the committee. The North Sea was divided into 278 blocks, each covering 500 sq.km – twice as big as Britain's – to keep interest awake. Very extensive labours had gone into this, so the claims that Norwegian oil history began on that day – 9 April 1965 – are not groundless.

From now on, things started to happen quickly in rapid succession: on 17 August of the same year, the Government awarded production licences for 78 blocks in all to nine applicants: Most of the world's large oil companies had applied, apart from British Petroleum, BP, whose head geologist claimed that there wasn't a drop of oil to be found in the North Sea. If there were, he would personally drink it all.

Figure 5. Accompanying the oil activity, major maritime operations also arrived in Norway. Here we see the first Condeep platform, Beryl A, being towed and steadied between the skerries and straits of Ryfylke in July 1978 by a team of tug boats fore and aft whose collected seaborne horsepower was the greatest ever witnessed.

In the spring of 1965, Stavanger also began its oil epoch when the first oil industry representative, Director R.J. "Dick" Loeffler from Esso began to search for a land base for supplies to the oil industry in the region between Kristiansand and Bergen. In Stavanger, Loeffler met shipowner Torolf Smedvig and they agreed that the obsolete herring oil factory Fjeldberg Brug at Hundvåg was suited for its intended purpose.

There lay in this both a continuity and a beginning for Stavanger. The town's ties to the sea have always been evident; its rise and fall in keeping with the health of marine resources and shipping trade cycles, has brought both joy and sorrow.

No-one knew at that time how great, how vigorous it would be, but the town authorities gambled boldly: In the autumn of 1965, the town's political bodies decided to give as much support as possible to companies who came to establish themselves in connection with the coming oil exploration in the North Sea: on 13 November 1965, Stavanger Aftenblad wrote:

"Stavanger is preparing for a new day – as the home port for oil exploration."

In the article, it was stated that apart from Esso Exploration Norway, both the Phillips and the Petronord groups had decided to operate from Stavanger, and from then on, one event followed the other: The first supply base was established in the town itself, in Strømsteinen. Already the same autumn, Smedvig's Tankrederi acquired a site at Dusavig for industrial use in connection with oil exploration, and later, the NorSea base was established here. In December, Aker Mekaniske Verksted purchased a site in Tananger and established the Norsco base there, while Helicopter Service with its far-ranging helicopters set itself up in hangars at Forus which had been shut down.

And not too much of 1966 had gone by before Esso Exploration Norway signed a contract with the American service company ODECO for leasing the drilling platform "Ocean Traveller", which was built in New Orleans for drilling operations in the Norwegian sector of the North Sea.

271

And one early June morning that same year, the populace around Dusavig woke up to a remarkable sight in the Byfjord: a strange vessel, floating on pontoons from which columns reared up and on which several decks with derricks, living quarters and helicopter deck rested.

The "Ocean Traveller" had been towed over the Atlantic Ocean: the trip had taken 45 days and thousands of crewmen in particular awaited its arrival: 1,000 people had applied for 35 positions on board: Sea men in Norway facing the North Sea also had faith in this new era.

On 21 June 1966, the "Ocean Traveller" set the first oil drill into the Norwegian continental shelf while the spring winds brushed past, on their way in towards the light Jæren beaches . . .

The dice had been cast. The game began and – as is always the case – fate knew more than did the oil explorers and we others. There was something at any rate. The North Sea did not submit so easily to these new maritime muscles.

– In the beginning, we often lay drifting without knowing what to do, said North Sea pioneer "Dick" Loeffler when he received the medal of St. Olav in 1978, at a point in time when Norway had long since cast the seventh and last veil and opened up for oil exploration north of 62 degrees latitude in the teeth of gusts from the Arctic.

But it wasn't only the maritime craftsmanship and the nautical challenges which presented themselves at sea: the oil and gas would not come either. Thirty-one dry holes at a price of NOK 750 million (Norway's running costs for many, many years at that time) were drilled without the great find: Small finds were made at such localities as Cod, but they were not viable. The oil industry was on the verge of packing up and going, but had to complete the agreed drilling program first.

On the basis of Norwegian indications, the Phillips group thus started to drill down to the agreed depth in Block 2/4 – in the far

Figure 6. Gas being landed in Norway. The pipelaying barge LB 200 is here seen leaving port from Kalstø on the western coast of Karmøy with the pipeline which is destined to receive gas from the Statfjord field via the Kårstø process refinery in Tysvær. Here the more refined gases, that cat's whiskers of hydrocarbon depletion, will be separated out before shunting the gas on via the Ekofisk system to Emden in West Germany.

Figure 7. The North Sea port of Stavanger is the oil capital of Norway, administratively as well as for operations.

Stavanger's Moss-Rosenberg Verft is a key fabrication yard for major building projects. The picture shows the Statfjord B topside during its construction phase.

An idea of the dimensions of the Statfjord B deck is given by the cruise liner Queen Elizabeth II as she sails past.

south of the Norwegian sector, 220 km from Stavanger. On the day before Christmas Eve 1969 the change came: The Norwegian-built drilling platform "Ocean Viking" struck an oil and gas field which has later been called Ekofisk, and which appeared to be among the 30 largest in the world.

The find was kept secret until 1970, but now the matter seemed clear: Norway had become an oil producing nation, a member of the world's most exclusive elite.

Now the North Sea had to be conquered.

And so it was; while everyone knew how easily the wheel of fortune could have stopped at other values:

The Ekofisk block was number 7 on the Phillips group's list of priorities.

Well then, it was here that the foundation stone was laid at any rate. Slowly but surely, the building up of the Ekofisk town and the Ekofisk complex was begun, and in time it was to consist of 24 platforms and 24 ports, in the new North Sea. The slow growth of an oil nation was thus initiated:

In 1971, production commenced on Ekofisk, or more correctly stated, trial production, with subsea systems, a temporary production platform and buoy loading: In this way, the sceptics, who feared not least the sea's living environment, were also challenged.

1971: New block distributions. The young oil nation wants more.

1973: Perhaps the most important year in the history of Norwegian trade and industry until then: Den norske stats oljeselskap, Statoil, was established with its head office in Stavanger after a previous resolution to the Storting, together with the Norwegian Petroleum Directorate, who were also given headquarters in the same town: If the truth be known: The NPD was probably established first.

As the North Sea acted as a magnet on the oil explorers of the world, these two institutions started to attract members of the Norwegian workforce educated in geology, geophysics, engineering subjects, economics and law to an extent never before seen in this country, and one which would enable both institutions, each in its

Figure 8. Oil and gas installations in the North Sea stand like navigation lights in the night. This is the Frigg field midway between Ekofisk and latitude 62 degrees north. Frigg supplies one third of the UK demand for gas through the Franco-Norwegian operator, Elf Aquitaine Norge.

273

Figure 9. The Ekofisk Center – an artifical town in the North Sea. Here oil and gas are processed and dispatched by pipeline to West Germany and Teesside in northeast England.
Ekofisk was Norway's first oil boom town. Offering tenants a life on steel stilts in the sea, Ekofisk was nevertheless organized according to the old pattern which segregated production, drilling and accomodation, unlike the integrated enormity of the monster Statfjord installations.

own way, to mind the regulations and the money flow.

It came as no surprise to the world's oil companies, which advocate private capitalism, that the Norwegian state wanted to have full national control of the oil activity.

It had been on the cards right from the start, but Norway was somewhat reticent with risk capital at the first distribution of concessions: With Statoil, the country became involved with 50% and above, a condition which the large companies accepted – in this way, oil prices developed through the 1980's. Through its high participation, Statoil was able to sit in on all important decisions and thus in every way, build itself up to be a fully integrated oil company, which in time took over all relevant operator tasks on the continental shelf, with five exploration platforms in operation at one and the same time.

But at one point, in 1970, when Norway brought in extra tax, a typical oil American snapped: You Norwegians are blue-eyed Arabs, he said. – It will never work.

But it has. The North Sea's history as regards oil is most eventful – for better or worse. Some of the events are as follows:

1971: First oil production on Ekofisk.

1972: New round of concessions.

1973: Statoil and the Norwegian Petroleum Directorate in active service.

1974: The world's largest oil and gas discoveries at sea are made by the Statoil-Mobil group. The field is called Statfjord.

1975: Norway exports more oil than we ourselves use.

1976: Proposal on opening up for exploration drilling north of 62 degrees latitude.

1977: Production from the world's largest pure gas field at sea – Frigg is in swing.

1978: The Ministry of Petroleum and Energy is founded.

1979: Production commences on Statfjord.

1980: Green light for oil exploration north of the 62nd parallel.

1980: On 1 June, the drilling platform "Treasure Seeker" sets its drill bit into the

Figure 10. Concrete found immediate favour as a constructional material in the North Sea in competition with traditional steel jacket concepts. Here we see Ekofisk 1, the Ekofisk Tank, under construction in Jåttåvågen in Stavanger in 1972.

Our experience with concrete wharves in fjords and inlets along the Norwegian coast had taught our engineers that concrete becomes even harder and more solid in the sea.

Norwegian designed concrete gravity based platforms conquered the British and Norwegian sectors of the North Sea alike.

North Norwegian continental shelf: The North Sea was stretched a step further. From now on, only the Norwegian continental shelf is referred to. The 62 degree limit is extended: Norway has a new maritime environment which it handles with its own technology. Huge concrete oil rigs were constructed in Stavanger and oil bases grew up at the coast of Norway.

The first gas pipeline is brought to land in Norway at Kårstø from Statfjord under Statoil's operatorship. Gullfaks is under development with Norwegian planners and workers.

But there is also a negative side to it.

On 22 April 1977, the first major blow came: Just before 2200 hours, the operators on board the drilling and production platform Bravo in the Ekofisk complex lost control of Well No. 14 and the North Sea's first uncontrolled blow-out was a fact. The ghost in the Norwegian oil debate since 1966 now suddenly appeared in the living form of a boiling oil and gas column out at sea, 220 km south-west of Stavanger:

We were all, and not least the world Press, reminded of the largest maritime and industrial drama in the history of the

North Sea, and what had been said by the American oil worker in his ballad to the oil ruffian's work site out there, was no longer valid:

You can see that rig from far away
It's shining clear and bright
In the early morning light.

The society on steel legs at sea was evacuated and the oil explorers – and the politicians – looked either forwards or backwards in time, depending on their outlook:

How had it developed: In the beginning, the drilling platform could operate 20–25% of the year. With the passage of years, a limit had been reached which covered 90% of the weather outlook: It was not harsher anywhere else in the world. Even the 100-year wave, a natural phenomenon which will hit all seas in the space of a one hundred year period, was rejected. In the autumn of 1972, the one followed after the other. Several hundred years were used up in advance!

The Norwegians began to be self-assured, but then it came . . . 22,000 tons of oil poured into the sea before the Bravo blow-out could be stopped on 30 April. The opening north of 62 degrees latitude was delayed. Focus was once again set on safety. Safety for people, the environment and investments – the triple safety concept. The Norwegian Petroleum Directorate began to clean up the sea floor: Many hundreds of fishermen received compensation for loss of equipment in collisions with the oil industry's cast-offs.

Activity in the North Sea had negative effects in other ways too:

1975: A gas-carrying riser on Alpha (Ekofisk) bursts and three people are killed during evacuation.

1976: The drilling platform "Deep Sea Driller" capsizes during a storm. Six people died.

1977: The Bravo blow-out. No loss of life.

1978: Fire in one of the legs on the Statfjord A platform. Five dead.

1980: On 27 March – the worst accident of all occurs. The accommodation platform "Alexander L. Kielland" overturns near the Edda platform on Ekofisk and 123 people are killed; the darkest chapter in Norwegian oil history.

The wreck of the platform was sent to Nedstrandsfjorden in the spring of 1984, but the last word has still not been uttered about the accident which will go into maritime history on a footing with the "Titanic": How did it happen? Why did it happen?

Faithless North Sea? What Alexander L. Kielland wrote is probably true: On this score, the sea has never promised us anything. On the contrary. Today, the oil and gas towns exist under our responsibility in a row from Ekofisk to Statfjord: High technology which goes and goes and which needs fastidious care: And Sleipner awaits maturation, as does Troll – the new gas giant in Western Europe, for something like NOK 2,500 billion if the stock exchange could swallow it all today.

And at the same time, the eternal wheel pulses in the closed sea chamber: The winter herring shall return; Winter herring which, at it's peak, had an egg-laying potential which equalled four times Europe's population by weight, and which carried a tidal wave of protein towards our coasts each year.

It also has its home in the North Sea: The world's largest stock of fish also has its feeding grounds there where the steel and concrete have erected their new maritime monuments and there where the oil and gas roads run like blood arteries along a rough sea bed.

Will it last? Yes. But for how long? Perhaps 100 years more, for all we know.

List of Contributors

Mr. Egil Bergsager
Deputy Director
Norwegian Petroleum Directorate
Stavanger
Norway

Dr. Alan Binns
Formerly Senior Lecturer (Anglo-Saxon &
Old Norse)
Hull University
Hull
England

Mr. Jarle Bjørklund
Education Officer
Norsk Sjøfartsmuseum
Oslo
Norway

Dr. Philippus Meesse Bosscher
Naval Officer. Teacher of naval history at
the Royal Netherlands Naval College and
curator of the Navy Museum, Den Helder
The Netherlands

Prof. Dr. J.R. Bruijn
Rijksuniversiteit te Leiden
Leiden
The Netherlands

Dr. Carl Olof Cederlund
Senior Curator
Statens Sjöhistoriska Museum
Stockholm
Sweden

Dr. Helen Clarke
University College of London
London
England

Dr. Detlev Ellmers
Director, Deutsches Schiffahrtsmuseum
Bremerhaven
Western Germany

Dr. Angela Evans
British Museum
London
England

Mr. Jan Hagland
Journalist
Stavanger Aftenblad
Stavanger
Norway

Mr. Bård Kolltveit
Director
Norsk Sjøfartsmuseum
Oslo
Norway

Emeritus Professor Hubert H. Lamb
Director of the Climatic Research Unit
University of East Anglia
Norwich
England

Mr. Alan Pearsall
Historian
National Maritime Museum
London
England

Mr. Alan Hjorth Rasmussen
Director
Nordsømuseet
Hirtshals
Denmark

Professor Anthony Nicholas Ryan
The School of History
University of Liverpool
Liverpool
England

Dr. Atle Thowsen
Senior Curator
Bergens Sjøfartsmuseum
Bergen
Norway

Dr. Geoffrey Till
Principal Lecturer
Department of History and International Affairs
Royal Naval College Greenwich
London
England